Selected Essays of
DELMORE
SCHWARTZ

Selected Essays of DELMORE SCHWARTZ

Edited by

Donald A. Dike

&

David H. Zucker

With an Appreciation by Dwight Macdonald

THE UNIVERSITY OF CHICAGO PRESS

CHICAGO AND LONDON

International Standard Book Number: 0–226–74212–1
Library of Congress Catalog Card Number: 76–123357
The University of Chicago Press, Chicago 60637
The University of Chicago Press, Ltd., London

Printed in the United States of America

Contents

Preface

Long overdue even then, this collection of essays by Delmore
Schwartz began in the fall of 1963, a year after its author came to
Syracuse University as a professor of English. The collection began in conversations between Delmore Schwartz and its editors,
conversations at first tentative that became increasingly focussed
and programmatic. The book should have appeared in 1964, 1965
at the latest. That it did not then appear, that, the possible contents
ready for final selection, it could not even be published during the
lifetime of Delmore Schwartz, is cause for sorrow.

The delay was due to Delmore Schwartz himself. He was, inter-
mittently, eager to see his best essays collected in a single volume;
he spent a great deal of time choosing and arranging. But as the
project matured, he grew more and more hesitant: invented reasons for postponement, withheld himself for increasingly longer
periods, until, during the unhappy last year of his life, the plan
for publication had regretfully to be suspended.

Such explanation of this hesitancy as may be ventured here is
bound to be tentative and incomplete. A combination of intellectual modesty, humility even, and intellectual pride had certainly a good deal to do with it. Delmore was reluctant to recommit
to print any of his past critical writing that failed to satisfy an
incredibly fastidious standard: a standard equivalent not only
to what he currently knew and thought but also to what he might
subsequently know and think. Like Yeats, whom he so much admired, he wanted to bring his work up to date, establish through
impossible, endless revision a consistency between his past and
present views and, further, those future views that would be based

on knowledge—about T. S. Eliot for example—as yet unavailable. Had this imagined revision been possible, had it been accomplished, it would, surely, have produced a book of great interest and power, but a book precisely lacking in one value of the present collection: the value of topicality, of immediateness of response. For though the essays are not arranged chronologically, their temporal eventfulness, their relation to historical time and even, in some cases, to journalistic occasion are a part of their relevance. The essays have their diverse subjects, but together they have a single subject. They are the inconsecutive record of an extraordinarily intelligent and sensitive mind, a mind nurtured on Joyce, Yeats, Rilke, Eliot, the heroes of modernism, but alert to changes in the tradition before and after World War II; they are the record of this mind thinking promptly and energetically—talking to his typewriter, Delmore would say—about literature and culture over a span of a quarter of a century.

Another reason must be mentioned for Delmore Schwartz's failure to see his essays through to publication. It is that during the last years of his life his personal suffering became so intense and demanded so much of him as virtually to dominate his consciousness. He did not stop writing—he could almost as easily have stopped talking—but he no longer, it must be inferred, wrote with real interest in a public audience. His writing no longer rose to occasions; he altogether gave up reviewing; and the fiction and poetry on which he was working seemed to have no particular end in sight. Increasingly, his own anguish and the measures he took to endure it became for him the important reality; in contrast, the publication of a book was unimportant, a trivial irrelevance, and he had no patience for those who tried to persuade him otherwise. By the time of his death, he had chosen isolation for his condition: severed all functional connection with the outer world.

Delmore Schwartz was born in Brooklyn on December 8, 1913. He came to his vocation early. While still an undergraduate at New York University, he edited a little magazine called *Mosaic;* his fiction, poetry, and translations of Rimbaud were published there and elsewhere while he was still in his early twenties. His first book, *In Dreams Begin Responsibilities*, appeared in 1939. The title story of this book, which also contains poetry and a play, had previously been published in *Partisan Review*. Almost overnight it brought its author a reputation for precocious brilliance, and it remains one of his best known and most widely anthologized pieces of writing. Other books followed quickly: a translation with introduction (substantially the same as the essay that is included in this volume) of Rimbaud's *Une Saison en Enfer* in 1940; *Shenandoah*, a verse play, in 1941; a long poem, *Genesis, Book I*, in 1942. A second book to this poem was intended and worked on but never finished.

Throughout the forties Schwartz continued to write fiction, and in 1948 he produced *The World Is a Wedding*, a volume of stories that are too successfully realized to be called experimental but that are strikingly original in conception and technique. After this volume came *Vaudeville for a Princess and Other Poems* (1950) and *Summer Knowledge* (1959), a selection of past and new poems, which won the 1960 Bollingen Prize in Poetry and the Shelley Memorial Award. The last published work, *Successful Love and Other Stories*, appeared in 1961. At the time of his death, on July 11, 1966, Schwartz had in progress a novel, a verse play, and a collection of stories to be called *A Child's Universal History*. The manuscripts, regrettably, have disappeared.

Meanwhile, his immense intellectual energy was otherwise and diversely employed. For seven years, from 1940 to 1947, he taught at Harvard University; during the ensuing fifteen years he taught for a while at Princeton and was visiting lecturer at a number of universities; in 1962 he went to Syracuse University for what was hoped and expected to be a permanent stay. His editorial career was equally crowded. While at Harvard he joined the staff of *Partisan Review*: as an editor from 1943 to 1947, as an associate editor until 1955. During the early 1950s he was an editor of *Perspectives USA* and literary consultant to New Directions. From 1955 to 1957 he was poetry editor of *The New Republic*, for which he also reviewed moving pictures. And from the middle 1930s to 1962, from early maturity to four years before his death, he wrote criticism, a criticism ranging in kind from brief review to sustained and elaborated essay. The bibliography of his critical writing includes at least one hundred and twenty entries. Of these the present book is a selection.

Poet, fiction writer, teacher, editor, critic—to summarize Delmore Schwartz under these headings may suggest something of the range of his powers. It only begins to suggest the extent and kind of his involvement in the intellectual life of the mid-century. As poet and short story writer he made a contribution to American literature that has not yet been properly assessed. As teacher, his personal magnetism and his compassionate interest in postwar generations of students put him into intimate contact with the young; some of his best, his most memorable teaching was done outside the classroom. As editor and critic he was quick to recognize and identify changes in the cultural weather—from the depression years to the uneasily prosperous early sixties. His connection with *Partisan Review* began shortly after that magazine had withdrawn its support of the Communist movement but at a time when it was still a theater for political, as well as literary, debate; it was, further, more than most other literary magazines of the era, in touch with intellectual attitudes and currents in Europe, existentialism for an obvious example, and it took special responsibility for making these attitudes known to its readers. New Directions, which Schwartz advised during the fifties, was of course specifically created to be an organ for avant garde and otherwise serious literature. And movie reviewing for *The New Republic* served not only his interest in film as art medium but also his continuing preoccupation with the various levels of popular culture.

Despite the extent of his involvements, at no time could Delmore Schwartz be identified with an organized sectarian or institutional position or cause. From beginning to end he remained his own man: unconforming, without ever seeming erratic or arbitrary; a genuine independent, no more tempted to programmatic dissent than to programmatic assent. His allegiances were to individuals, to friends and to the minds that could stimulate, enrich, and help shape his own, rather than to schools. So he taught in a number of universities but never belonged to the academy. He

greatly admired Karl Marx—his own early training was in classical philosophy, and this training showed in all his thinking—but
he was never attracted to international Communism. He was profoundly occupied by his own Jewish middle-class background and
used this background resourcefully in much of his fiction; it is
not, however, his exclusive or final subject, and his loyalty to the
circumstances of his birth and identity did not interfere with his
respect, his support for Ezra Pound.

Delmore Schwartz's proximity to the centers of intellectual activity and his simultaneous aloofness from formed, fixed, doctri-
naire attitudes are a clue to his quality as critic. Engrossment and
detachment, close awareness and sympathetic disinterest combined
in his intelligence. His mind was never passive, never merely re-
sponsive; he seized on facts and ideas actively, almost predatorily,
from whatever source. He appraised them, engaged with them,
took possession of them, found room for them in his extraordinarily capacious memory, from which they would issue at unexpected moments to surprise and astound. He thought about virtually everything that came to his attention; he had opinions virtually
about everything; he talked, with eloquence and endurance, about
everything. He was, as everybody who knew him knows, remarkable for his talk, remarkable not only because of the bravura
rhetoric but also because in the improvisations of his speech he
was thinking out loud.

Thinking did not finally make him happy, although it is not
possible to assign his unhappiness to any single source. The high
degree in which he was conscious may, however, be supposed to
have intensified his quarrel with the world. Always sensitive to
possibilities, he grew persuaded that they were actualized before
him. His imagination, turned so valuably on a variety of situations,
themes, subjects, was finally turned on himself. Whatever the
origin of his paranoia, his early abhorrence of injustice developed
into an obsessive conviction of its omnipresence. Because of this
conviction, ingenious at distortion, old friends loomed as enemies.
A passionate believer in the supreme importance, the sheer necessity of love, Delmore proved himself incapable of permanent relationships. Endlessly curious, endlessly fascinated by the world,
he discovered it to be relentless in its hostility, and he constructed

elaborate defenses against its threats. His duality, the contradictions that for a while strengthened and then sapped his powers, became his disaster. But the disaster is exemplary. Writing of it in a reminiscence and tribute, reprinted in this volume, Dwight Macdonald suggested that "the American climate is still not suited for poets," that in this country "poetry is a dangerous occupation." Delmore's persuasion that happiness was forbidden, his ultimate preoccupation with the reality of persecution, was, in Conrad's phrasing, "the imaginative exaggeration of a correct feeling."

Some of the criticism included in this collection was written during times when Delmore Schwartz was acutely troubled. That this is so could not be guessed. His essays never reflect his personal unhappiness nor suggest it. On the contrary they suggest his capacity to free his mind from contingencies, to disengage it for the matter at hand from whatever might impede or prejudice its activity. Thus one quality of the criticism is its consistent reasonableness. Its logic is informal and frequently wears the guise of common sense, impatient alike with received opinions and with obscurantism; it is rarely if ever scanted for the sake of a random conjecture or capricious speculation. A second quality of the criticism is its generosity: the ungrudging admiration for excellence, an openness to its potential existence in any quarter, a concern that goes far beyond mere fairness to recognize value and praise it. Reasonableness and generosity, these cohere with the authentic modesty which informs all the essays and which strengthens rather than weakens the judgments made. Tone and manner are altogether without pretentiousness; the critic makes no claim to special, privileged authority. This is not to say that the effect of the essays is impersonal. The quality and stamp of Delmore's intellect can everywhere be felt. He himself can be felt most directly, perhaps, in those recurring moments when his astringent wit, his exuberance, his instinct for the ridiculous and for the preposterous combine to discover and reveal comic possibilities inherent in his subject.

The humor is not relief from the seriousness of the criticism; it is an instrument of the seriousness. Delmore Schwartz was deeply, morally, concerned with the condition of literature in his own time: with its nature, its potentialities, its well-being; with the cultural landscape in which it had to survive; with the situation and role of the modern poet. This is why he wrote almost nothing about the literature of the past, despite the fact that his acquaintance with past literature was close and his enthusiasm for it continuous. Another omission is more surprising. This volume contains nothing on James Joyce. Two short pieces could have been included, but the editors thought them too perfunctory, too hastily journalistic to represent adequately Delmore's vast knowledge of the work of his chief literary hero. A likely guess would be that an extended essay or book on Joyce was one of Delmore's long entertained projects and that he never accomplished the project precisely because he thought of it as crucial.

The arrangement of the essays and reviews is based on their subject matter and to some extent on their length and tone. Parts I and II are devoted respectively to general commentary on the condition of modern poetry and to the examination of a number of modern poets, from Rimbaud to Roethke. Part III contains essays on some twentieth-century fiction; it is introduced by "The Duchess' Red Shoes," an essay that, uniting polemic, humor, and passion, is probably the fullest single statement of Delmore's deep feeling about the morality of literature. Part IV is devoted to modern literary criticism, mainly as practiced by four critics. Part V is composed of miscellaneous short pieces, their subjects ranging from existentialism to comic-book adaptations of the classics; and Part VI consists of nine film reviews and two reviews of Hollywood biographies.

The essays and reviews were written over a period of nearly twenty-five years. Their publication dates, consequently, not only are likely to be of interest but are in some cases indispensible to the reader. In order to avoid footnotes that would clutter the text and distract from Delmore Schwartz's own voice, the dates have been included in the table of contents. For the eleven magazines and journals from which the essays have been taken, the reader is referred to the acknowledgments. An appendix lists all of Delmore Schwartz's publications, not including reprints or republications.

The editors wish to thank Elizabeth Pollet and Dwight Macdonald for their help in facilitating publication and Susan Zucker
for her work on the manuscript.

DONALD A. DIKE
DAVID H. ZUCKER

Delmore Schwartz
1913-1966

Dwight Macdonald

In the fall of 1937, when *Partisan Review* was about to be re-
vived as a non-Communist literary magazine, a writer with the
unlikely name of Delmore Schwartz sent in a short story, "In
Dreams Begin Responsibilities," which I and my fellow editors
had the sense to recognize as a masterpiece and to make it the first
item in our first issue. There were also contributions from Wallace
Stevens, Edmund Wilson, Agee, Trilling, Picasso, Farrell, Mary
McCarthy, and William Troy—we tried to make it a "strong"
issue, for obvious tactical reasons—but I think Delmore's story
deserved its primacy. It is as good as a story can be, I'd say after
reading it again for the fifth or sixth time, comparable with Kafka,
Babel, or *Through the Looking Glass.* "I think it is the year 1909,"
it begins. "I feel as if I were in a moving-picture theatre, the long
arms of light crossing the darkness and spinning, my eyes fixed
on the screen. It is a silent picture, as if an old Biograph one, in
which the actors are dressed in ridiculously old-fashioned clothes,
and one flash succeeds another with sudden jumps, and the actors,
too, seem to jump about, walking too fast. The shots are full of
rays and dots, as if it had been raining when the picture is photographed. The light is bad." The movie is about his parents' courtship, mostly an excursion to Coney Island that ends in a disastrous
quarrel, a clash of temperaments, and obstinacies, that is all the
more ominous because the causes are so trivial. As he watches this
banal home movie that tells more than it means to, the author
becomes more and more upset, weeping at first ("There, there
young man," an old lady sitting next to him says, patting his
shoulder, "all of this is only a movie, only a movie"), and then

shouting warnings, to the scandal of the audience, at the images of his parents-to-be as they flicker on their unalterable course across the screen: "Don't do it! It's not too late to change your mind, both of you. Nothing good will come of it, only remorse, hatred, scandal, and two children whose characters are monstrous. . . . Don't they know what they are doing? Why doesn't my mother go after my father and beg him not to be angry? . . . Doesn't my father know what he is doing?" The story ends with his being ejected by the usher ("hurrying down the aisle with his flashlight") and his waking up "into the bleak winter morning of my twenty-first birthday, the windowsill shining with its lip of snow, and the morning already begun." An original literary idea that works imaginatively, I think, and that combines the freest, most specific self-revelation with a form that controls the expression of these deep, personal fears partly by "distancing" them in time and medium (a movie is just what suits) and partly by a classical concision (the story is only seven pages long) in which every word counts, as in the opening paragraph quoted above. This unusual combination of expressive candor and tight form is characteristic of Delmore's poetry in general—we were surprised to find, though we shouldn't have been, that he was a poet also, and essentially.

> What curious dresses all men wear!
> The walker you met in a brown study,
> The President smug in rotogravure,
> The mannequin, the bathing beauty.
>
> The bubble-dancer, the deep-sea diver,
> The bureaucrat, the adulterer,
> Hide private parts which I disclose
> To those who know what a poem knows.

So he wrote in the copy of his first book (New Directions, 1938) he gave me—the verses haven't been printed, so far as I know— and so it was with his work, the private disclosure and the public form, concealment on one level but all the more revealing on another, that of art, or of "those who know what a poem knows."

Delmore was twenty-four that year, but his open, ardent manner and his large, dreaming eyes, sensitive mouth, and proud good looks as of a newly fledged eaglet made him seem younger. We took to each other right away. We were alike: New Yorkers by

birth and upbringing, restless, impatient, fond of argument, push-
ing ideas as far as they would go, and farther, assuming that talk
was not necessarily, or intimately, related to action so that we could
say almost anything to each other without hurt feelings, or bloody
noses, and urban (though not urbane) types to whom "the country" was like the moon, interesting but alien and a little scary. We
also found each other exotic. Delmore was always ironic about my
Yale-gentile background—we were both middle-class, so that
wasn't involved—which struck him as picturesque but slightly
primitive; while I couldn't understand what seemed to me his
obsession with his Jewish childhood. Sometimes I felt like a teacher
—I was only seven years older, but that was a big gap at our ages—
dealing with a bright student whose affection was greater than
his respect. But most of the time, in the almost thirty years I knew
him, we were equals, friends, and I can't think of anyone who gave
himself in friendship more generously and whose conversation,
and companionship, I enjoyed more.

There was always something doing when Delmore was around.
He was a great talker and he never held back, no hedging around
with small talk and cautious civilities, unpacking his mind instantly like one of those Armenian peddlers who used to come to
our summer house in New Jersey and who would have their
enormous cardboard suitcases unstrapped and displaying their
treasures of lace and linen before my mother could get the door
shut. He was a master of the great American folk art of kidding,
an impractical joker—words were his medium—outraging dignity
and privacy, present company most definitely not excepted, press-
ing the attack until it reached a comic grandeur that had even the
victim laughing. An intellectual equivalent of the Borsch Circuit
tummler, or stirrer-upper, his wide mouth grinning, his speedy
raucous New York voice running up and down the scale of sar-
casm, invective, desperate rationality, gasping ridicule, his nervous
hands clutching his head in despair at the obtuseness of his antagonist or flung wide in triumphant demonstration or stabbing
the air with a minatory forefinger. And he could take it as well as
dish it out. I can't remember him irritated by the most drastic
counterattack; indeed he seemed to welcome direct onslaughts on
himself and his ideas like a skillful swordsman who knows he can

deflect the thrust. In more placid talk, he was even more impressive, quick on the uptake, bringing to bear on the point a richness of reference and of imagination. He was a conversationalist, not a monologist, his style of discourse being dialectical, depending on the other person, or persons, to stimulate him to his greatest reaches. He was both witty and humorous, the shrewd wisecrack slipped into the interstices of an argument like a quick knife thrust, and also the expansive comic "turn," like one of Mark Twain's leisurely, endlessly climaxing anecdotes, which left us both breathless with laughter as Delmore, with objections or additions from me—he welcomed interruptions, as a clever speaker welcomes hecklers, converting them to his own use and making them part of his improvisation—built up one of his realistic fantasies about an audience with T. S. Eliot, or the minutely characterized variations in the reactions of mutual friends to the James family plot in Mount Auburn cemetery or some other item in the tour of Cambridge he took them on while he was teaching at Harvard. These set pieces were as detailed as a Dutch genre painting; he seemed to have total recall, and while I suspected many of the details were invented, and sometimes when I had been present knew they were (or was Delmore just a better observer?), the general effect was always so true to life that it was extremely funny.

There was a genial shimmer over Delmore's talk—as the Irish say, he knew how to put a skin on it—generous, easy and, no matter how outrageously exaggerated, never envious or malicious; like Jove's laughter. He was egoistic without vanity: he was curiously modest, or perhaps "detached" or "objective" might be better words, about himself and his extraordinary talents. Even in his darkening later years, when paranoia was more and more spreading in his mind, his delusions were not of grandeur. He thought he was persecuted but not because of any imagined preeminence on his part; rather did he seem to see himself as the victim, merely, of powerful people—the Rockefellers figured prominently, for reasons as ingeniously complicated as they were tenuous—who were sending out rays from the Empire State Building to damage his poor brain, so superior to those of his fancied persecutors, and yet so vulnerable.

For all the exuberance and even violence with which he expressed himself—an emotional, not a physical violence, it should be noted; even when he came to denounce at last most of his old friends, including me, no blows were struck, so far as I know—Delmore's was a remarkably *reasonable* mind, immune to the passions and prejudices of our period. He was not a joiner. Although he didn't hesitate to throw in with us on *Partisan Review*, first as a contributor, then as an editor at a time when there was some risk in taking an anti-Communist stand, he seemed to feel no need for any political commitment as a writer; at least I can't recall his signing any of my manifestoes or joining any of my committees. And although he was very conscious of his Jewish family background and returned to it constantly in his work—he was one of the first of the Jewish school that has now succeeded the Southern school—his attitude toward it was sometimes ironical but never chauvinistic. Even after the war and the death camps he never made me feel uncomfortable as a *goy;* he could even discuss the Arab question without undue excitement, and if he poked fun at my gentile-ity, he also mocked his own Jewishness, beginning with his name: he used to say he had been named after a Pullman car on a Riverside Drive apartment house, making endless fun of the discrepancy between his first and last names, as in his long narrative poem about a hero named Shenandoah Fish.

In this detachment from ideological fashion, Delmore resembled James Agee, another inspired talker, though tending more toward the monological than the dialectical mode. There are other similarities: both combined, in a way unique in my generation, an extraordinary talent for writing, the sheer gift of technique, in prose and poetry, with an intellectual passion, and a capacity for dealing with ideas, even to the point of writing a good deal of excellent criticism—Agee's movie reviews are now well known; it might be interesting to collect Delmore's reviews, in *The New Republic* and elsewhere, of films, TV, and books—that is not usual in our "creative" writers today. Both died youngish of heart attacks, and both had a positive genius for self-destruction. The gap between what they might have done and what they actually realized in their work is heart-breaking. "Cut is the branch that might have grown full straight/And burned is Apollo's laurel bough/That sometime grew within this learned man."

At Delmore's funeral, M. L. Rosenthal of New York University read one of his later poems:

> All of the fruits had fallen,
> The bears had fallen asleep,
> And the pears were useless and soft
> Like used hopes, under the starlight's
> Small knowledge, scattered aloft
> In a glittering senseless drift:
> The jackals of remorse in a cage
> Drugged beyond mirth and rage.
>
> Then, then, the dark hour flowered!
> Under the silence, immense
> And empty as far-off seas,
> I wished for the innocence
> Of my stars and my stones and my trees
> All the brutality and inner sense
> A dog and a bird possess,
> The dog who barked at the moon
> As an enemy's white fang,
> The bird that thrashed up the bush
> And soared to soar as it sang,
> A being all present as touch,
> Free of the future and past
> —Until, in the dim window glass,
> The fog or cloud of my face
> Showed me my fear at last!

Poetry is a dangerous occupation in this country, as the careers of too many of our best twentieth-century poets show, from Ezra Pound on, including the recent deaths of Randall Jarrell and Theodore Roethke. This is not a new thing. Writing of our first major poet, Baudelaire often seems to be describing the subject of this memoir:

> His conversation deserves particular mention. The first time that I asked an American about it, he laughed a good deal and said: "His talk is *not at all consecutive.*" After some explanation I understood that Poe made long digressions in the world of ideas, like a mathematician making demonstrations for advanced students. . . . It seems that Poe was not at all difficult about his audience. He cared little whether his listeners were

able to understand his tenuous abstractions, or to admire the glorious conceptions which incessantly illuminated the dark sky of his mind. He would sit down in a tavern, beside some dirty scapegrace, and would gravely explain to him the grand outlines of his terrible book, *Eureka*. . . . No man ever freed himself more completely from the rules of society, or bothered himself less about passersby. . . . In Paris, in Germany, he would have found friends who could easily have understood and comforted him; in America he had to fight for his bread. Thus his drunkenness and his nomadic habits are readily explained. He went through life as if through a Sahara desert, and changed his residence like an Arab. . . . For Poe the United States was nothing more than a vast prison which he traversed with the feverish agitation of a being made to breathe a sweeter air.

No, the American climate is still not suited for poets. "Dazzling a young and unformed country by his mind," Baudelaire writes, "Poe was fated to become a most unhappy writer. Rancors were aroused, solitude settled around him." Our country is middle-aged but still unformed and, granting that in both poets psychological difficulties were also important, still I cannot but see Delmore, too, as "a being made to breathe a sweeter air." He found it mostly among the young. "Delmore was a regular Pied Piper," one of his students said to me after the funeral, where the attendance was sharply divided between the very young and the very middle-aged, one of the two limousines that went to the cemetery being filled with students who had known him at Syracuse University or in one of the Village bars he frequented. "I suppose that by the time the war is over, we will be outmoded characters, even such a Yale man as you," he wrote to me in 1942 from Harvard, groaning about "forty Freshman themes a week to correct," but adding: "If you come to one of my classes, you will see how far I am from the Genteel Tradition and with what shameless gestures I seek to find the post-war soul." His search continued to the very end; he was always a good teacher, in or out of the classroom, open to the young. For what made Delmore—nobody thinks of him as anything but "Delmore"—precious was his candor, his invincible innocence (like the Catholics' "invincible ignorance"), his un-calculating generosity of response—all that Meyer Schapiro finely calls "his ever-resurgent hopes of light."

Acknowledgments

Acknowledgment is made to *Accent* for permission to reprint "The Writing of Edmund Wilson" (Spring 1942); to *Kenyon Review* for permission to reprint "The Two Audens" (Winter 1939) and "The Isolation of Modern Poetry" (Spring 1941); to the Louisiana State University Press for permission to reprint from *Southern Review* "John Dos Passos and the Whole Truth" (1938), *"Primitivism and Decadence* by Yvor Winters" (1938), "Poetry and Belief in Thomas Hardy" (1940), "The Poetry of Allen Tate" (1940), "The Fiction of William Faulkner" (1941), "An Unwritten Book" (1942); to *The Nation* for permission to reprint "The Genius of W. C. Fields" (February 11, 1950); to *Poetry* for permission to reprint "Ezra Pound's Very Useful Labors" (March 1938), "The Critical Method of R. P. Blackmur" (October 1938), "Rimbaud in Our Time" (December 1939), "The Vocation of the Poet in the Modern World" (July 1951), "T. S. Eliot's Voice and His Voices" (December 1954, January 1955), "The Cunning and the Craft of the Unconscious and the Preconscious" (June 1959).

The following essays and reviews are reprinted by permission of *The New Republic,* copyright in the year of publication by Harrison-Blaine of New Jersey, Inc.: "Our Literary Critics: An Appreciation" (May 24, 1954); "In the Orchards of the Imagination" (November 1, 1954); film review, *Animal Farm* (January 17, 1955); film review, *Underwater, Blackboard Jungle* (April 11, 1955); "Mary Pickford: Little Girl in Curls" (June 6, 1955); film review, *The Long Gray Line, Captain Lightfoot, Untamed, Mambo* (June 27, 1955); "Films—TV" (July 18, 1955); film review, *The Seven Year Itch* (August 8, 1955); "Wallace Stevens: An Appreciation" (August 22, 1955); "French Taste in American Writing" (September 5, 1955); film review, *To Catch a Thief* (November 28, 1955); film review, *The Big Knife* (January 9, 1956); film review, *The Court Jester* (March 5, 1956); "Novels and the News" (April 13, 1959); "Ezra Pound and History" (February 8, 1960).

"The Fiction of Ernest Hemingway" and "Faulkner's *A Fable*" are reprinted from *Perspectives USA* (1955) by permission of Intercultural Publications, Inc., New York City, © 1955 by Intercultural Publications, Inc. "Ring Lardner: Highbrow in Hiding" is reprinted with permission from *The Reporter* (August 9, 1956), © 1956 by The Reporter Magazine Company. "Instructed of Much Mortality: A Note on the Poetry of John Crowe Ransom" is reprinted with permission from *The Sewanee Review* (July 1946), © 1946 by The University of the South. "The Present State of Poetry," a lecture delivered January 20, 1958, under the auspices of the Gertrude Clarke Whittall Poetry and Literature Fund in the Library of Congress, was first published by the Library of Congress in the brochure, *American Poetry at Mid-century, 1958.*

The following essays are reprinted from *Partisan Review*, permission and copyright by *Partisan Review* in the year of publication: *"The Man with the Blue Guitar, and Other Poems"* (February 1938); "The Poet as Poet" (Spring 1939); "T. S. Eliot as the International Hero" (Spring 1945); "The Meaningfulness of Absurdity" (Spring 1946); "Film Chronicle: *Henry V"* (Summer 1946); "Does Existentialism Still Exist?" (December 1948); "The Literary Dictatorship of T. S. Eliot" (February 1949); "Views of a Second Violinist" (December 1949); "Smile and Grin, Relax and Collapse" (March 1950); "The Grapes of Crisis" (January 1951); "The Fabulous Example of Andre Gide" (July–August 1951); "Masterpieces as Cartoons" (July 1952); "Our Country and Our Culture" (September–October 1952); "The Duchess' Red Shoes" (January 1953).

"Delmore Schwartz (1913–1966)" by Dwight Macdonald is reprinted from *The New York Review* (September 8, 1966) by permission of the author and of *The New York Review*.

The Poet and Poetry
·I·

The Isolation of
Modern Poetry

The characteristic of modern poetry which is most discussed is of course its difficulty, its famous obscurity. Certain discussions, usually by contemporary poets, have done much to illuminate the new methods and forms of contemporary poetry. Certain other discussions have illustrated an essential weakness inherent in all readers, the fact that the love of one kind of writing must often interfere with the understanding of another kind. Wordsworth was undoubtedly thinking of this weakness when he wrote, in his justly well-known preface, that

> It is supposed that by the act of writing in verse an Author makes a formal engagement that he will gratify certain known habits of association; that he not only apprises the reader that certain classes of ideas and expression will be found in his book, but that others will be carefully excluded.

This seems to me to be a perfect statement of the first barrier which intervenes between the reader and any kind of writing with which he is not familiar. But it is far from being sufficient as a defense of modern poetry. Wordsworth was engaged in defending his poetry against the habitual expectations of the reader accustomed to Dryden, Pope, and Johnson. It is necessary now to defend the modern poet against the reader accustomed to Wordsworth. The specific difference between such a poet as Wordsworth and the typical modern poet requires a specific explanation.

There is another defense of the modern poet which seems utterly insufficient to me. It is said that the modern poet must be complex because modern life is complicated. This is the view of Mr. T. S. Eliot, among others. "It appears likely," he says, "that poets in our

[3]

civilization, as it exists at present, must be *difficult*. Our civilization comprehends great variety and complexity, and this variety and complexity, playing upon a refined sensibility, must produce various and complex results." Mr. Eliot's explanation seems to me not so much wrong as superficial. I need hardly say that Mr. Eliot is seldom superficial in any regard; here, however, I think he is identifying the surface of our civilization with the surface of our poetry. But the complexity of modern life, the disorder of the traffic on a business street or the variety of reference in the daily newspaper is far from being the same thing as the difficulties of syntax, tone, diction, metaphor, and allusion which face the reader in the modern poem. If one is the product of the other, the causal sequence involves a number of factors on different levels, and to imply, as I think Mr. Eliot does, that there is a simple causal relationship between the disorder of modern life and the difficulty of modern poetry is merely to engender misunderstanding by oversimplification.

Now obscurity is merely one of the peculiar aspects of modern poetry. There are others which are just as important. Nothing could be more peculiar than the fact that modern poetry is lyric poetry. Almost without exception there is a failure or an absence of narrative or dramatic writing in verse. With the possible exception of Hardy and Robinson, it is impossible to think of any modern poet who will be remembered for his writing in any form other than that of the lyric.

It is obvious by contrast that the major portion of the poetry of the past, of poetry until we reach the latter half of the nineteenth century, is narrative and dramatic as well as lyrical in its most important moments; and it is equally evident that all of that poetry is never obscure in the modern sense.

I need not mention further characteristics of modern poetry which coexist with its obscurity and its limitation to the lyric form. The two characteristics seem to me to be closely related to each other and to spring from the essential condition of the modern poet. The way in which this condition, if that is the adequate word for what I mean, the way in which this essential circumstance affects the modern poet is a rather involved matter, but had better be stated bluntly and crudely at this point. The modern poet has been very much affected by the condition and the circumstance that he has been separated from the whole life of society. This separation has taken numerous forms and has increased continually. It is a separation which occurs with an uneven development in all the matters with which the modern poet must concern himself. Different poets have been differently affected, and their efforts to cope with this separation have been various. But there is a common denominator which points to a common cause.

The beginning of the process of separation, if one can rightly discern a beginning in such things, is the gradual destruction of the world picture which, despite many changes, had for a long time been taken for granted by the poet. Amid much change, development, and modification, the Bible had provided a view of the universe which circumscribed the area in which anyone ventured to think, or use his imagination. It would of course be a serious mistake to suppose that this view of the universe had not been disturbed in numerous ways long before the modern poet arrived upon the scene. But it is doubtful if the poet before the time of Blake felt a conflict between two pictures of the world, the picture provided by the Bible and the one provided by the physical sciences.

In Blake's rage against Newton and Voltaire, in his interest, as a poet, in the doctrine of Swedenborg, and in his attempt to construct his own view of the universe, we come upon the first full example of this difficulty of the poet. There is a break between intellect and sensibility; the intellect finds unreasonable what the sensibility and the imagination cannot help but accept because of centuries of imagining and feeling in terms of definite images of the world. Milton's use of a Ptolemaic cosmology, though he knew that the Copernican one was mathematically superior, is an example from a still earlier period; it shows with exactitude the extent to which the poet depended upon the traditional world picture of Western culture. After Blake, the Romantic poets are further instances; not only were they intensely interested in new conceptions of the world, new philosophies; but in turning to Nature as they did, they displayed their painful sense that the poet no longer belonged to the society into which he was born, and for which, presumably, he was writing his verse.

But these authors are not modern poets. And it was not until

[5]

the middle of the nineteenth century that the progress of the physical sciences brought forth a body of knowledge which was in serious and open conflict with the picture of the world which had been in use for so long a time. This conflict had been going on, of course, for centuries, but it was not until we come to an occasion like the publication of the Darwinian theory that the conflict becomes so radical and so obvious that no poet of ambition can seriously avoid it. I am not referring to any conflict between religious doctrine and scientific knowledge, for this conflict, if it actually exists, is hardly the direct concern of the poet at any time. It is a question of the conflict between the sensibility of the poet, the very images which he viewed as the world, and the evolving and blank and empty universe of nineteenth century science.

The development of modern culture from Darwin and Huxley to Freud, Marx, and the author of *The Golden Bough*, has merely extended, hastened, and intensified this process of removing the picture of the world which the poet took for granted as the arena of his imagination, and putting in its place another world picture which he could not use. This is illustrated broadly in the career of such poets as Yeats. Hearing as a young man that man was descended from the ape, Yeats occupied himself for many years with theosophy, black magic, and the least respectable forms of psychical research, all in the effort to gain a view of the universe and of man which would restore dignity and importance to both man and the universe. We may invent an illustration at this point and suppose that when Yeats or any other modern poet of similar interests heard of how many million light years the known regions of the universe comprise, he felt a fundamental incongruity between his own sense of the importance of human lives and their physical smallness in the universe. This is merely a difficulty in imagining—one has an image of a very small being in an endless world; but that's just the point, the difficulty with images. The philosopher and the theologian know that size is not a particularly important aspect of anything; but the poet must see, and what he has had to see was this incongruity between the importance man attributes to himself and his smallness against the background of the physical world of nineteenth century science.

Now this is only one aspect of the poet's isolation; it is the aspect in which the sensibility of the poet has been separated from the theoretical knowledge of his time. The isolation of the modern poet has, however, taken an even more difficult form, that of being separated by poetry from the rest of society. Here one must guard against a simple view of what this separation has amounted to in any particular context. It is not a simple matter of the poet lacking an audience, for that is an effect, rather than a cause, of the character of modern poetry. And it is not, on the other hand, the simple matter of the poet being isolated from the usual habits and customs and amusements of his time and place; for if this were the trouble, then the poet could perhaps be justly accused of retiring to his celebrated ivory tower; and it would then be quite reasonable to advise the poet as some have done: to tell him that he ought to get "experience," see the world, join a political party, make sure that he participates in the habitual activities of his society.

The fundamental isolation of the modern poet began not with the poet and his way of life; but rather with the whole way of life of modern society. It was not so much the poet as it was poetry, culture, sensibility, imagination, that were isolated. On the one hand, there was no room in the increasing industrialization of society for such a monster as the cultivated man; a man's taste for literature had at best nothing to do with most of the activities which constituted daily life in an industrial society. On the other hand, culture, since it could not find a place in modern life, has fed upon itself increasingly and has created its own autonomous satisfactions, removing itself further all the time from any essential part in the organic life of society.

Stated thus, this account may seem abstract and even implausible. It would be best before going further to mention certain striking evidences of what has taken place. There is, for instance, the classic American joke about how bored father is at the opera or the concert; the poet too has been an essentially comic figure, from time to time. But this homely instance may seem merely the product of vulgarity and lack of taste. A related tendency which has been much observed by foreigners is the belief in America that women were supposed to be interested in literature, culture, and "such things," while men had no time for such trivial delights because they were busy with what is called *business*. But this instance may seem local in that it is American and inconclusive since it has to do with the poet's audience rather than with the poet himself. There is then a third example, one which seems almost dramatic to me, the phenomenon of American authors of superior gifts going to Europe and staying there. Henry James is the most convincing case; one can scarcely doubt that he lived in Europe because there the divorce between culture and the rest of life, although it had begun, had by no means reached the point which was unavoidable in America. George Santayana, Ezra Pound, and T. S. Eliot are cases which come later in time; we do not know exactly why these men went to Europe; the significant fact is that they do not come back to America. I do not merely wish to suggest a critical view of the role of culture in American life, for the same process was occurring in Europe, though at a slower rate and with local modifications. The important point is the intuitive recognition on the part of both the artist and the rest of the population that culture and sensibility—and thus the works by means of which they sustained their existence—did not belong, did not fit into the essential workings of society.

At this point, it might be objected that culture has never played a very important part in the life of any society; it has only engaged the attention and devotion of the elect, who are always few in number. This view seems utterly false to me, and for the sake of showing briefly how false it has been historically, I quote one of the greatest living classical scholars on the part that dramatic tragedy played in the life of Periclean Athens. Werner Jaeger writes that

> After the state organized the dramatic performances held at the festival of Dionysus, tragedy more and more evoked the interest and participation of the entire people. . . . Its power over them was so vast that they held it responsible for the spirit of the whole state . . . it is no exaggeration to say that the tragic festival was the climax of the city's life. (*Paideia*, p. 245–246.)

No contrast could be more extreme than this one between the function of the Greek dramatist and that of the modern poet in their respective societies.

One significant effect of this divorce has been the poet's avowal of the doctrine of Art for Art's Sake, a doctrine which is meaningful only when viewed in the context in which it is always announced, that is, to repeat, a society which had no use and no need for Art, other than as a superfluous amusement or decoration. And another significant and related effect is the sentiment of the poet, and at times his convinced belief, that he has no connection with or allegiances to anything else. Nowhere is this belief stated with more clarity than in the following prose poem by Baudelaire, who in so many ways is either the first or the typical modern poet:

> "Whom do you love most of all, enigmatic man, tell me? Your father, your mother, your brother, or your sister?"
> "I have neither father, mother, brother, nor sister."
> "Do you love your friends then?"
> "You have just used a word whose meaning remains unknown to me to this very day."
> "Do you love your country, then?"
> "I ignore the latitude in which it is situated."
> "Then do you love Beauty?"
> "I love her with my whole will; she is a goddess and immortal."
> "Do you love gold?"
> "I hate it as you hate God."
> "Well then: extraordinary stranger, what *do* you love?"
> "I love the clouds . . . the clouds which pass . . . far away . . . far away . . . the marvelous clouds!"

It would be possible to take this stranger who is the modern poet with less seriousness, if he were merely affecting a pose, attempting to dramatize himself or be clever. The shocking passages in modern poetry have sometimes been understood in this way as Bohemianism, and the conventional picture or caricature of the poet has been derived from this Bohemianism, considered as a surface. But the sentiments which Baudelaire attributes to his stranger are the deepest feelings of the modern poet. He does feel that he is a stranger, an alien, an outsider; he finds himself without a father or mother, or he is separated from them by the opposition between his values as an artist and their values as respectable members of modern society. This opposition cannot be avoided because not a government subsidy, nor yearly prizes, nor a national academy can disguise the fact that there is no genuine place for the

[9]

poet in modern life. He has no country, no community, insofar as he is a poet, and his greatest enemy is money, since poetry does not yield him a livelihood. It is natural then that he should emphasize his allegiance, his devotion to Beauty, that is to say, to the practice of Art and the works of art which already exist. And thus it is that Baudelaire's stranger announces that what he loves most of all is to look at the clouds, that is, to exercise his own sensibility. The modern poet has had nothing to do, no serious activity other than the cultivation of his own sensibility. There is a very famous passage in Walter Pater advising just this course.

From this standpoint, the two aspects of modern poetry which I marked at the start can be seen as natural and almost inevitable developments. In cultivating his own sensibility, the modern poet participated in a life which was removed from the lives of other men, who, insofar as they could be considered important characters, were engaged in cultivating money or building an industrial society. Thus it became increasingly impossible for the poet to write about the lives of other men; for not only was he removed from their lives, but, above all, the culture and the sensibility which made him a poet could not be employed when the proposed subject was the lives of human beings in whom culture and sensibility had no organic function. There have been unsuccessful efforts on the part of able poets to write about bankers and about railroad trains, and in such examples the poet has been confronted by what seems on the surface a technical problem, the extraordinary difficulty of employing poetic diction, meter, language, and metaphor in the contexts of modern life. It is not that contemporary people do not speak or think poetically; human beings at any time in general do not speak or think in ways which are immediately poetic, and if they did there would be no need for poetry. The trouble has been that the idiom of poetic style and the normal thought and speech of the community have been moving in opposite directions and have had little or no relationship to each other. The normal state of affairs occurs when poetry is continually digesting the prose of its time, and folk art and speech are providing sustenance for major literary efforts.

Since the only life available to the poet as a man of culture has been the cultivation of his own sensibility, that is the only subject

[10]

available to him, if we may assume that a poet can only write about subjects of which he has an absorbing experience in every sense.[1] Thus we find that in much modern poetry, the poet is writing about other poetry, just as in modern painting the art works and styles of the past have so often become the painter's subject. For writing about other poetry and in general about works of art is the most direct way of grasping one's sensibility as a subject. But more than that, since one can only write about one's sensibility, one can only write lyric poetry. Dramatic and narrative poetry require a grasp of the lives of other men, and it is precisely these lives, to repeat, that are outside the orbit of poetic style and poetic sensibility. An analogous thing has, of necessity, happened in the history of the novel; the development of the autobiographical novel has resulted in part from the inability of the novelist to write about any one but himself or other people in relation to himself.

From this isolation of poetic sensibility the obscurity of modern poetry also arises. The poet is engaged in following the minutest movements, tones, and distinctions of his own being as a poetic man. Because this private life of his sensibility is the chief subject available to him, it becomes increasingly necessary to have recourse to new and special uses of language. The more the poet has cultivated his own sensibility, the more unique and special has his subject, and thus his method, become. The common language of daily life, its syntax, habitual sequences, and processes of association, are precisely the opposite of what he needs, if he is to make poetry from what absorbs him as a poet, his own sensibility.

Sometimes, indeed, the poet has taken this conflict between sensibility and modern life as his subject. The early fiction of Thomas Mann concerns itself repeatedly with the opposition be-

1. The connection between the way in which an author lives and his writing is of course a complicated one. But how close the connection is and how effective can be seen if we ask ourselves: would Eliot have written *The Waste Land* as we know it, if he had lived in London? would Pound have written the later Cantos, if he had not lived on the Italian Riviera? would either have written, using culture as they have, if they were not expatriate Americans? Certainly Joyce might not have written *Finnegans Wake* if he had not taught in a Berlitz school and Perse could not have written *Anabase* if he had not been sent to Asia as a diplomat, and Yeats might not have written his later poetry, if he had lived on Lady Gregory's estate.

[11]

tween the artist and the bourgeoisie, and in such a story as "Tonio Kröger" we see the problem most explicitly; the artist feels at home nowhere and he suffers from an intense longing to be normal and bourgeois himself. Again, there is the famous device of modern poetry which was invented by Laforgue and used most successfully by T. S. Eliot, the ironic contrast between a past in which culture was an important part of life and the present in which the cultural monument sits next to vulgarity and insensitivity. This has been misunderstood very often as a yearning to go back to a past idyllically conceived. It is nothing of the kind; it is the poet's conscious experience of the isolation of culture from the rest of society.

I would like to cite one more instance of this condition. Four years ago one of the very best modern poets lectured and read his own poetry at Harvard. As a normal citizen, this man is an executive of an important corporation. It may reasonably be presumed that most of his writing is done on holidays and vacations. At the conclusion of his reading of his own poetry, this poet and businessman remarked to one of the instructors who had welcomed him: "I wonder what the boys at the office would think of this."

But I have spoken throughout as if this isolation was in every sense a misfortune. It is certainly a misfortune so far as the life of the whole community is concerned; this is evident in the character of popular taste, in the kind of fiction, play, and movie which is successful, as compared with the popular authors of the nineteenth century, who were very often the best authors also. But on the other hand, it seems to me that the period of modern poetry, the age which begins with Baudelaire, is undoubtedly one in which the art of poetry has gained not only in the number of fine poets, but in technical resources of all kinds. If the enforced isolation of the poet has made dramatic and narrative poetry almost impossible, it has, on the other hand, increased the uses and powers of languages in the most amazing and the most valuable directions.

I have also spoken as if this isolation of the poet had already reached its conclusion. Whether it has or not, and whether it would be entirely desirable that it should, may be left as unanswered and perhaps unanswerable questions. It is true, at any rate, that during the past ten years a new school of poets has attempted to free itself from the isolation of poetry by taking society itself as the dominant

[12]

subject.[2] The attempt has been a brilliant and exciting one in many ways; the measure of its success is not yet clear, particularly since it has been inspired by the present crisis of society; and its relative popularity may also be limited to contemporary and transient interests. But the very nature of the effort testifies in its own way to the isolation which haunts modern poetry, and from which these poets have been trying to escape.

2. These are the poets who, significantly enough, have invented the recurrent figure of "the island," as a symbol of isolation. From the point of view of this essay, the leading themes of the Agrarian-Regionalist poets, such as Tate and Ransom, would represent another, very different effort to get back to the center of the community and away from the poet's isolation.

The Vocation of the Poet
in the Modern World

To have a vocation is to have a calling, to be called. One may be called by the powers of evil as well as the powers of good, but it is clear that one must respond with the whole of one's being. In this sense it is also clear that to have a vocation is very much like being in love. Being in love and being called to write poetry are often linked, and many people feel the need to write poetry when they are in love. As there are many errors in love, so there are many errors in the writing of poetry. And as there is puppy love, there is adolescent poetry.

Since there are errors and since a calling is a very important matter, since one is called during the formative and decisive years of existence, there is much doubt and hesitation about the fact of having a calling, and a period of trial is prescribed in some vocations, while one of the reasons for going to school, after a certain point, is to determine if one has a true vocation, if one has truly been called; and it is in some kind of school that we prepare ourselves to be adequate to our vocation.

In poetry, it is particularly true that many are called and few are chosen. And to be a poet in the modern world means a certain important renunciation which does not hold of all vocations: it means that there is little hope or none of being able to earn a living directly by the writing of poetry; and this has been true in the past, although in other ways, as well as in the modern life; for example, Dryden speaks of "not having the vocation of poverty to scribble." In the modern world, it is hard to think of any poet who has had from the start any real economic support for the writing of poetry. There are prizes, grants, patrons, and poetry is honored by much generosity and much prestige. Unfortunately, these are provided after the poet has established himself—and not always then —but during the first and perhaps most difficult years of being a poet, the best a poet can do is to get some other job to support his effort to be a poet. In recent years, the job of teaching English has provided a good many positions which help the poet during his first years, but it is not entirely clear that this is a good thing. For to have a vocation means that one must respond with the whole of one's being; but teaching should be a vocation too, and not a job, and when the poet takes teaching as a job, he may injure or weaken himself as a poet, or he may not be adequate to all that the task of teaching requires. All the temptations of the world, the flesh, and the devil combine to lure the poet to success as a teacher and to the rewards of successful academic ambition. At the same time that the poet resists these temptations, he must resign himself to the likelihood that a genuine poetic reputation can be achieved only among others who are poets—for it is mostly poets who read any poetry except what is to be found in anthologies—and the kind of fame (that last infirmity of noble mind, as Milton said) which he would like will come to him, if it comes at all, only in middle age.

What I have just said should distinguish roughly the difference between being a poet in the modern world from what it may have been in other historical periods. If we turn again to the wisdom, tried and inherited for so many years, to be found in the origins of words, we remember that to be a poet is to be a maker, to be the maker of something new, to make something new by putting things and words together. The distinguishing mark of the poet, that aptitude which more than any other skill of the mind makes him a poet, is metaphor, according to Aristotle. Now metaphor is literally a bearing-across, or a bringing-together of things by means of words. And composition, which is what the poet accomplishes by all the elements of his poem when they are brought together in a unity, structural, formal, intuitive, and musical—composition means putting things together, bringing them together into a unity which is original, interesting and fruitful. Thus the poet at any time may be said to be engaged in bringing things together, in making new things, in uniting the old and the new, all by the inexhaustible means which words provide for him. In this

[15]

way, the poet as creator, and metaphor-maker, and presiding bringer of unity is a kind of priest. He unites things, meanings, attitudes, feelings, through the power, prowess and benediction of words, and in this way he is a priest who performs a ceremony of marriage each time he composes a poem. Unfortunately, not all marriages are happy.

In the modern world, the poet who has been truly called cannot respond as poets did in idyllic and primitive periods when merely the naming of things, as Adam named the animals, was enough to bring poems into existence. On the contrary, he must resist the innumerable ways in which words are spoiled, misused, commercialized, deformed, mispronounced, and in general degraded. We can see clearly how much this resistance is part of the vocation of the poet if we consider the recurrent references to language itself in the poems of that truly modern poet, T. S. Eliot. These references occur in his poems from the very start, continue in each volume he has published, and culminate in a passage in his most recent book of poems, *Four Quartets:*

> So here I am, in the middle way, having had twenty years—
> Twenty years largely wasted, the years of *l'entre deux guerre*—
> Trying to learn to use words, and every attempt
> Is a wholly new start, and a different kind of failure
> Because one has only learnt to get the better of words
> For the thing one no longer has to say, or the way in which
> One is no longer disposed to say it.

Elsewhere in his work there is a sensitivity to colloquial speech— and a kind of horror or anguish about it—which arises from the fact that for a modern poet, as for any poet, words are the keys to what he wants.

Eliot's play in verse, "Sweeney Agonistes," is the best example of this aspect of his feeling about language, which is used to express a profound anguish about human beings and human existence. When language is degraded in speech, then the basis in community life for the art of poetry is diseased; and it is appropriate and perhaps inevitable that the great modern poet who should have felt this fact with as much acuteness as any other poet should at the same time be an author who acquired an English accent after arriving at the age of reason. Nevertheless, just as certain kinds of disease make for a greater sensitivity to experience or a more precise observation of reality (the blind know more about how things sound and how they feel to the touch than those who have normal vision), so, too, the disease which degrades language in the modern world may help to bring about the remarkable and often multilingual sensitivity of the modern poet to the language which is the matrix from which he draws his poems.

Degradation and disease are strong words of condemnation, and a great claim is also made when one says that the degradation and disease to which poetry is subjected in the modern world are also one of the fruitful and necessary conditions of genuine poetry and of a genuine vocation for the art of poetry. For the sake of justifying these claims, let us examine small and convenient examples. The word, *intrigue*, is a noun which has four legitimate meanings. It means something which is intricate; it means "a plot, or a plotting intended to affect some purpose by secret artifice"; thirdly, it is "the plot of a play or romance"; fourthly, it is "a secret and illicit love affair; an amour; a liason" (this fourth meaning probably derives from the third). And the synonyms of intrigue are *plot, scheme, machination,* and *conspiracy.* Notice that there is no sense in which the word means something overwhelmingly attractive and fascinating, unless one thinks of secret and illicit love affairs as overpowering in their fascination. However, at present, the use of the word as a noun has fallen into decay. Although there are still references to schemers who engage in conspiracies and intrigues, the noun has become a verb in popular usage: anyone who is said to be *intriguing* is said to be very attractive, in fact, fascinating like a Hollywood star, or like the spy Mata Hari. An intrigue was something unpleasant, dishonorable, underhand, and immoral. But now to be intriguing is to be wonderfully desirable or interesting and has no unfavorable or dishonorable association. The sense of the same word has thus been turned upside down; it has changed, in popular usage, from signifying something unscrupulous to representing in a vague but unmistakeable way something which is extremely interesting, desirable, or beautiful, and has no immediate connotations of moral disrepute.

What has happened to one word has happened to many words

[17]

and can happen to many more. And the causes are not, as is sometimes supposed, limited to a poor teaching of English, or a disregard of the dictionary. In this instance, the shift is probably involved in the radical trial which conventional morality has undergone in the last twenty-five years, and certainly there is also involved the influence of newspapers, the stage, the films, and the *literary* zest with which most people read of the sins of others.

This example does not make clear how a degradation in the meaning of a word can be fruitful as well as foolish. There is a shift of meaning and a new richness of meaning, of course, but some of the exactness has already been lost and more is going to be lost. Let me point out two more examples in which the complicated and mixed benefits and losses of the change may appear more fully. For a number of years I taught English composition. I taught because I was unable to support myself by writing poetry (for the most part, however, I like to teach very much). When I began to teach, I was confounded by simple misuses of languages of which *intrigue* is a fairly representative example. One student wrote that "swimming is my chief *abstraction*," and another student said that "a certain part of my native city is *slightly ugly*." A third student who was attempting to describe the salutary effects of higher education upon all members of the fairer and weaker sex said that it was good for a girl to go to college because "it makes a girl *broader*." When I corrected the last word in accordance with my instructions as to the proper usage of English —and with a physical sense of one of the meanings of broader— the student protested that I had a peculiar mind; otherwise I would not object to the way in which she used *broader* instead of *broadens*.

These errors—errors at least from the point of view of conventional and prescribed usage—made me reflect upon the character I played as a teacher of composition. The students thought I was pedantic when they did not think I was idiosyncratic. The difficulty was that so many of them made the same errors that, in a way, they were no longer errors. Moreover, the longer I thought about some of the errors, the more they seemed to be possible enlargements of meaning and association which might be creative. There was a real sense in which swimming, for an urban human

[18]

being, was an abstraction as well as a distraction. So too, to say that something was slightly ugly was to suggest that a word or words denoting degrees of ugliness from homeliness and plainness to what was utterly ugly were lacking in English. And finally, it was true enough that education might make a girl broader as well as broaden a girl's outlook, although I doubt that this would have occurred to me if it had not been for this fruitful error.

The experience of teaching English literature and English poetry directly confronts the poet who teaches English with what can only be described as the most educated part of the population. Before the poet has taught English, he may well have been under the impression that no one except poets read modern poetry (with a few and misleading exceptions). When he teaches poetry in the classroom, he finds out something which may be a great hope or a great delusion. It may be a delusion now and a hope for the future. At any rate, he does discover that he can persuade any student to understand any kind of poetry, no matter how difficult. They understand it as long as they are in the classroom, and they remain interested in it until they depart from school. Since so many poets have more and more undertaken the teaching of English and of poetry, it does seem possible that this may be the beginning of a new audience trained in reading and aware of how marvelous and exalted the rewards of poetry can be. But this is a matter which must be realized in the future. In the present, it is true that as soon as the student leaves school, all the seductions of mass culture and middle-brow culture, and in addition the whole way of life of our society, combine to make the reading of poetry a dangerous and quickly rejected luxury. The poet who teaches has immediate experiences in the classroom which give him some reason to hope for a real literary and poetic renaissance. As soon as he departs from the pleasant confines of the university, he discovers that it is more and more true that less and less people read serious poetry. And the last straw may be the recognition that even poets do not read very much poetry: Edwin Arlington Robinson confessed that during the latter half of his life, he read hardly any poems except his own which he read again and again, and which may explain the paralysis of self-imitation which overcomes many good poets in mid-career. Here then is another trait which

[19]

distinguishes the vocation of the modern poet from poets of the past: he not only knows how language is inexactly and exactly used, he also knows that for the most part only other poets will read his poems.

One reason that language is misused, whether fruitfully or not, is that in modern life experience has become international. In America itself the fact of many peoples and the fact that so large a part of the population has some immigrant background and cherishes the fragments of another language creates a multilingual situation in which words are misused and yet the language is also enriched by new words and new meanings. To make fun of errors in the use of language and to make the most comedy possible of foreign accents—or for that matter, an English accent—is an important and vital part of American humor, which is itself a very important part of American life. Moreover, the pilgrimage to Europe has for long been an important episode in the national experience. The American tourist in Europe, Baedeker in hand, has for generations spelled out the names of places, and works of art, and delicious foods. And most crucial of all, the experience of two world wars has made Americans conscious of the extent to which the very quality of their lives depends upon the entire international situation. Whether the danger is from Germany or from Russia, whether a banking scandal occurs in Paris, or Spain becomes Fascist, or the Vatican intervenes in American politics and American morality and American education, no one at this late date can fail to be aware of the extent to which the fate of the individual is inseparable from what is happening in the whole world.

These facts are, of course, in one sense platitudes; and yet it may not be clear how they affect the modern poet in his vocation as such. I want to resort to examples again before trying to define the way in which the international scene and an involvement with it affect the poet as a poet and have to do with his calling.

To quote once more from that truly modern poet, T. S. Eliot, here is a passage from one of his best poems, "Gerontion." Christ, the protagonist says is:

> To be eaten, to be divided, to be drunk
> Among whispers; by Mr. Silvero
> With caressing hands, at Limoges
> Who walked all night in the next room;
>
> By Hakagawa, bowing among the Titians;
> By Madame de Tornquist, in the dark room
> Shifting the candles; Fraülein von Kulp
> Who turned in the hall, one hand on the door.

Let us think a little merely of the names of the people he remembers, Mr. Silvero, Hakagawa, Madame de Tornquist, Fraülein von Kulp. Is it not evident that the experience which provides the subject-matter of the poet or inspires him to write his poem is not only European, but international, since Hakagawa is presumably Japanese; and involves all history, all culture, since the reference here to Titian is matched elsewhere by allusions to ancient Egypt, Buddhist sermons, and the religion of classical Greece? Another aspect of the same involvement and of how it has a direct impact on the writing of the poetry is illustrated in "Sweeney Agonistes" where "two American gentlemen here on business" arrive in London and rehearse the clichés of colloquial American speech: London, one of them explains with great politeness to his English friends, is "a slick place, London's a swell place,/London's a fine place to come on a visit—," and the other adds with equal politeness: "Specially when you got a real live Britisher/A guy like Sam to show you around/Sam of course is at *home* in London,/And he's promised to show us around." In the same work, at a moment of great anguish, another character reiterates the poet's extreme sensitivity to and concern for language when he says: "I gotta use words when I talk to you."

If Eliot as a transplanted American in Europe seems to be a special case (a great poet, however, is always a special case, if one chooses to regard him in that light), the example of James Joyce should help to reinforce the somewhat complicated .(because ubiquitous) thesis I am trying to elucidate. Joyce was an impoverished Irishman. As Eliot had to toil for some time in a bank while he tried to write poems, Joyce supported himself during the composition of *Ulysses* by teaching in a Berlitz school in Trieste during the first World War. The publication of *Ulysses*—an event which was described by a French critic as marking Ireland's spectacular reentry into European literature—was sufficiently a success to make a rich Englishman provide Joyce with financial security almost until the end of his life. Two years before, Joyce had completed his last and probably his best work, the stupendous *Finnegans Wake*, a book which would in itself provide sufficient evidence and illustration of the vocation of the modern poet[1] in modern life. All that has been observed in Eliot's work is all the more true of *Finnegans Wake:*—the attention to colloquial speech, the awareness of the variety of ways in which languages can be degraded and how that degradation can be the base for a new originality and exactitude, the sense of an involvement with the international scene and with all history. But more than that, the radio and even television play a part in this wonderful book, as indeed they played a part in the writing of it. Joyce had a shortwave radio with which he was able to hear London, Moscow, Dublin—and New York! In *Finnegans Wake*, I was perplexed for a time by echoes of American radio comedy and Yiddish humor until I learned about Joyce's radio and about his daily reading of the Paris edition of the New York *Herald-Tribune*. The most important point of all, however, is that *Finnegans Wake* exhibits in the smallest detail and in the entire scope of the work the internationality of the modern poet, his involvement in all history, and his consciousness of the impingement of any foreign language from Hebrew to Esperanto upon the poet's use of the English language.

It is foolish to speculate about the future of anything as precarious as the vocation of poetry—an eminent critic said some years ago that the technique of verse was a dying one, but Joyce may

1. Joyce's two best works, *Ulysses* and his last book, are not poems in the ordinary sense of the word; and he wrote several volumes of poetry, most of which consist of verses far inferior to anything in his major books. But any view of poetry which excludes *Finnegans Wake* as a poem and Joyce as a poet merely suggests the likelihood that Joyce transformed and extended the limits of poetry by the writing of his last book. If we freeze our categories and our definitions, (and this is especially true in literature) the result is that we disable and blind our minds.

have persuaded him to change his mind—but to think of the future is as inevitable as it is dubious. Joyce's last book suggests certain tentative formulations about the future of the writing of poetry. It suggests that there can be no turning back, unless civilization itself declines as it did when the Roman Empire fell. Yet it is also clear that poets cannot go forward in a straight line from the point at which *Finnegans Wake* concluded. What they can do is not evident in the least, apart from the fact that a literal imitation or extension of Joyce would be as mechanical as it is undesirable: too much in the very nature of his work depends upon personal and idiosyncratic traits of the author, his training as a Jesuit, his love of operatic music, the personal pride which was involved in his departure from Ireland and the infatuation with everything Irish which obsessed him in this as in his other books. There are other important elements in Joyce's work and in his life which do lead, I think, to some tentative generalization about the future of poetry and the vocation of the poet. One of them was pointed out to me by Meyer Schapiro (who has influenced me in much of what I have said throughout) : the question has been raised as to why Joyce, both in *Ulysses* and in *Finnegans Wake*, identified himself with Jews, with Leopold Bloom, an Irish Jew, and with the character of Shem in his last book (Shem is, among other of his very many kinships, a son of Noah, and he is compared with Jesus Christ, to the ironic denigration of both beings). The answer to the question of Joyce's identification with Jews, Schapiro said, is that the Jew is at once alienated and indestructible, he is an exile from his own country and an exile even from himself, yet he survives the annihilating fury of history. In the unpredictable and fearful future that awaits civilization, the poet must be prepared to be alienated and indestructible. He must dedicate himself to poetry, although no one else seems likely to read what he writes; and he must be indestructible as a poet until he is destroyed as a human being. In the modern world, poetry is alienated; it will remain indestructible as long as the faith and love of each poet in his vocation survives.

Views of a Second Violinist
Some Answers to Questions about Writing Poetry

Questions about the practice of writing make me very nervous because my answers look strange after a newspaper reporter has rendered them. For instance, one time, I replied to a question about meter by saying that there was no such thing as free verse, but only different kinds of rhythm. By the time this careless remark reached the printed page, it turned out that I had denied the existence of poems which were called free verse. This inexactitude may not seem important, but I feel that there is too much misunderstanding in the world as it is, and if that is the best that can be done in the way of accurate repetition, I would rather shut up. However, it is necessary that one be polite, no matter what or how great the provocation. This requirement of politeness nearly ruined me, however, once when I was questioned as to whether the most important element in modern poetry was the intellectual factor or the emotional factor. Naturally I was stupefied. But politeness made me reply that it was just like the weather, sometimes it was too hot, sometimes it was too cold, sometimes the weather was just plain boring, and the less attention one paid to it, the better. My questioner, a very kind lady, who was just trying to make conversation, looked so alarmed at my answer that I hastened to assure her that Plato and Dryden were wrong when they declared that poets were practically insane. The next questioner was the feature writer, whatever that is, for a fashionable fashion magazine which printed literary prattle and the like to break the flow of gorgeous garment prose. Needless to say, I was on guard. The first question was as to how I had decided to become a poet, so I explained that as an infant in the cradle I had cried loudly and received immediate and unanimous attention; consequently, putting two and two together, I had tried crying out loudly in public and in blank verse, and the results had on the whole been most gratifying. My questioner seemed to like this answer very much, for she wrote it down quickly in shorthand and then inquired as to what was the greatest influence upon me? I was about to say Shakespeare and the depression of 1929-1937, but this was all too true, and since the truth had been distorted so often in all previous exchanges, I answered: prenatal experiences, for this was the first thing that came into my head. She took it as a *double entendre*, I think, for she left in a rage.

Since then, feeling badly about how all these well-meant inquisitions have turned out, I've given the whole subject cool and careful thought. The chief dangers, I've decided, are as follows: one may be too technical; or fleeing from technical observations and shop-talk, one may become oracular and thus very pretentious about poets as unacknowledged legislators and similar braggadocio; and from this extreme, one swings to facetiousness and receives a sickly, uneasy grin because poets are supposed to be very serious; and then, worst of all, one becomes too personal, thus infuriating other poets, although other people just love these intimate disclosures.

Conscious of these dangers, and others I have not troubled to mention, I've often resorted to or been reduced to silence. But I feel now that no amount of circumspection will protect me, so I might as well speak freely. I choose two professional problems which have long preoccupied me.

One of these problems is that of how much poetry one ought to write and how much one ought to publish. After much reflection, I've decided that one ought to write as much as possible and publish as little as possible. The latter conclusion follows from the glum fact that most poetry is likely to be bad, if judged by any standards which would justify the assertion that some poetry is good. On the other hand, one ought to write as much as possible because, among other reasons, there is no way of telling in advance whether the poem one is about to write is going to be good. Moreover, the writing of bad poems is often a way of arriving at the writing of good poems. By publishing only work which one is reasonably comfortable about, or work which is in an idiom one no longer cultivates, one escapes the remorse of looking at one's bad poems in print and the paralyzing effects which may ensue. Horace advises one to wait for nine years before publishing a poem; and a very gifted modern poet told me that it is best to publish as much as possible, for one can always write more poems. Both pieces of advice may be good for some poets or good under certain conditions; but for most poets to wait, to be patient, to rewrite and keep looking at one's poems is the best possible method of procedure, if one is interested in writing good poems rather than in being regarded as a poet. There is nothing wrong in wanting to be known as a good poet, but the desire to write good poems is more fruitful in the long run. Many good poets have been spoiled by the belief that they had to rush into print with a new book every year, and only a few have been weakened by revision, patience, and privacy.

This question is important in itself now, since the example of Auden has intensified the natural desire to appear in print very often; and it is also a significant problem because in trying to face it, one has to face the whole problem of the nature of poetry.

So too with the second problem, the relationship of any modern poet to his audience and to the well-known difficulty of modern poetry, a difficulty which obviously involves the audience. Anyone who wants to understand modern poetry can do so by working about half as hard as he must to learn a language, or acquire any new skill, or learn to play bridge well. The real problem is the effect upon the poet himself of the reader's feeling that modern poetry is difficult. His most frequent response of late has been one of panic, a panic which leads to false moves and desperate oversimplifications. One fashion or tendency for the last fifteen years, at least, has been to try to write poetry which would be intelligible to any audience. And meanwhile the extent of the difficulty has somehow increased in the public's mind, perhaps because the public has been preoccupied with matters other than literature. For a long time, "The Waste Land" seemed the perfect example of modern poetry's obscurity, but nowadays even the beautifully lucid poems of Robert Frost are said to be obscure. Perhaps this development is all to the good, since it may prevent poets from forcing themselves to try to be popular. But the fundamental problem presents itself falsely as long as it is supposed that the kind of poetry one produces is solely a matter of choice or will. Choice and will are involved, of course, but there is also present a large and inescapable relationship, a relationship which may well be prior because it has had a great deal to do with making the poet interested in writing poetry from the very start. Any modern poet exists in an inescapable relationship to all the modern and modernist poetry which has been written since Baudelaire. He can choose to disregard or forget about this complicated relationship; but if he does, he is depriving himself of what is an important part of his inheritance as a poet, and a powerful presence in the minds of everyone who is capable of reading poetry.

Consequently the modern poet is bound to be drawn in two apparently opposed directions. On the one hand, it is natural that he should want to write as directly and clearly as Yeats and Frost at their best (which is not to forget that their directness and clarity were accomplished only by means of a great deal of intellectual toil and obscure or esoteric delvings). On the other hand, he is bound to be drawn toward an emulation of the marvellous refinements in the uses and powers of language which have occurred since the symbolists appeared.

The best convenient example of this cultivation of language is this little poem which appears in James Joyce's *Ulysses:*

> White thy fambles, red thy gan,
> And thy quarrons dainty is.
> Couch a hogshead with me then
> In the darkmans clip and kiss.

(I choose this example not only for its convenient brevity, but also because it is an omen or beginning of *Finnegans Wake*, an overwhelming work which, if it concludes an epoch, also initiates a new one.) The obscurity of the little poem in *Ulysses* is not reduced very much by its context in the novel. And even when the reader finds out, as he may not unless he reads Stuart Gilbert's commentary on *Ulysses*, that the words he does not understand, or only imperfectly understands, are gypsy slang, he may be disturbed by the poem or resent the author's use of unfamiliar and special words. Indeed, it can be argued (in a misleading way or in an illuminating one) that the beauty of this poem and the powerful emotion it communicates come through best of all when the reader does not know exactly what the exact gypsy meanings of the words are. For example, "couch a hogshead" means "lie down and sleep," and if one knows this in advance, some of the richness of connotation may be blocked off.

Every modern poet would like to be direct, lucid, and immediately intelligible, at least most of the time. In fact, one of the most fantastic misconceptions of modern literature and modern art in general is the widespread delusion that the modern artist does not want and would not like a vast popular audience, if this were possible without the sacrifice of some necessary quality in his work. But it is often not possible. And every modern poet would also like to be successful, popular, famous, rich, cheered on Broadway, sought by Hollywood, recited on the radio, and admired by Mr. J. Donald Adams. The renunciation of popularity does not arise from any poet's desire to punish himself and deprive himself of these glorious prizes and delectable rewards. The basic cause is a consciousness of the powers and possibilities of language, a consciousness which cannot be discarded with any more ease than one can regain one's innocence.

Some will doubtless continue to be irritated by the cultivation of language of which Joyce's poem is a somewhat extreme instance. And they will waste time, mind, and energy in defensive attitudes, denouncing or denying the virtues of this kind of writing.

And some will try to imitate and extend literally and mechanically the direction which Joyce represents.

And some will try to find a point at which the clarity of Yeats can be sought at the same time as one seeks the richness which Joyce possessed.

This last effort or ambition may be as quixotic and contradictory as an attempt to square the circle. But given the consciousness of literature likely in any one who wants to write good poetry, anything less than the reconciliation of these extremes is far from enough. As some Indian chief once said at a dinner in the White

House after he had had two portions of everything but remained hungry: *A little too much of everything is just enough for me.*

Orpheus once visited a colleague. His name was Agathon and he was a famous poet and critic of the time. Indeed he was much better known than Orpheus then, for the latter had not yet attracted to himself the widespread publicity which followed upon his sensational adventures in trying to get his wife to return to him.

Orpheus showed Agathon his most recent work, requesting a critical opinion, but hoping for praise and admiration.

"Frankly," said Agathon, "these poems are worthless. Even a fellow-poet like myself has a hard time understanding them. You can imagine what the common reader will and will not make of them. Why don't you write the way the old boys did? *This is not what the public wants.*"

"I do my best," said Orpheus meekly (he was very disappointed but grateful for his friend's candor), "I write whatever I can."

This story is endless. I hope to discuss it at greater length in the future. One must not be deceived by Orpheus' subsequent career which was largely in the nature of an escapade and *tour de force.* Every genuine poet is now in the same boat as Orpheus was then. Agathon was right to say what he did say. What would have been the point of being other than sincere, if that was the way he felt?

"*Amor omnia vincit,*" muttered Orpheus under his breath as he left, "Love always wins out. Poetry is its own reward. Maybe Agathon is right. Maybe he is wrong."

Obviously the above interview may be interpreted in several different ways.

The Present State of Poetry

On a number of other occasions, some of them fairly recent, some of them very long ago, I have written or spoken, or I have heard what others have written and spoken about the subject of tonight's lecture, the condition of poetry in America at present. I intend to describe some of these occasions in a while, but right now, as a starting point, it is important to say that the present occasion is quite different from every past occasion, although the subject is the same; and all those past occasions seem quite different now than at the time that they occurred.

In the past, there has been little or no reason to feel as I felt when, in preparing to speak tonight, I reviewed the subject in my mind. For as I thought of the present state of poetry in America, in the middle of the twentieth century, I had two very unlike and wholly conflicting impressions. One impression was that of bewilderment and reminded me of a film I once saw in which a minor but complicated character, whenever anyone said to him, "How are you?", invariably replied, "I don't know!" So far as I can remember, this answer displeased everyone else: some were irritated, others were infuriated, no one was satisfied, and yet there was more to the answer than a simple statement of ignorance or a simple unwillingness to make a clear and unequivocal statement about one's state of being, and this was made evident when one irritated questioner said: "What do you mean, you don't know how you are?" When one says, "I don't know," whether one is speaking of one's state of being or one is speaking of the state of poetry, the answer possesses a genuine accuracy. It would be inaccurate to say that poetry at present is in a state of perfect health; at the same time, it would be still more inaccurate to say that it was in a state of severe illness or decline, as it has been, from time to time, during the latter half of the nineteenth century and the first fourteen years of the twentieth century. Perhaps to say that the condition of poetry at present is one of complicated transition is the closest one can come to a positive statement. But one must immediately add that it is in a state of a special and new kind, a state of groping and uncertainty. It should be almost needless to say that this attitude toward the present is not limited to poets and the condition of poetry, nor is it confined to the United States. The second strong feeling which tonight's subject repeatedly suggested to me was not in the least a sense of doubt and perplexity, but on the contrary it was very much of an embarrassment of riches: I felt as I think Baudelaire must have felt when he wrote, in one of his best poems, "I have more memories than if I had lived for a thousand years!" There are various reasons for this abundance and excess of memory, which is common, I feel almost certain, to all the poets of my own generation, and particularly true of those who like myself have been critics, teachers, and editors as well as poets. So many changes have occurred since the time when we were adolescents: this was the time when it seemed the most wonderful thing in the world to be a poet, when any older person who had appeared in print seemed to have a godlike aura, a supernatural radiance, and when the experience of reading the work of older poets was the cause of overwhelming excitement, and at times, indeed, of an intense exaltation comparable to no other kind of experience, however pleasant or joyous.

For the poets of my own generation as for myself, some twenty, twenty-five, or thirty years of chronological time have passed since the time of adolescence or the time when we first began to appear in print. Most of us thought when we first appeared in print that all our problems were over and we were entirely unaware that on the contrary, all our problems had just begun. But even if we had possessed the knowledge of our elders, we would not have been prepared for the changes which have continually occurred during the past twenty years, changes which make the time of adolescence and of first youth appear to belong to another century and to the experience of some human being other than oneself.

The apocalyptic events which have occurred since 1938 throughout the world, and in particular the five years of the Second World War, would be sufficient to make the past of twenty years ago seem far more distant from us than twenty years of chronological time. But the changes which have occurred in the state of poetry, changes which could hardly have been anticipated or indeed imagined very often, can best be summarized by citing a series of examples: these examples should indicate, in one or another way, that the changes have sometimes been profound, sometimes superficial, and sometimes misleading, and it is their rapid succession during the past twenty years which makes the state of poetry very different and more difficult to define now than in 1938, or indeed at any time, in America, since the Civil War.

My first example, which may be an illustration of the most important change of all, is the visit of T. S. Eliot to America during 1932 and 1933 when, in addition to teaching and lecturing at various schools, he read his own poetry in public. My own direct experience is limited to a lecture on Milton which Mr. Eliot gave at Columbia and another lecture in New York City in which he quoted verse quite often, but I am sure that I am not mistaken in supposing that Mr. Eliot's public appearances were very different from what occurred when Dylan Thomas read his poetry in public on his visits to America between 1949 and 1953. Eliot was already famous then: his authority as a critic was already that of a literary dictator, and hence his appearances inspired a sense of awe which went beyond the admiration one would have felt in the presence of other creative writers of the same rank, such as William Butler Yeats, James Joyce and Thomas Mann. His manner of lecturing as well as the way in which he read poetry, his own or another poet's was extremely impressive. But Eliot's public appearances only served to confirm what his audience already felt: namely, that he was a very great poet indeed and the greatest living literary critic. The experience of attending one of his lectures or readings was like that of reading his poems or his criticism; it did not create a new impression of his work. In contrast, this is exactly what Dylan Thomas' readings in public accomplished when they took place many years after. Until these readings Thomas was known in America merely as one of a number of fairly well-known poets. His readings in public made him as famous, in a short period of time, as T. S. Eliot, Robert Frost, and William Butler Yeats had become only after a good many years. And indeed if not for these readings, it is likely that he would have remained comparatively unknown to the general public. Many of the people who were excited to intense admiration by hearing his poems aloud were people who had found his poetry, when it appeared in print, opaque, impenetrable, difficult, obscure, and in a word, unreadable. Thus what Thomas accomplished by his public readings is meaningful in ways which extend far beyond the unquestionable importance of his work. He demonstrated by direct, eloquent, and vivid example of a truth about the nature of poetry which no amount of critical elucidation could have communicated—the truth that the actuality of a poem is not merely a matter of the explicit meanings contained in each successive line. For many years the majority of readers had been puzzled and irritated by modern poetry's obscurity and difficulty, its esoteric allusions, sudden transitions, or the appearance of a lack of transition, connection and logical order. The irritation of many readers almost always developed into the conviction that the obscurity and difficulty of modern poetry was too great for the uninstructed reader to overcome. Yet when the same readers heard Thomas' poetry aloud, they immediately forgot about their previous impressions. The aural experience of a poem, when read as well as Thomas could read his own poetry and the poetry of others also, communicated to his listeners an experience of the truth that the total being of a poem is far more than its explicit meanings, and this made the poem very different from what it had seemed to be when it was encountered upon the page and seemed very much like an inferior crossword puzzle, an unrewarding exercise in discovering concealed meanings. The living voice communicated to Thomas' readers the intensely felt attitudes and emotions which were the actual poem in its complete and concrete reality.

There would be a good deal more to say if tonight's subject were restricted to the public's skill or lack of skill in reading poetry as it appears upon the page. Here I must limit my comments to the bearing which Thomas's readings have had upon the present state of poetry. Thomas' readings initiated what may very well be an immense change in the public's whole conception of the nature of modern poetry. The enthusiasm he awakened suggests that for the majority of readers a poem as it appears in print has the same relationship to the total reality and being of a poem as a musical score of a symphony has to the orchestral performance of that symphony. I must immediately add that it would be very easy to overestimate—or to underestimate the advance, and to overlook the very real dangers inherent in the aural experience of poetry. Thus, those who hear a poem aloud do not invariably feel moved to seek out the poem in print. This might well lead to the neglect of the kind of poetry in which there is a richness of style and language that requires the eye as well as the ear, and conversely it might encourage the writing of that kind of poetry which lends itself best to being read aloud. It might also encourage one or another kind of histrionic elocutionism and the vulgarity of most forms of oratory and declamation. A great and powerful voice can be extremely hynoptic and deceptive, and it can disregard the inferiority of the text: thus Sarah Bernhardt is said to have been able to reduce an audience to tears by reciting the multiplication table.

These and other dangers are all the more difficult to avoid because few poets read aloud very well or indeed with any degree of the eloquence and power which Thomas possessed. The fact that many of the good poets of our time read poetry poorly may be temporary and due to a lack of training and experience. But it is also true that few human beings know how to read poetry aloud: few actors possess this skill, however good they may be as actors. This is evident in the way in which Shakespearean blank verse is spoken in most productions of Shakespeare; it is spoken as if there were no difference between speeches in blank verse and speeches in prose. Hence it must be said that for the time being one must guard against any unqualified optimism about the effectiveness of public readings, and the need of being critical will continue until there exists for poetry as there already exists for music and the drama an independent class of performers trained in the aural realization of poetry. Those who are devoted to music do not expect a great virtuoso to be a great composer, or the reverse: there is just as little justification for expecting the situation to be otherwise in poetry.

The purpose of my second example is to illustrate another very important change which has occurred in recent years and which makes the present state of poetry very different from what it was in the past, some twenty years ago, or for that matter forty and fifty years ago. In 1936 I heard Wallace Stevens, one of the best of all American poets, read his poetry at Harvard: it was the first time Stevens had ever read his poetry in public, and this first reading was at once an indescribable ordeal and a precious event to Stevens: it was precious because he had been an undergraduate at Harvard some thirty-seven years before, at the turn of the century, and he had not returned since that time in his own person, although he had often gone to the Yale-Harvard football games incognito. Before and after reading each poem, Stevens spoke of the nature of poetry, a theme which naturally concerned him very much, and he said, among other things, that the least sound counts, the least sound and the least syllable. He illustrated this observation by telling of how he had awakened after midnight the week before and heard the sounds made by a cat walking delicately and carefully on the crusted snow outside his house. After each comment, Stevens returned to his own poems: but at one point an old Cambridge lady, holding an ear trumpet aloft and dressed in a style which must have been *chic* at the inauguration of Rutherford Hayes, shouted out, hoarse and peremptory as crows, that she must ask Mr. Stevens to speak loudly and clearly, loudly and clearly, if you please. She might just as well have been shouting at President Hayes. Stevens continued to read his poems in a very low voice, although a good many of them were written in a style as high-flown and passionate as that of any Elizabethan playwright. And throughout his reading Stevens was extremely nervous and constrained, although since this state of mind showed itself only as a rigid impassivity, his overwhelming nervousness must have been invisible to most of his audience. When the reading ended, Stevens said to the teacher who had introduced him: "I wonder what the boys at the office would think about this?' The office was the Hartford Accident and Indemnity Co., the boys were those who knew Stevens as the vice-president and legal counsel of the company and thus the most solid of citizens.

A good deal more might be said about the significance of this remark and how much it helps to illuminate Stevens' poetic career and the very quality of his poetry. But right now the point which must be emphasized as much as possible is this: no poet of my own or the rising generation of poets would feel as Stevens did when he made the remark, for, among other things, if one said: "I wonder what the boys at the office would think about this," it is a matter of overwhelming probability that one would be referring to the office of the English department at a university.

This is the change which has affected the condition of poetry more than any other during the past generation. The fact that in 1958 so many poets are teachers of literature and that in 1938, 1928, and 1908, this was very seldom true, constitutes a radical change which involves not only the poet and the poetry which he writes, but the readers of poetry and their concept of the poet and of poetry. Primary and important as this change is, it cannot, however, be regarded in isolation from changes of other kinds which have also taken place and which are rooted in the changing character of American life: for example, the college-educated population of the entire country has more than doubled in two generations, and since this increase is likely to continue, more and more poets may be welcomed as teachers of literature in the colleges.

The effect upon the poet of being a teacher of literature is a complicated and independent topic; what I want to point out now is the effect upon the poet's conception of himself as a poet and indeed as a human being. In the past, the poet had a sense of what he seemed to most other human beings which was identical, in one or another way, with the feelings of Wallace Stevens not only when he read his poetry for the first time in public but throughout his entire life.

Today, since so many poets are teachers, it is no longer true that the poet is regarded by most other human beings as a strange and exotic being. Moreover, as a teacher the poet makes direct use of the entire past of American and English poetry and he is in direct communication several times a week with what is known in advertising circles as a trapped audience: he has as an audience human beings at the most impressionable and receptive stage of existence, and he soon discovers that in the classroom it is possible to persuade almost all students that poetry is extremely interesting and that it is never too difficult or too obscure to be understood. This is true to such an extent that at times the problem becomes one of persuading the student that a poem is not good merely because it is difficult, or bad because it is simple and lucid. Indeed, this experience may encourage the most sanguine illusions in the poet himself. He may very well forget that the conditions which exist in the classroom do not exist outside of the classroom and hence he may suppose that the intense love of poetry which he has awakened with ease in his students will continue permanently. He may also suppose that the teaching of literature is sufficient in itself, granted the proper support, to create and sustain a genuinely literate reading public immune to all the corruptions of mass culture. Whether or not he suffers from these illusions, one thing is incontestable and makes an immense difference. The poet as a teacher has a status within the confines of the academic community which gives him a very different sense of himself and a very different sense of how he is regarded by other human beings: he is a useful and accepted member of society and not a peculiar and strange being, since the writing of poetry is clearly a natural pursuit for the teacher of literature. The fact that he is a poet is not something which in itself isolates him from most other human beings, an isolation which the poet and indeed the artist in every medium felt profoundly during every generation in the past.

My examples thus far have illustrated the extent to which the state of poetry as a whole is superior at present to what it has been for the most part during the past. Now I want to go on to a series of examples which are of a mixed character and which indicate that the present superiority is incomplete and may very well be misleading. For the advantages involve disadvantages. It is possible to overestimate or misunderstand both what is positive and what is negative.

I have just described the positive advantages of the tendency of poets to be teachers of literature. The best way I can deal with the disadvantages, which are inseparable from the advantages, is to speak directly of my own experience as a poet who has been a teacher. I feel no doubt whatever that the paradoxical character of my own experience is typical in every way of most if not all the poets of my own generation, and typical also of the experience, during the past twenty years, of poets older and younger than myself.

During the past twenty years I have been employed as a teacher of English composition, English literature, American literature, and creative writing at eight universities. I have also been a lecturer, the editor of a literary review, the poetry editor and film critic of a weekly periodical, the literary consultant for a philanthropic foundation, and in general I have been provided with a good deal of work which not only enabled me to earn a modest livelihood, but also enabled me to acquire interesting and useful skills, so many, in fact, that there was a period of fifteen months during which I had five jobs, only two of which, however, were full-time. The important and paradoxical point is that I would seldom if ever have been employed in these capacities if I had not been a poet, and my first teaching appointment certainly would not have been offered to me if I had not published my first book of poems some time before. I was asked to do many things because I was a poet: the one thing I was not asked to do very often was to write poetry. I will speak of the two occasions, seventeen years apart from each other, which are exceptions to this statement in a moment. Right now I want to try to be as concrete as possible about what I mean. When a poet is asked to teach, or to act as an editor, or to write book reviews and critical essays, the basis of his employment is such as to enable him to earn a living. When, however, he writes a poem, this is not true in the same way: for the most likely result of the writing of a poem and its publication is that he will have one or another opportunity to earn a living in some way other than that of writing poetry.

It must be said immediately that during the past twenty years the number of prizes, awards, grants, and honors given to poets has increased a great deal, and it would be ungrateful as well as untrue to say that they have not helped matters a good deal, and made the lot of the poet fortunate in ways which hardly existed at all twenty and thirty years ago. At the same time it would be wrong to suppose that the generosity with which poetry is supported does more than reduce the problem of economic necessity, which is more difficult for the poet than for other human beings precisely because he is a poet. During two of the past seventeen years, in 1940 and in 1957, I have been given sums of money sufficient to enable me to devote myself entirely to the writing of poetry: but these grants, which I was delighted, I need hardly say, to get, are based precisely on the fact that it is impossible to earn even the most modest livelihood unless, in addition to writing poetry, one does a good many other things.

The attitude of the public toward poetry and the poet is, as much that I have said should indicate, very important too. And here again it is only after one has taken account of positive and negative complications that one avoids oversimplification and arrives at an adequate conclusion.

Here is a negative piece of evidence: "A recent survey showed that sixty percent of the adult population of America did not read a book other than the Bible in 1954." And here is an even more negative piece of evidence: "If the American Festival Academy can help it, the Bard of Avon will not be the formidable bore that he is to so many students across the land." I need not mention the measures which are going to be taken to make Shakespeare something other than a formidable bore, but it is worth remarking, in passing, that if to many millions of Americans Shakespeare is a formidable bore, there is no justification for attributing the public's indifference to or dislike of modern poetry to its difficulty and obscurity. It can also be maintained that Shakespeare has stopped being a formidable bore, since the Broadway stage has discovered that Shakespeare really wrote musical comedies, a truth which remained unknown for centuries.

In any case, the negative evidence in both instances is misleading if either instance is regarded in isolation or if, with Whitman, one believes that "To have great poets one must have great audiences," a statement which can certainly be understood in a numerical sense. To assume, however, that mere quantity or the mere largeness of an audience is of absolute and decisive importance is just as false as to assume that the indifference of the public toward poetry and the poet makes no difference at all. To have great poetry it is necessary to have great poets: during the past hundred years and more, there have been great poets who had little or no audience at all during their lifetime, and if the mere numerical quantity of the audience were as crucial a matter as it is often supposed to be, the best sellers of each year would be far more important than they are. One has only to ask more readers of fiction: "What were the best sellers of five years ago and ten years ago?" to discover that their very names have been forgotten and thus that as best sellers they have really made no lasting impression at all on the reading public.

The fact that sixty percent of the adult population does not read any book other than the Bible during the year is regrettable; and it is equally regrettable that Shakespeare is regarded as a bore by millions of human beings. But the attitude of those who do not read books at all is far less important than the attitude of those who do read books. The comments of John O'Hara when he lectured here last December, and his comments at other times, will illustrate what I mean in several ways. Mr. O'Hara is of course a very gifted novelist and he is also, it is clear, an avid reader. The dissatisfaction he expressed because some of his novels had sold no more than one hundred thousand copies should show that the possibilities of dissatisfaction are unlimited. Mr. O'Hara has made other comments of a critical kind which illustrate the fact that even a very gifted novelist and a devoted reader may not be a desirable addition to the reading public. Thus Mr. O'Hara spoke of how delighted and honored he was to have the company of "a foremost intellectual like Thornton Wilder" and yet how distraught he became when Mr. Wilder mentioned the names of Søren Kierkegaard and Franz Kafka. In a like way, Mr. O'Hara, reviewing a novel by Ernest Hemingway several years ago, declared that Hemingway was the greatest writer since Shakespeare, a statement which immediately made one wonder: what makes Shakespeare better? It also suggests that Mr. O'Hara's disgust with Kierkegaard and Kafka may extend to Shakespeare too, or at any rate to those modern poets who have been influenced by Kierkegaard, Kafka, and Shakespeare.

Mr. O'Hara's impressions as a reader are a negative illustration of what may be most defective in the reading public's attitude toward poetry at present. In the past, when a reader found that a poem or a novel did not interest him, he usually said, with humility, "I don't understand it, it's over my head."

During recent years and at present, more and more readers have adopted an attitude of extreme arrogance, declaring that a poem or novel which they were unable to understand was clearly worthless precisely because they were unable to understand it.

The number of readers of poetry is far less important than the quality of their attitude toward poetry. One hundred thousand readers who felt as passionate and devoted and sustained an interest in the work of living poets as they feel towards a good many games, sports, and avocations, would be far more desirable than a reading public of several millions who felt that their attitude as readers was an unquestionable criterion of the intrinsic value of any work of poetry or fiction.

At present, it is clear that the reading public as a whole regards the anthology as the best of all books of poetry. And the increasing popularity of anthologies during the past twenty years has certainly been the cause of more anthologies and better anthologies. It remains true that the anthology is very often a substitute for the reading of the books of any poet in particular. But again, it is also true that many readers of anthologies would not read contemporary poetry at all, if anthologies were not available to them and they had to choose among the books of individual poets.

The attitude of the American public as a whole toward poetry and the poet can be further defined by describing how *Life* magazine noted the death of Dylan Thomas in the autumn of 1953, and then, a few months after, the death of Maxwell Bodenheim. Thomas' death was mentioned in a brief paragraph of tribute which made one of the millions of readers or beholders of *Life* curious enough to write to the editors and ask: "Who is Dylan Thomas?" The letter was printed along with a small photograph of Thomas. Bodenheim's death, on the other hand, was the subject of two full pages of photographs and captions, reviewing thirty years of Bodenheim's life. Clearly poetic merit and public fame had nothing to do with the extreme contrast, since Thomas not only was a far more important poet than Bodenheim but a far more famous one. The extreme contrast in coverage, which of course would have been reversed if poetic merit had been the cri-

[41]

terion, has only one explanation: Bodenheim was murdered; Thomas' death was the result, on the surface at least, of what are sometimes called natural causes and thus hardly sensational enough to excite and gratify the curiosity of the vast number of human beings who view *Life* weekly. This instance is grotesque and special; nevertheless it certainly suggests that a poet can succeed in attracting national attention by being murdered or by being involved in some other activity of a spectacular, scandalous or extraordinary character: the intrinsic poetic value of his work is certainly not going to win him the same attention of the entire public at present or at any time in the foreseeable future.

Two further and final examples should complete the picture and demonstrate why any positive statement about the state of poetry at present requires a negative qualification and any negative formulation the converse, so that an adequate generalization is possible only if one can say without emotional contradiction: The present state of poetry in America is superior to what it has ever been in the past; yet at the same time, the present state of poetry is not in an unquestionably flourishing state in any full sense.

Thus, when one poet of my own generation sent a copy of his first book of poems to his brother, he received a letter of acknowledgment from which I quote only the first paragraph:

> Dear Brother,
>   I received your book and really liked it very much except that I don't like poetry as I don't understand it. I showed your book to a few people and they were very much impressed and except for the fact that they didn't have a spare $2.50 they would have bought a copy.

This letter was written nineteen years ago; since then, it must be said again, there have continually been changes which make the present very different from the past. The far greater number of prizes, awards, grants, fellowships, public readings and recordings, and teaching appointments are the result of a public interest and solicitude which hardly existed a generation ago. Thus there are now five major prizes for poetry each year, and there was only one, the Pulitzer Prize, twenty years ago. And this is very important, since it does a great deal to encourage publishers to publish new books of poetry, despite the likelihood of financial loss. But on the whole the greatly increased interest of the public is an interest in the poet, far more than an interest in poetry itself. The purchase of a new book of poems of most poets represents but a small fraction of the number of human beings who attend poetry readings. And this is but one indication that it is the poet, in person, as an interesting human being, rather than his poetry, which attracts the majority of those at any poetry reading, although it is certainly true that the poet is regarded as an interesting human being only because he writes poems. So too, time again, other poets have spoken of the experience of being invited to dinner or for a weekend and being the object of the most generous hospitality solely because they were poets. They would otherwise have been unknown and thus out of the reach of the kindness of those who entertained them. Yet at the same time their hosts seldom showed any sign of a serious and passionate interest in their own poetry or the poetry of other writers. Nevertheless, I doubt very much that any poet does not prefer this split in interest to the total indifference which characterized every other period in the past.

Thus far I have said nothing about the kind of poetry which is being written at present, although the subject of the present state of poetry in America might be understood as requiring first of all an attempt to describe and evaluate the work of particular poets and of leading poetic tendencies and movements. The fact that the changing status of the poet and poetry, the changing attitude of the public, and the changing set of conditions under which the poet writes seemed to have a prior importance is significant in itself. It indicates how profound these changes are or may be in the future. It is also significant of the fact that there are no new poetic movements and schools as clearly defined and as strong as Imagism and the free verse movement of some forty years ago or the powerful emergence of social consciousness during the years of the depression. Indeed the very poets who first became famous as advocates of political and social revolution—for example, Auden, Spender, and C. Day Lewis—have for the past decade and more written poetry which seems so unrelated to the subject matter of their early work that no reader who knew only their later work would suspect that in their early work they called for the death of the old gang, and for the working class revolution, at-

[43]

tacked capitalism, fascism, and war, and dismissed all other themes as unimportant. The theme of political revolution has vanished as if it had never been a preoccupation excluding all other themes. But another revolution which began before the social and economic crisis of the depression, has continued all the while: I mean the poetic revolution, the revolution in poetic taste which was inspired by the criticism of T. S. Eliot. This revolution has established itself in power so completely that it is taken for granted not only in poetry and the criticism of poetry, but in the teaching of literature.

Once a literary and poetic revolution has established itself, it is no longer revolutionary, but something very different from what it was when it had to struggle for recognition and assert itself against the opposition of established literary authority. Thus the most striking trait of the poetry of the rising generation of poets is the assumption as self-evident and incontestable of that conception of the nature of poetry which was, at its inception and for years after, a radical and much disputed transformation of poetic taste and sensibility. What was once a battlefield has become a peaceful public park on a pleasant summer Sunday afternoon, so that if the majority of new poets write in a style and idiom which takes as its starting point the poetic idiom and literary taste of the genera-tion of Pound and Eliot, the motives and attitudes at the heart of the writing possess an assurance which sometimes makes their work seem tame and sedate.

Before saying something more detailed about the character of the poetry of the majority of new poets, some attention must be given to the only recent new movement and counter-tendency, that of the San Francisco circle of poets who, under the leadership of Kenneth Rexroth, have recently proclaimed themselves super-Bohemians and leaders of a new poetic revolution. According to Mr. Rexroth, the new rebels are rebelling against "the highly or-ganized academic and literary movement employment agency of the Neoantireconstructionists," the established poets and critics who are installed in the universities, and who form, he says, "a dense crust of custom over American cultural life." Since these poets recite their poems in bars and with jazz accompanists, and since one poet aptly calls his book of poems, "Howl," it is appro-priate to refer to them as the Howlers of San Francisco as a way of labelling their leading theme, the conviction that they must scream against the conformism which prevails in society and in literary circles. The San Francisco Howlers are, however, imaginary rebels since the substance of their work is a violent advocacy of a nonconformism which they already possess and which requires no insurrection whatever, since nonconformism of almost every variety had become acceptable and respectable and available to everyone. Unlike the Bohemianism of the past, which had to attack the dominant Puritanism and Victorianism of respectable society in a variety of forms, including the censorship of books, Prohibition, and a prudery enforced by the police, the new nonconformism has no genuine enemy: it is unopposed and permitted to exist in freedom, hence the new rebel bears a great deal of resemblance to a prize fighter trying to knock out an antagonist who is not in the ring with him. The essential conviction of the San Francisco Howlers is that they are fighting the conformism of the organization man, the advertising executive, the man in the grey flannel suit, or the man in the Brooks Brothers suit. The rebellion is a form of shadow boxing because the Man in the Brooks Brothers suit is himself, in his own home, very often what Russell has called an upper Bohemian. His conformism is limited to the office day and business hours: in private life—and at heart—he is as Bohemian as anyone else. And it is often true indeed that the purpose of the job which requires conformism is solely to support his personal idiosyncracies, tastes and inclinations. Even if this were not true, the fact remains that the nonconformism proclaimed by the new rebels is not prohibited, proscribed, regarded as immoral and antisocial by the community as a whole, and no social pressure exists to compel the nonconformist to wear a grey flannel suit instead of a turtleneck sweater, slacks, and a sport jacket. The new rebel is fighting for what he has already won and fighting against a threat which does not exist, since he does not want a grey flannel suit, he is not forced to wear one, he need not compromise or conceal his Bohemianism in any respect, he is free to dress as he pleases and behave as he feels like behaving without being guilty of disorderly conduct, vagrancy, or even eccentricity.

The extent to which the San Francisco Howlers are engaged in an imaginary rebellion becomes entirely clear when Mr. Rexroth's statements take on a political and global character, attempting to connect literary tendencies in America with Russian totalitarianism in Europe. Outside of San Francisco, Mr. Rexroth declares, there is only fear and despair: "Poets are coming to San Francisco," he adds, "for the same reasons that so many Hungarians have been going to Austria recently." This is enough to make one feel that Mr. Rexroth does not recognize the difference between the Red Army and the *Kenyon Review* critics, between Nikita Khrushchev and John Crowe Ransom, or between the political commissars of a police state and the tyrants who write advertising copy on Madison Avenue.

Ludicrous as this attitude is, it does nevertheless point to one significant way in which the international state of affairs has had a serious and adverse effect upon creative writing in America. The leading motive of classical American literature and of twentieth century writing has been a criticism of American life. Sometimes the criticism has had a native basis: the actuality of American life has been criticized from the exalted point of view of the American Dream. And sometimes, in expatriate writers like Henry James and T. S. Eliot, the actuality of American life has been criticized by being compared with the culture of the Old World. But since the Second World War and the beginning of the atomic age, the consciousness of the creative writer, however detached, has been confronted with the spectre of the totalitarian state, the growing poverty and helplessness of Western Europe, and the threat of an inconceivably destructive war which may annihilate civilization and mankind itself. Clearly when the future of civilization is no longer assured, a criticism of American life in terms of a contrast between avowed ideals and present actuality cannot be a primary preoccupation and source of inspiration. For America, not Europe, is now the sanctuary of culture; civilization's very existence depends upon America, upon the actuality of American life, and not the ideals of the American Dream. To criticize the actuality upon which all hope depends thus becomes a criticism of hope itself. No matter what may be wrong with American life, it is nothing compared to the police state, barbarism, and annihilation.

This may be the most important cause of the tameness and the constrained calm which shows itself very often in the writing of the new generation of poets. An anthology of the work of new poets which has recently appeared and which is called the *New Poets of England and America* represents the character of their work as a whole very well. The editors say in their introduction: "What characteristics are to be discovered in the poetry of this generation, we leave the reader to discover." This statement is very revealing precisely because it is so different from the positive assertions, unquestioned convictions and intense rejections which have, in the past, marked the emergence of a strong poetic movement, school, or tendency.

The editors of this new anthology have restricted their selections to the work of poets under forty, who receive the blessing, in the form of an introduction, of Robert Frost, a very great poet indeed, and one who is now over eighty. Mr. Frost, unlike the editors, finds some positive generalization possible about the present state of poetry. The selections are gratifying evidence, Mr. Frost says, that "school and poetry come near to being the same thing." And he concludes by saying that as a result of the number of poets who have become teachers, "in a thousand, two thousand colleges," we now have "the best audiences poetry ever had in this world."

The characteristics which these new poets tend to have in common are matters of both style and subject matter. Most of these new poets have mastered poetic form and technique to a degree superior, on the whole, to that of any past generation. Until the generation of Pound and Eliot, American poets were for the most part inspired amateurs, and when deserted by inspiration, the habits of versification which they had acquired intuitively or through reading were too erratic to prevent them from writing verse which was painfully slipshod and uneven. The new generation of poets possess a trained and conscious skill, a sophisticated mastery of the craft of versification. And this professional competence may be strengthened by the disciplined knowledge of literary form which the teacher of literature must have.

The subject matter of these new poets is also revealing. One poem is about a toothache; and one poem is about a vacuum cleaner; and in general, the objects and experiences of daily life, which in previous generations were either supposed to be outside the realm of poetry or were introduced into poetry with a con-

[47]

scious daring and defiance, now appear in poem after poem in the most matter-of-fact way, as if their poetic quality had never been denied, questioned, or regarded as outrageous. In a like way, there is an explicitness about sexual experience without the self-consciousness or the assertive Bohemianism which characterized the poetry written during the first postwar period.

The perspectives which the generation of Pound and Eliot had to discover are now taken for granted: there is a clear and explicit consciousness of the international span of experience, and a pan-historical sense of culture, art, and literature which did not and indeed could not exist in the past. The subject matter of a good many poems is based upon travel in Europe, but these poets view Europe in a very different light from that of the poets of the past. Writers like Henry James and T. S. Eliot went to Europe with a Baedeker. Writers of the generation of Ernest Hemingway and E. E. Cummings went to Europe to drive an ambulance. The new poets often consult a Baedeker, but at the same time their awareness of the international sense is such as to make them ready to drop their Baedekers at any moment and seek out an ambulance, or at least transatlantic plane reservations to bring them back to America. Thus their point of view, in general, is that of the international tourist who, as an American, regards himself as an innocent bystander in a world in which an innocent bystander is continually faced by overwhelming and inexhaustible threat: in fact, there is often a feeling that to be an innocent bystander is in itself one form of guilt. The consciousness that experience is international, panhistorical, and multilingual is explicit and intense to a greater degree than ever before. Hence it can be said that for the poet today, English literature no longer exists as an independent entity. Whether the poet is reading, writing or teaching, the text is a text in comparative literature. This is a very great change indeed.

I can best summarize all that I have said so far about the present state of poetry by quoting two very different poems. One is one of Robert Frost's best and best-known lyrics; the other is by W. D. Snodgrass, a poet whose work I know only through the selections in *New Poets of England and America*. The two poems are hardly comparable in poetic value, but they are worth reading for the sake

of the contrast between them, a contrast which epitomizes the
changes which have occurred to make the state of poetry in the
middle of the twentieth century very different from what it was
during the first decade of the twentieth century.

STOPPING BY WOODS ON A SNOWY EVENING

Whose woods these are I think I know.
His house is in the village though;
He will not see me stopping here
To watch his woods fill up with snow.

My little horse must think it queer
To stop without a farmhouse near
Between the woods and frozen lake
The darkest evening of the year.

He gives his harness bells a shake
To ask if there is some mistake.
The only other sound's the sweep
Of easy wind and downy flake.

The woods are lovely, dark, and deep,
But I have promises to keep,
And miles to go before I sleep,
And miles to go before I sleep.[1]

APRIL INVENTORY

The green catalpa tree has turned
All white; the cherry blooms once more.
In one whole year I haven't learned
A blessed thing they pay you for.

. . . . .

The trees have more than I to spare.
The sleek expensive girls I teach
Younger and pinker every year,
Bloom gradually out of reach.
The pear-tree lets its petals drop
Like dandruff on a tabletop.

. . . . .

1. From *The Poetry of Robert Frost* edited by Edward Connery Lathem.
Copyright 1923 by Holt, Rinehart and Winston, Inc. Copyright 1951 by
Robert Frost. Reprinted by permission of Holt, Rinehart and Winston, Inc.,
and Jonathan Cape Ltd.

The tenth time, just a year ago,
I made myself a little list
Of all the things I ought to know;
Then told my parents, analyst,
And everyone who's trusted me
I'd be substantial, presently.
I haven't read one book about
A book or memorized a plot.
Or found a date I didn't doubt.
I learned one date and then forgot.
And one by one the solid scholars
Get the degrees, the jobs, the dollars.
And smile above their starchy collars.
I taught my classes Whitehead's notions;
One lovely girl, a song of Mahler's,
Lacking a source-book or promotions,
I showed one child the colors of
The lunar moth and how to love.

. . . . .

Though trees turn bare and girls turn wives,
We shall afford our costly seasons;
There is a gentleness survives
That will outspeak and has its reasons.
There is a loveliness exists,
Preserves us. Not for specialists.[2]

2. From "April Inventory," by W. D. Snodgrass. © 1957 by W. D. Snodgrass. Reprinted from *Heart's Needle,* by W. D. Snodgrass, by permission of Alfred A. Knopf, Inc.

On Poets
·II·

Rimbaud in Our Time

❧ Rimbaud inscribed upon a park bench the curse: "Merde à Dieu." The anger and hatred in him required for his insults the highest being conceivable. No one inferior could satisfy his hatred because he hated a whole world. Beginning as the bourgeois adolescent who finds his family intolerable, Rimbaud moved with the greatest speed to a recognition of his essential enemy, the whole bourgeois culture. The age in which one exists is the air which one breathes. Rimbaud was left breathless by his age. He inhaled the new day of industrial capitalism, an air in which all that had been holy to European man decayed: "The inferior race has covered everything—the populace, as we say, Reason, the Nation, and Science." And at first he thought Europe and even Christianity were identical with the systematic abomination of bourgeois society.

In order to free himself, he made two efforts, which are not entirely distant from one another. First, he attempted to return to an ancient purity, a time previous to Europe, and Christianity, a pagan culture: "I am a beast, a Negro," "I bury the dead in my belly." "It was of Eden that I was thinking," "I depart from Europe," "I have never been of these people, I have never been Christian." But he cannot accomplish this departure because Europe reaches everywhere: "The white men land. The cannon! One must submit oneself to baptism, dress oneself, work." And as one cannot change one's father and mother, so one cannot change one's nature of being a European. In running away, the European carries himself and Europe with him.

But another and greater need presents itself, that of attaining a new understanding of life, since the old one had produced so much evil and has been seen as false. Christianity is dying, therefore the need which one cannot deny will only be satisfied by a new discovery of the truth. The poet must make himself a seer, he must find out "the meaning" of life, if he wishes to continue to live: "I am going to unveil all the mysteries: mysteries of religion or of nature, death, birth, future, past, non-existence, cosmogony." Rimbaud supposed that by a new method of poetry, by "the alchemy of the word," by deliberate hallucination, he could attain to the whole truth: "I wrote down silences, nights, I noted the inexpressible. I fixed vertigos." At the same time, this practice made possible an attack upon the habitual bourgeois forms of life, and united with the attempt to get back to a primitive innocence previous to Christianity.

But as violence cannot compel love, although every terror is used, so a great violence of the spirit cannot bring about insight and understanding. This attempt to build a Tower of Babel in order to see God must fail, as did the attempt to go back to the Eden of the negro; and the consequence is that, like Faustus and like Lucifer, one lands in Hell.

Rimbaud endured his season in Hell until he was certain that he could not become God—as he had desired when he wrote: "Oh! je serai celui-là qui sera Dieu!"—and until he thought he saw Christianity as the ambiguous key to his need: "Charity is that key," "Divine love alone can provide the keys of knowledge." It is not that he finds it necessary to say that he has been in Hell, for he now must use the Christian language. And yet he rejects that key —"This inspiration proves that I have dreamed!"—although he can see no other way: "I saw the consoling Cross arise," "By the spirit one attains God! Heartrending misfortune!" But whether or not Christianity provides salvation, it is certain that poetry does not; hence Rimbaud finds that he can no longer be a poet: "I must bury my imagination and my memories! A beautiful glory of artist and storyteller cast aside!" For it is salvation, not poetry, that he wants, although it was the practice of poetry which made more acute and more precise his need of salvation, his need *to possess the truth in a soul and a body.*

What happened after Rimbaud had come to this conclusion need not concern us. It is assumed, as with so many others, that his life interprets his poetry. One gets much more illumination by permitting our lives to interpret his text. It is true that in the chapter which is the "confession of a companion in Hell" one can hardly help supposing that it is Verlaine who is speaking, that Rimbaud is presenting Verlaine's vision of Rimbaud during the time when he was in Hell because he believed that he could unveil the whole truth. And for those who do not know that the child is the illegitimate father of the man, it is perhaps interesting to hear about Rimbaud's school days, or that Rimbaud may have attributed colors to the vowels in the celebrated vowel sonnet because of a childhood memory of colored alphabet blocks. But *A Season in Hell* can best be understood when one forgets the infant prodigy, the adolescent Lucifer whom Verlaine tried to kill, and the Abyssinian gunrunner. And it is not necessary to devote too much attention to the provincial France of Rimbaud's boyhood, nor the France of the Second Empire, the Franco-Prussian War, and the Paris Commune, although the intense conflicts of that time must have had something to do with the overwhelming haste of Rimbaud's career.

The true context of *A Season in Hell* begins with Blake, who was perhaps the first poet to feel the need for a new vision of life, and who cursed Voltaire, Rousseau, and Newton, married Heaven and Hell, and used his poetry in order to reveal a system of theology he had himself invented. The Romantics come next, seeking in Nature for what the social order no longer provided. Wordsworth, long before Rimbaud, recognized what was lacking:

> Great God! I'd rather be
> A pagan suckled on a creed outworn,
> So might I, standing on this pleasant lea,
> Have glimpses that would make me less forlorn;
> Have sight of Proteus rising from the sea;
> Or hear old Triton blow his wreathèd horn.[1]

1. It ought to be remembered that this sentiment, of a religious need, arises from what we would call social criticism, for this sonnet begins:

> "The world is too much with us; late and soon,
> Getting and spending, we lay waste our powers;
> Little we see in Nature that is ours . . ."

And if Wordsworth seems an example from the too distant past, it is worth remembering how much more difficult the need had become a hundred

[55]

and managed to persuade himself that Nature was the concrete embodiment of the highest values. Coleridge, by contrast, turned to German transcendentalism, the comfort of a world deduced from the abstract nature of consciousness, and Keats turned to the beauty of art and the artistic beauty of Nature. The next stage begins with Baudelaire, who tried to regain in the experience of degradation and vice the knowledge of good and evil which seemed to be dying with a dying Christianity, just as, during the next generation, George Eliot would write her stories endeavoring to maintain Christian morality without Christian belief. In America, Poe had found it necessary to construct a naive metaphysics, vainly named "Eureka", and Whitman denied what Baudelaire had tried to regain by poems in which he *accepted* everything, just as Nietzsche was later to abuse Christian morality, compose his own Bible, and announce that he wished to be beyond good and evil; while in Russia, Tolstoy found it necessary to seek to return to a primitive Christianity, and Dostoievsky, some of whose characters resemble Rimbaud, rejected Western Europe because he saw it as opposed to Russian Christianity, its science and liberalism denying the love of God and the sense of guilt and of human nothingness.

After Rimbaud and until the present day, the need becomes more intense and more ingenious of various fulfillments. Some return to Christianity by new routes, by a picturesque medievalism, to use the most vulgar example. And some, like D. H. Lawrence, find in sexual fulfillment the Eden and the innocence which Rimbaud wanted. William Butler Yeats and Hart Crane construct, like Blake, a new system of belief, in which they do not believe. The Symbolists, the Dadaists, and the Surrealists also resume in their own way different moments of Rimbaud's efforts. It is in this

---

years later, when, during the World War, Hardy wrote of the story that on Christmas Eve the oxen kneel because of the birth of Christ:

> "If someone said, on Christmas Eve,
> 'Come see the oxen kneel
> " 'In the lonely barton by yonder coomb
> Our childhood used to know,'
> I should go with him in the gloom,
> Hoping it might be so."

sense that Rimbaud can be said to have *tried out* the whole century to come *in advance.*

Man cannot live without an interpretation of the whole of life which will tell him or seem to tell him what is good, what is right, what is important, and which will relate nature, man, man's economy, and man's art, so that they are not opposed in a conflict in which one or the other is abused and denied. As the city must have avenues, names, and numbers, if the citizen is to be able to go from one place to another, so some map of life is necessary as soon as human activity is concerned with anything more than the fulfillment of animal needs; and it is useful for that purpose also.

The increasing inadequacy of Christianity, at least in a definite period of history, to provide that map of life for Europe is only part of the condition which inspired Rimbaud, and then defeated him. An equally important part is the social order which in its whole development was in conflict even with the new and diluted versions of Christianity which weakly attempted to come to terms with it. The whole condition became a problem for every serious poet, as in the sequence of examples just cited. The poet above all is the one who feels the central lack in what men do, know, and believe, because he works in terms of consciousness as in terms of words. We ought to remember that perhaps the greatest evil of capitalism is its oppression or perversion of all values and thus of all lives, not only the lives of the working class (although one does not wish to underestimate that oppression for a moment). And it is in the lives of the most intelligent and the most sensitive that the greatest harm is done, at least to the intelligence and the sensibility.

The history of poetry since Blake, from this important perspective, is the history of men who found the social order into which they were born increasingly inadequate in every *human* respect and wholly deficient in satisfying the inevitable human need for a whole view of life. Rimbaud knew this need and knew certain characteristic attempts at its satisfaction with a sensitivity which is incomparable. The satisfaction is far from being in sight, even today, or rather today least of all. That is why *A Season in Hell* is a text which deserves our endless study.

Poetry and Belief in Thomas Hardy

I

It is natural that beliefs should be involved in poetry in a variety of ways. Hardy is a rich example of this variety. For that reason, it would be well to distinguish some of the important ways in which belief inhabits poetry.

Some poetry is written in order to state beliefs. The purpose of the versification is to make the doctrine plain. Lucretius is the obvious and much-used example, and Dante is probably another, although there is some dramatic justification for most passages of philosophical statement and discussion in the *Paradiso*.

Some poetry employs beliefs merely as an aspect of the thoughts and emotions of the human characters with which it is concerned. Almost every dramatic poet will serve as an example of this tendency. Human beings are full of beliefs, a fact which even the naturalistic novelist cannot wholly forget; and since their beliefs are very important motives in their lives, no serious poet can forget about beliefs all of the time. One doubts that any serious poet would want to do so.

It is not difficult to distinguish the two poetic uses of belief from each other. The first kind is generally marked by the forms of direct statement, the second kind by a narrative or dramatic context. And when there is a shift in purpose, when the dramatic poet begins to use his characters merely as mouthpieces to state beliefs, the shift shows immediately in the surface of the poetry. The poet's use of his medium and his attitude toward his subject are always reflected strikingly in the looking glass of form.

Between these two extremes, there exist intermediate stages of which Hardy provides a number of examples. It is commonplace, in addition, that a poet may begin with the intention of stating a belief—or perhaps merely some observation which interests him—and conclude by modifying belief and observation to suit the necessities of versification, the suggestion of a rhyme or the implication of a metaphor.

But there is a prior way in which beliefs enter into a poem. It is prior in that it is inevitable in the very act of writing poetry, while the previous two ways may conceivably be avoided. The poet's beliefs operate within his poem whether he knows it or not, and apart from any effort to use them. This fundamental operation of belief can be seen when we consider a Christian poet's observations of Nature, and then compare them to similar observations on the part of a Romantic poet, such as Wordsworth or Keats. The comparison can be made more extreme with ease, if we substitute a Russian or a Chinese poet, using descriptive passages. It should be evident that poets with different beliefs when confronted with what is nominally the same object do not make the same observations. The same shift because of belief occurs in the slightest detail of language; such common words as *pain, animal, night, rock, hope, death, the sky* must of necessity have different power of association and implication for the Christian poet and one whose beliefs are different. It is a simple fact that our beliefs not only make us see certain things, but also prevent us from seeing other things; and in addition, or perhaps one should say at the same time, our understanding of the language we use is changed.

In Hardy's poetry, these three functions of belief all have an important part. Another and equally important factor is at work also. With the tone, the attitude implied by the tone, and often with the explicit statement of his poem, Hardy says with the greatest emphasis: "You see: this is what Life is." And more than that, he says very often: "You see: your old conception of what Life is has been shown to be wrong and foolish by this example."

One hesitates to make a simple synopsis of Hardy's beliefs. It is not that there is anything inherently obscure in them, but that they exist in his poetry so close to the attitudes, feelings, tones, and observations which make them different from their abstract formulation. For the purpose of lucidity, however, it is worthwhile saying that Hardy believed, in the most literal sense, that the fundamental factor in the nature of things was a "First or Fundamental Energy," as he calls It in the foreword to *The Dynasts*. This Energy operated without consciousness or order throughout the universe and produced the motions of the stars and the long development of the forms of life upon our own planet. Hardy did not hold this view simply, though on occasion he stated it thus. Stated thus, his writing would be an example of philosophical poetry. But this view is only one moment of his whole state of mind and does not by any means exist by itself. It is a view which Hardy affirms in active opposition, first of all, to the view that an intelligent and omnipotent Being ruled the universe; second of all, in active opposition to what he knew of the nature of human life as something lived by human beings who in their conscious striving blandly disregard the fact that they were merely products of the First or Fundamental Energy. Thus Hardy's state of mind is one example of the conflict between the new scientific view of life which the nineteenth century produced and the whole attitude toward life which had been traditional to Western culture. Hardy is a partisan of the new view, but acutely conscious always of the old view. He holds the two in a dialectical tension. Indeed there are moments when it seems that Hardy is merely taking the Christian idea of God and the world, and placing a negative prefix to each of God's attributes. The genuine atheist, by contrast, is never so concerned with the view which he has rejected. Or if he is so concerned, he is, like Hardy, a being who is fundamentally religious and essentially possessed by a state of mind in which an old view of Life and a new one contest without conclusion.

There are certain poems in which this conflict is stated explicitly. In the lyric called, "A Plaint to Man," the false God of Christianity is personified and given a voice, and with that voice he addresses mankind, resuming the doctrine of evolution:

> When you slowly emerged from the den of Time,
> And gained percipience as you grew,
> And fleshed you fair out of shapeless slime,
>
> Wherefore, O Man, did there come to you
> The unhappy need of creating me—
> A form like your own—for praying to?

[60]

This false God, being told that mankind had need of some agency of hope and mercy, tells mankind that he, God, dwindles day by day "beneath the deicide eyes of seers," "and tomorrow the whole of me disappears," so that "the truth should be told, and the fact be faced"—the fact that if mankind is to have mercy, justice, and love, the human heart itself would have to provide it.

In another poem, "God's Funeral," the ambiguity of Hardy's attitude becomes increasingly evident. The God of Christianity is being escorted to his grave by a long train of mourners who are described in Dantesque lines and who have thoughts which are overheard by the protagonist of the poem and which rehearse the history of monotheism from the standpoint of a higher criticism of the Bible. Among the funeral throng, however, the protagonist sees many who refuse to believe that God has died:

> Some in the background then I saw,
> Sweet women, youths, men, all incredulous,
> Who chimed: "This is a counterfeit of straw,
> This requiem mockery! Still he lives to us!"

> I could not buoy their faith: and yet
> Many I had known: with all I sympathized;
> And though struck speechless, I did not forget
> That what was mourned for, I, too, long had prized.

This confession that Hardy, too, had prized what he was so concerned to deny must be remembered for the light it gives us upon Hardy's poetry as a whole. In other poems, the wish to believe in the dying God is frankly declared. "The Oxen," a poem which will require detailed attention, tells of an old Christmas story that the oxen kneel at the hour of Christ's nativity, and the poet declares in the most moving terms that if he should be asked at Christmas to come to the pen at midnight to see the oxen kneel, he would go "in the gloom," "Hoping it might be so!" In *The Dynasts*, this desire is given the most peculiar and pathetic form of all. The hope is stated at the very end that the Fundamental Energy which rules the nature of things will continue to evolve until It takes upon itself the attribute of consciousness—"Consciousness the Will informing till It fashions all things fair!"—and thus, or such is the implication, becomes like the God of Christianity, a God of love, mercy, and justice.

At the same time, there is a decisive moment of Hardy's state of mind which is directly opposed to this one. Hardy works without end to manipulate the events in the lives of his characters so that it will be plain that human life is at the mercy of chance and the most arbitrary circumstances. Hardy not only makes his Immanent Will of the universe an active power of evil, but he engages his characters in the most incredible conjunctions of unfortunate accidents. There is such an intensity of interest in seeing chance thwart and annihilate human life that the tendency of mind seems pathological until one remembers that chance and coincidence have become for Hardy one of the primary motions of the universe. It is Providence, which is functioning in reverse; the poet has attempted to state a definite view of life in the very working out of his plot.

And at the same time also, the older and stronger view of life inhabited the poet's mind at a level on which it was not opposed. Hardy inherited a substratum of sensibility of a definite character and formed by definite beliefs which denied the scientific view his intellect accepted. He inherited this sensibility from his fathers, just as he inherited the lineaments of his face, and he could as soon have changed one as the other. Hardy was convinced that the new scientific view was the correct one; he was convinced intellectually, that is to say, that Darwin, Huxley, Schopenhauer, Hartmann, and Nietzsche had attained to the truth about Life. But at the same time, he could not help seeing Nature and human life in the light which was as habitual as walking on one's feet and not on one's hands. He could not work as a poet without his profound sense of history and sense of the past, his feeling for the many generations who had lived and died in his countryside before him; and his mind, like theirs, naturally and inevitably recognized human choice, responsibility, and freedom, the irreparable character of human acts and the undeniable necessity of seeing life from the inside of the human psyche rather than from the astronomical-biological perspective of nineteenth-century science. But more than that, he could not work as a poet without such entities as "spectres, mysterious voices, intuitions, omens and haunted places," the operations of the supernatural in which he could not believe.

II

The cosmology of nineteenth-century science which affected Hardy so much has had a long and interesting history in the culture of the last forty years. Its effects are to be seen in the novels of Theodore Dreiser, in the plays of Bernard Shaw, the early philosophical writing of Bertrand Russell, the early poetry of Archibald MacLeish, and the poetry of Robinson Jeffers. A prime American example is Joseph Wood Krutch's *The Modern Temper,* where it is explicitly announced that such things as love and tragedy and all other specifically human values are not possible to modern man. The example of Bertrand Russell suggests that of I. A. Richards, whose sincerity ritual to test the genuineness of a poem works at least in part by envisaging the "meaninglessness" of the universe which follows or seemed to follow from the scientific view; and the example of Krutch suggests some of the best poems of Mark Van Doren, where the emptiness of the sky, the departure of the old picture of the world, is the literal theme. This array of examples, and the many others which might be added, should not only suggest how modern a poet Hardy is; they should also suggest how variously the scientific view may enter into the poet's whole being, what different attitudes it may engender, and how differently the poet's sensibility may attempt to handle it.

It is nothing if not fitting that I. A. Richards should look to Hardy for his perfect example in *Science and Poetry,* the book he has devoted to precisely this question, the effect of the scientific view upon the modern poet. Mr. Richards is at once very illuminating, I think, and very wrong in what he says of Hardy. It would not be possible for anyone to improve upon the appreciation of Hardy's virtues implicit in the three pages Mr. Richards devotes to him; but it would be equally difficult to invert the truth about Hardy as completely as Mr. Richards does in the interests of his general thesis. He quotes a remark about Hardy made by J. Middleton Murry: "His reaction to an episode has behind it and within it a reaction to the universe." And then his comment is: "This is not as I should put it were I making a statement; but read as a pseudo-statement, emotively, it is excellent; it makes us remember how we felt. Actually it describes just what Hardy, at his best, does not do. He makes no reaction to the universe, recognizing it as something to which no reaction is more relevant than another."

On the contrary, Hardy is almost always bringing his reaction to the universe into his poems. It is true that he sees the universe as something to which no reaction is more relevant than another; but it is just that view of the neutral universe which prepossesses Hardy almost always and gives much of the power to the most minute details of his poems. Perhaps one ought not to say Hardy's beliefs, but Hardy's disbeliefs; whichever term is exact, the fact is that his beliefs or disbeliefs make possible the great strength of his verse. We can see that this is so if we examine some of the poems in which Hardy's beliefs play a direct part.

THE OXEN

Christmas Eve, and twelve of the clock.
"Now they are all on their knees,"
An elder said as we sat in a flock
By the embers in hearthside ease.

We pictured the meek mild creatures where
They dwelt in their strawy pen,
Nor did it occur to one of us there
To doubt they were kneeling then.

So fair a fancy few would weave
In these years! Yet, I feel,
If someone said on Christmas Eve,
"Come; see the oxen kneel,

"In the lonely barton by yonder coomb
Our childhood used to know,"
I should go with him in the gloom,
Hoping it might be so.

The belief in this poem is of course a disbelief in the truth of Christianity. The emotion is the wish that it were true. But it must be emphasized that this emotion, which obviously motivates the whole poem, depends upon a very full sense of what the belief in Christianity amounted to; and this sense also functions to provide the poet with the details of the Christmas story which serves as the example of Christianity. It is Hardy's sensibility as the son of his fathers which make possible his realization of the specific scene and story; this sensibility itself was the product of definite beliefs, to refer back to the point made at the beginning that we see what we do see because of our beliefs. But for the whole poem to be written, it was necessary that what Hardy's sensibility made him conscious of should be held against the scientific view which his intellect accepted. Both must enter into the poem. This is the sense in which a reaction to the universe, if one must use Mr. Murry's terms, is involved in Hardy's reaction to the Christmas story. Hardy, remembering the Christmas story of childhood, cannot help keeping in mind the immense universe of nineteenth-century science, which not only makes such a story seem untrue, but increases one's reasons for wishing that it were true. His sensibility's grasp of the meaning of Christmas and Christianity makes such a choice of detail as calling the oxen "meek mild creatures" likely, perfectly exact, and implicit with the Christian quality of humility. His intellectual awareness of the new world picture engenders the fullness of meaning involved in the phrase, which is deliberately emphasized by the overflow, "In these years!" A reaction to the universe is involved in this phrase and in addition a reaction to a definite period in Western culture.

If we take a negative example, one in which Hardy's beliefs have operated to produce a poor poem, this function of belief will be seen with further definition. The following poem is as typical of Hardy's failures as "The Oxen" is of the elements which produced his successes:

THE MASKED FACE

I found me in a great surging space,
　　At either end a door,
And I said: "What is this giddying place,
　　With no firm-fixéd floor,
　　That I knew not of before?"
"It is Life," said a mask-clad face.

I asked: "But how do I come here,
　　Who never wished to come;
Can the light and air be made more clear,
　　The floor more quietsome,
　　And the door set wide? They numb
Fast-locked, and fill with fear."

[65]

> The mask put on a bleak smile then,
> And said, "O vassal-wight,
> There once complained a goosequill pen
> To the scribe of the Infinite
> Of the words it had to write
> Because they were past its ken."

Here too Hardy's picture of the universe is at work and Hardy is intent upon declaring his belief that Life is beyond human understanding. But there is a plain incongruity between the vaguely cosmological scene which is declared to be Life in the first stanza and the stenographic metaphor for human life in the last stanza, which, apart from this relationship, is grotesque enough in itself. There is no adequate reason in the poem why a giddying place with no firm-fixed floor should be beyond understanding, and it is not made so by being entitled: Life. It reminds one rather of the barrel rolls at amusement parks and by no means of the revolutions of day and night which Hardy presumably had in mind. The masked face is probably intended to designate the Immanent Will; but here again, there is a gulf between what Hardy meant by that Will and any speaking face, and the gulf cannot be annulled merely by the device of personification. Moreover, it is difficult enough to see the human being as a goosequill pen; when the pen complains, the poem collapses because too great a weight of meaning has been put upon a figure which was inadequate at the start.

In poems such as these, and they are not few, Hardy has been merely attempting to versify his beliefs about the universe, and neither his mastery of language nor his skill at versification can provide him with all that he needs. He needs his sensibility; but his sensibility works only when the objects proper to it are in view. When it is required to function on a cosmological scene, it can only produce weak and incommensurate figures. It is possible for a poet to make poetry by the direct statement of his beliefs, but it is not possible for such a poet as Hardy. The true philosophical poet is characterized by an understanding of ideas and an interest in them which absorbs his whole being. Hardy was interested in ideas, too; but predominantly in their bearing upon human life. No better characterization could be formulated than the one Hardy wrote for his novel, *Two on a Tower*: "This slightly-built romance was the outcome of a wish to set the emotional history of two infinitesimal lives against the stupendous background of the stellar universe, and to impart to readers the sentiment that of these contrasting magnitudes the smaller might be the greater to them as men."

III

Hardy failed when he tried to make a direct statement of his beliefs; he succeeded when he used his beliefs to make significant the observations which concerned him. This contrast should suggest that something essential to the nature of poetry may very well be in question. It is a long time since the statement was first made that poetry is more philosophical than history; the example of Hardy provides another instance of how useful and how illuminating the doctrine is. The minute particulars of Hardy's experience might have made a diary, history, or biography; what made them poetry was the functioning of Hardy's beliefs. The function of belief was to generalize his experience into something neither merely particular, which is the historian's concern; nor merely general, which is the philosopher's; but into symbols which possess the qualitative richness, as Mr. Ransom might say, of any particular thing and yet have that generality which makes them significant beyond their moment of existence, or the passing context in which they are located. And here again an examination of a particular poem will make the discussion specific:

A DRIZZLING EASTER MORNING

And he is risen? Well, be it so. . . .
And still the pensive lands complain,
And dead men wait as long ago,
As if, much doubting, they would know
What they are ransomed from, before
They pass again their sheltering door.

I stand amid them in the rain,
While blusters vex the yew and vane;
And on the road the weary wain
Plods forward, laden heavily;
And toilers with their aches are fain
For endless rest—though risen is he.

It is the belief and disbelief in Christ's resurrection which not only make this poem possible, but make its details so moving. They are not only moving; the weary wain which plods forward heavily and the dread men in the graveyard are envisaged fully as particular things and yet become significant of the whole experience of suffering and evil just because the belief exists for Hardy and provides a light which makes these particular things symbols. *Without the belief, it is only another rainy morning in March or April.* In passing, it should be noted that both belief and disbelief are necessary; the belief is necessary to the disbelief. And both are responsible here as elsewhere for that quality of language which is Hardy's greatest strength. The mere use of such words as *men, doubting, door, rain,* has a richness of implication, a sense of generations of human experience behind it; this richness is created immediately by the modifying words in the content, *pensive, weary, plod, vex, heavily,* and other workings of the words upon each other; but fundamentally by Hardy's ability to see particulars as significant of Life in general. He would not have had that ability without his beliefs and disbeliefs, though it is true that other poets get that ability by other means and other beliefs.

IV

Once we remember that good poems have been produced by the use of different and contradictory beliefs, we are confronted by the problem of belief in the modern sense.

There are good reasons for supposing that this is not, in itself, a poetic problem. But at any rate, it is true enough that many readers are profoundly disturbed by poems which contain beliefs which they do not accept or beliefs which are in direct contradiction to their own. Hardy's beliefs, as presented explicitly in his poems, offended and still offend his readers in this way.

In turn, the poet is wounded to hear that his poems are not enjoyed because his beliefs are untrue. Throughout his long career, both as poet and as novelist, Hardy was intensely disturbed by criticism on such a basis.

In the "Apology" to *Late Lyrics and Earlier,* Hardy spoke out with the tiredness and anger of an author who has suffered from reviewers for fifty years. His answer is curious and defective, however. He points out that the case against him is "neatly sum-marized in a stern pronouncement . . . 'This view of life is not mine.'" But instead of defending himself by pointing to all the great poetry which would be eliminated if it were judged merely on the basis of its agreement with the reader's beliefs, Hardy concedes the basic issue to his critics by claiming that his beliefs are better than they have been painted. He defends himself by saying that he is not a pessimist, but "an evolutionary meliorist." No one but another evolutionary meliorist could be persuaded by this kind of argument.

On another occasion, in the introduction to *The Dynasts*, Hardy attempts to solve the problem by requiring Coleridge's temporary "suspension of disbelief which constitutes poetic faith." But this formula would seem to provide for no more than the convention of theatrical or fictive illusion. When the curtain rises, we must suspend disbelief as to whether we see before us Elsinore, a plat-form before the castle. If we do not, then there can be no play. The case seems more difficult, at least on the surface, when we are asked to accept alien beliefs.

Now there are two ways in which we tend to handle alien be-liefs. One of them is to reject those poems which contain beliefs we regard as false. This is an example of judging poetry in terms of its subject, considered in abstraction, and the difficulties are obviously numerous. For one thing, as has been said, we would have to reject most great poetry. Certainly we would have to do without Homer, and without Dante or Shakespeare.

The other alternative, which is in any case preferable to the first, is to judge poetry wholly in terms of its formal character. But this is an act of unjustifiable abstraction also. For it is evident that we enjoy more in a poem, or at least the poem presents more to us, than a refined use of language.

What we need, and what we actually have, I think, is a criterion for the beliefs in a poem which is genuinely a poetic criterion. In reading Hardy when he is successful, in "A Drizzling Easter Morning," we find that the belief and disbelief operate upon the particular *datum* of the poem to give it a metaphorical significance it would not otherwise have. To repeat, without both belief and disbelief it is only another rainy morning in the spring. Con-

[69]

versely, in "The Masked Face," the asserted belief, instead of generalizing the particulars of the poem, merely interferes with them and fails to give them the significance they are intended to have.

In both instances, we are faced with a relationship between the belief in the poem and its other particulars. This is a relationship *internal* to the poem, so to speak. It is not a question of the relationship of the poet's beliefs to the reader's. In "The Masked Face," for example, the inadequacy proceeds from the relationship between the belief that Life is beyond human understanding, and the goosequill pen which is required to represent the human mind.

It might be objected that this internal relationship between the belief and the rest of the poem is in turn good, or not good, in terms of what the given reader himself believes. Thus it might seem that for a reader who shares Hardy's beliefs, the goosequill pen was an adequate figure for the human mind. Actually this cannot be so, unless the reader is not interested in poetry but merely in hearing his beliefs stated. If the reader is interested in poetry, the poem itself cannot give him the poetic experience of Life as beyond human understanding, which is its intention. The details of the poem, as presented in the context which the belief and the versification provide, do not do the work in the reader's mind which is done by such an element in "A Drizzling Easter Morning," as the weary wain, which plods forward, laden heavily. And one reason why they lack that energy is their relationship, within the poem, to the belief the poem asserts. Whether or not the reader shares Hardy's beliefs, even if he shares them completely, the goosequill pen is an inadequate figure for what it is intended to signify in the context. The belief in the poem fails to make it adequate, and this is a poetic failure, just as, in "The Oxen," the kneeling animals are a poetic success because of the disbelief, whether the reader himself disbelieves in Christianity or not.

And again, it might be objected that only valid beliefs, in the end, can operate successfully upon the other elements of any poem. Once more we must refer back to the fact that poets have written good poetry based upon opposed beliefs, and then to the point made at the start, that there is a basic way in which beliefs have much to do with the whole character of a poet's sensibility, with what he sees and does not see. The subject of poetry is experience, not truth, even wh en the poet is writing about ideas. When the poet can get the whol e experience of his sensibility into his poem, then there will be an ad equate relationship between the details of his poem and the belief s he asserts, whether they are true or not. For then he is getting th e actuality of his experience into his poem, and it does not matter whether that actuality is illusory or not; just as the earth may be seen as flat. The functioning of his sensibility guarantees his asserted beliefs; it guarantees them as aspects of experience, thoug h not as statements of truth. The philosophical poet, as well as any other kind, must meet this test. The details of his poem are neither dramatic, nor lyrical, but there is the same question of the relationship between his asserted ideas and the language, tone, attitude, and figures which constitute the rest of the poem.

At any rate, by adopting this point of view, we avoid the two extremes, the two kinds of abstraction, which violate the poem as a concrete whole. And it is especially necessary to do this in Hardy's case, for it is unlikely that many readers will hold Hardy's beliefs as he held them. In the future we are likely to believe less or more; but we will not be in the same kind of intellectual situation as Hardy was.

The important thing is to keep Hardy's poetry, to keep as much of it as we can, and to enjoy it for what it is in its utmost concreteness. And if this is to be accomplished, it is necessary that we keep Hardy's beliefs *in* his poetry, and our own beliefs outside.

The Poet as Poet

   "A miracle of development!" Thus one critic describes the contrast between the early and the later poetry of Yeats. The astonishment, the phenomenal applause contained in this phrase and in much that was said of the poet's last two volumes of verse are compelled by the complexity of a literary career which lasted for fifty years, and which exhibits, looking backward, the process of a bad poet of the nineties becoming a great poet in middle age. Henceforth no poet can be regarded as utterly hopeless: the possibility of a Yeatsian miracle will always present itself.

During the first half of his career, the poems which Yeats wrote were full of a verbal glitter, an effect of being very "poetic," a soft mellifluous speech to please the reader who delights in the most obvious aural quality—the Shelleyan-Swinburnian quality—of language. Yeats was the son of a painter friendly with the pre-Raphaelite group, to whom he was introduced and with whom he himself became very friendly, and certain poems may be affected by that visual example. During this period, too, Yeats visited Mme. Blavatsky (though she had recently been discredited by the Society for Psysical Research), so that Indian dieties join the Irish ones in some poems. The young poet's interest in such matters and his experimental attitude toward them is but one more example of the desperate shifts to which the poetic sensibility was reduced by the world picture presented by nineteenth-century science: "I am very religious," Yeats explains in his *Autobiographies*, "and deprived by Huxley and Tyndall, whom I detested, of the simple-minded religion of my childhood, I had made a new religion," an activity which continued throughout his life. From beginning to

[72]

end, Yeats was evidently prepared to try anything, Socialism or hashish, once or twice. The idiom in which he wrote, however, was the period style, based upon a misunderstanding of Baudelaire and Mallarmé by an emphasis of their superficial qualities. A just example of this writing is this stanza from a poem in Yeats' fourth book of poems, "The Wind Among the Reeds":

> Dim Powers of drowsy thought, let her no longer be
> Like the pale cup of the sea,
> When the winds have gathered and sun and moon burned dim
> Above its cloudy rim;
> But let a gentle silence wrought with music flow
> Whither her footsteps go.

During the latter half of his life, a genuine revolution in style occurs, although the subjects of the poems remain the same, as did the poet's interests. Instead of a general effect, a specific one is always intended; instead of dim images musically sounded, the precise word and the precise observation are used to get a specific emotion upon the page. The poet's initial gift for versifying has become the power to get into verbal behavior, into meter and diction, the slightest shift in emotion, the least movement of attitude and tone. Here he is writing of the same woman as in the poem just quoted, although she is now old:

> Her present image floats into the mind—
> Did Quattrocento finger fashion it
> Hollow of cheek as though it drank the wind
> And took a mess of shadows for its meat?
> And I though never of Ledaean kind
> Had pretty plumage once—enough of that,
> Better to smile on all that smile, and show
> There is a comfortable kind of old scarecrow.

The mastery of the poet is displayed in the ease with which he shifts from a description of the beautiful woman as old to the personal emotion with which it is involved and the irony consequent upon it which completes itself in the phrase "pretty plumage," while the further shift in emotion is contained perfectly in the brief mark of punctuation and the colloquial phrase which follows, "enough of that." It is this ability to represent emotion with the greatest vividness, directness, and dramatic justification which constitutes Yeats' peculiar gift, rather than the understanding and insight or the brilliance of observation or the freshness of attitudes and values which are the more usual marks of the great poet.

It is natural to try to explain the transformation of the poet in terms of his life or the life of his times, the fact, for example, that he participated in the Irish Nationalist movement for a time and attempted to participate in the life of the people. But Yeats, in the *Autobiographies,* says nothing of decisive events which would compel a great change of heart and of style, nor does he attribute the change to any interest apart from his will as a poet to go from an over-decorative style to a bare one. Such an explanation begs the question, which is the reason for wishing the modification and the source of the means to accomplish it. One concludes, then, that the explanation is to be found in a culmination of factors, just as the change is displayed gradually through ten years in his poems.

During the years in which the change began to show itself, Yeats was faced with failures of various sorts. His early fame had begun to wane, his long courtship of one woman had ended in emptiness. The Abbey Theatre, on which his hopes for a poetic theatre rested, had received little but abuse and misunderstanding, the whole Irish literary renaissance had faded, and many of his most gifted friends, Wilde, Dowson, Lionel Johnson, and Synge, had died in misery and degradation. This would be enough to make most men forget about the land of dreams and the Irish fairyland of the early poems.

Something much more complicated than a mere forgetting happened or would seem to have happened to Yeats. He seized upon the opposition between the land of dreams and the actuality about him, and engaged in a continual seesaw between the two. The structure, so to speak, of thought and of feeling became what Yeats came to call *antithetical.* Antithesis as a dynamic process of the conflict and interchange of opposites, became the movement and the framework which he saw everywhere, just as a man who has donned rose-colored glasses sees the color of rose on all things. The antithesis took many forms—day and night, life and death, the sun and the moon, the natural and the supernatural—but the fundamental opposition was between what Yeats called subjectivity and objectivity; or less ambiguously, between introversion and extroversion, for Yeats was really concerned with psychological attitudes. A whole philosophy of history and of human nature in these terms is the result: everything that happens to man and to society is viewed as a stage in the passage from objectivity to subjectivity or from subjectivity to objectivity.

Yeats began with subjectivity, that is to say, with ART, spelled with capitals, and opposed to Life, which was sordid, sodden, and soiled, or, as Lionel Johnson said of the poems of Arthur Symons, constituted by "a London fog, the blurred tawny lamplight, the red omnibus, the glaring gin shop, the slatternly shivering women." Yeats literally inhaled the doctrine of Art for Art's Sake as a young man; from his father, who quoted only poetry significant of intense emotion, believing only such poetry was genuine, or from Oscar Wilde, who told him that his narrative verse was like Homer, or from Walter Pater ("we looked consciously to Pater for our philosophy"), Yeats and many of his friends learned that nothing was as important as "Beauty." Not only ought one to occupy one's daily life with aesthetic experiences above all, but there was only one justification for other experiences, the possibility that they might be a means to the creation of a great work of art. To be a poet for Yeats actually included a deliberate appearance, the pale dreamer of mussed hair, flowing tie, and ethereal look which caricature has now established in the popular mind as the figure of the poet and which is established as Yeats' image by the portraits next to the title-page of many of his books. Lionel Johnson, whom he admired as the most learned of his friends, had told Yeats that "Life is ritual," and Yeats never stopped seeking ritual, formality, and ceremony, as traits of Art. One more attitude of the young Yeats is important because he adheres to it throughout his life and it enters into many of his poems, the romantic conception of woman: "Woman herself was still in our eyes romantic and mysterious, still the priestess of her shrine, our emotions remembering the *Lilith* and the *Sybilla Palmifera* of Rossetti."

The Priesthood of Yeats' shrine was Maud Gonne, who was

[75]

devoting her whole life to Irish Nationalism, an activity on her part which Yeats never stopped regretting, even in the poems of his latest volume. Partly in the hope of winning her, Yeats entered the movement himself and what occurred then, by his own confession, seems the fundamental motion of his life: "I went hither and thither speaking at meetings in England and Scotland, and occasionally at tumultuous Dublin conventions, and endured the worst months of my life," "I took pride in an evening spent with some small organizer into whose spittoon I secretly poured my third glass of whiskey, I dreaded some wild Fenian movement, and with literature perhaps more in my mind than politics, dreamed of that Unity of Culture which might begin with some few men controlling some form of administration."

With literature perhaps more in my mind than politics! This is precisely the equivocal attitude which Yeats maintained everywhere. The poet of the nineties was dragged again and again from his tower into the most alien and the least desired circumstances. In the midst of them he did not for one moment surrender his notion of himself as Poet, nor his belief that Art was the most important value of life. In this sense he was intransigent; and yet, on the other hand, he was the most flexible member of his generation. And this double character, the capacity to be both intransigent and yet to be drawn into many circumstances of existence which have little to do with Art, shows itself in his best poems.

Consider "Easter 1916," which is supposedly a political poem. What is said, in crude brevity, is that the poet has known the leaders of the Easter Rebellion who were executed and had thought of them as casual and unimportant acquaintances; the fact that they have become a part of a national tragedy suggests not a political nor a patriotic conclusion to Yeats, but he speaks from the standpoint of a man long obsessed with being a poet when he writes, as the refrain of the poem:

A terrible beauty is born.

Again, he writes a short poem during the World War about an Irish airman, in which the airman is supposedly revealing his reasons for participating in the war on the side of Great Britain:

> Those that I fight I do not hate,
> Those that I hate I do not love. . . .
> My countrymen Kiltartan's poor,
> No likely end could bring them loss,
> Or leave them happier than before.
> Nor law nor duty bade me fight,
> Nor public men nor cheering crowds,
> A lonely impulse of delight
> Drove to this tumult in the clouds. . . .

The lonely impulse of delight, the rejection of law, duty, public men, and cheering crowds, betrays the voice as that of the poet of the nineties who has lived into the next generation. Yeats has transformed his hypothetical airman into a romantic poet, or we may say, if we consider this poem in relation to his work as a whole, that even when confronted with the World War, the poet succeeds in sustaining the romantic attitude with which he began; but not, however, without being perfectly aware of the difficult circumstances in which he is sustaining it.

And once more, in the volume of verse which was published in 1929, Yeats writes of two beautiful women who, like Maud Gonne, had devoted their lives to politics, and he remains utterly unchanged in the sentiment which motivates his poem:

> Two girls in silk kimonos, both
> Beautiful, one a gazelle. . . .
> The older is condemned to death,
> Pardoned, drags out lonely years.
> I know not what the younger dreams—
> Some vague Utopia—and she seems,
> When withered old and skeleton-gaunt,
> An image of such politics. . . .
> Dear shadows, now you know it all,
> All the folly of a fight
> With a common wrong or right.
> The innocent and the beautiful
> Have no enemy but time.

To think that the innocent and the beautiful have no enemy but time is probably not a Shakespearean nor a Biblical wisdom, if taken in itself as a literal statement. But the emotion which this poem is concerned to represent transfigures the statement, for the poem concludes with a dramatic statement of the poet's longing to destroy time altogether, a desire which is related, as in other poems, to the poet's awareness that it is history, the movement of his age, which has greatly altered the bases and the assumptions with which he began to practice his art.

Many other later poems concern this hatred of time and the change which attends all natural things, and this hatred takes several significant forms. There is the emotion, in such a poem as "Sailing to Byzantium," to be outside of time and a part of "the artifice of eternity"; the poet longs to be free of birds, beasts, and the young in one another's arms, and to become what? a work of art! Eternity or heaven is conceived by the poet as being like Byzantium, a civilization in which artificiality and ritual dominate, where all that is natural is suppressed, where the unchanging is the good, where art is the structure of existence:

> A starlit or a moonlit dome disdains
> All that man is,
> All mere complexities,
> The fury and the mire of human veins.

The next best thing to being free of the fury of human veins in a Byzantine civilization is to exist in a society where a landed aristocracy rules. In every poem on the subject of the landed aristocracy as the good society, the figure of the artist appears in the doorway, works of art abound, the rich man, or the rich woman, Lady Gregory, has been the patron of artists, and by means of the country house and its tradition, ceremony, and continuity, a victory over change and history is made possible, though only for a while. "I meditate," he says in writing his two poems about Lady Gregory and her country house, "upon an aged woman and her house." What are the leading virtues of this lady and her house? "Great works constructed there in nature's spite," "Beloved books that famous hands have bound, Old marble heads, old pictures everywhere." In the midst of these poems, the poet always remembers how precarious is the existence of such a society:

> And maybe the great-grandson of that house,
> For all its bronze and marble, 's but a mouse.

[78]

And this awareness is usually accompanied by the feeling that the fate of poetry is inseparable from the fate of that society, so that, when he returns to Coole Park after Lady Gregory has died, where "whatever most can bless The mind of man or elevate a rhyme" was composed with the help of her hospitality, he finds everything altered:

> But all is changed, that high horse riderless,
> Though mounted in that saddle Homer rode
> Where the swan drifts upon a darkening flood.

The fact that he was to say three years later in prose that the past sixty years have been a very great period of poetry contradicts that sentiment only if we forget the context in which it is felt, the end of the society in which Yeats came to be a poet.

Then there is one short poem called "The Dolls," another symbol for Yeats of the artificial and unnatural object which is art and not life. In this poem, when the doll-maker's wife has a child, the dolls scream that the house has been disgraced by the filthy thing which the child is, and the doll-maker's wife apologizes humbly to the guility doll-maker who has been shamed by the dolls: she tells him the child was an accident. The hatred of the natural and the biological in this poem is obviously related to a like obsession in the poetry of T. S. Eliot—it is the same "birth, copulation, death" which the poet abhors—and there is also the connection with the opposition of Art and Life in Thomas Mann, which is the significant inheritance of all the writers who came to maturity during the first decade of the present century. In another famous poem, "Among School Children," the poet turns from the children to the image of the beautiful woman he has loved all his life (the identity of the beautiful woman and the work of art had been established in the earliest poems) in the distortion of old age; and in his anger at old age and the changes of life, he sees all philosophy as a denial of Nature and time, he compares a mother's love of the living child with the nun's love of a bronze image, preferring the nun's love to the mother's, and he concludes by calling before his mind with longing a realm where process—and history—do not exist.

The substance of the later poetry is, then, the *emotion* of the

Poet as Poet (in the romantic sense) when faced with modern times, when forced to exist and to practice his art in the circumstances of the last forty years. If every generalization is bound to omit or to distort, and if this must be especially so of a generalization about the work of a poet, yet, in terms of this emphasis, the nature of the shift from the early to the later style becomes entirely plain. Yeats shifted from the effort to write the "poetic" poetry of the nineties to the concern, as poet, with what it was to be a poet amid the alien circumstances of his age. That is why he is so often, in his later poetry, writing about the artists, scholars, and beautiful women he has known, and their unfortunate lives. And that is perhaps why the unknown instructors or spirits who dictated a supernatural system to him through the mediumship of his wife, and prompted Yeats to offer to use the rest of his life explicating what had been dictated, rejected his offer, saying: "No, we have come to give you metaphors for poetry." Those spirits, it is certain, recognized their man. The poet intent upon Art so exhausted his intention and learned so much about that intention from others who were of like mind that his poetry became a revelation of the fate of Art and the emotion of the Artist in modern history. The will to seek one's opposite, the doctrine that one must seek one's anti-self, is at once the method by means of which Yeats found his genuine and peculiar theme, and one more example of the concern with acting a part which flows from the obsession with Art. The result has been a group of poems which will be known as long as the English language exists.

An Unwritten Book

When Maud Gonne speaks of William Butler Yeats, the great poet, as Willie, does it not suggest thoughts of the veritable *ding-an-sich?* Her essay in *Scattering Branches,* a volume of English and Irish tributes to Yeats, is devoted and full of a respect for Yeats which is not destroyed by misgivings about his patriotism. But what is the English language—what is the gulf between Ireland and America—if the diminutive, Willie, does not suggest a guffaw, rather than the dignity of the great poet with "the stately head." Does it not seem even stranger when one thinks of the mask of the poet in the poems written about his love for Maud Gonne?

Perhaps this example is slight or wrong. Yet it may stand for many false notes which have been audible since the death of Yeats. At one extreme, there has been the false note that Yeats was a fop and a fool who by some miracle of a gift for language wrote great poetry. At the other extreme, a distinguished poet has permitted himself to say that, so far as he was concerned, Yeats had written more good poems than any other author in the history of English poetry.

But much more than false notes, much more than stupidities, too much praise or too much blame, or too little of each, or the wrong kind of each, have surrounded the dead poet and the deathless poetry. It is the sense of many points of view which makes one ask such endless questions as, What was in himself, beneath the deliberate mask? How shall we understand the greatness of his poetry? How shall we view his long career and many volumes, so different and various, and yet having the unity of one human being?

Some understanding can be gained merely by declaring some of the points of view from which Yeats has been looked at, and much more can be gained, perhaps, by taking some of the questions, problems, and mysteries which Yeats makes inevitable and considering them under the figure of an unwritten book, the unwritten book about Yeats which would tell the whole truth about him; or if not the whole truth, the truth we need to hear. It should be possible to state the nature of such a book, however far one is from being able to write it.

The very question—what kind of author will write this unwritten book?—may shed some light. Is it not clear that this author will not be Irish? Not only have the Irish admirers and followers of Yeats seemed to miss a great deal, so that they are hardly able to distinguish Yeats from AE; but, as more than one critic has observed, Yeats's career and work must for some time be bound up with many native feelings about Ireland, both in the past which was Yeats's lifetime and in the present.

Yet, on the other hand, an American will not write this book because he will not know enough about Ireland, being an American. He may even know as little as the present writer, who must look into the fourteenth edition of the *Encyclopaedia Britannica* in order to understand many of the names and references in Yeats's political poems—feeling then only that the information there is but a dark surface, at best; for what is said is often the kind of smugly judicious half-truth intended to make little of the long conflict between England and Ireland.

This must suggest that no Englishman will write our unwritten book, not even an unhappy Englishman who desires the death of the old gang. Might our author then be Anglo-Irish, like Yeats himself? Or perhaps Irish-American?

Conjectures such as these might go on forever. Perhaps they had better be exhausted by an extreme, that is, by suggesting that the unknown author of this unwritten book will be a poet and a critic who, although not Irish, enjoys and suffers a place in his time and country which is analogous to Yeats's: the poet of an oppressed country, during a period of nationalist activity, who has been educated in the country of the oppressor and must be read and understood and published there, although he must also give himself to the cause of national freedom and the native language and art. Perhaps—if the fancy and metaphor will be forgiven me—this author will be French-Canadian or Chinese, educated in Japan during the latter half of the twentieth century.

Consider, if it seems that too much is being made of the problem, merely the chief subjects of Yeats's poetry—romantic love, nationalist Ireland, distinguished friends and artists, the Irish aristocracy, the stories of a remote countryside, and a homemade philosophy of history and of the supernatural. In each of these subjects, how can we help feel that there is much more worth knowing than what we know as common readers? This difficulty and need of knowledge does not exist in all poets because all poets are not, like Yeats, engaged in dramatizing their own lives; not as directly, not to the same extent, not in the same way. R. P. Blackmur has shown how, for example, one cannot understand some of Yeats's best poems if one does not apply to them Yeats's views about magic. Perhaps it is not necessary to know much about political Ireland in order to understand the political poems: but what richness of particularity such knowledge gives to the poems. It is probably not necessary to know at all about Yeats's long relationship with Maud Gonne, if we are nothing more than readers of poetry. But some readers will always look for the private life in the public poems—if in Dante and Shakespeare, then everywhere in all poets—here, at this level, the exact and particular fact would help to keep the poems free of romantic misunderstanding; they are full enough of romantic understanding.

Thus one important part of our unwritten book would consist of the valuable information which makes possible footnotes from line to line wherever proper names or special references occur, or when the rhyme depends upon the way in which Yeats pronounced some English words. That the poems of Yeats require more footnotes than most other poets might serve as a working principle with which to begin. This is made only more true by the fact that Yeats himself provided some of the material for footnotes in his prose. For the labor then becomes one of seeing and making explicit the connections in question, and also of being critical of the poet's intention, since he was not only engaged in creating an image of himself, but often he may not have known himself what the truth was, as is the case with passages in *A Vision*.

This need of the information of footnotes is more than obvious. No poet is free of particularity, nor would any poet wish to be; the need of information is a general thing and only the degree and kind required by Yeats has to be mentioned. So too with other topics which are generic traits of an adequate book. But as soon as one sets up a sharp distinction between the general subjects of a satisfactory book about a poet and the specific problems which Yeats presents, there is so much to think about that it is hard to keep one's thoughts in order. The easy order of a review of specific problems is perhaps best, beginning with the most inclusive and going forward by trying to close in on the unique and irreducible thing which is the poetry.

Yeats in Europe. What a high-sounding title! But it is impossible to avoid a recognition of how important Europe is in thinking of Yeats. Born at the height of the Victorian period, becoming a writer during the nineties, living through the years which culminated in the first World War, arriving at his true mastery and power during the postwar period, and dying four months after the signing of the Munich Pact, Yeats suggests, just to begin with, the kind of table of contemporary events which is often found at the beginning of a great poet's collected poems. But it is much more than a matter of interesting correspondences. Yeats died the same month that *The Criterion* was suspended, because, as the editor said, the Munich Pact seemed to make no longer possible the assumptions on which the magazine had been based. Let this stand as a sign of the international causes which have a serious effect upon the literature of our time. The Munich Pact destroyed or helped to destroy an important magazine. In Yeats himself, from the beginning of his career to the very end, what happened in the Europe of his time penetrated his whole being as a poet, despite his serious sincere belief that he was writing, for the most part, sub specie aeternitatis. Thus one of his last poems, "Lapis Lazuli," at once expresses this belief and reproves the fear in Europe of the coming war:

[84]

> For everybody knows or else should know
> That if nothing drastic is done
> Aeroplane or Zeppelin will come out,
> Pitch like King Billy bomb balls in
> Until the town lie beaten flat.

What can the London reader think of these lines at present? What anyone can think of the characteristic attitude involved in this poem is something to be considered carefully later on. The point here is not merely the number of poems which are concerned—some of them explicitly—with the long agony of Europe. Often it is the effect of Europe on the fate of Ireland which occupies the poet's mind. But it is just as often true that we cannot but see how Yeats was a European man, intensely interested in and moved by what was happening in Paris, where the Symbolist movement reigned as he began to write, and in England, where his books were published.

To take one difficult instance which suggests the *Zeitgeist,* or perhaps, as Yeats would have said, the *Anima Mundi,* we find the obsessive symbol of the doll being used by Rilke, Stravinsky, and Yeats. Is it the same kind of feeling, the love of the artifact against the love of the natural thing, in all three? Did performances of the Russian Ballet bring Rilke and Yeats to the same symbol? Is this love of the artifact and hatred of the natural an expression of the isolation of the modern artist from the rest of society, as well as a metaphysical hatred of natural life and of change? Such are some of the questions, among many, which our unknown author might be able to answer, although we are too ignorant to do more than guess. The problem is neither general nor vague: what was happening in Europe during Yeats's career was a factor in bringing about minute details of the structure and texture of his poems. We need not take an obvious example like "Easter, 1916" or other poems in which the World War and Irish Nationalism are involved. For there is a large-scale example of great complexity and impressiveness, clear perhaps only from an angel's point of view: the shift from romantic dimness to sharp- and clear-cut harshness of texture which took place in music and painting as well as in poetry during the years that Yeats was developing his later style. Needless to say,

Yeats's later style is part of this shift. From the pre-Raphaelites to Picasso, from Debussy to Stravinsky, from Swinburne, Symons and Dowson, to the Imagists, Pound, and Eliot, the transformation is such that we can hardly doubt that the source is the same, the character and changes in European civilization, whatever the diversity and individuality of all these artists. Is it not this factor which must be the source of such another resemblance amid difference of the affirmation by Yeats, Eliot, and Rilke, among others, of the landed aristocracy as the good society? We can hardly fail to see Yeats's writing of *A Vision* as being at least suggested by the movement of history in this time. We know that never before has the character of society changed as quickly as in the fifty years of Yeats's adult life. And we know that in times of rapid social change, men are moved to study the philosophy of history more frequently. Given these two generalizations, a reading of *A Vision* together with the autobiographical writings and the poems would bring forth further major problems for our unknown author.

He would undoubtedly note that "objectivity" and "subjectivity," the basic terms of Yeats's philosophy of history, are analogues or equivalents for thought and action. Their opposition, their mixture, and their cycle look like projections—although not merely projections—of the life Yeats lived and the lives of his friends who were also artists, so that the whole framework of this view of history from beginning to end must be suspect as a vast sublimation of a special and limited experience. This suspicion would merely be reinforced when one took into account Yeats's method in elucidating his system. To illustrate the kinds of human beings produced by each phase of the moon which was an analogue of each phase of history, Yeats chooses almost always as his examples poets, artists, or intellectuals of some kind—"Flaubert, Herbert Spencer, Swedenborg, Dostoyevsky, Darwin," "Keats, Giorgione, many beautiful women," the few exceptions being obvious: Queen Victoria, Napoleon and Parnell. Thus it would seem on the surface that when Yeats looked at Europe and at history, he could see only his own face or the faces of his friends or what was already in his mind. But we soon see that the being of all the things which concerned Yeats was bound up with what was happening in Europe, and that as Yeats follows what interests him, in his poems and in his autobiographies, he is following, in his own way, the effect of Europe upon his own life.

Another generalization inevitably suggests itself, once we have seen the poet against the background of Europe from 1890 until 1939, the generalization that the center of the work is the poet as romantic poet, just as so much other work during this period has, as its subject, art as art, because the artist is isolated from the rest of society.

Starting with a desire to write the poetic poetry of the nineties, Yeats went through a complete experience of what it is for the poet to exist and practice his art during modern times and thus came upon a subject peculiarly fit for the romantic poet, namely, what it is to be a poet in modern times. The experience of his generation, the fate of such gifted authors as Wilde, Dowson, Lionel Johnson, and Synge, who died in misery and degradation, might by itself be taken as a sufficient cause for turning to this subject. But there is much else which makes it seem natural that the later poetry should be full of references to the artists, poets, scholars and beautiful women the poet has known, and should speak of the country house where life is ceremony, where works of art abound, where the rich are patrons of the arts. The poet intent upon Art for Art's sake so exhausted his intention and learned so much about Art from others who were of like intent that the underlying subject of his later poetry became the fate of Art and the emotion of the Artist in modern life.

Given this generalization, how much seems to be explained: the hatred of time in the later poetry is, in part, the hatred of the movement of history, which has greatly altered the bases and assumptions with which the poet began to practice his art. The ideal of a landed aristocracy is the expression of a desire for a society in which the artist can thrive, for the ruling class of industrial and finance capitalism does not need the artist and, unlike other ruling classes, when it turns to art buys Old Masters, partly because culture has become international, partly because the millionaire, like the artist, is, in his own way, removed from the rest of society. Thus too the opposition of Byzantium to nature is the opposition of a civilization in which art, artificiality and ritual dominate, to modern civilization. At the same time, it is the expression of the artist's need of fixed forms, traditions, and stability.

Another point to be emphasized is that it was the poet's experience of ceaseless social change which brought him the desire for permanence and the metaphors of permanence.

Yeats in Ireland. What has just been said of Yeats's relationship to Europe would be even more true of his relationship to Ireland. Perhaps this second instance will make it clear that when one speaks of Europe one is not summoning up an empty abstraction or convenient abbreviation for many things taken together. The most rigorous nominalist could hardly say that Ireland was some kind of abstraction endowed with illusory powers by the patriot or Platonist. And Ireland's fate was of course bound up with that of Europe and in particular with the course of the British Empire. The working principle of our gifted author here would probably be an invariable sense of his own ignorance, a knowledge that one cannot feel the full quality of the words and emotions when Yeats writes of Ireland. One must understand, knowing that one cannot feel, what names like Parnell, O'Leary, Pearse, and Connally mean to the Irish nationalists, even to such a one as Yeats, whose ambiguous and ambivalent sentiments can be heard in many poems; most directly perhaps in such a poem as "I am of Ireland," where a woman cries to a man with "a stately head," "Come dance with me in Ireland," and the man replies that the orchestra seems to be insane in Ireland, only to have her repeat her invitation, as if forever.

The question of how well the poet has generalized his experiences as an Irishman is one that can be quickly answered after explicit admission has been made of how most readers must fall short of grasping the local or national feelings. We can see how, with a knowledge of the particular references, the Irish names and events mentioned so often in the poems become signs of the common experience of human beings: the history has become poetry in that the particular event signifies a typical kind of event. Thus in "I am of Ireland," the dramatic relationship, far from being local or national or personal, is significant of any human being's effort in the disorder of our time.

But another problem which is more difficult would present itself at this point for our author, the task of making out the part that

Irish Nationalism played in Yeats's career as a poet. Undoubtedly it played a great part from beginning to end, but in mixed and opposed ways. Some have said that it was Yeats's experience as a political organizer which made him a poet of the later style. Yet in his *Autobiographies,* Yeats says that the few months of his political activity were the worst months of his life, he was an utter failure at it, and he soon gave it up. Again, it is said that politics brought him in direct contact with the speech of the people; yet, in "Estrangement," written in 1909, he says that he has always been unable to speak with strangers, with any but intimate friends. If one wishes, one can rescue the worth of Yeats's political experience by means of the dialectical sleight of tongue whereby every habit, trait, or action brings forth its opposite; this was of course one of Yeats's favorite doctrines. But surely our adequate author would not rest with this kind of explanation which, since it can explain everything, really explains nothing.

The part that Yeats took in the Irish Renaissance,[1] closely connected as it is with Irish Nationalism despite such conflicts as the one over *The Playboy of the Western World,* must bring to the fore another large-scale generalization, the fact that the few great periods of the drama in Western culture have been periods of strong or triumphant nationalism; for example, Periclean Athens, Elizabethan England, and the France of Louis XIV. This should suggest a connection between nationalism and the audience which the dramatist needs more than any other kind of author. In Yeats's case, it suggests the possibility that it was here, in the Abbey Theater, hearing again and again plays by authors who were closer to the people and their speech than Yeats could ever come directly, that Yeats acquired that knowledge of how to use speech in verse which is so important an element in his later style. The relationship of Yeats to Synge, who, on Yeats's advice, went among the people in order to hear and copy down their speech, the extreme admiration which Yeats felt for Synge—an admiration far in excess of what Synge's plays now seem to justify—may have been in part Yeats's intuitive anticipation of the nature of his later style.

Whatever the truth, in detail, about the effect of Irish nationalism

1. It is worth remarking that Yeats's first prose work appeared in 1894 and was entitled "The Celtic Twilight."

and the Irish theater upon Yeats, one important rule we must note, and see exemplified in Yeats as well as other authors, is the rule that authors seek the conditions which make them what they are just as much as the conditions seek out authors. Irish nationalism must have made authors of a number of men who might otherwise have spent their lives in peace; it must have dictated their subject matter often enough and given them an audience. But in Yeats's case one cannot avoid the notion that Yeats came to Irish nationalism from deliberate choice, seeking out a cultural and literary *milieu* in which he might fulfill himself as an author. How this process occurred, what factors of pride, careerism, and immediate need began it, the influence of childhood attachments in Yeats's case, and the influence of Maud Gonne, how the process reached beneath such motives and became deeply-rooted—what a difficult chapter this would make in the book that is not yet written. Perhaps in Yeats, the whole process could be followed step by step, despite the evasions and gaps in the *Autobiographies*.

One fact in the back of one's mind throughout, whenever one seeks the connection between a man and the conditions of all kinds which have surrounded him and penetrated him, is the unique poet who cannot be reduced to any causes or circumstances. Yeats alone of his generation became a great poet: what cause or circumstance explains this greatness?

Yeats in Himself. The first thing that meets the reader in most volumes by Yeats is a portrait of the author next to the title page, showing the poet at a stated age. No matter how intent we are in distinguishing between a body of poetry and the poet who composed it, we cannot do so when we come to Yeats. For he is his own chief character—from the languishing and pale "I" of the early love poems to the "sixty-year-old smiling public man," Senator Yeats, of "Among School Children." The *Autobiographies* increase this connection in numerous ways because no one will read the poems without wishing to see what is in the *Autobiographies*.

Yet this dramatized projection of himself in prose and verse is only one view, and a most charitable one. Other views of the same human being exist and seem to contradict it. To use the most striking example, when we read *Dramatis Personae*, we cannot forget

the Yeats presented by George Moore. Just as we can hardly
doubt that the Yeats presented by George Moore and the George
Moore of Yeats are far from being the whole truth, so too we are
aware, whenever Yeats uses himself as a character in one of his
poems, that this is a version made by the poet to suit his own
idea of himself and of what a poet should be. What, for example,
does an Irish Republican think of the Yeats who appears in "Easter,
1916"? We can be certain that he does not see Yeats as Yeats sees
and presents himself.

In the *Autobiographies,* Yeats was not trying to tell the truth
about himself, but to use whatever part of the truth would help
him to achieve a dramatic image. When we read in the *Autobiographies* the judgment that Oscar Wilde made of *The Wander-
ings of Oisin,* comparing it favorably with Homer, if we have read
that poem or even if we have not, we know that we are confronted
with vanity and blindness; not Wilde's only, but Yeats's also.

So too when we read of Wilde himself in the *Autobiographies,*
or when we come upon the many references to Maud Gonne in the
prose or the verse: we know that this is not the truth about
them because other people saw them so differently. And it is not
only different views of the same person, but almost always a view
on Yeats's part which seems the product of a will to see only what
he wants to see, and a will to forget the rest. Yeats's poetry will
never be separated from his *Autobiographies,* and neither work
will ever be separated from the human being who was not what he
wished to be and not what he saw himself as being.

How difficult it is to keep the human being and the work
separate can be seen in a few more very recent instances. One
reviewer of Yeats's *Last Poems and Plays* remarked that he was
disgusted by the explicit sexuality displayed in these poems by
a man who was, after all, over seventy. Whether or not disgust
is justified in this case the present writer does not pretend to know,
but it is certain that the protagonist of these poems is manifestly
an old man full of sexual longings and regrets. Again, in *Scattering
Branches,* L. A. G. Strong writes that several critics have attributed
"the riot of copulation" in the last poems to "the gland operation
Yeats underwent some five or six years before he died." Mr.
Strong believes that the way to answer such an attribution is to

"look to that in him which made him demand the operation: to the manner of man he was." Louis MacNeice is similarly concerned in his book on Yeats about the poet's virginity until the age of forty: how shall we tell the poet from the poem? Although we know how to make the distinction and ignore all Yeats did to dramatize himself as a human being, some will always refuse to make the distinction. Perhaps it is for this reason that Homer and Shakespeare have sometimes ceased to exist.

And finally, our unknown author will perhaps engage in comparisons; Yeats against Arthur Symons, for the sake of what light may be shed on why one became a great poet in middle age while the other, better educated and better equipped in other ways, did not; Yeats against A. E. Housman, to show, among much else, how Yeats did perfectly what Housman did mechanically in verse; Yeats against James Joyce and against Ezra Pound; Yeats against Arnold Bennett and André Gide, both of them born almost at the same time as Yeats and both of them authors of journals which make a rich comparison with Yeats's *Autobiographies.*

His Lyric Poems. It is possible to read Yeats's prose for its beauties of style, although those beauties never arrive at the sustained coherence and unity which constitute a complete book. But it is clear that neither his plays nor his prose writings[2] make Yeats what he is for us. The poems which begin with the volume called *The Green Helmet* and end with *Last Poems and Plays* are for most readers the only reason why the rest of Yeats's work has anything but incidental interest. They are the center of interest, the justification of our interest, and inevitably the source of fresh instances of old problems about the nature of literature. Our gifted author, confronted with these problems, will probably be content with stating them once more as well as possible in their relationship to Yeats.

For example, there will certainly once more be the problem of what the reader who does not share Yeats's beliefs in the super-

2. Perhaps Yeats was a great lyric poet, but a poor dramatist and fragmentary prose writer because of the self-absorption, obvious throughout, which kept him from being interested in other human beings, except as they were directly related to himself.

natural can take as a workable attitude while he reads. This problem is further complicated by the difficulty of knowing whether or not Yeats held those beliefs himself, and still further complicated by the grab-bag character of Yeats's view of the supernatural, arrived at through such intermediaries as Irish peasants, Madame Blavatsky, and Mrs. Yeats, whatever the ultimate ontological source. But another ancient problem, which in a way contains the problem of belief and must arise even for those who believe exactly what Yeats believed, is the question of the relationship of the formal perfection of some of the poems to the kind of insight which it for the most part embodies. I mean to say that the insight is far from being the equal of the writing itself taken in abstraction.

It is true that some of Yeats's poems are full of a wisdom which must commend itself to and convince every man, Buddhist to Seventh Day Adventist. The second part of "A Dialogue of Self and Soul" is a passage the equal of Dante and Shakespeare at their best. But in general, the point of view of Yeats's verse is romantic in its assumptions and in its conclusions. Romantic love, the romantic view of death, the romantic view of the poet, the private self-made philosophy of the romantic poet—these are all basic elements of Yeats's mind as it manifests itself in his lyric poems. Even when he sees and understands much more than the romantic poet, the lurid glow of romanticism nevertheless hangs over the scene. And very often it is pure romantic perception, the consequence of all the romantic assumptions, that we find in poems which, considered as verbal expression, are faultless.

An easy instance is such a poem as "The Scholars." These academic figures, bald-headed, coughing, and respectable, would be dumbfounded, the poet suggests, if they met Catullus or the other poets whom they edit and annotate, making a learned text of the lines

> That young men, tossing on their beds,
> Rhymed out in love's despair
> To flatter beauty's ear.

How utterly banal a view! No doubt, some scholars are worthy of contempt for the reasons advanced by the poet. It is not a question

of the character of the scholar, past or present, nor is it necessary
to suppose that scholars are handsome and heroic figures. What
one finds essentially wrong here is the romantic triteness and stupidity of the attitude, the implied contempt for learning because it
is painstaking and not spontaneous, the schoolboy's view of the
absentminded professor, and the Bohemian's notion of aca-
demicism: "All (that is, all the scholars) think what other people
think," Yeats wrote, thinking what other people think. What
would Catullus have thought of this poem? We are told of the
Alexandrian sources of his poetry.

Again, to take a more striking and more characteristic example,
in "An Irish Airman Forsees His Death," consider the following
lines, in which the airman is supposedly revealing his reasons for
participating in the first World War on the side of Great Britain:

> Those that I fight I do not hate,
> Those that I guard I do not love . . .
> My country is Kiltartan Cross,
> My countrymen Kiltartan's poor,
> No likely end could bring them loss,
> Or leave them happier than before.
> Nor law nor duty bade me fight,
> Nor public men nor cheering crowds,
> A lonely impulse of delight
> Drove to this tumult in the clouds.

The rejection of law, duty, public men, and cheering crowds, and
the apotheosis of one motive, "A lonely impulse of delight," shows
with exactitude how complete a romantic Yeats was.

For one more even more obvious example of the height, width
and depth of Yeats's romanticism, there is the first poem of the
sequence, "A Woman Young and Old" in Yeats's next to last
volume of verse:

> FATHER AND CHILD
> She hears me strike the board and say
> That she is under ban
> Of all good men and women,
> Being mentioned with a man
> That has the worst of all bad names,
> And thereupon replies
> That his hair is beautiful,
> Cold as the March wind his eyes.

This is of course a quasi-dramatic lyric. Hence it may be wrong to suppose that the poet is expressing an admiration without reservations for the lady's reply. Yet is it not the same lonely impulse of delight, rejecting all other appeals, which motivates not only the lady's sentiments, and not only the father, who seems to be much impressed by his daughter's reply, but the whole poem? I certainly do not mean to raise any issue of moralism or didacticism, although whatever the worst of all bad names may be, traitor, murderer, or pimp, it is hard to accept beautiful hair and cold eyes as being a counterweight from any rational point of view. Nor is it that one would wish the poem always to declare that virtue is good, evil is bad, and the wicked will surely be punished. The issue I want very much to raise is the distinction in quality between the expression, considered in abstraction, and the wisdom or rather lack of wisdom in this poem. Some instance of this issue can be found in a majority of Yeats's later poems and it is only brevity and convenience which make the weight of argument rest on this short poem. The expression here as elsewhere seems to me to have every *literary* virtue which could possibly be required for a short lyric: it has clarity, simplicity, exactness of diction, metrical exactness and sensitivity, a fine dramatic framework which finds its counterpart in the order and structure of the lines. But, by contrast, the sentiments which are given this fine expression are part of the foolish bravado of romantic adolescence: the equivalent in literary expression would be irresponsible doggerel or perhaps a quick-moving limerick.

It is here then that our unknown author would have his most difficult problem. He would have to accept and elucidate the greatness of the writing without forgetting the inferior quality of the emotions and attitudes embodied in the writing. No doubt this raises the ancient and ever-new problem of the separation of form from subject matter. At the same time it raises the similar but more inclusive problem, stated precisely, and yet not, I think, sufficiently discussed by T. S. Eliot in an analogous context where the question was that of the religious attitude to literature: "The 'greatness' of literature cannot be determined solely by literary standards; though we must remember that whether it is literature or not can be determined only by literary standards." Our gifted unknown author will have to make that distinction again and again in writing of Yeats's poems, explicating the nature of literary standards by considering the verse as expression and at the same time making clear, in all humility, how often Yeats fell short of the wisdom which is in the Bible, Dante, and Shakespeare, and in every rational being when he thinks well enough and acts well enough to survive as a human being. There are passages and whole poems in which Yeats has that wisdom as well as any poet, but the dominant tendency of his work derives, in the direct way we have seen, from the tenets, the assumptions and the conclusions of romanticism in some of its most familiar forms.

Only if one subscribes to the theory of the identity of form and subject matter—which can always be heard and which is never explained—is such a separate enjoyment of expression apart from doctrine, attitude, and sentiment impossible. Is it not necessary, in fact, to grasp the quality of language and expression in Yeats's later poetry without taking its romanticism with equal seriousness, or permitting a rejection of its romanticism to interfere with one's enjoyment of it as expression?

His Mastery of Expression. As expression, Yeats's later poetry suggests the possibility of endless study. The use of speed and slowness in going from word to word, the use of line lengths, of repetition, of off-rhymes, and similar devices of the versification, are matters which would be analyzed in detail in our adequate book. But it is the use of meter, above all, which would require and reward study. The metrical mastery which accomplishes so much works through variations of the iambic structure of a complexity which is such that the proper names for all the devices do not, so far as I know, exist:

> '*Old lov*ers yet may have
> *All* that time denied—
> *Grave* is heaped on grave
> That they be satisfied—
> *Over* the blackened earth
> *The old troops* parade,
> *Birth* is heaped on birth
> That such *cannonade*
> May thunder time away,
> *Birth-hour and death-hour meet,*
> *Or, as great sages* say,
> *Men dance* on deathless feet.'

I have italicized the variations of the iambic trimeter of this quotation in order to show briefly the extraordinary variety Yeats could manage with ease and without the least hint of a wrenching of accent or an imperfection of tone. I do not know the name for such a variation as is contained in "*The old troops* parade." But the expressiveness of this variation and of the wonderful last line, "*Men dance* on deathless feet," should illustrate the riches in Yeats's versification which require elucidation and analysis as well as enjoyment.[3]

Another example which illustrates more broadly the difference between formal excellence and insight which is inferior, slight, or absent is such a poem—there are many like it in this respect—as "A Thought from Propertius":

> She might, so noble from head
> To great shapely knees
> The long flowing line,
> Have walked to the altar
> Through the holy images
> At Pallas Athena's side,
> Or been fit spoil for a centaur
> Drunk with the unmixed wine.

The extraordinary effect of this short poem is largely the result of the inverted sentence structure[4] in the first three lines—"So noble from head/To great shapely knees/The long flowing line," and the delayed rhyme of "line" and "wine," which binds the third line with the conclusion of the poem. The image of the poem simulates the visual without being visual and the classical references do not have any profound associations for the modern reader, and in any case hardly account for the beauty of the verse. This instance suggests in fact that any great translation shows how mastery of language and expression can exist in isolation from mastery of or insight into subject matter.

Interpretation. Most important of all, I think, will be the labor of providing a system of interpretation for Yeats's poems. We have

3. There is also the question of why Yeats wrote such weak, unorganized blank verse in his plays; why, when he gave up rhyme, his metrical mastery disappeared. In the lyrics, the use of anapests and spondees is another matter worth studying.

4. It is with this device of style that Yeats achieves some of the beauty of his prose: this device in the middle of artful simple declarative sentences.

[97]

heard enough by now of the four kinds of levels of meaning in *The Divine Comedy*. A like system will have to be made and worked out for Yeats. R. P. Blackmur's emphasis on the magical kind of meaning is exemplified, in his essay on Yeats, in what he says of one of Yeats's best poems: " 'Leda and the Swan' can be read on at least three distinct levels of significance, none of which interferes with the others: the levels of dramatic fiction, of condensed insight into Greek mythology, and a third level of fiction and insight combined, as we said, to represent and hide a magical insight."

Yet, since this possibility sometimes brings about a drunkenness or wantonness of interpretation, perhaps it is worthwhile citing an extreme example, an example of fruitful misunderstanding, in order to show not only how real the problem of interpretation may be, but what dangers it creates.

In another of Yeats's best poems, "Among School Children," there is a passage which becomes, I think, very much better *when it is misunderstood*. Or rather when Yeats's intended meaning is mistaken for another one. In the fifth stanza of "Among School Children," the "I" of the poem turns from the school children who have reminded him of the old age and the childhood of a woman who was once a great beauty. Her old age and her loss of beauty have made him question the worth of any natural life.

Quite naturally and appropriately, this leads to thoughts about what famous philosophers have said of Nature, and of human life as a natural process:

> Plato thought nature but a spume that plays
> Upon a ghostly paradigm of things;
> Soldier Aristotle played the taws
> Upon the bottom of a king of kings;
> World-famous golden-thighed Pythagoras
> Fingered upon a fiddle-stick or strings
> What a star sang and careless Muses heard:
> Old clothes upon old sticks to scare a bird.

Given the first two lines of the stanza, which are certainly an effort to describe Plato's view of nature, suppose one takes the next two lines as a description of Aristotle's cosmology. "A king of kings" would thus be Aristotle's Prime Mover or God; the taws or marbles[5] would be the concentric spheres which constitute the world for Aristotle and to which the Prime Mover gives impetus or movement. The reference is playful and ironic, and also exact in saying that the taws or celestial spheres were played against the bottom of the Prime Mover, since he is, in Aristotle's description of his life, turned away from all nature and wholly engaged in eternal thought about himself. And the whole sense of the passage, taken in this way, is a good extension, by example, of the contempt for nature which Yeats is trying to state. The succeeding four lines, as well as the preceding two, help this interpretation by their reference to Pythagoras on the same level of discourse, namely, different philosophies of nature expressed in concrete figures. There is nothing special to or limited to Aristotle about this interpretation of the two lines concerning him, for the Ptolemaic cosmology must be known in order to understand many other authors: the last line of the *Divine Comedy*, "The Love which moves the sun and the other stars," depends on the same cosmology and is a reference to the same Prime Mover, which should suggest that the educated reader might naturally and even spontaneously seize upon this interpretation.

Moreover, this interpretation seems to tally with what one takes to be a misprint; "Soldier Aristotle" (which appears on page 251 of the American edition of the *Collected Poems* of 1933) should then read "Solider Aristotle," a correction enforced not only by the obvious contrast between Aristotle and Plato, but also by the meter which is wrenched by "soldier."

It seems fairly certain, however, that Yeats intended nothing of the sort. "Taws" means whips, as well as marbles. The king of kings is Alexander, Aristotle's pupil, often referred to in antiquity

5. In *Webster's New International*, a taw is defined as follows: "1. *Colloq. & Dial.* A line or mark from which players at marbles shoot. 2. A marble to be used as a shooter; also, a game at marbles." This is all that is given for taw as a noun.

If taws are taken as marbles, then their application to the Aristotelian-Ptolemaic cosmology might mean the sun and the stars, which are part of the celestial spheres, as well as their celestial spheres themselves. For the sun and the stars are more like marbles than the spheres, which are concentric to each other, so that the whole of nature resembles, to use a homely example, an onion, at the approximate center of which is the earth and outside of which is the Prime Mover.

as the king of kings. "Soldier Aristotle" may not be a misprint, but a reference to Aristotle's interest in military strategy, and the whole intention of the poet becomes a biographical-historical example, the supposition that Aristotle whipped his noble pupil.

Further evidence that Yeats had this in mind is to be seen in another of his poems, "The Saint and the Hunchback," in which it is impossible to doubt that by taws, Yeats meant whips:

> I lay about me with the taws
> That night and morning I may thrash
> Greek Alexander from my flesh.

This historical-biographical interpretation seems to me obviously inferior, in terms of the poem itself, so far as significance goes; they seem to stick out wrongly from the rest of the stanza: what has Aristotle's whipping of his noble pupil to do with contempt for nature? It would seem rather to be contempt for monarchy.

The whole problem of the meaning or meanings of any poem is raised by this example. This particular example is extreme, as I have said, and possibly freakish, but in one form or another much of Yeats's verse raises the same question for any reader, namely, What are the limits which define legitimate interpretation? Are there any limits? To what extent can we disregard the author's intention?

One answer fairly popular at present I suppose would be that the reader is justified in giving as many interpretations as he can to a poem: the more, the better; the more, the richer the poem. In William Empson's terms, there are any number of possible types of ambiguity, and we ought to get all we can from all of them.

This answer seems to be involved in countless difficulties. For example, some interpretations contradict one another. In "Among School Children," one cannot at the same time take the two lines in question as referring to Alexander and to the Prime Mover.

Another answer might be, An interpretation is valid only if it is consistent with the whole context of the poem taken as a literal statement. But this criterion of the whole literal context breaks down quickly. One sees that it enforces the philosophical interpretation by being consistent with the consideration of Nature which is the subject of the two preceding and the four succeeding lines. One also sees how the interpretation which makes the two lines describe Aristotle's whipping of his pupil would be also consistent, with a slight straining of one's ingenuity, with a poem which is about schoolchildren.

Whatever the answer to the whole problem of interpretation or this particular instance of it may be, this problem and all the problems I have shifted to an unknown author should add up to a definition of ignorance. Yet this defined ignorance assumes, knows, and depends upon an inexhaustible substance, like Life itself. Only admiration of this substance could bring one to a concern with its problems and mysteries. It is with this admiration, with a conviction of the greatness of this poetry, that our author will begin and end. All will begin and end with admiration and love of the greatness of this poetry.

Ezra Pound's Very Useful Labors

This is the thirtieth year since the publication of Ezra Pound's first book of poems. The occasion, for it is an occasion, is marked, as it should be for so faithful a poet, by the publication of ten new cantos of his long poem,[1] and it is obvious that a response of congratulation and gratitude is precisely what he deserves. The fact that Pound himself has from time to time fired twenty-one gun salutes to his own efforts ought not to deter us. An enormous transformation of sensibility has occurred since the printing of the first volume of *Personae*, and no man can have had more to do with this transformation than Ezra Pound. The contrasting states of culture in 1908 and 1938 are subjects for the literary historian, but what has happened can be suggested briefly and by a mere array of names. No complacency, no great satisfaction with 1938 need be assumed. Some of the names for 1908 are Hamilton Wright Mabie, William Dean Howells, Richard Harding Davis, and George Woodberry. American culture was an insupportable desert from which Pound, and before him, Henry James, and but a few years later, George Santayana and T. S. Eliot found it necessary to depart. They left for various reasons—both Eliot and Pound seem to have gone merely for a year of study—but the significant fact is that they did not return. What has happened in the interim cannot, it is clear, be attributed to the operation of any individual mind; the World War, to take the big example, broke down a great deal in the region of attitudes and feelings which Pound, though he had shouted one hundred times more loudly than his usual wont, could never have moved. But here is another array of

1. *The Fifth Decad of Cantos*, by Ezra Pound. Farrar & Rinehart.

names: James Joyce, William Butler Yeats, Robert Frost, Wyndham Lewis, William Carlos Williams, Marianne Moore, and many more could be added. They have at least this fact in common, that at one time or another, one way or another, Pound helped them very much, often howling their merits in the ineffable jargon of his public epistles. Joyce has said publicly that it was Pound who secured a publisher for *Ulysses*, and there was, before this, all that Pound said and wrote about Joyce's first two books. There is also the famous story of how, after years of the hardship of loneliness, Robert Frost went to England and was discovered by Pound immediately upon the reading of his poetry. Besides these quasi-editorial activities, there is the profound effect which Pound's verse has had upon the writing of T. S. Eliot: not only obviously in poems like "The Journey of the Magi," and *The Waste Land*, but in the most minute details: the first line of *Ash Wednesday*, "Because I do not hope to turn again," is a translation of Cavalcanti's *Perch'io non spero tornar già mai*, and thus probably derives from Pound's early translation of Cavalcanti. The very variety of Pound's services is impressive and one cannot but be amazed at the examples of generous attention on Pound's part which crop up from time to time. To take an instance which is not well known, John Peale Bishop writes in his essay on Hemingway that "in Paris, Hemingway submitted much of his apprentice work in fiction to Pound. It came back to him blue-penciled, most of the adjectives gone." And then there is all that Pound has done in Chinese poetry, in Provençal poetry, in Latin poetry, and from the very beginning in 1912, in *Poetry: A Magazine of Verse*. So many more fruitful activities of this nature could be rehearsed that it is necessary to stop here in order to avoid a mere list.

The Cantos ought to be regarded as arising from this whole complex of interests. They are the production of one who has devoted himself almost wholly to literature, setting up literature, whether knowingly or not, as his ruling value. When in 1934 Pound declared that he was giving up literature for economics, no one really interested in the matter was disturbed, and there was no reason to be, for ten new cantos appeared a short while after. When we consider this devotion to literature, we come upon the essential characteristic of the Cantos: their philological discussions, their

[103]

translations, their textual references, their peculiar and unceasing interest in how things are said, not to speak of the various dialects and slangs which are introduced, and the habitual quotation, of letters, codices, and other documents.

The standpoint from which the various heroes of the Cantos are represented is also a good indication of this point. Mozart is celebrated in *Canto XXVI* not as the great musician, but because of an insulting letter to the Archbishop of Salzburg, Mozart's epistolary style of invective being so interesting that it must be quoted. T. E. Hulme, whose thought affected so many of Pound's generation so much, is mentioned not as a philosopher of great promise, but as the soldier who went to the trenches with books from the London Library, and when the books were lost in a trench explosion, the London Library became very annoyed, and when Hulme was wounded and in the hospital, he read Kant "and the hospital staff didn't like it." Andreas Divus is mentioned because he was a good translator of Homer, and Helen of Troy is introduced briefly by means of several puns in Greek and a quotation, finely translated, from *The Iliad*. Another figure held up for admiration is old Lévy, a German scholar of Provençal whom Pound visited in order to find out the meaning of the word "noigandres": Lévy's dialect is reproduced and the sensuous character of the place where the interview occurred, Freiburg, is described, the philological interest apparently giving rise to the whole passage, which is one of the most beautiful in the Cantos. The Italian nobles of the Renaissance and Thomas Jefferson are both sung by the poet partly because they were patrons of the arts, partly because they wrote interesting letters. And as for the villains, the same attitude determines their choice, and we get as an example of complete stupidity such an anecdote as this one from *Canto XXVIII*:

> "Buk!" said the Second Baronet "eh. . . .
> "Thass a funny lookin' buk" said the Baronet
> Looking at Bayle, folio, 4 vols., in gilt leather," Ah. . . .
> "Wu . . . Wu . . . wot you goin' eh to do with ah. . .
> ". . . ah read-it?"

The generalization which flows from these instances is almost too obvious to be mentioned: Pound has been the pure literary man,

[104]

the complete man of letters; the concern with literary things, with the very look of print upon the page, is at the center, the source, of his writing. It would be possible, but difficult, to exaggerate this attachment, for it infects the Cantos at every point, and even in this latest volume under review, which is devoted to a long history of the origins of usury proceeding through many cantos (with typical interruptions), the presentation of the facts is made in terms of textual references, signatures upon documents, their dates, and the idiom in which the documents were written. From this standpoint the Cantos are the long poem of a wandering scholar without chair, without portfolio. And it is tempting, but not sufficiently tempting, to attribute this kind of prepossession to the fact that when Pound went to Europe to study texts for a thesis on Lope de Vega, he left a country where a thoroughgoing devotion to literature as an important element in the life of an educated man had for a long time been a rare or academic or sterile thing.

Much is to be gained by keeping this in mind when we read the Cantos. We understand why a poet with such interests resorts so often to allusion, and we see that if we want to know what the poem is about, we had better read it as it was written, in the shadow of many books. But more than that, the values by which men and things are judged seem actually to be determined by a belief, or rather feeling that literature is the greatest good in the life of mankind. In the Kung canto, where the dominant values of the poem are explicitly declared, we have, to begin with, a quotation from the books of Confucius. And among the emphases, order, fit ritual, a temple, mandolins, and other things related to art, we are given the key statement about government:

> And "When the prince has gathered about him
> "All the savants and artists, his riches will be fully employed"

and this is one of the central motives behind the later concern with usury and economics, the fact that good writers are not adequately supported and published, as Pound has explained in his prose. Or again, as Kung says in conclusion:

> "Without character you will
> be unable to play on that instrument
> Or to execute the music fit for the Odes."

[105]

The implication is that we ought to have character merely for the sake of being good poets. The opposite extreme, as of I. A. Richards, is to suppose that the Odes exist in order to make character possible.

The facile thing would be to say that Pound's vision was "one-sided," or a version of the ivory tower and sheer aestheticism, or a picture of the nature of things through the medium of books. The truth, however, is that Pound has been standing still on this basis, occupying this particular balcony, but has turned his gaze in a great many directions, so that the Cantos represent and contain a good deal more than the perspective from which they were written, although so much of what they contain is naturally in terms of that perspective. If then, before going on to consider the Cantos in themselves, we examine them as a source of literary influence and a profound modification of poetic practice, we find immense profits. The most important and impressive fact about what Pound has done to extend the medium of poetry is clearly the versification. It is not only that some great modes of poetry—direct statement, description, speech, and the movement of the poem itself—have been given fresh kinds of rhythm, but that, above all and extreme as the claim may seem, our capacity to *hear* words, lines, and phrases has been increased by the Cantos. In this new volume, for example, in *Canto XLV* and again in *Canto XLI*, there is this chant:

> With *Usura*
> With usura hath no man a house of good stone
> each block cut smooth and well fitting
> that design might cover their face,
> with usura
> hath no man a painted paradise on his church wall
> *harpes et luthes*
> or where virgin receiveth message
> and halo projects from incision

and so, through many repetitions and specifications which heighten the song, concluding with

> Azure hath a canker by usura; cramoisi is unbroidered
> Emerald findeth no Memling
> Usura slayeth the child in the womb
> It stayeth the young man's courting

It hath brought palsey to bed, lyeth
between the young bride and her bridegroom
CONTRA NATURAM

They have brought whores to Eleusis
Corpses are set to banquet
at behest of usura.[2]

To observe the way in which the emphasis is variously shifted and the key word brought in differently and monotony avoided, it would be necessary to quote the whole Canto. There is nothing like it in English, except perhaps for a like chant against pity in *Canto XXX*. And in order to show adequately how many times and with what variety the Cantos display a progress, actually, in hearing, it would be necessary to quote at great length. No one seriously interested in writing ambitious poetry during the next hundred years will fail to be affected by those aural developments; if not directly, then through some poet who has himself digested Pound. T. S. Eliot is in part an example of such a poet, and it is Eliot who has pointed out that the Cantos "are a mine for juvenile poets to quarry." Related to this aspect of Pound's writing, and perhaps merely the same thing at another point is the effort throughout the Cantos to incorporate speech, to make verse out of speech, and if in this the poem is often distorted by Pound's love of the weirdest slangs and dialects, represented in his own kind of phonetics, the experiment is valuable even in its failure, and provides the basis for a dramatic verse which would attempt to display contemporary speech. And there is, in addition, what has been noted often before, the demonstration of style which is clean-cut, hard, sharp, and visual, the utter rejection of certain types of rhetoric, and the use of subject matters which have not previously or recently been considered "poetic."

2. It is interesting to observe in passing that in this particular canto, the attack on usury as a poetic statement can be separated from its connection with a particular economic theory by the mere device of substituting another three-syllable word with the same accents, for example, "capital." The point cannot be pressed very far, since the canto in question ties up with other discussions of economic theory throughout the poem, discussions which would prevent such a substitution. Nevertheless the possibility of substitution may exist wherever we are confronted with a good poem whose beliefs we do not accept.

But most of all, literary practice benefits by the effort of the Cantos to digest a great many diverse elements, and to speak, in one poem, of many different *kinds* of things. This is a matter important enough to deserve a digression. It is clear that at the present time, the poet is confronted by an environment which, on the level of perception at least, is extremely disordered; perhaps one should say: un-ordered. One who rides in a subway train knows very well how advertisements, lights, stations, the faces in another passing train, are all shuffled together. Or when one walks in crowds one is amid thousands unknown to each other. Or in reading the daily newspaper, one is faced with a fund of events which are together mainly because they occurred upon the same date. The subway, the crowds, and the newspaper are merely easy examples. The point is that the writer who has a sense of his own time and a sense of intellectual responsibility toward his own experience must of necessity attempt to digest into his poetry these types of disorder. It is not a question of yielding to modern experience and merely reflecting it in one's writing by an equivalent disorder upon the verbal level; nor, except for certain kinds of lyric writing, is it possible merely to disregard the kind of experience which has become a part, to put it bluntly, of the nervous system. The difficult and ineluctable task is to say something intelligent and just about modern experience, and to be sure that modern experience is actually contained in the poem and the intelligence and the justice made relevant to it; not, on the contrary, to permit the poem to be absorbed wholly in edifying sentiments.

When, then, the *unrelatedness*, on all sides, of modern experience is recognized, it becomes simple to understand the way in which the Cantos are put together, and we can see what a lesson they afford for further acts of ordering. *The Waste Land, The Orators*, of Auden, and *The Bridge*, of Hart Crane, are further examples of the actuality of the problem, and if it is only in the instance of the first poem that anything has been gained from Pound, all these poems reinforce our understanding of what confronts the modern poet and of how the Cantos have to do with it. Thus in this new volume which brings us to *Canto LI*, we find Pound attempting to get no less than the subject matter of economics into his poem.

Once, however, that we narrow our attention to the Cantos in themselves, forgetting their usefulness as a basis for future poetry, a somewhat different story seems to present itself, at least to one reader. Taking this long poem in itself, we must of necessity see it not as an integral part of a literary period, but in the company of other long poems of like ambition. The first lack to be noted from this standpoint is the absence of a narrative framework such as sustains every long poem which has become a portion of the whole corpus of poetry. Pound himself has declared that it is above all by its story that a literary work gains its lasting interest,[3] and it is difficult to see what basis for unity in an extended poem would be superior to that of plot. Pound's own words, in a letter to *Poetry* for August 1936, can be used against him:

> "Whether the present generation of local talents think they are being superior in eschewing topics which interested Dante, Shakespeare, and Ovid, must be left to the local book trade to determine. . . . Whether anyone will rise to VITAL ethics remains to be seen. Whether poetry can get on without taking count of those motivations without consideration of which no novel can rise to being *historie morale contemporaine* I very considerably doubt."

Pound's object in this letter is merely to state that he thinks other poets ought to write about economics, and in passing it ought to be noted that the purposes of the Cantos is stated in two succinct phrases, "VITAL ethics" and *histoire morale contemporaine,* but the citation of authorities, Dante, Shakespeare, Ovid, is very interesting since all of these poets depended upon plot in one fashion or another. The Cantos have no plot, although as the poem continues, the repetition of key phrases, characters and situations, makes more and more clear the kind of unity which the Cantos do have, a wholeness based upon certain obsessions or preoccupations, deriving itself from the character of Pound's mind, and displaying itself not in conjunction with the numerical order of the Cantos, but, so to speak, against the grain of continuity, which itself seems to

---

3. "Narrative sense, narrative power can survive ANY truncation. If a man have the tale to tell and can keep his mind on that and refuses to worry about his own limitations, the reader, in the long or short run, will find him."

be determined by the requirements of musical order, *melopoeia*, as Pound calls it. Or to put the whole issue differently, here we have a long poem without a hero, such as Achilles or Odysseus or *Virgilio mio*, or Agamemnon or Hamlet. Or if there is a hero, it is not Thomas Jefferson, Sigismundo Malatesta, and the other letter writers, but it is, in fact, Pound himself, the taste of Pound, above all his literary taste, that is to say, his likes and dislikes among books and the men who in some way have had to do with books or documents of some kind.

And when we examine the texture of the verse, we find lacking, amid much beauty of language and observation other elements which have been characteristic of great poetry. The Cantos, as others have noted, consist of many surfaces, presented with great exactitude, but with nothing behind them. We get what is upon the surface, whether the idiom of a text which Pound is translating or the particular quality of the sunlight upon the water which Pound is describing; but we do not get anything more than this. Many touchstones from very different poets could be cited for comparison, but one example, the following line from Yeats, may suffice because the meaning itself states what is wholly absent from the Cantos:

> The uncontrollable mystery on the bestial floor

and as against this, as an example of the moments when the Cantos are seeking sublimity, the following passage may be taken as characteristic:

> The small lamps drift in the bay
> And the sea's claw gathers them.
> Neptunus drinks after neap-tide.
> Tamuz! Tamuz!!
> The red flame going seaward.
>   By this gate art thou measured.
> From the long boats they have set lights in the water,
> The sea's claw gathers them outward.
> Scilla's dogs snarl at the cliff's base,
> The white teeth gnaw in under the crag,
> But in the pale night the small lamps float seaward

Beautiful as is this writing, the difference must be apparent. It is not the absence of a particular belief in any "uncontrollable mystery"—Yeats is no more a Christian than Pound—but the lack of interest in some of the most significant attitudes of the human spirit, which displays itself at times in the absence of seriousness as a *literary* quality. What is held up for our gaze most often in the Cantos is one man's brutal forthrightness, another's explosive speech, "verbal manifestations" of all sorts, and the quality of Mediterranean seascapes. We get as an interesting personality:

> (Az ole man Comley wd. say Boys! . . .
> Never cherr terbakker! Hrwwkke tth!
> Never cherr terbakker!

It is the entrance of the cuspidor into the medium of epic poetry, and it is a very interesting entrance, witnessing Pound's wide sense of fact, but if *The Iliad, The Divine Comedy,* and the plays of Shakespeare are our actual criterion of good, better, best in literature, then we must say that such presentations (and the Cantos abound in them) are sometimes good, but never best. And sometimes they show a triviality of interest, and they show how oppressive "personality" often must be.

The obscurity of the Cantos, their dependence upon quantities of information which are not readily available is at once another definition of the poem, and yet not at all as important a handicap and burden as some suppose. The amount of learning necessary in order to understand the manifold allusions of the Cantos can easily be exaggerated, and could quite simply be put together in one supplementary volume such as has already been provided for Joyce's *Ulysses.* Pound is not as learned as he seems to be—the scattered character of his learning leads to the mistaken impression —and at any rate the amount of information which must be acquired is nothing compared to what must be done in order to read *The Divine Comedy,* or the effort we make when we learn a foreign language. It is curious, of course, that a writer of our own time and language should require so much external help, but the only question is: is the poem good enough? It is.

Another fact to be remembered is that if we take Pound's writing as a unity and read his criticism as well as the Cantos, we have another good light in which to read the poem. Peire Vidal, Actaeon, Andreas Divus, Henry James, Sordello, the Homeric Hymns have all been mentioned explicitly in the criticism before the poem had been written, a point significant with regard to the whole pattern. And most of the relevant essays are to be found gathered together again in the book called *Make It New*, which selects from the previous books of criticism. Here, for example, there is a statement which illuminates the whole intention of the poem: "Most good poetry asserts something to be worthwhile, or damns a contrary; at any rate asserts emotional values." And here as one more example we find the very beginning of passages in the Cantos, such a passage as

> And the great domed head, *con gli occhi onesti e tardi*
> Moves before me, phantom with weighted motion,
> *Grave incessu,* drinking the tone of things,
> And the old voice lifts itself
>   weaving an endless sentence.

It is Henry James, a patron saint of all literary craftsmen, as we are told in the prose:

> The massive head, the slow uplift of the hand, *gli occhi onesti e tardi,* the long sentences piling themselves in elaborate phrase after phrase, the lightning incision, the pauses, the slightly shaking admonitory gesture. . . . I had heard it but seldom but it is all unforgettable.

Thus the poem rests upon the various stilts of Pound's criticism and other sources of information. But very few things are not so crippled in one way or another.

The justification of the whole is thus not the poem taken in itself, not yet, at any rate, before the poem is completed. The virtue which we can be certain of at present is, to sum up and repeat, the immense usefulness for future writing. Pound fits one of his own categories: he has been a great *inventor* in verse, and we know how few can be supposed to know the satisfaction of fulfilling their own canons of excellence.

Ezra Pound and History

As one reads these thirteen new cantos[1] of Ezra Pound's long poem and then rereads the ninety-five which have preceded it, one's first strong impression is that little change or genuine development of theme and attitude have occurred throughout the entire work. Through the years Pound has remembered a great deal, but he has learned nothing—nothing that could be called a new insight into the attitudes with which he began to write. Thus Canto 100 begins with

> "Has packed the Supreme Court
> so they declare anything he does
> constitutional."
> —*Senator Wheeler, 1936*

Here, in this denunciatory reference to Franklin D. Roosevelt and the New Deal, as elsewhere in these cantos, it is clear that Pound's view of the New Deal and the Second World War have not been altered since the lamentable attempt to pack the Supreme Court. And this is but one instance of the fact that Pound has not reviewed, in the light of recent experience and recent knowledge, his attitude toward the Second World War: he has not asked himself what would have happened to Western civilization, America, modern literature and his own poetry, if Germany had won the Second World War. And yet Pound must know—in some sense—that to the Nazis his own kind of work and the creative work he admired and helped to bring into being was regarded as an intolerable and

1. *Thrones de los Cantares* (Cantos 96–109).

barbaric manifestation of *Kulturbolscheivismus* and decadent cosmopolitanism.

Since the Cantos as a whole aspire to be a kind of philosophy of history, it is necessary to point out how, despite their frequent passages of great beauty, learning, metrical invention and prophetic significance, they are often no more than Pound's discursive monologue about his own *personal* experience of history, particularly 20th Century history, and particularly in relation to his own understandable obsession with the relationship of the creative artist and the statesman. This is perhaps the chief reason that he writes so often about economics and politics.

As a poet whose theme is the nature of history, Pound is inadequate in two important ways: he has an intense tendency to over-interpret and overgeneralize experience from a purely personal point of view or from the point of view very often of the assumed supremacy of the creative artist (as if other human beings were not necessary to the existence of creativity); and this inadequacy is made worse, time and again, by Pound's undisciplined and very often uninformed abstractions.

Here is a somewhat elaborate example: if the Cantos had been concerned with the fall of the Roman Empire as they are concerned again and again with the rise and fall of other great civilizations, Pound clearly would have blamed the fall of Rome upon the weakness and stupidity of a Caesar, or the personal strength of a Barbarian general, or perhaps upon the rise of debt and usury in Rome and the corruption of the aristocracy. What actually happened to cause the fall of Rome, according to J. B. Bury, was something seemingly trivial and implausible: the extraordinary advent of historical *coincidence* or historical *luck*. For centuries, the Barbarians had attacked Rome in great strength: it was only when the unique moment of Barbarian attack and Roman weakness occurred *at the same time* that the huge event of Rome's fall occurred and a great civilization perished. It can be argued that sooner or later this unique historical coincidence was bound to occur unless a great and wise Caesar extirpated the deeply-rooted causes of Roman weakness, and thus that political leadership is very important. But nowhere in this long poem about the nature of history is a sustained effort made to rise to the level of generality necessary to the extreme ambition of the poem; nor is there very much evidence of the intellectual awareness necessary to deal with the questions Pound raises about the nature of history.

The new cantos have many interesting passages, some passages of unique lyrical beauty, and too many passages when inspiration and excited self-indulgence have been confused with one another.

Thus, at one point, in a passage dealing, I think, with the Byzantine Empire, Pound writes

> Some sort of embargo, Theodora died
>   in the 19th Justinian.
> And the money sellers Ablavius and
>   Marcellus
> Thought they would just bump off
>   Justinian.
> A flood of fads swelled over Europe.
>
> But there could have been two Ab-
>   duls
> And it would not have annoyed one.
> That is something to note. I mean as
>   personality, when one says "ori-
>   ental." The third bahai
> Said nothing remarkable. Edgar Wal-
>   lace had his kind of modesty.

Here Edgar Wallace, a detective story writer once as well-known as Agatha Christie and Erle Stanley Gardner, suddenly emerges, and as suddenly departs from the 20th Century and appears in Byzantium as part of a discussion of the virtues and defects of an obscure historical regime's political luminaries. The relevance of a popular mystery story writer to a political discussion of a distant and for the most part very obscure historical period is, I think, tenuous but real. Edgar Wallace, of whose mystery fiction Pound avowed himself to be very fond in a book published more than twenty years ago, probably was *modest*, and it is probably true that Pound believes in and likes modesty—in other human beings. But the entire passage which is fairly characteristic of Pound's political discourses in the cantos, is a good example of how easy it is to confuse inspiration and self-indulgence, and childishness.

The reference to Edgar Wallace's personal modesty in a passage dealing with Byzantine politicos is not bad in itself, but it is, in addition, quite self-indulgent and personal in the worst way. It does not matter that Pound takes a childish pride in being fond of Wallace and knowing him and bringing his character into an epic poem; and the passage is not bad because of the sudden transition to Wallace's modesty or because of the obscurity of Byzantine history. It is bad because some other and better embodiment or touchstone of modesty would have made the poetic point less tangential and lessened the strain upon the reader who not only has to find out or know who the third bahai and the two Abduls are, but in what way Edgar Wallace possessed the same kind of modesty as his predecessors. To be self-indulgent myself for a moment, I am willing to entertain the possibility that the third bahai was a really important personage, but I don't see what Wallace had to be modest *about*, although I am sure he did the best he could and received adequate compensation.

Nevertheless it must immediately be added that what is bad and self-indulgent in this passage is inseparable from Pound's poetic genius at its best: in other passages, the suddenness of transition and apparent randomness of historical juxtaposition and range are necessary to create the historical perspective of the cantos, the sense that all history is relevant to any moment of history, and the profound belief that the entire past, at any moment and in any place, is capable of illuminating the present and the whole nature of historical experience.

The prose of the book jacket of *Thrones de los Cantares* can serve as a summary of what is good and what is bad in this new section of the cantos. As a description of the new cantos, it is neither better nor worse than most book jacket prose. This is how the preceding section of the cantos, *Rock Drill*, is described:

> " 'The human soul is not love, but love flows from it . . . it cannot, ergo, delight in itself, but only in the love flowing from it'. This is the major theme as the Cantos move into their final phase: 'The domination of benevolence'. Now the great poem has progressed into the realms of the 'permanent'; the poet has passed through 'the casual' and 'the recurrent' and come to values that endure like the sea.
>
> "The *Cantos* are a poem containing history; it is their purpose to give the true meaning of history as one man has found it: in

the annals of China, in the Italian Renaissance, in the letters and diaries of Jefferson, the Adamses and Van Buren, in the personalities and currents of his own time. The truth must be hammered home by reiteration, with the insistence of a rock drill 'Drilling it into their heads . . . much in the way that a composer does in music'."

As a description of Cantos 85–95 and the new Cantos this is not only adequate, it has a good deal of the obscurity of unavoidable truth and the immense confusion of reality. And it participates in the barbarous contempt for most human beings—unless they are creative artists or patrons of the arts—which recurs throughout Pound's great poem. For it should be clear, by inspection, that the domination of benevolence is a bad and impractical description of both love and statesmanship. It was, I think, Tallyrand who said to Napoleon, pointlessly enough: "Sire, you cannot sit on bayonets." And it should not be necessary to say, at this late date, that power which is maintained through domination of any kind—benevolent paternalism, for example—is worthless because it is temporary and must be sustained by tyranny. It should be a truism by now that genuine power depends upon consent, just as genuine love requires requited love. Finally to say that the truth must be hammered home by reiteration, with the insistence of a rock drill, is revealing in ways which the author of the jacket did not intend: revealing and novel. This must be the first time that the acetylene torch has been advocated as a method of teaching the truth to human beings or writing poetry. One might just as well try out the surgeon's scalpel, psychoacoustical bombing, brainwashing and all the other forms of psychological warfare. And to compare the insistence of a rock drill with the repetition of musical phrases is to reveal a complete ignorance of music and to show how metaphor may be a means of justifying anything, if one is also eager to deceive oneself. If the insistence of a rock drill and the repetition of musical phrases resembled each other in any way whatever, the interest in good music, which is small enough as it is, would not exist at all.

I have dwelt at length on the book jacket for several reasons. One is that it is a good summary of Pound's intention and what is wrong with it. But there is a more important reason. In recent years, for extra-literary reasons of all sorts, Pound's work has been praised too often and for the wrong reasons, without qualification or reservation, by ardent admirers and friends, in such a way as to antagonize readers who are not very well acquainted with his work. Indeed, Pound has been praised by his friends—sometimes, perhaps, out of sympathy for his personal plight, rather than his poetry—in so lavish and uncritical a way as to have exactly the reverse of the effect which was intended. The mixed feelings of the reading public toward complicated new poetry are such that uncritical praise is at best merely bewildering. Indeed, the effort and ardor of most of Pound's friends are unfortunate enough to make one think, again: any human being who has friends of this kind has no need of enemies.

There is also an unfortunate and unnecessary antagonism to Pound's work which takes a variety of forms and which, whatever its form, is unjustified. Sometimes the antagonism is purely personal; sometimes the antagonism is political; sometimes it is literary; sometimes it is literary and asserts itself as political liberalism and sometimes it is political and literary; as in the critics who dislike modern poetry and Pound's kind of modern poetry and his political views which Pound makes explicit, from time to time in his poetry. The reference to Roosevelt and the New Deal which I have already quoted is but one of a good many in the present volume. Here is another explicit passage concerning Hitler:

> Adolf furious from perception.
>   But there is a blindness comes from inside—
> they try to explain themselves out of nullity.

This is enough to make the uninformed reader—or the reader who has been told that Pound is a Fascist and an anti-Semite—dismiss Pound as a bad poet, or dismiss that which is valuable and beautiful in Pound's writing as trivial when the basic attitude of his work is anti-human. But here is another passage from an early Canto which would illustrate, among other things, the way in which Pound became a great poet:

> The boughs are not more fresh
> where the almond shoots
> take their March green.
>   And that year I went up to Freiburg,
> And Rennert had said: "Nobody, no, nobody

Knows anything about Provençal, or if there is anybody
It's old Levy."
And so I went up to Freiburg,
And the vacation was just beginning,
The students getting off for the summer,
Freiburg im Breisgau
And everything clean, seeming clean, after Italy.

There is a great deal more to be said about Pound's work and about the passages which disfigure it. For example there are several other passages—the description of a synagogue in Italy and its religious ceremonies and cantos which contain the passionate denunciations of modern war which show that if Pound is, at times, anti-Semitic, he is also, at other times, philo-Semitic; and if he is anti-human, it is, at least, in part, partly through a disappointed and embittered love of mankind. Certainly no one who was wholly misanthropic could be so avidly interested in what happens to human beings and to so many forms of human art and culture. But this is a complicated subject which cannot be discussed with brevity. The first and most important thing to say about Pound's Cantos is that they ought to be read again and again by anyone interested in any form of literature.

T. S. Eliot as the
International Hero

A culture hero is one who brings new arts and skills to mankind. Prometheus was a culture hero and the inventors of the radio may also be said to be culture heroes, although this is hardly to be confounded with the culture made available by the radio.

The inventors of the radio made possible a new range of experience. This is true of certain authors; for example, it is true of Wordsworth in regard to nature, and Proust in regard to time. It is not true of Shakespeare, but by contrast it is true of Surrey and the early Elizabethan playwrights who invented blank verse. Thus the most important authors are not always culture heroes, and thus no rank, stature, or scope is of necessity implicit in speaking of the author as a culture hero.

When we speak of nature and of a new range of experience, we may think of a mountain range: some may make the vehicles by means of which a mountain is climbed, some may climb the mountain, and some may apprehend the new view of the surrounding countryside which becomes possible from the heights of the mountain. T. S. Eliot is a culture hero in each of these three ways. This becomes clear when we study the relationship of his work to the possible experiences of modern life. The term, possible, should be kept in mind, for many human beings obviously disregard and turn their backs upon much of modern life, although modern life does not in the least cease to circumscribe and penetrate their existence.

The reader of T. S. Eliot by turning the dials of his radio can hear the capitals of the world, London, Vienna, Athens, Alexandria, Jerusalem. What he hears will be news of the agony of war. Both the agony and the width of this experience are vivid examples of how the poetry of T. S. Eliot has a direct relationship to modern life. The width and the height and the depth of modern life are exhibited in his poetry; the agony and the horror of modern life are represented as inevitable to any human being who does not wish to deceive himself with systematic lies. Thus it is truly significant that E. M. Forster, in writing of Eliot, should recall August 1914 and the beginning of the First World War; it is just as significant that he should speak of first reading Eliot's poems in Alexandria, Egypt, during that war, and that he should conclude by saying that Eliot was one who had looked into the abyss and refused henceforward to deny or forget the fact.

We are given an early view of the international hero in the quasi-autobiographical poem which Eliot entitles: "Mélange Adultère Du Tout." The title, borrowed from a poem by Corbière, is ironic, but the adulterous mixture of practically everything, every time and every place, is not ironic in the least: a teacher in America, the poem goes, a journalist in England, a lecturer in Yorkshire, a literary nihilist in Paris, overexcited by philosophy in Germany, a wanderer from Omaha to Damascus, he has celebrated, he says, his birthday at an African oasis, dressed in a giraffe's skin. Let us place next to this array another list of names and events as heterogeneous as a circus or America itself: St. Louis, New England, Boston, Harvard, England, Paris, the First World War, Oxford, London, the Russian Revolution, the Church of England, the postwar period, the world crisis and depression, the Munich Pact, and the Second World War. If this list seems farfetched or forced, if it seems that such a list might be made for any author, the answer is that these names and events are *presences* in Eliot's work in a way which is not true of many authors, good and bad, who have lived through the same years.

Philip Rahv has shown how the heroine of Henry James is best understood as the heiress of all the ages. So, in a further sense, the true protagonist of Eliot's poems is the heir of all the ages. He is the descendant of the essential characters of James in that he is the American who visits Europe with a Baedeker in his hand, just like Isabel Archer. But the further sense in which he is the heir of all the ages is illustrated when Eliot describes the seduction of a typist in a London flat from the point of view of Tiresias, a character in a play by Sophocles. To suppose that this is the mere exhibition of learning or reading is a banal misunderstanding. The important point is that the presence of Tiresias illuminates the seduction of the typist just as much as a description of her room. Hence Eliot writes in his notes to *The Waste Land* that "what Tiresias *sees* is the substance of the poem." The illumination of the ages is available at any moment, and when the typist's indifference and boredom in the act of love must be represented, it is possible for Eliot to invoke and paraphrase a lyric from a play by Oliver Goldsmith. Literary allusion has become not merely a Miltonic reference to Greek gods and Old Testament geography, not merely the citation of parallels, but a powerful and inevitable habit of mind, a habit which issues in judgment and the representation of different levels of experience, past and present.

James supposed that his theme was the international theme: would it not be more precise to speak of it as the transatlantic theme? This effort at a greater exactness defines what is involved in Eliot's work. Henry James was concerned with the American in Europe. Eliot cannot help but be concerned with the whole world and all history. Tiresias sees the nature of love in all times and all places and when Sweeney outwits a scheming whore, the fate of Agamemnon becomes relevant. So too, in the same way exactly, Eliot must recognize and use a correspondence between St. Augustine and Buddha in speaking of sensuality. And thus, as he writes again in his notes to *The Waste Land*, "The collocation of these two representatives of eastern and western asceticism as the culmination of this part of the poem is not an accident." And it is not an accident that the international hero should have come from St. Louis, Missouri, or at any rate from America. Only an American with a mind and sensibility which is cosmopolitan and expatriated could have seen Europe as it is seen in *The Waste Land*.

A literary work may be important in many ways, but surely one of the ways in which it is important is in its relationship to some important human interest or need, or in its relationship to some new aspect of human existence. Eliot's work is important in relationship to the fact that experience has become international. We have become an international people, and hence an international hero is possible. Just as the war is international, so the true causes of many of the things in our lives are worldwide, and we are able to understand the character of our lives only when we are aware of all history, of the philosophy of history, of primitive peoples and the Russian Revolution, of ancient Egypt and the unconscious mind. Thus again it is no accident that in *The Waste Land* use is made of *The Golden Bough,* and a book on the quest of the Grail; and the way in which images and associations appear in the poem illustrates a new view of consciousness, the depths of consciousness and the unconscious mind.

The protagonist of *The Waste Land* stands on the banks of the Thames and quotes the Upanishads, and this very quotation, the command to "give, sympathize, and control," makes possible a comprehensive insight into the difficulty of his life in the present. But this emphasis upon one poem of Eliot's may be misleading. What is true of much of his poetry is also true of his criticism. When the critic writes of tradition and the individual talent, he declares the necessity for the author of a consciousness of the past as far back as Homer, when he brings the reader back to Dante, the Elizabethans and Andrew Marvell, he is also speaking as the heir of all the ages.

The emphasis on a consciousness of literature may also be misleading, for nowhere better than in Eliot can we see the difference between being merely literary and making the knowledge of literature an element in vision, that is to say, an essential part of the process of seeing anything and everything. Thus, to cite the advent of Tiresias again, the literary character of his appearance is matched by the unliterary actuality by means of which he refers to himself as being "like a taxi throbbing waiting." In one way, the subject of *The Waste Land* is the sensibility of the protagonist, a sensibility which is literary, philosophical, cosmopolitan and expatriated. But this sensibility is concerned not with itself as such, but with the common things of modern life, with two such important aspects of existence as religious belief and making love. To summon to mind such profound witnesses as

[123]

Freud and D. H. Lawrence is to remember how often, in modern life, love has been the worst sickness of human beings.

The extent to which Eliot's poetry is directly concerned with love is matched only by the extent to which it is concerned with religious belief and the crisis of moral values. J. Alfred Prufrock is unable to make love to women of his own class and kind because of shyness, self-consciousness, and fear of rejection. The protagonists of other poems in Eliot's first book are men or women laughed at or rejected in love, and a girl deserted by her lover seems like a body deserted by the soul.

In Eliot's second volume of poems, an old man's despair issues in part from his inability to make love, while Sweeney, an antithetical character, is able to make love, but is unable to satisfy the woman with whom he copulates. In *The Waste Land,* the theme of love as a failure is again uppermost. Two lovers return from a garden after a moment of love, and the woman is overcome by despair or pathological despondency. A lady, perhaps the same woman who has returned from the garden in despair, becomes hysterical in her boudoir because her lover or her husband has nothing to say to her and cannot give her life any meaning or interest: "What shall I do now?" she says, "what shall I ever do?" The neurasthenic lady is succeeded in the poem by cockney women who gossip about another cockney woman who has been made ill by contraceptive pills taken to avoid the consequences of love; which is to say that the sickness of love has struck down every class in society: "What you get married for, if you don't want children?" And then we witness the seduction of the typist; and then other aspects of the sickness of love appear when, on the Thames bank, three girls ruined by love rehearse the sins of the young men with whom they have been having affairs. In the last part of the poem, the impossibility of love, the gulf between one human being and another, is the answer to the command to give, that is to say, to give oneself or surrender oneself to another human being in the act of making love.

Elsewhere love either results in impotence, or it is merely copulation. In "The Hollow Men," the hollow men are incapable of making love because there is a shadow which falls between the desire and the spasm. The kinship of love and belief is affirmed when the difficulty of love and of religious belief are expressed in the same way and as parallels, by means of a paraphrase and parody of the Lord's Prayer. In "Sweeney Agonistes," Sweeney returns to say that there is nothing in love but copulation, which, like birth and death, is boring. Sweeney's boredom should be placed in contrast with the experience of Burbank, who encountered the Princess Volupine in Venice, and found himself impotent with her. A comparison ought also to be made between Sweeney and the protagonist of one of Eliot's poems in French who harks back to a childhood experience of love: "I tickled her to make her laugh. I experienced a moment of power and delirium." Eliot's characters when they make love either suffer from what the psychoanalysts term "psychic impotence," or they make love so inadequately that the lady is left either hysterical or indifferent when the episode is over. The characters who are potent and insensitive are placed in contrast with the characters who are impotent and sensitive. Grishkin has a bust which promises pneumatic bliss, while Burbank's kind, the kind of a man who goes to Europe with a Baedeker, has to crawl between the dry ribs of metaphysics because no contact possible to flesh is satisfactory. The potent and the insensitive, such as Sweeney, are not taken in by the ladies, the nightingales and the whores; but Burbank, like Agamemnon, is betrayed and undone.

This synoptic recitation might be increased by many more examples. Its essence is expressed perfectly in "Little Gidding": "Love is the unfamiliar name." But we ought to remember that the difficulty of making love, that is to say, of entering into the most intimate of relationships, is not the beginning but the consequence of the whole character of modern life. That is why the apparatus of reference which the poet brings to bear upon failure in love involves all history ("And I Tiresias have foresuffered all") and is international. So too the old man who is the protagonist of "Gerontion" must refer to human beings of many nationalities, to Mr. Silvero at Limoges, Hakagawa, Madame de Tornquist, Fräulen von Kulp and Christ [the tiger] and he finds it necessary to speak of all history as well as his failure in love. History is made to illuminate love and love is made to illuminate history. In modern life, human beings are whirled beyond the circuit of the constellations: their intimate plight is seen in connection or relation with the anguish of the Apostles after Calvary, the murder of Agamemnon, the insanity of Ophelia and children who chant that London bridge is falling down. In the same way, the plight of Prufrock is illuminated by means of a rich, passing reference to Michelangelo, the sculptor of the strong and heroic man. Only when the poet is the heir of all the ages can he make significant use of so many different and distant kinds of experience. But conversely, only when experience becomes international, only when many different and distant kinds of experience are encountered by the poet, does he find it necessary to become the heir of all the ages.

Difficulty in love is inseparable from the deracination and the alienation from which the international man suffers. When the traditional beliefs, sanctions and bonds of the community and of the family decay or disappear in the distance like a receding harbor, then love ceases to be an act which is in relation to the life of the community, and in immediate relation to the family and other human beings. Love becomes purely personal. It is isolated from the past and the future, and since it is isolated from all other relationships, since it is no longer celebrated, evaluated and given a status by the community, love does become merely copulation. The protagonist of "Gerontion" uses one of the most significant phrases in Eliot's work when he speaks of himself as living in a *rented* house; which is to say, not in the house where his forbears lived. He lives in a rented house, he is unable to make love, and he knows that history has many cunning, deceptive, and empty corridors. The nature of the house, of love and of history are interdependent aspects of modern life.

When we compare Eliot's poetry to the poetry of Valèry, Yeats and Rilke, Eliot's direct and comprehensive concern with the essential nature of modern life gains an external definition. Yeats writes of Leda and he writes of the nature of history; Valèry writes of Narcissus and the serpent in the Garden of Eden; Rilke is inspired by great works of art, by Christ's mother and by Orpheus. Yet in each of these authors the subject is transformed into a timeless essence. The heritage of Western culture is available to these authors and they use it many beautiful ways; but the fate of Western culture and the historical sense as such does not become an important part of their poetry. And then if we compare Eliot with Auden and with Pound, a further definition becomes clear. In his early work, Auden is inspired by an international crisis in a social and political sense; in his new work, he writes as a teacher and preacher and secular theologian. In neither period is all history and all culture a necessary part of the subject or the sensibility which is dealing with the subject. With Pound, we come closer to Eliot and the closeness sharpens the difference. Pound is an American in Europe too, and Pound, not Eliot, was the first to grasp the historical and international dimension of experience, as we can see in an early effort of his to explain the method of the *Cantos* and the internal structure of each *Canto*: "All times are contemporaneous," he wrote, and in the *Cantos*, he attempts to deal with all history as if it were part of the present. But he fails; he remains for the most part an American in Europe, and the *Cantos* are never more than a book of souvenirs of a tour of the world and a tour of culture.

To be international is to be a citizen of the world and thus a citizen of no particular city. The world as such is not a community and it has no constitution or government: it is the turning world in which the human being, surrounded by the consequences of all times and all places, must live his life as a human being and not as the citizen of any nation. Hence, to be the heir of all the ages is to inherit nothing but a consciousness of how all heirlooms are rooted in the past. Dominated by the historical consciousness, the international hero finds that all beliefs affect the holding of any belief (he cannot think of Christianity without remembering Adonis); he finds that many languages affect each use of speech (*The Waste Land* concludes with a passage in four languages).

When nationalism attempts to renew itself, it can do so only through the throes of war. And when nationalism in America attempts to become articulate, when a poet like Carl Sandburg writes that "The past is a bucket of ashes," or when Henry Ford makes the purely American remark that "History is the bunk," we have only to remember such a pilgrimage as that of Ford in the Peace Ship in which he attempted to bring the First World War to an end in order to see that anyone can say whatever he likes: no matter what anyone says, existence has become international for everyone.

Eliot's political and religious affirmations are at another extreme, and they do not resemble Ford's quixotic pilgrimage except as illustrating the starting point of the modern American, and his inevitable journey to Europe. What should be made explicit here is that only one who has known fully the deracination and alienation inherent in modern life can be moved to make so extreme an effort at returning to the traditional community as Eliot makes in attaching himself to Anglo-Catholicism and Royalism. Coming back may well be the same thing as going away; or at any rate, the effort to return home may exhibit the same predicament and the same topography as the fact of departure. Only by going to Europe, by crossing the Atlantic and living thousands of miles from home, does the international hero conceive of the complex nature of going home.

Modern life may be compared to a foreign country in which a foreign language is spoken. Eliot is the international hero because he has made the journey to the foreign country and described the nature of the new life in the foreign country. Since the future is bound to be international, if it is anything at all, we are all the bankrupt heirs of the ages, and the moments of the crisis expressed in Eliot's work are a prophecy of the crises of our own future in regard to love, religious belief, good and evil, the good life and the nature of the just society. *The Waste Land* will soon be as good as new.

T. S. Eliot's Voice and His Voices

The sea has many voices,
Many gods and many voices.

I

𝕭 When the beautiful blue book of Eliot's collected poems (familiar to many of us for so long) was replaced last year by *The Complete Poems and Plays of T. S. Eliot,* the new volume naturally suggested a new effort to define and characterize Eliot's kind of poetry as something different and unique. The attempt at definition has been made many times and will have to be made many times again—if only because the situation of poetry, in relation to itself and to the rest of life, often changes. But there is a special reason for making a new attempt now; Eliot's recent plays in verse, *The Cocktail Party,* and *The Confidential Clerk, appear* to be out of relation to most of Eliot's other writings, so much so that they obscure the uniqueness of his style and idiom as a poet.

The versification of these new plays has been called "a carefully concealed verse," a view which the author himself has seemed to support. But verse which is carefully concealed is a little too close to "inaudible music" and "invisible painting." One would be more doubtful of this impression, as of course one must be with the new work of any great author, were it not that there is so much else in these plays—their subject matter, for example, and their vision of life—which one cannot connect with the same source and genius as *Ash Wednesday, Sweeney Agonistes,* and other wonderful, representative, and various poems.

The lack of connection would not matter very much—there remains so much more in Mr. Eliot's work which one admires not only very much but more and more—except for the fact that the pedestrian, carefully concealed verse of these plays is likely to be identified and assimilated to that miraculous poetic resurrection of all words, however abstract, prosaic, unpoetic or anti-poetic, which is an essential characteristic, a necessary and very important part of the uniqueness of his poetry.

Uniqueness is an unfortunate but unavoidable term. It does not of course exclude resemblance and kinship, influence and similarity, but on the contrary the aim and the effect of the recognition of both kinship and uniqueness is a heightened sense of both. And if the uniqueness of any poet is fundamentally as indefinable as the uniqueness of blue or any color, nevertheless an adequate circumscription of the uniqueness is possible and valuable.

The uniqueness of Eliot's poetry is recognizable perhaps first of all in the diction. It is clear from the beginning, in his first poems, that the poet has discovered the hidden, or latent, seed or light of the poetic in prose words; which is to say, in words commonly supposed to be too unpoetic to be used in poetry. Thus on the very first page of Eliot's first book the reader comes upon "etherised," "tedious argument," "insidious intent," "overwhelming question" (a word which recurs many times and is entirely representative and significant). Then, in the same poem, "indecisions and revisions," "snicker," "*slightly* bald," "afternoons," and "coffee spoons" are important words. In this poem and in the same volume, this particular choice of words, this consistent diction is intensified by many rhymes, such as "fate," "at any rate"; "ices," "crisis"; "matter," "platter"; and the like. No matter how familiar one may be with Eliot's poetry, the number of examples of this kind of diction, when they are counted, is likely to surprise one because there are so many of them in so few pages. And the quality of the diction must be seen as it functions in a phrase: in such a phrase as "My necktie rich and modest, but *asserted* by a simple pin—," the word "asserted" is given a physical and visual meaning which it usually lacks.

It is true that the whole of modern poetry has moved in the direction of this kind of diction. We have only to think of the diction of Yeats' early and his later poetry to see how profound the movement has been. And long before the first poems of the mature Yeats, there is in Baudelaire, in Laforgue, in Rilke—in almost every important poet—an effort to assimilate the everyday

[130]

world, the modern world, and colloquial speech by the use of everyday or prosaic words. Moreover, on the surface Eliot's diction does not seem very different from that necessary and important transformation or assimilation of prose into poetry which characterizes Ezra Pound, Marianne Moore, and William Carlos Williams, among others.

Not until *Ash Wednesday*—which is lyrical in a way that Eliot had not been before: a lyricism stripped of almost all particularity of time and place (*The Waste Land* exemplified the other extreme of complete particularity)—not until that very beautiful poem do we have an adequate means of discriminating between Eliot's transformation of prose into poetry and that of his peers and compeers. In the first part of *Ash Wednesday,* the reader encounters "because" (eleven important times, making it comparable to the recurrence of "question"), "usual," "veritable," "positive," "consequently," and "construct." And "time," "place," and "actual" are used as abstractions—that is, at the highest level of conceptual meaning, and yet given the greatest particularity because of the intense emotion of their context.

We have only to connect these examples with such prior words and phrases as "asserted," "his dry and passionate talk," "I concentrated my attention with careful subtlety to this end," "the eternal enemy of the absolute," "these cogitations," "we have not reached conclusion," "controversial, polymath," "between the idea and the reality"—we have only to make the connection (which, once instituted, attracts and orders many other words and phrases into a recognizable constellation and *gestalt*) to perceive the consistent operation of a unique mind and sensibility moving in a unique direction: the particular kinds of words commonly used in prose and thought of as prosaic or unpoetic which Eliot converts into poetry do not, as the careless reader and critic has often supposed, derive their quality chiefly from their reference to the surfaces of modern life: the idiom is not a matter of breakfast plates and the smell of steaks, though this element is of course present. What does mark and differentiate Eliot's diction and phrasing is the *intellectual* source, the *conceptual* burden and connotation of his language. At a deeper level, once we have examined the characteristic words again and again, the states of mind and emotion exhibit a close and consistent relationship: within the under-lying intensity of thought, the emotions which motivate the words and thus the poems, are identifiable as those of self-doubt, self-argument, hesitation before the torment of choice, hyperconsciousness, and self-consciousness: "*Because* I do not *hope* to *turn* again," "*Consequently* I rejoice, having to construct something / Upon which to rejoice," and the like. The experience of introspection *and* of conceptual thought *and* of difficult analysis is involved in this choice of words. At bottom, at rock bottom, at the depth where it is difficult to formulate anything whatever with certainty, the reader must feel that this use of language has its origin in an attitude toward experience which is at once the love and the fear of experience—the fear and the love being inseparable—and equally in the need to subject all experience, actual and possible, to conscious scrutiny, calculation, and judgment.

It should be needless to say that thus to isolate Eliot's diction from his poetic style as a whole, particularly his sense of rhythm, may easily be very misleading: the phrasing has the same character, metaphors and subject matter have a like character; attitude and tone have the same source.

II

The intellectualized character of Eliot's diction is immediately related to another leading characteristic of his writing, one which really requires an independent essay full of the detailed analysis of examples. I mean Eliot's poetic and creative use of the printed word and of his reading not only as a source of inspiration but as the material of the actual poem. This is close to the sources of his diction and phrasing partly by virtue of the fact that it is so often prose as well as poetry, and prose of all kinds, including philosophical exposition and theological discourse, which serves as a creative springboard. How natural it is that a poet who has converted prose into poetry should be inspired to write by prose and by the printed word. The most representative example is the versifying of part of a sermon by Lancelot Andrewes (previously quoted in an essay on him) as the beginning of "The Journey of the Magi." It is equally meaningful and natural that the poet's

[132]

critical essays and the verse of other poets quoted in these essays should also be a source of poetic inspiration.

This process of composition may have taken two forms. It may be that the poet's encounter with prose inspired a poem or a passage in a poem. And it may be that the poet deliberately looked for what he wanted, in the books of others, after the poem had been begun. One process hardly excludes the other; and one would guess that the experience of finding poetic inspiration unexpectedly (in such unlikely places as Conan Doyle, P. G. Wodehouse, Gilbert and Sullivan, Edmund Husserl) might very well have led to a systematic cultivation of reading as a method of writing poems, or parts of poems. This is almost certainly what occurs in passages of *Four Quartets*, but it is important to remember that Eliot never permitted the practice to degenerate into a mechanical method, as other poets, Pound particularly, sometimes have. Invariably, when we are able to compare the original with Eliot's creative use of it, it is clear that he is always inventive when he is derivative; he always either improves or makes something new of what he has found in the work of another author. Thus one of Eliot's most famous lines (which the poet was sufficiently pleased with to use more than once), "At the still point of the turning world," has as its probable source a sentence in a detective story by Dorothy Sayers where it occurs in this, I think, inferior form: "At the still point of the spinning world."

A good deal of ingenuity, some of it stupid or malicious, has been devoted to the titles of Eliot's poems and to his choice of names. Sometimes the names and titles originate in the same sense of language and are motivated by the same abiding constellation of emotions as the poetic style. As with so many novelists and dramatists, the names function to suggest character—Burbank, Grishkin, Sweeney, Stetson. But not enough has been said about the spare and delicate elegance of certain names and titles. Some of the names, De Bailhache, Mr. Silvero, Boudin, Gutierriez, are immediately poetic; and the poet's sensitivity to this aspect of names shows itself explicitly when he speaks, in his essay on Cyril Tourneur, of that playwright's name as beautiful. In these and other instances both names and titles again exemplify the conversion of the prosaic into poetry—in a title like *Burnt Norton,*

[133]

the adjective's suggestiveness and the matter-of-factness of the noun combine as virtually an epitome of the poet's style.

A few titles verge on preciosity—*For Lancelot Andrewes*, perhaps (instead of *to* Lancelot Andrewes); and it is possible to think of *Murder in the Cathedral* as a little affected. But for the most part one cannot help but sense a profound unity and necessity in the titles, as in the names, the kind of unity which for most poets as for most human beings has its source in some unconscious or only partly conscious depth of the author's mind, however conscious some of his reasons for choosing a title or a name may have been. Thus there is the recurrence of burning, of waste, and of sanctity in such titles as *The Sacred Wood, Ash Wednesday, Burnt Norton, Murder in the Cathedral, The Waste Land,* and *The Rock.*

III

Mr. Eliot has recently published an essay entitled *The Three Voices of Poetry,* which was delivered as a lecture to a particular audience, at the annual meeting of the Book League in London and has appeared in an abridged version in the April 1954 issue of *The Atlantic Monthly.* Part of Mr. Eliot's purpose in this essay may be to instruct the reader of poetry in how to read his new plays, and how *not* to read them: "if you have to listen to a verse play, take it first at its face value, as entertainment, for each character speaking for himself with whatever reality his author has been able to endow him." Whatever Mr. Eliot's purpose may be, however, he provides a classification of the voices of poetry which has an immediate relevance to any attempt to characterize his poetry as a whole:

> "I shall explain at once," Mr. Eliot says at the very outset, "what I mean by the 'three voices.' The first is the voice of the poet talking to himself—or to nobody. The second is the voice of the poet addressing an audience, whether large or small. The third is the voice of the poet when he attempts to create a dramatic character speaking in verse."

This classification, as it is elaborated, and despite many valuable and interesting observations, seems to me deceptive when it is not false. But it is foolish to comment upon an essay which one had seen only in an abridged version; and in any case, what is in question here is not this classification as true of all the kinds and varieties of poetry, but only its relationship to the poetry which Eliot himself has written.

To speak then only of Eliot's poetry, his poems contain far more than three voices: they contain many voices. But more than and apart from this point, his poems are often dominated by a *listening* to other voices—the voices of other poets, in other centuries and countries; the voices of various human beings of differing classes and stations in society, a diversity of beliefs, values, habits of speech, and views of life.

My point at first glance may hardly seem more than a quibble: it will seem, of course, that the poet has listened to a variety of voices merely as one phase, and an early one, in the process of composition; and what he has done is to use various voices as a means or material for the invention of characters and the dramatization of situations. And it is certainly true that the speech of other voices is carefully chosen and selected in terms of the poets' governing intentions and motives in particular poems.

There is nothing wrong with this view in itself. It becomes inadequate and inaccurate only insofar as it makes the reader overlook the particular quality of the use of other voices as he encounters them in the actual experience of the poem. I mean to say—and perhaps this is only a point of emphasis—that the poet is listening to (or perhaps *quoting* is a more exact term) the speech of other voices in a way which is blurred over when regarded as only the familiar technique of dramatizing character through speech. Eliot is doing something which includes what that kind of poet does.

Thus when the reader encounters

> O O O that Shakespeherian rag
> It's so elegant
> So intelligent

he hears neither the voice of the poet, nor another's voice. When he reads, in the same poem

> You ought to be ashamed to look so antique.
> (And her only thirty-one.)

he hears the voice of another very different human being as heard and quoted by the poet. And when the reader comes upon this passage in *Portrait of a Lady,*

> ". . . But what have I, but what have I, my
> friend,
> To give you, what can you receive from
> me?
> Only the friendship and the sympathy
> Of one about to reach her journey's end.
>
> I shall sit here, serving tea to friends . . ."
> I take my hat: how can I make a cowardly
> amends
> For what she has said to me?

The overwhelming comment of the protagonist, the complexity of his feeling in contrast with the lady's insensitivity and unawareness, loses much of its force if the reader brushes over the, so to speak, expressed gulf between the lady's speech and the protagonist's comment; between the protagonist as listening or quoting and the protagonist's resumption of his own voice. Which is to say: the distinction between listening and speaking is a concrete part of the poem itself; and it is more than the customary dramatic framework of voices in dialogue.

Again in *Sweeney Agonistes,* when Sweeney says

> . . . Death is life and life is death
> I gotta use words when I talk to you
> But if you understand or if you don't
> We all gotta do what we gotta do.

surely this is not the voice of the poet, speaking to himself, or another; it can of course be taken as the voice of Sweeney, an invented character: but if it is, there is again a loss of meaning in the first line quoted, for example, as in other utterances elsewhere which become remarkable in the wrong way when they are viewed as *solely* the expression of Sweeney's mind.

There are many other instances in other poems which illustrate the primary actuality of listening to other voices. But to repeat the point, which is as slippery as it is important: the reader may regard the process of listening as a phase in the conversion of observation into drama, the transformation of another human being's voice and speech into the material of an invented mask through which the poet's voice is speaking. But once this emphasis is made (and Eliot as a critic recommends it), there is a dimness of focus and hence a weakness of apprehension: the reader misses, over-looks, looks through or looks past the purity and the exactness with which the poet has listened to and quoted and recorded the speech of another human being; the reader misses something which is actually there upon the page, in the poem itself, and in his experience as a reader.

In passing, it is worth invoking the often illustrated fact that numerous critics and readers have misunderstood and misinterpreted Eliot's poems precisely because they took all the voices in it as being essentially the voice of the poet, or essentially a dramatization of the voices of invented characters, and have not seen that quite often the actual substance of a passage is first of all a listening or a quoting.

The presence of quotation in this sense is clearly and closely related to the creative use of reading, perceptions encountered in the medium of print. The poet as a listener, as, in this way, sibylline (to use a term which *The Waste Land* first suggests as appropriate) leads to further elaboration, elaboration to a point which comprehends Eliot's poetic method as a whole. At this point Eliot's originality is most marked, and at this point the inseparable connection between poetic method and profound insight is clearest.

More than one critic has remarked that in Eliot the overall organization of the poem as a whole is not lyrical in any recognizable and traditional way; nor is the poem organized in terms of narrative; nor is it dramatic in the literal theatrical sense; and it is certainly not logical, argumentative, or expository. One critic has spoken of musical structure, which, although suggestive, is as much a metaphor as dramatic structure is; and the organization of the dramatic monologue is a starting point as the interior monologue or stream of consciousness is an influence. But neither one nor the other is adequate as a description of the total and binding organization of a poem by Eliot from beginning to end, as an explanation of the poetic basis upon which one passage succeeds another. Where poets in the last would have used a logical, emotional, dramatic, or narrative basis for the transition from part to part, Eliot either uses each one of these kinds of transition

[137]

freely and alternatively and without committing himself to any one of them or to any systematic succession of them; or he omits the connection between one passage and the next, one part and the part which succeeds it: it may be possible to read *The Love Song of J. Alfred Prufrock* as organized in terms of a dramatic monologue, though the customary framework of a definite time and place is absent. But surely it is impossible to do this with *The Waste Land* and *Ash Wednesday* and *Four Quartets* unless we impose our own scenario upon the poem. Moreover, it is true that this kind of organization is not present in Eliot's plays in verse, but the absence of this method of organization may account for the diminution of the poetry from play to play, as Eliot concentrates more and more upon being a playwright first of all.

The characteristic overall organization of the whole poem—of which *The Waste Land* is the vividest example—can be called, for the lack of a better phrase, that of sibylline (or subliminal) listening. Whatever it is called, all the other and prior terms which describe the total organization of a poem cannot fit; and partly, perhaps, as a result of their unsuitability, not enough attention has been given to the originality and the importance of this new method of organization. The method of the sibylline or subliminal listener must seem, at first glance, to be no method at all precisely because it is the method which permits all other methods to be used freely and without predetermination; and which allows no particular method to interfere with the quintessential receptivity which opens itself to any and all kinds of material and subject matter.

The value of this method can best be illustrated by comparisons of an extremely heterogeneous variety. First there is the example of Swift's *Journal to Stella:* no matter how much we admire Swift's fiction or verse (and it is impossible to admire some of his writings too much), we have to recognize that in the journal Swift articulated areas of consciousness and emotion which the prevailing forms and structures of eighteenth-century writing excluded from his fiction and his verse. It was thus not that these areas were not available to Swift; nor can one suppose that they did not seem important or beautiful to him. But he had no comprehensive form, apart from the journal and the letter, which would draw them forth and order them. Then, there are the like examples of

Samuel Johnson's *London* and *The Vanity of Human Wishes,* and
Oliver Goldsmith's *The Deserted Village:* I choose to cite these
poems for a reason similar to the reference to Swift: all three poems
may be said to have roughly the same subject matter as *The Waste
Land,* just as Eliot's sensibility in certain respects resembles
Swift's.

Compare the lines from *London:*

> Though grief and fondness in my breast rebel,
> When injur'd Thales bids the town farewell,
> Yet still my calmer thoughts his choice
>   commend,
> I praise the hermit, but regret the friend;
> Resolv'd at length, from vice and London far,
> To breathe, in distant fields, a purer air.

and these from *The Deserted Village:*

> Ill fares the land, to hastening ills a prey,
> Where wealth accumulates and men decay:
> Princes and lords may flourish, or may fade;
> A breath can make them, as a breath has made;
> But a bold peasantry, their country's pride.
> When once destroyed, can never be supplied.

with a representative passage from *The Waste Land:*

> Summer surprised us, coming over the
>   Starnbergersee
> With a shower of rain; we stopped in the
>   colonnade
> And went on in sunlight, into the Hofgarten,
> And drank coffee and talked for an hour.
> Bin gar keine Russin, stamm'aus Litauen,
>   echt deutsch.
> And when we were children, staying at the
>   archduke's,
> My cousin's, he took me out on a sled,
> And I was frightened. He said, Marie,
> Marie, hold on tight. And down we went.
> In the mountains, there you feel free.
> I read, much of the night, and go south in the
>   winter.
> What are the roots that clutch, what
>   branches grow
> Out of this stony rubbish?

[139]

The likeness of attitude and subject may not be immediately apparent when these passages are taken out of their contexts. But whatever one's comparative judgment of these passages and these poets, it can hardly be denied that the modern poet possesses, by virtue of his method, an immense energy and mobility, which is new. Moreover, he still possesses, to a degree, the power of the older methods as one part or resource of his new method, a fact evident in *The Waste Land* in that part which describes the seduction of the typist by means of traditional organization and recognizable narrative organization. It is also true, and it should be insisted, that in using the new method certain qualities commanded by Johnson and Swift have had to be sacrificed, of necessity.

In addition to energy and mobility, and a number of other desirable qualities, the new method of organization gives the poet an immediacy and a scope not available to the older poets because, above all, the new method makes it possible to bring into the poem certain depths of experience directly and explicitly. Here again the evidence of comparison is perhaps the best proof. The excellence of Hawthorne's fiction is the same in kind, if not in degree, as Swift's. Yet when we read Hawthorne's notebooks and his letters, we find again that Hawthorne like Swift omitted from his creative writing—and with greater loss, being the kind of an author that he was—important material of which he was very much aware and which he recorded in his notebooks precisely because it seemed related to the writing of fiction.

What the literary methods and the conceptions of structure of Swift and Hawthorne exclude from all but the privacy of the journal or the letter is brought to the surface and exposed to direct examination by the new method. Whether this is entirely desirable is a separate question, a question apart from this attempt at characterization and definition. It must be admitted that the new method is a dangerous one, requiring not only a great deal of passive receptivity but also the operation of a severe critical sense to assure the genuineness and the purity of what is received: the listening and the quotation can easily become self-indulgent; can become an intolerable looseness, emotionalism, or self-revelation for their own sake or for the purpose of sensationalism. Here it is worth remarking on how integral and organic a part of the composition of poetry the presence and practice of criticism and of critical habits of mind have been to Eliot. And the new method is also immensely more useful to a poet with Eliot's genius for rhythm and versification (a subject which I have had to slight in this essay): without the utmost sensitivity and command of rhythm, the power of a method which uses any and all methods is much reduced; and the reduction is in exact proportion to the poet's command of different kinds of versification; and also in exact proportion—to return to our first concern—to the poet's sense of the vast poetic potential locked up or latent in prose, and his skill in converting prose into poetry.

We can hardly afford to forget the dangers inherent in the new method, nor fail to recognize the gifts of technique necessary to any poet who uses it. But once we have been sure that we do not underestimate the dangers or the difficulties, we are prepared to see that Eliot's use of the method, wonderful as it is in itself, is merely the beginning of a pioneer: it is a starting point from which poets in the recent past and in the present have drawn back. For a variety of understandable reasons they have moved in other fruitful directions, influenced by the equally great poetry of Yeats, by the pressure of life itself, and by the interminable or recurrent crises of society in depression or war.

But the starting point inherent in Eliot's method can hardly be entirely neglected if the future of poetry is bound up with the sense of existence which no human being, and certainly no poet, can escape, at this moment in history, or any moment in the future which is likely soon to succeed the present: the development of the historical sense and the awareness of experience which originate in psychoanalysis are two aspects of the view of existence which is natural to a modern human being and which makes the scope and the mobility of this new method of organization congenial. Certainly it cannot be said that great poetry is possible only by means of this method—Yeats, Valéry, and Rilke, as well as Swift and Hawthorne show how foolish such a belief would be—nor can one say that this method is the one, which, given the character of modern consciousness alone will lead to the greatest poetry. Indeed there is something unbearable in the prospect of many poems

[141]

which resemble *The Waste Land* very closely. But the new method does not and should not mean poetry which has the same emotional quality: to see that this is so, we have only to think of Pound's *Cantos*, which, whatever their virtues and faults, set the same example of poetic method to such an extent that Pound is not only the prior innovator, and the model and influence upon Eliot, he is a much more extensive practitioner of the method, so that, if my subject had been the elucidation of the method, Pound's poetry would have had to be the primary example.

Whenever in a critical essay, one begins to speak of the future, the conclusion ought to be near at hand, or one ought to be prepared to don the attire, awkward and uncomfortable as a knight's armor, of a prophet. But the past is involved in the present and future of poetry in a way which I have hardly touched upon; as the new method of organization marks a revolution in poetic form and structure, so it is also the continuation of the revolution in versification which has been going on since Christopher Smart and William Blake, which can be discerned in Coleridge, Hopkins, and Whitman; and which, with the onset of the Imagist movement, helped Pound and Eliot in the first part of their careers. If instead of using the term, free verse, one speaks of open and closed versification, then one can relate the new method of organization to the revolution in versification in this way: as the new method of total organization includes any and all other kinds of organization within it, without requiring any particular one at any particular point, so open versification includes all the closed forms of versification and the older open forms exemplified in the Bible, Whitman, Marianne Moore, and William Carlos Williams, without being committed to any particular one at any time. This is illustrated with the greatest fullness in Pound's *Cantos*, so far as versification itself is in question. And the richness and the fullness which are now possible can be summed up by paraphrasing the words about the sea in *The Dry Salvages*:

> The future has many voices,
> Many gods and many voices.

The Two Audens

Auden moves fast, like a good boxer. His subject, his opponent, present-day England, is moving fast also. Perhaps the fate of the poet is bound up with the fate of England. For the poet is "contemporary" in a special sense, the sense of being completely dependent on his time. Thus we are told that he is "so English", and what is meant is that his subject and his tone have their full meaning only for readers who are also English. The difficulty of defining such a poet is fairly clear. Any definition may become inadequate tomorrow, as the social crisis takes a new form and the poet attempts a new attitude or adjustment because of serious changes.

Nevertheless, no modern poet shows himself so obviously in two quickly discriminating parts, almost two poets, or at any rate two voices. The two voices are sometimes at war, sometimes reconciled and singing together, and sometimes one drowns out the other. One voice is that of the clever guy, the Noel Coward of literary Marxism:

> You were a great Cunarder, I
> Was only a fishing smack.
> Once you passed my bows
> And of course you did not look back.
> It was only a single moment, yet
> I watch the sea and sigh
> Because my heart can never forget
> The day you passed me by.

It is when he speaks in this voice that Auden is called "a schoolboy" and "the radical Kipling." He is attempting to be at once popular entertainer, propagandist, and satirist, and since a deliberate effort is involved in this kind of writing, no matter what aspect of it is examined, let us call this voice the Ego, thus using a terminology in which the poet himself is interested, and suggesting that this mode of writing does, in fact, spring from the conscious motives of the poet.

Then the other voice will have to be called the Id. From this one, we get many images of the greatest import and power. This one, to complicate the metaphor, is a kind of sibyl who utters the telltale symbols in a psycho-analytic trance. What strikes one immediately is the quality of the language, its toughness, its crabbedness, and the fact that it seems to be significant of so much without our being able to say why. We can render an explanation, however, when we examine the verse with its social background in view:

> Because I'm come it does not mean to hold
> An anniversary, think illness healed,
> As to renew the lease, consider costs
> Of derelict ironworks on deserted coasts.
> Love was not love for you, but episodes,
> Traffic in memoirs, views from different sides.

It is plain that the healing of illness, the lease renewed, the memoirs, the costs are items of modern life, and this reference is secured not merely by a naming of objects, but by their conjunction, the work of the poet's language. But much more is involved. Consider, in fact, the costs of derelict ironworks on deserted coasts. Auden refers repeatedly to industrial ruins, always with the foreboding of some plot, some explosion. The social basis for this recurrent symbol is the decay of mining in England and Wales during the 'twenties, and the wider fact of industrial breakdown all over the world. The social fact explains the power of the image. But it is the poet's language which makes possible its power.

Another example will serve to show how sensitive this poet is to the society in which he has lived:

> Certain it became while we were still incomplete
> There were certain prizes for which we would never
>   compete;
> A choice was killed by every childish illness,
> The boiling tears among the hothouse plants,

[144]

> The rigid promise fractured in the garden,
> And the long aunts.

The appearance of the long aunts ought certainly to surprise the reader and make him suspect the necessity of the rhyme (which, as so often before, has actually induced a fresh perception). For we discover that the poet has been inspired by his social context to this particular rhyme. We are being told that among the factors which determine certain childhoods are the spinster aunts, who communicate their sense of shame and their prudery to the child. The basis of the rhyme and the insight which it contains is a fact about English society, the existence of a spinster class.[1]

May one speak of the collective unconscious and suggest that when Auden is writing in this fashion he is delivering its obsessions to the page? Let one astounding example serve to give some warrant to the notion of an unconscious mind and the belief that certain poets find intuitions there. The example is from another poet of great fame, Rupert Brooke.[2] In May, 1913, Brooke wrote, as one would expect that poet to write: "I want to walk 1,000 miles and write 1,000 plays, and sing 1,000 poems, and drink 1,000 pots of beer and kiss 1,000 girls, and oh, a million things." A month later his appetite is somewhat less enormous: "All I want is life in a cottage, and leisure to write supreme poems." A year later, however, the desire to run away has come upon him: "I want to live in a hut by the river and pretend I'm a Polynesian" (one thinks of the celebrated Sweeney under the bamboo tree with Doris). By July, 1914, the World War being a few weeks away, he is genuinely afraid: "I'm so uneasy—subconsciously. All the vague perils of the time—the world seems so dark—and I'm vaguely frightened." The difference between the two poets in their poetry need

1. We are told that there are more women than men in England, partly as a result of the World War. The *New York Times* in August, 1938, carried two news stories concerning the class of womanhood which has resulted. One story stated that the spinster class had formed a union and demanded pensions after fifty. The other told of a lady betrayed by her fiancé who spent the next fifteen years robbing men involved in breach of promise suits, no one else, and giving the fruits of her crime anonymously to the mistreated women.

2. I have taken these quotations from a page of the English magazine, *New Verse*, where they are printed as an advertisement or warning to the young men of 1938 that the present year may be another 1914.

not be emphasized. One finds nothing of these fears and changes in Brooke's poems, while Auden writes directly from his awareness of them. At least this honesty, we may exult, has been accomplished for poetry since 1914.

The point has been worth laboring because it is this voice of Auden which seems to me to be the valuable one. We have, on the other hand, various indications of the poet's attitude to his medium. The deliberate conduct of the poet can only be attributed to the Ego. Many of Auden's poems have as their subjects mere occasions, which is true of much good poetry. But the poems seem also to be mere occasions in the poet's career, not independent objects which had better be well equipped for a dangerous life. Private joke, charade, jingle, and birthday poem are manners in which this attitude betrays itself in the texture of Auden's writing. And Christopher Isherwood writes, in the Auden number of *New Verse*, that Auden, at least in that earliest or Oxford period of the poet's poetry, "hated polishing and making corrections. If I didn't like a poem, he threw it away and wrote another. If I liked one line, he would keep it and work it into another poem. In this way, whole poems were constructed which were simply anthologies of my favorite lines, entirely regardless of grammar or sense. This is the explanation of much of Auden's celebrated obscurity." Such an account is not as damning as it may at first seem, for what counts is the end-product, anthology of favorite lines or not. But another example renders more dubious some of the end-products. One poem in *On This Island* appeared first in a volume of contemporary English writing called *New Country*, where, however, it was more than twice as long. What Auden had done was merely to cut the poem in two and discard one part and print the other part as a new unity, a procedure which resembles that of Miss Gertrude Stein, who was able to diminish her novel *The Making Of Americans* to half its initial length for its American publication. What the reader can get from writers who write works upon which they can perform such operations is a certain sense of things, a certain vision; but not a complete and self-contained object which is worth making part of one's memory. And it is the Ego or clever young man who writes with this idea of the poem and of the art of poetry.

A different question suggests itself with regard to the fruits of the Id. One finds in Auden a romantic set of symbols, which continually recur and which are used at very important moments of the poem. There are "mornings," "islands," "mountains," "frontiers," "waters," "birds," and "stones" as symbols which purport to signify a great deal. Indeed, on the basis of his method, a school has sprung up after Auden, and engages in a kind of Pre-Raphaelite Freudianism, from motives which are sometimes alleged to be religious or Surrealist or Freudian or derived from D. H. Lawrence, some names of this sect being Dylan Thomas, Frederic Prokosch, and George Barker. In Auden, one finds it necessary to ask whether these recurrent metaphors, along with like elements, do not often hide a residue of undigested meaning. This question makes more exact the distinction between poet as Ego and poet as Id. To be of great sensibility is not identical with the ability to understand the fruits of one's sensibility. The Id in this example is far ahead of the Ego, which is merely clever and ingenious; and it is upon the Ego that the business of understanding depends. In the very nature of the case, it would be a great expectation to hope that this poet in writing his poetry would perform an act of understanding upon all that his immense awareness impresses upon him. One must be grateful for what Auden's words contain, even if what they contain is not illuminated very often. The poet with a less difficult subject can do more, although with less. Moreover, not all subjects are completely and equally open to the understanding. Auden has been writing about the present.

II

But by this time it will seem that the use of Freudian terms in describing a poet is a mere reification and undue manipulation of aspects of his poetry. The proof that these terms are relevant (and that they are used not clinically, but in a genuine critical sense) is to be found where all proof of judgment awaits us, in the text itself.

In the text of Auden's initial volume, the *Poems* of 1930, most of the writing issues from the voice of the Id. It is true that the jocular slanging tone, half apology and half on the difficulty of being serious, sometimes produces what will undoubtedly be known as the Auden jingle. Sometimes in the middle of a poem, the writer of doggerel gets his way and has his say: "It's no use raising a shout./ No, Honey, you can cut that right out." But in the same poem occurs the true note: "In my veins there is a wish,/ And a memory of fish." And at the end of the poem, there is one couplet in which both voices are represented: "A bird used to visit this shore;/ He isn't going to come any more." But in the best poems of this first volume, the Id is dominant and—significantly enough —always in terms of a style which is a new grasping or synthesis of many important elements in the complex tradition of English poetry. Ezra Pound's translation of "The Seafarer," the style of Laura Riding, Emily Dickinson, Gerard Manly Hopkins, and John Skelton, the technique of Anglo-Saxon verse and of the Icelandic sagas, something of the kind of comment of choruses in Greek dramatic poetry—all these idioms and habits appear in a new order of style, and certain elements which inevitably belong to the genius of the language, though they have long been suppressed, are given full rein. As Eliot might say, the organism of English poetry has been modified by a new addition, an addition in which certain past styles are carried forward and grasped anew for a different subject-matter.

In Auden's second book, *The Orators*, every tendency in the first book is continued. But the subject is a large one, namely, the state of England. Consequently the poet's difficulties and conflicts as a poet are increased and displayed broadly. Apparently *The Orators* was started with a good plot in mind, that of a romantic quasi-Fascist conspiracy to purge and reform England under the leadership of an airman and by means of subversive speeches throughout the countryside, especially to school children and especially against the parasitic habits and values of the lower middle-class. But this substantial plan never manages to get a progressive narrative for itself, and instead there is a suite of excerpts expressive of the difficulties of the conspirators, their intense devotion to their Leader, and their meager ideas of the kind of society which they wish to create. This too in turn is left behind for the journal of the Leader himself, who is shown as very much like his disciples. Towards the conclusion of his journal, his desire for revolution, his profession of airman, and his homosexuality are all curiously identified as aspects of alienation from society. At this point, the plot is re-vived, and the method of revolutionary action is made clear—the practical joke! It is the practical joke, it seems, that will destroy the mentality of the status quo. And thus a new identification presents itself, for if, as we are told, homosexuality is most often an infantile regression, so, we may add, is the practical joke, and not only does the Airman's method of revolution betray him in the act of returning to his childhood, but the jocular tone of the doggerel writing is also placed.

The revolution of the practical joke is defeated, and once more the book shifts radically, and the poet gives up his plot completely in order to write a series of Odes addressed to his friends and repeating the theme, the sickness of England, in terms of personal relationships. The disorder is made entire by the last Ode, a very fine poem in itself, which is addressed to God, who has arrived on the scene much too late to be welcome. The habit to be noted and emphasized is the apparent cause of the disorder. Beginning with an objective narrative, or at least the plan for one, the plot has broken down repeatedly because of the intrusion of the poet's irreducible subject, psychic illness. One may say that this constant breakdown or intrusion occurs because it is identical with the poet's style, or one may say that the character of the poet's style is a function of his intuitions of psychic life. One is saying the same thing. The Id has insisted upon being heard, despite the deliberate plan of the poet. Or perhaps this is to dramatize the problem too neatly, and we had better say that the poet was working towards a form, but not working in the region where the form "proportionate" to his genuine intuitions could be found. And in the end the quality of his language and the energy of his perceptions satisfied the poet and appeared sufficient to him.

The next effort, a short play called "The Dance Of Death," represents the other extreme, the victory of the Ego: "We present to you this evening a picture of the decline of a class, of how its members dream of a new life, but secretly desire the old one, for there is death inside them." This might indicate that the theme would be presented in terms of intimate images of a way of life, which would obviously fit Auden perfectly in his subliminal rôle. Instead, there is a verbalization of Marxian formulas in a style derived, as I have said, from musical comedy. It is not at all that an emphasis on politics must betray this particular poet; on the contrary, the lower middle-class aware of its grave and insoluble problems always appears in the background of Auden's typical neurotic, biting his nails in his lonely room. But it is true that Auden's gifts seem to necessitate that the politics be grasped at a lower and more personal level, and in terms, for example, of neurotic fears. This is, in fact, what happens in the best parts of *The Orators*. Of the satire in "The Dance of Death," however, the best one can say is that it is flat and very laborious: "You are responsible./ You are impossible./ Out you go./ We will liquidate,/ The capitalist state/ Overthrow." Here again it is not that satire is not one of Auden's gifts, but that it pierces its target only when its terms are derived from a less conscious, less theoretical source.

The work Auden has done since, his two long plays in collaboration with Isherwood, his travel book, his poem on Spain, and his second volume of lyrics, are full of varied examples in which all tendencies try to operate together. The choruses in his *The Dog Beneath the Skin* possess a lucidity gained by a long verse line (a derivation in part from the *Anabase* of Perse and from the later Eliot as affected by Perse) which actually dilutes and weakens the power and spring and richness of the images. Dilution and expansiveness are the price of the lucidity, in place of the previous terseness, just as doggerel, musical comedy style, is the price of the cleverness. In *The Ascent of F6* another cost is made clear. The motivation of the hero is understood alternately in Freudian and in Marxian terms—he is betrayed in successive turns by an Oedipus complex and by imperialism. The style displays the effect of alternation, for when the crisis is reached, a very weak blank verse issues exactly where Auden was most powerful in the play of his first book, *Paid on Both Sides*, and although Auden has previously written one poem in a masterly blank verse. The conjunction of Freud and Marx is a very interesting one, and it is probably unavoidable for some poets in our time. But the use of their concepts appears to be foreign to Auden's whole drive, since he is not an intellectual poet in the full sense, and he lacks entirely a genuine interest in theory of any kind. Freud leads him to the brink where his true Muse lies; Marx reveals the interweaving of social process and personal life. But the direct use of their doctrines awaits the poet concerned with intellectual matters for their own sake. The glib speech about the lies of the radio and the press represents a very thin adoption of Marxism, not that of the Marxist poet who naturally and without conscious plan sees people and their habits always in terms of their social class and in the unity of the way of life and the way of producing the means of life. In this sense of a certain perspective native to the poet, Auden is, however, a Freudian poet.

The poems in *On This Island,* and the poem called "Spain," and the verse-writing by Auden in his book on Iceland display a reconciliation of tendencies gained by means of nothing less than a vulgarization of his gifts. This is not to say that there is not much good writing in various parts. But the edge of the verse has been softened. The poems are trim and obvious, although their subjects are just as complex as ever. The clever young man writes: "Gosh, to look at we're no great catch;/ History seems to have struck a bad patch./ We haven't time—it's been such a rush—/ Except to attend to our own little push." And this, one notes, is a birthday poem to a friend, while the symbol of History, an entity which has taken on most of the powers and functions of a deity, is tossed about with no discrimination. The poet who in his first book called for "death, our death/ Death of the old gang," now pleads as an established public poet for Love, which sometimes means the uninhibited libido, sometimes the spirit of political liberalism. Many of the images are almost heraldic—"lions," "scarlet soldiers," "florid music"—and the lyrics are sometimes imitative of A. E. Housman. Even the curse is pronounced in a rhyme-scheme which verges on the limerick idea:

> Let fever sweat them till they tremble
> Cramp rack their limbs till they resemble
>   Cartoons by Goya:
> Their daughters sterile be in rut,
> May cancer rot their herring gut,
> The circular madness on them shut,
>   Or paranoia.

The metre makes the savagery meek. The revolution which will purge the land induces in the poet no better symbol than that of a flood, although we know from other sources that such a revolution requires not only a class-consciousness and a deliberate will of the working-class, but also a profound modification of emotions and attitudes. And thus it is that in "Spain," we are given an itemization of the beautiful future, which is childish: "Tomorrow for the young the poets exploding like bombs"—although one would venture to hope timidly that the future and Auden will permit the poets a less explosive activity, even in the mercy of metaphor. This poem concludes with a stanza which is typical of Auden's present style:

> The stars are dead. The animals will not look.
> We are left alone with our day, and the time is short and
>   History to the defeated
> May say Alas but cannot help nor pardon.

A style in which all depends upon what meaning we can give to abstract symbols.

This shift from irony and the need of destruction to Love is at once the peace and adjustment of the Ego, which is in full control of its subliminal energies; and it is something more than that individual modification, precisely because Auden depends on his own time so much. The change corresponds with the day of the Popular Front in the international radical movement, and the correspondence suggests that what will come next depends upon our times and upon that movement, rather than upon the poet himself. Only a sharp break with the public poet which has been fashioned by a conscious will, and a return to the rôle of obedience to the passive, subconscious self would, it seems, free Auden from so perilous and immediate a relationship.

Will Auden suffer Kipling's fate, which is that of many another poet who was too intimate with the *Zeitgeist*, just as Kipling's Muse cohabited with the White Man's Burden? One does not know what is in store for present-day England, which is undoubtedly Auden's evil genius. With England, Auden now exists in the shadow of the Munich Pact of September, 1938. This is not true, at least in the same sense, of such poets as Yeats, Valéry, and Wallace Stevens. Such is the price of being completely contemporary. It may be a price worth paying or one may be unable to help oneself. At any rate, the fact remains that Auden's sheer natural gifts are incomparable, and it may be that with an immense gift for language one can survive social catastrophe, international terror, and the solicitations of the Ego.

[152]

The Poetry of Allen Tate

I

An honest man is one incapable of deceiving others. An honest poet, however, is one incapable of self-deception, at least in his poetry. This requires much difficult labor. One of the essential facts about Allen Tate's writings is the tireless effort and strained labor to be honest as a writer. The effort, the strain, the labor, and the honesty are, in a sense, a dominant quality of the very surface of his verse. I say: in a sense, because strictly what we know as the surface is a certain unique harshness of diction and meter, and an equally curious violence of imagery and sentiment. It is only when we have grasped the writing as a whole vision that we recognize a consistent intention in the quality of specific details, reading from line to line.

But where, before this, have we heard of the honesty in poetry? T. S. Eliot, in his essay on Blake in *The Sacred Wood,* speaks of the peculiar honesty to be found in genuine poetry:

> It is merely a peculiar honesty, which, in a world too frightened to be honest, is peculiarly terrifying. It is an honesty against which the world conspires because it is unpleasant. . . . Nothing that can be called morbid or abnormal or perverse, none of the things which exemplify the sickness of an epoch or a fashion, have this quality; only those things which, by some extraordinary labour of simplification, exhibit the sickness or strength of the human soul. And this honesty never exists without great technical accomplishment.

There is a lack of great technical accomplishment in Tate's poetry, but its place is taken, I think, by Tate's critical powers, operating in his verse. The relationship of Eliot's essay to the subject

[153]

of this essay is a fecund one by that accident of agreement which is no accident at all when we come to see how writers with like concerns must often arrive at like observations. Thus, as if by accident, the title page of Tate's first volume of verse contains a stanza from Blake, which is also quoted by Eliot in his essay as an example of "the naked vision" of that honest poet. Blake's stanza speaks of London, where often at midnight the poet has heard how the harlot's curse blasts the newborn infant's ear and blights with plagues—with a social disease, shall we say?—the marriage hearse. And what Eliot has quoted as an example of honesty is quoted by Tate to characterize the particular judgment of our time to be found in his book.

This connection may seem a labored coincidence. We get a further coincidence when we continue in Eliot's essay and come to Eliot's explanation of the defects of Blake's later poetry:

> What Blake's genius required, and what it sadly lacked, was a framework of accepted and traditional ideas which would have prevented him from indulging in a philosophy of his own, and concentrated his attention upon the problems of the poet. . . . The fault is perhaps not with Blake himself, but with the environment which failed to provide what such a poet needed.

This is, to begin with, Tate's leading doctrine as a critic, and one which he has extended and made specific in many ways not envisaged by Eliot. And both as poet and as critic, Tate's effort has been to recover, define, and possess the only framework of accepted and traditional ideas available to him. The effort of honesty to exhibit the essential strength or sickness of the human soul, becomes in the example of Tate's poetry an exhibition of the state of man when the framework of ideas which he accepts is rejected, ignored, and opposed by his environment. To state the matter so, however, is to say too much with too little definition. What is needed is an explicit outline of the kind of mind involved essentially in the poetry, and this is to be found by disengaging the whole view of the writer from the particular subjects and occasions of his prose.

II

Thus, in his criticism, Tate defines a comprehensive view of the genesis and the meaning of a framework of traditional and accepted ideas. Man is located in nature. He cannot get along without "ideas" or generalizations about his experience in nature. Without such generalizations, he would be unable to survive from day to day. In like manner, a society cannot survive from generation to generation without generalizations about both nature and the desirable behavior of men when they live with one another; and they must live with one another, just as they must live in nature. But how are such generalizations obtained? Not by a constitutional convention, abstruse speculations, or the reading of edifying works of literature; but by the difficult accumulation of experience from father to son and from generation to generation. Tradition is the habitual way of acting which has been found satisfactory, which has enabled men to cope with nature and with their own need, and which has made possible the realization of desires and objectives which are peculiarly human. The source of a framework of ideas is tradition, and the source of tradition is the concrete experience of men who have lived in a definite time and place. What this emphasis on traditional experience means is illustrated in the following example, where the source of morality is in question: "Jefferson calls his judgment 'taste'—reliance on custom, breeding, ingrained moral decision. But Adams needs 'a process of moral reasoning,' which forces the individual to think out from abstract principle his rôle at a critical moment of action."

Now nature is inexhaustible and unpredictable in many respects; it is what Tate calls (using terms I want to avoid) "an open realm of Quality," which always threatens man with evil and disintegration. Man's traditional experience protects him to a certain extent from the inexhaustible contingency of nature by abstracting a version of the past to serve as a provisional version of the future. Just as the mariner upon the ocean depends upon an inherited and concrete version of sailing in order to cope with the dangers of the ocean, so does man operate in history and in nature. But there are two extremes which he sometimes tends to embrace. The first extreme is that of giving himself over to nature as an irreducible and mystical process which he cannot control, but in which he can only immerse himself; the second extreme is that of regarding nature as a machine which works in certain immutable ways, a machine which can be operated and completely controlled by man. In the former, there is a lack of abstraction; in the latter, there is complete abstraction. Nature is regarded either as an unknowable flux, or as a checkerboard on which all possible moves can be known in advance. Man is faced by the peril of pure mysticism, or by the peril of pure industrialism. What is necessary in one's framework of ideas is a view of experience which grasps both extremes. A horse, to use Tate's vivid example, may be regarded as an irreducible quality, or as horsepower; the whole horse "cropping the blue grass on the lawn" is both an irreducible quality and horsepower.

Science (and here Tate fails to distinguish between the theoretical investigation and the practical use of that investigation)[1] reduces experience to predictive patterns, so that things can be made to work. Religion, by contrast, provides us with "the organized meaning of the encounters of man and nature, which are temporal and concrete," and by doing so, gives us "a living center of action and judgment" which enables us not only to know how things work and how to make them work, but above all to maintain an adequate attitude and behavior toward *the whole of life,* a phrase which is perhaps unfortunate, but nevertheless unavoidable. Birth, love, death, the inexhaustible vitality of nature, the continuity of past and present, the nature of the good society, the good life, and the good man—it is because religion provides us with the technique for grasping these things without violating them, for seeing them in their connection with one another, and for maintaining

1. This is not the occasion for more than a passing remark about Tate's prose, considered in itself. What should be said is that a defective and eclectic terminology leads him to superficial contradictions when, rightly understood, he has made available genuine and original insights in a prose of almost savage power. An example of one kind of fault would be such a statement as "For this is what a principle is—the way things will work." Another defect is that of posing false dilemmas to destroy his opponents. For example, "Mr. Moore is among other things, a Platonist. What is a Platonist? Is he a man who believes what Plato believed? Or is he a man who uses the Socratic method for the exposure of contradiction? . . . Since Mr. Moore obviously believes things that Plato did not, he is, if he be a Platonist at all, one by virtue of his use of the Socratic method." It is obvious that Mr. Moore could have been a Platonist, believed certain things which Plato did not, and yet not have used the Socratic method. And yet, despite such logic-chopping, the essay from which this passage is quoted is probably the best of all discussions of Neo-Humanism.

an adequate behavior toward them, that religion may be said to have to do with the whole of life.

But the means which religion provides is often curious. The basis of religion is tradition once more, that is, an inherited version of experience and of certain famous events. But these events are often not natural, but supernatural, that is to say (in this context), contrary to nature. And here in order to understand Tate, it is necessary to turn to the writing of John Crowe Ransom, who is evidently with T. S. Eliot one of Tate's two instructors. In *God Without Thunder,* Ransom defends the supernatural terms of religion by asserting that these terms are not intended to be taken as matters of fact, but rather as symbols, metaphors, fables, deliberate fictions which prescribe to us an adequate attitude, an adequate way of looking at the whole of life in all of its inexhaustible fullness and particularity. This is not the context in which one can be just to Ransom's argument; what is relevant here is that Tate has taken over Ransom's view of the metaphorical character of religious belief and extended the notion not only to poetry, but even to the very detail of our sense-experience. What we see with our eyesight is determined by the ways in which we look at nature and by our fundamental values, by what we are looking for. Thus Tate writes: "It is still a nice question among higher critics whether the authors of the Gospels were deliberate mythmakers or whether their minds were simply constructed that way." The best explication of how and why one's mind may be constructed that way is in *God Without Thunder.* Another one is to be found in Tate's recent novel:

> There are days when we consciously guide the flow of being towards the night, and our suspense is a kind of listening, as if the absence of light, when it comes, will be audible just because sight and touch are frustrated. Of course this is what we all know. But how many of us know that there are times when we passionately desire to hear the night? And I think we hear it: we hear it because our senses, not being mechanisms, actually perform the miracles of imagination that they themselves create: from our senses come the metaphors through which we know the world and in turn our senses get knowledge of the world by means of figures of their own making. . . . To hear the night, and to crave its coming, one must have deep inside one's being

[157]

a vast metaphor controlling all the rest: a belief in the innate evil of man's nature, and the need to face that evil, of which the symbol is the darkness, of which again the living image is man alone. Now that men cannot be alone, they cannot bear the dark, and they see themselves as innately good, but betrayed by circumstances that render them pathetic.

One must have deep inside one's being a vast metaphor controlling all the rest: it is such vast metaphors, the symbols by means of which we are enabled to live our lives, which constitute the essential subject of Tate's poetry. Not, however, in a simple way: the metaphors are grasped by the poet *existentially,* and by this is meant that the poet contemplates the metaphors by which he lives with an intense sense of the concrete circumstances of his being. He is a Southerner; an intellectual much concerned with literary, cultural, and historical problems; an American critical of the domination of finance-capitalism and industrialism; a Western man who recognizes the origin of his culture, even of the very language he speaks, in the Mediterranean, and yet who remains at the same time wholly conscious of his own age, the twentieth century. And at the center of this awareness, there is a particular human being who possesses a private life of his own, who must face the darkness, night, and death by himself.

One acquainted with Tate's poetry will recognize in this review the explicit subject of many of his poems. It may be less evident that this complicated and "intellectual" sensibility is made manifest throughout any given poem and in overt conscious ways. There is much poetry which is the deliberate allegorization of ideas; and all poetry can be interpreted as merely example and fable which illustrate general principles of one sort or another, if that is what one wants from a poem. But in Tate's writing we get neither deliberate allegorization (although certain poems must be excepted), nor dramatization of particular histories or emotions (and this again must be qualified). What we do get predominantly is the dramatization of such moments of experience as are intensely significant of the generalizations, the framework of ideas, about history and nature which I have just attempted to summarize. The poet brings into his poem a sensibility dominated not by particular characters, events, scenes, or landscapes, but dominated

[158]

by general ideas about the basic metaphors which are involved in all the scenes and events of our lives. This must be illustrated in characteristic poems and in some of its special phases.

III

One special phase is the steadfast recognition of the fate of his symbols. The Christian story (I want to avoid the term *myth,* as one which has intolerable connotations) is perhaps the most important of the metaphors controlling all the rest. But that story and that metaphor are in a state of decay; or perhaps one should say that the civilization which lived by means of that story is in a state of decay. The poet knows how important that story is to all that he means by civilization. But he knows too the concrete circumstances of that story in the present age. Thus there is for him the difficulty of possessing that vast metaphor as a modern man, a difficulty which he does not evade but embraces. The problem of belief achieves perfect formality in this short poem:

SONNET AT CHRISTMAS

This is the day His hour of life draws near,
Let me get ready from head to foot for it
Most handily with eyes to pick the year
For small feed to reward a feathered wit.
Some men would see it an epiphany
At ease, at food and drink, others at chase
Yet I, stung lassitude, with ecstasy
Unspent argue the season's difficult case
So: Man, dull critter of enormous head,
What would he look at in the coiling sky?
But I must kneel again unto the Dead
While Christmas bells of paper white and red,
Figured with boys and girls split from a sled,
Ring out the silence I am nourished by.

The sonnet-form has been mastered here to the point where it can be used for an expressiveness of the most minute shifts of emphasis, as in the neat point which begins the sestet, "So," and is made possible by an overflow of the eighth line; as in the subtle shifts of tone in the fifth and sixth lines; and as in the triple rhyme which brings the poem to its conclusive line, which is made to flow forth

with the consummate ease of a Miltonic last line by beginning with
a verb. The mastery of the form makes actual the immense plight
in question: the ego of the poem is incapable of enjoying this
Christmas as a day of feast partly because he is a dull critter of
enormous head, an intellectual animal; partly because of the great
difficulty of belief. He cannot believe; nor can he disbelieve. His
difficult case is that he must kneel—to one whom he must call the
Dead, with but an hour of life—he must look at the sky, and he
must argue his difficulty. In the twelfth line, the Christmas bells
upon the ceiling appear as a full image of the holiday and of the
character of the holiday for the protagonist. In the thirteenth
line, the innocent decoration upon the Christmas bells extends
itself into an implication of human fate by means of the connotations of the phrase, boys and girls, and by the verb, which spills
them. And in the brilliant antithesis, of the final line, the image
of the Christmas bells is raised to an irony which is both sensuous
and intellectual. The bells are artificial bells, not true ones, which
is what the protagonist fears may be true of the being whose birthday is being celebrated. The bells do not ring, although by their
symbolic character they ring out silence, and the protagonist is not
nourished, for he is nourished by silence. The intense desire to
believe is in conflict with the silence, which is a lack of light or
grace, and the whole conflict finds its expressive terms in the literal
contradiction that the false bells are ringing out silence. It is easier
to believe or to disbelieve than it is to maintain the poise between
belief and disbelief which this sonnet presents. The honesty in
question at the outset is fully exemplified in this difficult case. It is
an example also of the intellectual character of the poet's sensibility,
for the poet seizes the scene and its various aspects only as significant of his general concern with belief.

But if there is an honesty possible in the apprehension of belief
and idea, there is equally one in the sheer practice of versification.
In Tate's essay on the Elizabethan lyricists, there is a telling remark
which characterizes his own poetic style with precision: "It is the
resistance of language to full expression, the strain between images
and rhythm, opposites 'yoked by violence together,' that gives to
English lyrical verse its true genius." The perfect example is either

Webster or Donne. And it is this strain and tension which makes possible the aural quality, the diction, phrasing, and rhythm of Tate's verse both at its best and at its worst. At its best, the result is writing of great concentration and weight: the language is firm, emphatic, burdened with the proper tones of deliberateness and seriousness. The words resist the expectancies of the mind's ear, which by itself tends to be habituated to a metronome-like alternation of accents. At its worst, the strain of the two elements is too great and they break apart, so that the wrenching of accent falsifies the meaning of the verse. But this falsification is effect, not cause; as we can see if we examine another important poem in detail.

LAST DAYS OF ALICE

Alice grown lazy, mammoth but not fat,
Declines upon her lost and twilight age;
Above in the dozing leaves the grinning cat
Quivers forever with his abstract rage:

Whatever light swayed on the perilous gate
Forever sways, nor will the arching grass,
Caught when the world clattered, undulate
In the deep suspension of the looking-glass.

Bright Alice! always pondering to gloze
The spoiled cruelty she had meant to say
Gazes learnedly down her airy nose
At nothing, nothing thinking all the day.

Turned absent-minded by infinity
She cannot move unless her double move—
The All-Alice of the world's entity
Smashed in the anger of her hopeless love,

Love for herself who, as an earthly twain,
Pouted to join her two in a sweet one:
No more the second lips to kiss in vain
The first she broke, plunged to the glass alone—

Alone to the weight of impassivity,
Incest of spirit, theorem of desire,
Without will as chalky cliffs by the sea,
Empty as the bodiless flesh of fire:

All space, that heaven is a dayless night,
A nightless day driven by perfect lust
For vacancy, in which her bored eyesight
Stares at the drowsy cubes of human dust.

—We too back to the world shall never pass
Through the shattered door, a dumb shade-harried crowd
Being all infinite, function, depth and mass
Without figure, a mathematical shroud

Hurled at the air—blessèd without sin!
O God of our flesh, return us to Your wrath,
Let us be evil could we enter in
Your grace, and falter on the stony path!

Alice is perhaps the sister or the aunt of Gertrude Stein. She is, at any rate, a mammoth exponent of narcissism and of that "quantification" of nature which translates all things into merely measurable units and which makes the whole world merely a mathematical expanse, on the one hand, and merely a region for the ego to exploit, on the other hand. Is she adequate, however, to the meaning placed upon her?

We get an answer when we examine the formal surface at the crux of the poem, in the last two stanzas. Here the poem shifts from its particular symbol, Alice and her fate, to a generalization about the present age, and then to a prayer which can be glossed by T. S. Eliot's remark that "it is better, in a paradoxical way, to do evil than to do nothing." The shift at the crux makes desirable a formal equivalent, a shift in the movement and structure of the stanza-form, which had been established by the regularity of the first stanza. And there is indeed a modification in the movement of the poem, but one which wrenches the rhythm without being expressive of the particular shift in attitude and emotion. One feels that if the regularity is interrupted, the interruption can only be justified by its fusion with the meaning of what is said. Here, however, the overflow in the last line of the next to the last stanza and also in the last line of the last stanza, together with several violations of accents in the two stanzas, makes key lines unreadable, at least to one reader's ear. Instead of the hardness of diction which occurs when the poet is successful, we get a kind of stumbling and clumsiness, especially in the last stanza where the prayer and outcry seem separated from, not joined with and heightened by, the movement of the words.

But this failure, if it is indeed a failure, is not merely metrical. The strain and tension of the poet's style work too well elsewhere not to suggest that the difficulty inheres in the way in which the subject has been conceived. What the fable would seem to lack is a sufficiently concrete framework of circumstance.

We begin well enough with Alice as mammoth, the grinning cat, and the looking glass, but the paralysis of Alice as she gazes at her own image seems to annihilate the scene for the poet as well as for Alice, for there is a suite of statements which can be understood less and less in terms of a specific scene, and which seem to be *deduced* from, not engendered by, the abstract theme of the poem. Perhaps if the method of the poem had been that of bare general statement, such as is given toward the end, then one would feel no break, as one does when there is the transfer to increasing generality from what commenced as a particular scene and character.

The subject is an extremely difficult one, a difficulty which is evident when we recognize that Alice is required to signify a whole tendency of Western civilization. It is one more example of the poet's primary concern with basic ideas. What is lacking is lacking in the symbol, in its capacity to be complicated richly and yet concretely; from beginning to end, the problem of the poet rests upon symbols. This illustrates perhaps the chief peril of such a sensibility with such dominant concerns. There will always be the tendency or temptation to grasp the subject too intellectually and thus too abstractly. This is what has happened, for one reader, in "Last Days of Alice." The symbol, being seen too much as idea, does not yield the images which would give a dramatic existence to the idea, and hence the poet's habitual use of language also stands apart and dislocated from the symbol and the idea. If this judgment can be helped by the witness of comparison, then one comparison would be with T. S. Eliot's "Sweeney Among the Nightingales," or such a wholly successful example of an important relationship grasped dramatically as "The Oath," a poem in which Tate succeeds in making meter, diction, scence, symbol, and idea meet in the unity of a moment of experience.

IV

But to place all the emphasis of judgment upon particular poems is the distortion of the anthologist. Not only are all the books of a poet one book, as Tate has said, but in this one book the inferior poems provide the best writing with a definition and a background they would otherwise lack. What we get from any poet, if we get anything, is a vision. This vision is made increasingly available by being seen as directed upon a variety of subjects, and to this must be added, in Tate's example, the further definition which is given by the poet's prose. Thus, "Last Days of Alice," despite its defects, is valuable, for one thing, as an elucidation of the concluding stanzas of "To the Lacedaemonians," and the novel, *The Fathers,* illuminates all of the poems.

The whole vision of the poet can best be seen by grasping minute image, recurrent metaphor, symbol and idea, typical use of language, and single view of differing subjects in the unity from which they arise. Beginning with the minute image, we find that every element, from image to subject, tends to suggest itself as an example of some aspect of another part and of the writing as a whole.

Thus the images are often daring and daringly complicated, as in a stanza of the poem, "Death of Little Boys," in which, when a little boy has died, the ego of the poem remains at the bedside,

> Till all the guests, come in to look, turn down
> Their palms, and delirium assails the cliff
> Of Norway where you ponder, and your little town
> Reels like a sailor drunk in his rotten skiff.

The cliff of Norway would appear to be an extreme way of presenting the detached coldness and numbness of the bereaved ego, a metaphor immediately complicated by transforming the cliff of Norway into a little town, perhaps upon the cliff, which reels, to exhibit the mourner's tendency to be hysterical, like a sailor, who is not only reeling in his swaying boat, but also drunk, in a boat which is rotten, or shall we say, mortal also. The fact that the poem can *consistently* be complicated proves that the image was relevant at the very beginning.

The complication which strengthens the images is often intellectual, that is to say, the bond between the image and the subject depends upon the intellect, which has seen a relationship not given to visual observation, although often framed in visual terms. Thus in "The going years with an accurate glow,/ Reverse like balls englished upon green baize," the justice of the simile depends upon the understanding, not the sight of some scene, that the passage of years is a kind of reversal in that they bring the ageing man to a second childhood. This example may serve also as an instance of daring complication, just as the previous one may also serve as an instance of the working of the intellect among the images.

Hence the visual image is often, when taken in itself, qualified by terms which diminish its immediacy, but increase our sense of the mind which is involved in the poem. Thus the weather which attacks a graveyard is said to have "a particular zeal for every slab," a description of a physical effect in terms of a moral quality. Again, there is "The improbable mist of nightfall," where the use of "improbable" is another abstract word used for physical description. It is not only a particular effect which is attained by this use of language, but a kind of intellectual eyesight, which dominates the poet's sensibility.

Or, to view the matter from the other pole, the poet is obsessed with the precarious character of existence, with his sense of mortality. Hence there are an extraordinary number of images which have to do with dusk and people who have died. One hears "when dusk seals the window" and "the fire grows bright," "the dark pounding its head." The intuitions and the symbols by which one lives and dies become most intense "when the night's coming and the last light falls/A weak child among lost shadows on the floor." It is perhaps, in the whole vision of the poet's one book, the same weak child who dies in "Death of Little Boys." The obsession with twilight and with death are also one, for the twilight is an image of that dying of nature of which human mortality is an aspect. Two lovers, in a love poem which is full of terror, are seen as merely shades within the universal shadow which is night and nature.

Dusk is an event in the air, and the air, "the yawn of space," being another recurrent image, provides an extension of the unity

[165]

of vision. The air, "the burnt sea of universal frame," "the imponderable nowhere" in which "all lovers meet" is "the heaving jelly" in which is heard "some old forgotten talk," the speech which comes to be the meaning of time, the speech of one's fathers, "till now the air/Waits twilit for their echo."

But all that the air contains must be grasped by the staring eye. Hence the eye is another recurrent factor, which studies "the imponderable air," especially at dusk. Consequently one becomes aware of what "the eyes will never see"; one wishes, being a poet, to become nothing but straining vision and contemplation, "desire in the eye," "at night/When the long covers loose the roving eye/ To find the horror of the day a shape/Of life: we would have more than living sight."

We have, at any rate, a living sight in which what is seen is seen by the mind's eye. In these several aspects, a dramatic scene suggests itself as a kind of frontispiece to the poet's one book. It is a scene which continues one of the great modes of poetry, that of the ego isolated in some situation, whether we think of Dante in a gloomy wood astray, or of Wordsworth in "Resolution and Independence" and the great sonnets, or Coleridge in the "Ode to Dejection" and the other conversation poems. Here the self involved in the entire poetry is to be seen in solitude or with one other person, before the window or before the fire, at the hour of dusk, when the departure of the light is seen not merely as a change of impressions, but as a perpetual sign of the nature in which man must exist and find something permanent and human. What does the mind's eye see after "the evening star at a cold window"? What is "the twilit certainty of an animal"? The mind's eye sees the dead and recognizes that they are in a genuine sense more living than those who exist in the present.

The dead are the meaning of time in the sense that only the continuity of past and present makes our existence other than animal. Death is "the providence of life" in that death makes life a finite and concrete history, with genuine alternatives, with a beginning, middle, and end, as contrasted with "Infinity, that has nor ear nor eye," like the aforementioned Alice. "There is no civilization without death," although the ones "who have knowledge/Carried to the heart" must face the ones who have just died with an utter honesty about the blunt physical tragedy which confronts them, the corpse in which "the body's life," "deep as a foul well,/Instinctive as the wind, busy as May,/ Burns out a secret passageway to Hell." In the realism of such a vision, "the bleak sunshine shrieks its chipped music," and one says, "Come, now, no prattle/ Of remergence with the *ontos on*," no immortality with the "really real," for "Men cannot live forever/ But they must die forever" and all rationality, all pleasure and technique, all famous art, even Mr. Pope's, are bounded by the circumstance of mortality. It is this sense which, to return to the images with which we began, makes them of a tough and harsh "morbidity," even when an innocent description is their surface interest.

Yet if death is the conclusion of life, the dead were and are the beginning of life. One asks: "What is this flesh and blood compounded of/ But a few moments in the life of time?" What is the meaning of life? If life is "a black river full of eyeless fish/ Heavy with spawn," which is as pure and irreducible a view as the naturalist could require, then it is the relationships made possible by spawn which raise life to a level above the mere activity and exhaustion of animal energy.

The dead were the source of life and they remain the source of one's habits, memories, and beliefs, of all one possesses, indeed of one's way of life, and of the whole civilization in which one is able to breathe and speak. It is only in the most desperate irony that one says: "Gentlemen, let's/Forget the past." For one is united to the dead and to the past by the blood, "The track/We know so well, wound in these arteries," "The lifeblood that labors you so much," and that is why, aware of the nothingness which awaits each individual apart from "connections" of the blood, one says to the person one loves, "Companion of this lust, we fall,/ . . . , lest we should die alone," and that is also why the traveler, the seeker, the wanderer, who has been seeking through afternoon until night finds out that only "the dark shift within the bone/ Brings him the end he could not find," for that end was "the secret ones around a stone."

Moreover, the past and the dead to whom one belongs go far back from a particular countryside, "the road, red clay, suncracked and baked," through "Maryland Virginia Caroline," "Clay valleys rocky hills old fields of pine," through "Shiloh, Antietam, Malvern Hill, Bull Run" and the Confederate dead who fill the air, "the yawn of space," "With the furious murmur of their chivalry," to Aeneas, Troy, and the Mediterranean, which is the beginning of our civilization. Such is the continuity of past and present that on a day of festival in a Mediterranean bay one has the sense that one has "Devoured the very plates Aeneas bore" which made known his fatherland to him, and it is possible, on the other hand, to suppose Aeneas at Washington, regarding America, and thinking of the civilization he had begun, "what we had built her for." Aeneas is only one of the living dead who remembers that he was " A true gentleman, valorous in arms,/Disinterested and honorable," and one of the Confederate dead is another one, one who says "It is a privilege to be dead," who remembers "that everything but kin was less than kind," and who, remembering above all the war in which he fought to defend a way of life, condemns the present into which he has survived because now "All are born Yankees of the race of men," "by motion sired, not born." And if the present is condemned, the defects of the past are observed also; Jefferson Davis is viewed as receiving "Just preterition for his crimes," as in the prose the South is condemned for seeking salvation in politics alone and for trying to build a civilization on the basis of an enslaved peasantry.

And yet if one cannot truly know the present without a sense of the past, the only end in view when one is concerned with the past and the dead is an increased knowledge of the present in which one must exist and in which "Motors and urchins contest the city streets." Now "Narcissus is vocabulary. Hermes decorates/ A cornice on the Third National Bank"; now "Not power nor the storied hand of God/ Shall keep us whole in our dissevering air"; now "It is moot whether there be divinities," and "There are wolves in the next room, waiting," bearing inevitable evil. The present is seen and judged in terms of a way of life which, though with many lapses, was sustained for three thousand years, so that one's tongue still utters a "fierce latinity." When this criticism of the present shifts, however, from irony to direct satire, the writing becomes literary in the worst sense: "Every son-of-a-bitch is Christ, at least Rousseau," intended as an attack on liberalism and humanitarianism, merely makes one suppose that the terms of attack were derived from the writings of Irving Babbitt. But the way of life is seen not as a pattern of activity and enjoyment, but in terms of its basic conceptions of nature, man, and the good life. But, again, these conceptions are not stated abstractly as desirable ends, but their meaning is grasped within certain moments of experience and as the meaning of the images of nature and man, the meaning of night and the meaning of a man's dignity, courtesy, and honor. It is the experience of attempting to be a moral being and to lead "a private, self-contained, and essentially spiritual life," an experience which finds its metaphor in the sieve, which strains, searches, and separates whatever comes into it: "They ask us how to live./ We answer: Again try/Being the drops we sieve./What death it is to die!"

Thus, by such a reading as this laborious review is intended to represent, one is able to get the whole vision which motivates all of this poetry; and thus one is able to recognize its scope, seriousness, and ambition, which may be concealed by the allusive method and the great concreteness of particular poems.

V

Examples external to the poet's one book will also serve to define that book more exactly and to establish its relationship to concerns which are beyond poetry and beyond a particular American region.

One example which will free this poetry from being misunderstood as representing merely the piety of a man for his countryside or the peculiarity of a Southern intellectual is to be found by remembering a passage in which William Butler Yeats also pays tribute to the landed society, explicating with the economy of the great poet, the ideal of a society which is able to survive and nourish itself through generations:

> A spot whereon the founders lived and died
> Seemed once more dear than life; ancestral trees,
> Or gardens rich in memory glorified,
> Marriages, alliances, families,
> And every bride's ambition satisfied.
> Where fashion or mere fantasy decrees
> Man shifts about—all that great glory spent—
> Like some poor Arab tribesman and his tent.

We remember that in the present age many of us are even less fortunate than the Arab tribesman, lacking even a tent, and the particular character of our misfortune can be emphasized by quoting from a novelist who, writing in the first decade of the century and learning the lesson from France, not the South, nor Ireland, lends further generality to the vision of civilization which is in question in Tate's writing. Mrs. Wharton, in *The House of Mirth*, gives to her heroine a knowledge of the reasons for her complete failure; and the passage is too relevant not to be quoted at full length:

> It was no longer, however, from the vision of material poverty that she turned with the greatest shrinking. She had a sense of deeper impoverishment—of an inner destitution compared to which outward conditions dwindled to insignificance. It was indeed miserable to be poor—to look forward to a shabby, anxious middle-age, leading by gradual degrees of economy and self-denial to dreary absorption in the dingy communal existence of the boarding house. But there was something more miserable still—it was the clutch of solitude at her heart, the sense of being swept like a stray uprooted growth down the heedless current of the years. That was the feeling which possessed her now—the feeling of being something ephemeral and rootless, mere spindrift of the whirling surface of existence, without anything to which the poor tentacles could cling before the awful flood submerged them. Her parents too had been rootless, blown hither and thither on every wind of fashion, without any personal existence to shelter them from its shifting gusts. She herself had grown up without any one spot of earth being dearer to her than another: there was no center of early pieties, of grave endearing traditions, to which her heart could revert and from which it could draw strength for itself and tenderness for others. In whatever form a slowly-accumulated past lives in the blood—whether in the concrete image of the old house stored with visual memories, or in the conception of the house not built with hands, but made up of inherited passions and loyalties, it has the same power of broadening and deepening the individual existence, of attaching it by mysterious links of kinship to all the mighty sum of human striving. Such a vision of life's solidarity had never before come to Lily. She had had a premonition of it in the blind notions of her mating instinct; but they had been checked by the disintegrating influences of the life about her. All the men and women she knew were like atoms whirling away from each other in some wild centrifugal dance.

The illumination which this passage contains suggests the possibility of another kind of misunderstanding, a judgment which would condemn this view of the good life because it seems to depend essentially upon a social order which must issue in injustice and oppression. But if we take one key value, the emphasis throughout Tate's poetry of dignity as a necessary human good, another generalizing reference presents itself. We remember that a revolutionary writer justifies the social revolution by making this value a primary end. In André Malraux's *Man's Fate*, where the hero gives himself to the proletarian revolution with something of the sensibility of a symbolist poet, his life and his death are also directed to the possibility of human dignity:

> His life had a meaning and he saw what it was; to give to each of these men whom hunger, at this very moment, was killing like a slow disease, possession of their own dignity. He was one of them, they had the same enemies. There is no possibility of dignity, of a real life, where men work twelve hours a day without knowing what they are working for. This labor must take on a meaning, must become their country. . . . Revolution gives men only the *possibility* of dignity; it is for every one of them to turn that dignity into a possession.

One does not mean to say that these two writers mean precisely the same thing by dignity, and the difference in meaning obviously rests on a crucial issue, whether dignity is best to be secured by abolishing property or by winning for each man enough property to make him a self-sustaining being. It is a disagreement great enough to make each one willing to shoot at the other on the proper occasion. Nevertheless the common denominator of human values is significant.

One more reference will display the relationship, both agreement and disagreement, of the poet's whole view and the whole view of Marxism, the latter view being one which, however we accept or reject or qualify it, is part of the background of the age, against which all works are posed. In general, from both perspectives it is seen that values have their necessary roots in the whole social complex, in the complicated unity of a way of life. Hence, when in his prose Tate writes: "Economy is the secular image of religious conviction," he is not saying the same thing as "Religion is the theological rationalization of economic compulsion." But the

[171]

disagreement is less than the agreement, as we can see when, in relating Emily Dickinson to a declining New England theocracy, Tate recognizes the same cross-section of society as the Marxist would affirm; for he sees that decline of New England as being begun when the design of a cotton-spinner was brought to Massachusetts, until "the energy that had built the meeting-house ran the factory." The disagreement rests upon which factor is "fundamental," whatever that term may mean, the factor of economic compulsion or the factor of the moral choice by human beings of a way of life. And if Tate affirms the latter one, he does so "for the honor of man," an honor with which the Marxist is also concerned.

It is important to see that all these matters are essentially involved in this poetry, because it is then that we recognize the intelligence which the poetry makes available. Other writers have been more gifted with the habitual trappings of the poet, the facility which Tate lacks and the gaudy show of sensibility which always attracts the majority of readers. Ezra Pound, for an extreme example of comparison, undoubtedly has a better ear than Tate and takes hold of a greater amount of material, though with a proportionate lack of understanding. But in the end it is the discriminating intelligence, operating within the poetry, which makes one poet more important to us than another. And it is to the exact functioning of his intelligence in his verse that Tate has directed his energies. Despite this, despite the concern with all that is most important to us, there is a certain obliqueness, narrowness, and overconcentration, and there is the typical defect of the subject grasped too abstractly. The poet has not yet found the comprehensive form which will display his whole vision from every perspective. The reader must to a certain extent construe the whole view in its fullness. But otherwise that which concerns us most of all is presented with that honesty which Eliot spoke of as being so peculiar, rare, strange, unpleasant, and genuine.

[172]

Instructed of Much Mortality
A Note on the Poetry of
John Crowe Ransom

℥ The appearance of Ransom's *Selected Poems* (Knopf, 1945) suggest reflections, full of a modest joy, about the modest triumphs of virtue, both in poetry itself and in the weird, vague, treacherous amphitheatre of poetic reputation. When most of the poems in this book appeared, American poetry was dominated by such trumpeters and maestri as Carl Sandburg, Vachel Lindsey, Edgar Lee Masters, and Edwin Arlington Robinson. It is unfair to join Robinson with the other poets, except in terms of the functioning of poetic reputation. Reputation is the point; the poets who seemed significant and big and what I believe is known as major have suffered the fate of huge balloons. Meanwhile such poets as Marianne Moore, Wallace Stevens, and William Carlos Williams have emerged through the strength of a genuineness which was perhaps the reason for their not being recognized at their true worth immediately. Ransom is another such author, and there is a moral for publishers in the persistence of his reputation. Some authors, good as well as bad, appear to think that they must publish a book every year, if the great beast which is the public is to remember and read them. Ransom has published perhaps six new poems, some of them his best ones, in the past twenty years. Meanwhile, despite the absence of renewal, his poems have remained important in the one truly indubitable way that poetry can remain important: namely, they have been read again and again by other poets and—purest of all laurels—they have been read by those who are beginning to write poetry, those who want to write poetry, and those who are trying to learn how to write poetry. This may seem a somewhat meager existence; but it is the only alternative, given literary curiosity in America, to not being read at all.

A strange instance of this modest triumph of genuineness occurred when, in 1935 in England, Geoffrey Grigson suddenly published a brief essay in praise of Ransom's poetry. The instance is strange in several ways. No new volume by Ransom had appeared, for one thing; and then, it has been clear in general that, were it not for the existence of T. S. Eliot, America to British literati would be virtually indistinguishable from Australia; and strange most of all because Grigson had labored in vain to make head or tail of modern American poetry, finding only that Frost was provincial, James Agee wrote as if he had no roof to his mouth, William Carlos Williams was bogus, and Wallace Stevens was a "stuffed goldfinch," "a Klee without rhythm"! Yet Grigson's comments on Ransom, however inconsistent with his other judgments, were very perceptive. He guessed that Ransom had studied Hardy, he said that "there was not much else in American poetry like Ransom," and that Ransom "defended himself by irony against an inclination to the pathetic," and that, in fine, Ransom's two books, *Chills And Fever*, and *Two Gentlemen In Bonds*, were "two of the most delightful collections published since the War." Not too much ought to be made of this praise, though it is always cheering when American literature is not identified abroad with such authors as Steinbeck, Saroyan, Robinson Jeffers, and Carl Sandberg. For Grigson's remark that there was not much else in American poetry like Ransom is both true and false. It is true that the total effect of his poems is unlike that of any other poet. But nonetheless there is a significant resemblance to other poets so far as language and style are concerned, and the sum of this significant resemblance can perhaps best be stated by citing Wallace Stevens. Both poets make a like use of dandyism of surface, of irony, and of a mock-grand style. Here are samples which, so far as the texture of the style goes, might have been written by either poet:

> When this yokel comes maundering,
> Whetting his hacker,
> I shall run before him,
>
> Diffusing civilest odors
> Out of geraniums and unsmelled flowers.
> It will check him.

· · · · ·

[174]

I placed a jar in Tennessee
And round it was, upon a hill.
It made the slovenly wilderness
Surround that hill.

. . . . .

If the lady hath any loveliness, let it die.
For being drunken with the steam of Cuban cigars,
I find no pungence in the odour of stars,
And all my music goes out of me on a sigh.

. . . . .

But now, by our perverse supposal,
There is a drift of fog on your mornings;
You in your peignoir, dainty at your orange cup,
Feel poising round the sunny room

Invisible evil, deprived and bold.
All day the clock will metronome
Your gallant fear; the needles clicking,
The heels detonating the stair's cavern.

The first two are excerpts from Stevens, and the second two are passages in Ransom. I have deliberately chosen samples in which there is a likeness of subject-matter to some of Steven's best known poems. It is not, however, such a likeness which is important, but the way language is used and the attitude *toward* language. Both poets use the grand style with mockery and playfulness, and both poets correct the excess inherent in this mock grandiloquence by that use of the colloquial and the concrete which may seem to the future to be the most marked aspect of modern poetry. Of the two poets, Stevens has followed out the possibilities of this idiom with much greater intensity and consistency. But the irony in Stevens is defensive; he seems at times to be discounting or trimming the serious emotions with which he is concerned, as if he were suspicious of them. In Ransom, however, the irony is most often an expression of the very painfulness of the emotion:

The little cousin is dead, by foul subtraction,
A green bough from Virginia's aged tree,
And none of the country kin like the transaction;
Nor some of the world of outer dark, like me.

Here the wryness of tone accomplished by rhyming *subtraction* and *transaction* should serve as an instance of how the irony is part of the emotion, and not, as in Stevens, a kind of guard which surrounds it.

It is natural to speculate about this likeness in style, in attitude toward language, of the two poets. There can be no question of the influence of one poet upon the other, although, insofar as a period style may be said to be the source of the resemblance, it is true that there may be some common influence upon both. If one went through the files of *Poetry: A Magazine of Verse, The Smart Set*, and *The Dial*, one would come upon many poems—by such very different authors as Conrad Aiken, Maxwell Bodenheim, Donald Evans, and even Edna St. Vincent Millay!—in which the convention of the high poetic is used with irony. And there is even, I think, a resemblance to the exotic, foreign and bravura quality of the prose styles of H. L. Mencken and James Branch Cabell. But these resemblances, far from being a matter of literary influence, suggest a common situation which involves the whole human being, namely, the relationship of the author to the age. The way that the language is used would thus have as its fundamental cause the attitude of society to poetry and the consequent attitude of the poet to his art. When the poet is regarded as a strange, rare and abnormal being, it is natural that he should mock at the same time as he enjoys the language of the grand manner. Perhaps there is further illumination, in literary history which has not yet been written: the overstuffed upholstery which is the rhetoric of late Victorian poetry was rejected by the poets who began to write between 1910 and 1920. One has only to cite the concern with speech, direct statement, and concreteness which were the declared aims of the founders of the *vers libre* movement. Now if we suppose that poets like Stevens and Ransom were caught, so to speak, in the midst of this shift from rhetoric in the grand manner to the direct concreteness of (what was then) the new poetry, we have perhaps placed the kind of literary energy which is the source of their ironic styles and their resemblance to each other. The irony of their language can thus be attributed to the tension and conflict they felt with regard to the two conceptions of what poetry ought to be.

In "Philomela," a poem which has had the misfortune to be much anthologized so that, like a famous symphony, repetition

has imposed a transient triteness upon it, Ransom deals directly
with the fate of poetry in our time:

> Procne, Philomela, and Itylus,
> Your names are liquid, your improbable tale
> Is recited in the classic numbers of the nightingale.
> Ah, but our numbers are not felicitous,
> It goes not liquidly for us.
>
> .   .   .   .   .
>
> Up from the darkest wood where Philomela sat,
> Her fairy numbers issued. What then ailed me?
> My ears are called capacious but they failed me,
> Her classics registered a little flat!
> I rose and venomously spat.
>
> Philomela, Philomela, lover of song.
> I am in despair if we may make us worthy,
> A bantering breed sophistical and swarthy;
> Unto more beautiful, persistently more young,
> Thy fabulous provinces belong.

It is probably needless to suggest that to compare this poem with
Keats' "Ode to a Nightingale" is to see the distance between
the romantic and the modern poet. But since I have not quoted the
entire poem, perhaps it is necessary to emphasize the fact that the
poet's doubt of the nature of modern poetry—he has said in an
unquoted stanza that he felt "sick of my dissonance"—is a mixed
one. He is not entirely displeased that he belongs to "a bantering
breed sophistical and swarthy," and if he feels that "our numbers
are not felicitous" nor liquid, he also finds Philomela's classics "a
little flat." Indeed there is a pleasure in the use of the language
throughout which suggests that far from preferring felicitous and
liquid numbers, the poet prefers to be able to write verses in which
he can say that he "venomously spat," an instance of the kind of
diction which the Romantic poet would be incapable of using,
and which the Elizabethan dramatic poet found more and more
necessary as he moved from the liquid and empty felicity of Spen-
ser to the choppy and perception-burdened versification of Donne
and Webster.

To return to the comparison between Ransom and Stevens,
they are alike in their attitude toward language and their themes

are often alike. But the ultimate direction is quite different.
Stevens moves toward a contemplation of symbols and ideas abstracted from any time and place; and when in his recent poems
he returns to the time and the place of the present, the present
also becomes some kind of abstraction. Ransom on the other hand
returns always to the relationship of human beings to each other
and to the immediacy and particularity of existence. The human
beings are present chiefly for the sake of declaring an attitude
toward existence. Robert Penn Warren has pointed out that Ransom's characteristic form is "the little objective fable, with a kernel
of drama." *Kernel* is exact, for it is hardly more than a kernel of
drama. Neither the characters nor the drama are important for
their own sake, as in many of the lyrics of Robinson and Eliot. It
is the meaning of the fable which determines the place or rôle of
all the other properties of the poem. And this meaning comes
through so much by way of the tone of the poem,—a tone which
is by turns playful, charming, gay, off-hand, and sardonic—that
the seriousness of the meaning and of the whole poem may easily
be missed. Consider, for example, a poem such as "Conrad In
Twilight":

> Conrad, Conrad, aren't you old
> To sit so late in your mouldy garden?
> And I think Conrad knows it well,
> Nursing his knees, too rheumy and cold
> To warm the wraith of a Forest of Arden.
>
> Neuralgia in the back of his neck,
> His lungs filling with such miasma,
> His feet dipping in leafage and muck:
> Conrad! you've forgotten asthma.
>
> Conrad's house has thick red walls
> And chips on Conrad's hearth are blazing,
> Slippers and pipe and tea are served,
> Butter and toast, Conrad, are pleasing!
> Still Conrad's back is not uncurved
> And here's an autumn on him, teasing.
>
> Autumn days in our section
> Are the most used-up thing on earth
> (Or in the waters under the earth)

Having no more color nor predilection
Than cornstalks too wet for the fire,
A ribbon rotting on the byre,
A man's face as weathered as straw
By the summer's flare and winter's flaw.

Butter and toast, Conrad, are pleasing! How readily the careless reader may be put off by the seeming triviality of such a line, so that he misses its essential connection with the extraordinary last stanza and the theme of the body's decay and death over which this poem, like so many others by Ransom, agonizes. The prose quality of the last stanza, the shift in rhythm from the jingling with which the poem begins to the flat, direct statement of the last stanza, the significance of the image of "a ribbon rotting on the byre," the conclusiveness and the beauty of the last line (which is secured by means of assonance as well as by the visual and emotional connotations of "the summer's flare")—all of these qualities may be disregarded if the reader does not grasp the easy tone and jingling rhythm as a *preparation* for the last stanza.

As this poem is concerned with death, so the hard fact of death is the most frequent subject, and the reader encounters an astonishing number of funerals and corpses. (In one of his essays, Ransom remarks in passing that a man may go out of his mind if he thinks too much about death.) And where the conclusion is not as radical as that, there is frustration, disappointment, and despair. When the subject is not a dead boy or a dying lady, it is the impassable distress that lovers feel at the thought of death, as in "Vaunting Oak," where a lady *"instructed of much mortality"* cites a great oak as an instance of permanence and then, when the oak is struck, hears in the reverberance "like a funeral, a hollow tone." A mind instructed in mortality has a natural love of the body, and it is without sympathy for any denial of the body's beauty or actuality, a denial to which the mind is often tempted. Thus, in "The Equilibrists," two lovers who are separated by honor forever, are told that "great lovers lie in Hell," "they rend each other when they kiss," and "the pieces kiss again," while in Heaven there is not only no marriage, but the soul is bodiless; and the implication is that in this way Hell is preferable to Heaven. So, in another poem, the head is accused of seeking decapitation, of

[179]

seeking "to play truant from the body bush," of traducing the flesh, but "Beauty is of body," the body's love is necessary to the head, and without the body's love the living world is colorless and empty. So too, in "Address to the Scholars of New England," we hear that

> There used to be debate of soul and body,
> The soul storming incontinent with shrew's tongue
> Against what natural brilliance body had loved

In the psychomachia of this poet, the character of the debate has reversed itself, the soul storms against itself for being in the least faithless to the body. Furthermore, to be faithful to the body and to love the body is to be aware of its degradation, its decay, and its death. Here again a detailed comparison with Stevens would be fruitful. I have in mind particularly Stevens's "Sunday Morning," and "The Emperor of Ice Cream": "Let be be finale of seem/The only Emperor is the Emperor of ice cream." And Ransom's best poem must be quoted as a whole, if one is to see how this concern with death can mount to a vision of life in which everything (from children and "the pretty kings of France" to a dressing-gown, buckberries in blue bowls, the "warning sibilance of pines" and "the heels detonating the stair's cavern") is seen in the cold, cloudy light of the fact of mortality:

PRELUDE TO AN EVENING

> Do not enforce the tired wolf
> Dragging his infected wound homeward
> To sit tonight with the warm children
> Naming the pretty kings of France.
>
> The images of the invaded mind
> Being as the monsters in the dreams
> Of your most brief enchanted headful,
> Suppose a miracle of confusion:
>
> That dreamed and undreamt become each other
> And mix the night and day of your mind;
> And it does not matter your twice crying
> From mouth unbeautiful against the pillow

[180]

To avert the gun of the same old soldier;
For cry, cock-crow, or the iron bell
Can crack the sleep-sense of outrage,
Annihilate phantoms who were nothing.

But now, by our perverse supposal,
There is a drift of fog on your mornings;
You in your peignoir, dainty at your orange cup,
Feel poising round the sunny room

Invisible evil, deprived and bold.
All day the clock will metronome
Your gallant fear; the needles clicking,
The heels detonating the stair's cavern.

Freshening the water in the blue bowls
For the buckberries, with not all your love,
You shall be listening for the low wind,
The warning sibilance of pines.

You like a waning moon, and I accusing
Our too banded Eumenides,
While you pronounce Noes wanderingly
And smooth the heads of the hungry children

The Man with the Blue Guitar, and Other Poems

The poems of Wallace Stevens present an elegant surface. It has been mentioned often, and misunderstood even more frequently, but its affiliations are fairly clear. The same dandyism of speech and the same florid irony is to be found in such writers as James Branch Cabell and Carl Van Vechten, in certain poems of J. C. Ransom and Conrad Aiken, even in the prose style of Santayana, in the poems of the forgotten Donald Evans, and going further back in time, in the moonstruck poems of Dowson, Laforgue, and Verlaine, the Verlaine of "Fêtes Galantes," and the Laforgue who sighs that existence is so quotidian. This is a formidable family, but the resemblances are unmistakable. They are also superficial; Stevens has made a significant virtue out of the dubious verbal habits involved in the tendency from which he seems, in some way, to have derived his style. He is unquestionably a much better writer than most of the above authors.

Perhaps it is worthwhile attempting to account for the kinship by relating Stevens to the *milieu* which must have surrounded him when he began to write. As a hypothesis, one may suppose that his style crystalized in the days when *The Smart Set* was the leading literary magazine, when one knew French with pride, discussed sophistication, feared to be provincial, and aspired to membership among the élite. The backwash or lag of that day is still apparent in the Greenwich Village tearoom, and one can scarcely doubt that among the admirers of Miss Millay, there are some who still exist in that period of time. To be a poet at that time was to be peculiar; merely to be interested in the arts was to take upon oneself the burden of being superior, and an exile at home. It may be that as a result of some such feeling, Stevens called his wonderful discourse on love "Le Monocle de Mon Oncle," thus resorting to French, and thus mocking, as so often in his titles, the poem itself, as if the poet were extremely self-conscious about the fact of being a poet. It ought to be added that the title of the poem in question does, nevertheless, have a distinct meaning in the poem.

In the present volume, Stevens provides another example, the best one perhaps, of how much there is in his poetry beneath the baroque decoration. The surface would seem to be a mask, which releases the poet's voice, a guise without which he could not speak. But the sentiments beneath the mask are of a different order. If we rest with our impression of the surface, we get nothing but a sense of play and jocular attitudinizing:

> To strike his living hi and ho,
> To tick it, tock it, turn it true,

If we dig into just such usages and then come back to the poem as a whole, we understand the justice of such verbalism, its necessity, and we are confronted with a mind of the utmost seriousness, aware and involved in the most important things in our lives.

The imagination and actuality, the blue guitar which is poetry and things as they are, constitute the antithesis to which Stevens devotes a varied discourse in the present book. In the title poem or suite of poems, there are thirty-three short lyrics in which the various relationships between art and the actual world are named, examined, turned upside down, and transformed into the terms of Stevens' personal vision. In the opening lyric, we are given the suggestion of some lack in the nature of poetry. The poet is addressed by his audience:

> They said, "You have a blue guitar,
> You do not play things as they are"

The poet replies that the imagination must of necessity alter and distort actuality, and the audience then extends its demand:

> "But play you must
> A tune beyond us, yet ourselves,
>
> A tune upon the blue guitar,
> Of things exactly as they are."

The difficulty is that poetry is somehow insufficient. The incidence of that insufficiency, its present point, is made evident further on in the poem:

> The earth is not earth, but a stone,
> Not the mother that held men as they fell,
>
> But stone, but like a stone, no, not
> The mother but an oppressor

It is because of an enforced awareness that his time is one of immense conflict and derangement that the poet has been compelled to consider the nature of poetry in its travail among things as they are. The basic preoccupation, the apprehension which has produced two volumes in two years, was revealed most explicitly in the previous book, *Ideas of Order*:

> There is order in neither sea nor sun,
> There are these sudden mobs of men,
>
> These sudden clouds of faces and arms,
> An immense suppression, freed,
> These voices crying without knowing for what,
>
> Except to be happy, without knowing how.

This is the way, then, in which Stevens answers these sudden mobs of men, these sudden clouds of faces and arms: he justifies poetry, he defines its place, its rôle, its priceless value. Nothing could be more characteristic of this poet, of his virtues and also of his limitations, and one cannot think of an answer of greater propriety.

The second sequence of poems, "Owl's Clover," consists of five meditations in blank verse, all of them concerned with extending the theme of the fate of art amid terrifying change and destruction, and envisaging the kind of place toward which history is moving:

> Shall you,
> Then, fear a drastic community evolved
> From the whirling, slowly and by trial; or fear
> Men gathering for a final flight of men,
> An abysmal migration into possible blue?

The fear is in the foreground and is complicated by the themes which were Stevens' direct subject in *Harmonium*, the brutality and chaos of Nature, which is here figured forth in a new symbol,

Africa; and also the absence of belief, the departure of God, the angels, and heaven. The attitudes toward what is to come are complex and ambiguous, as they ought to be. The poet can only regard the possibilities which he fears and state his hope:

> Basilewsky in the bandstand played
> "Concerto for Airplane and Pianoforte,"
> The newest Soviet reclame. Profound
> Abortion, fit for the enchanting of basilisks. . . .
> What man of folk-lore shall rebuild the world,
> What lesser man shall measure sun and moon,
> What super-animal dictate our fates?
> As the man the state, not as the state the man.

But finally and unequivocally, in the last poem of the volume, the poet salutes the men that are falling, for whom God and the angels have become identical with the cause for which they are falling:

> Taste of the blood upon his martyred lips,
> O pensioners, O demagogues and pay-men!
>
> This death was his belief, though death is a stone
> This man loved earth, not heaven, enough to die.

This is clearly a poetry which flows from a mind in love not only with the beautiful, but also with the just.

There are, however, distinct limitations also. From beginning to end, in *Harmonium* as well as in the present volume, these poems are absorbed in "responses" to various facts. They are absorbed to such an extent that the facts can scarcely get into the poems at all. We may compare Stevens to William Carlos Williams, whom he admires and who may be said to represent the other extreme, a poet whose whole effort is to get facts into his poem with the greatest exactitude and to keep everything else out. One beautiful line in particular in "Owl's Clover" ("The sound of z in the grass all day") emphasizes by contrast how little direct observation there is in Stevens. There is no specific scene, nor time, nor action, but only the mind moving among its meanings and replying to situations which are referred to, but not contained in, the poem itself. "Rocks, moss, stonecrop, iron, merds," another poet writes, "The woman keeps the kitchen, makes tea, Sneezes at evening, poking the peevish gutter." By thus placing the fact within the poem, the response to the fact gains immeasurable strength and relevance. In Stevens, however, the poet "strides" "among the cigar stores, Ryan's lunch, hatters, insurance and medicines" without convincing the reader that he is walking on an actual street. There is always an abstractness present; everything is turned into an object of the imagination. Certain weaknesses result: the word-play does not always escape the adventitious frivolity for which it is always mistaken by the careless reader; the poem is sometimes extended not by a progress of perception, or of meaning, but one word and one phrase multiplies others; and, to sum up these defects, the poet is "too poetic." It may also be that the burden of this style is responsible for the faults which have always been present in Stevens' blank verse, a lack of variety in going from line to line, a difficulty with overflow, and lately, in "Owl's Clover," a tendency to anapestic substitution which unsettles the sonorous Miltonic period.

Virtue and defect, however, seem to be inseparable. The magnificence of the rhetoric necessitates an exclusion of narrative elements, necessitates the whole weight of the verbalism, and, on the other hand, makes possible the extreme range and freedom of the symbols. The blue guitar, the statue, the duck, the greenest continent, and above all the bread and the stone presented here for the first time are figures and metaphors of a richness and meaningfulness which justify the method. The poems taken as a whole constitute a special kind of museum, of a very familiar strangeness, located, because of the extent of the poet's awareness, in the middle of everything which concerns us.

In the Orchards of the Imagination

The occasion of Wallace Stevens' seventy-fifth birthday, marked as it is by the publication of his *Collected Poems*, suggests a variety of comments, a set of rhetorical statements suitable to a celebration. One must say, for example, that Stevens is certainly the best poet who has ever been the vice-president of an insurance company. This sentence is not an effort at a mere epigram, but has a great deal of bearing on the poet's work, the poet as an American, and poetry in America. One must also say: here is a poet who has been writing major poetry for more than half a century, here are more than five hundred pages of his thought and eloquence. Here is a modern poet who has celebrated the fact that it is good to be alive and that the goodness is magnified by that powerful way of being alive which is the writing of poems. For example, one of his poems begins: "What more is there to love than I have loved?" How many human beings, how many poets are capable of this sovereign affirmation?

Stevens' career requires some comment, since it is not only involved in his poetry as such, but it is also one way in which his poetry is important. He has had a double career. He has practised law since 1904, worked for the Hartford Accident and Indemnity Company since 1916, and has been vice-president since 1934. For all of these fifty years he has devoted himself to the writing of poetry, and although his first book was not published until 1922, the six books which have appeared in the past 20 years are characterized by an ever-growing mastery and power, all the more impressive in middle age, a time when most poets, good or bad, tend more and more to self-imitation, or worse.

Anyone who said in 1900, 1910, or even in 1920 that it was possible to be a successful executive and at the same time a first-rate poet would have been regarded as probably jocose and possibly insane: the fact that Pound and Eliot chose to live in Europe is enough to show how peculiar and isolated a poet felt in America. It is still true that there is a fundamental conflict between the vocation of poetry and the middle-class business community. Nevertheless Stevens' career is a parable of what is possible. Too much and too little can be made of Stevens' example. But one can be sure, at least, that Stevens has made the most of the conflict of his situation; has made a fecund virtue out of a difficult necessity.

This is clear in the very style and substance of his poems. The starting-point of Stevens' poems is often the aesthetic experience in isolation from all other experiences, as art is isolated from work, and as a museum is special and isolated in any modern American community. And if one limits oneself to the surface of Stevens' poetic style, one can characterize Stevens as the poet of Sunday: the poet of the week-end, the holiday, and the vacation, who sees objects at a distance, as they appear to the tourist or in the art museum. But this is merely the poet's starting-point. Stevens converts aestheticism into contemplation in the full philosophical and virtually religious sense of the word. The surface of his poetry is very often verbal, visual, and gay; beneath the surface, it is a deadly earnest scrutiny of attitudes toward existence, of "how to live, what to do." The reader begins with the impression that Stevens is a dandy and virtuoso of language, and too many readers have stopped with that impression; but the reader who persists discovers that Stevens is literally a poet of ideas, a philosophical poet; his discourses on thought, existence, nature, and destiny are suave and elegant—and also profound, uniting an underlying seriousness with an ultimate gaiety. The point of view of the man of art, the concert-goer, the student of French poetry—the point of view, in short, of the aesthete—has been transformed from a limitation into a window with "a good light" as the poet says, "for those who know the ultimate Plato."

Stevens has often been much underrated because readers fail to perceive this transformation. The reader begins with such sensuous observations as

The sound of z in the grass all day.

A crinkled paper makes a brilliant sound.

With my whole body I taste these peaches.

Each perception is in itself valuable and beautiful; hence it is understandable enough that the careless reader does not see how often the perceptions are essentially springboards leading to ultimate generalizations, to such formulations of insight and wisdom as

> The greatest poverty is not to live
> In a physical world.

> Adam in Eden was the father of Descartes.

> If sex were all, then every trembling hand
> Could make us speak, like dolls, the wished-for words.

Perhaps the best illustration is one of Stevens' best and most ambitious poems: "Le Monocle de Mon Oncle." The title itself is ironic and flippant and thus misleading; and the poem is written chiefly in the bravura style of such verses as

> Is it for nothing, then, that old Chinese
> Sat titivating by their mountain pools
> Or in the Yangtze studied out their beards.

and

> A frog
> Boomed from his belly odious chords.

But the poem is, in fact, a serious meditation on the nature of love. When the middleaged protagonist describes himself and his wife as "Two golden gourds distended on our vines . . . We hang like warty squashes, streaked and rayed," the mocking ironic grotesqueness is necessary to bring one to the conclusion, the delicate statement of the difficult belief that love makes human beings important and unique, no matter how they look in middle age or at any other time.

R. P. Blackmur was the first to remark (in a pioneer essay on Stevens, in 1932) that Stevens' poems "grow in the mind." They do. The growing continues, astonishing and inexhaustible, and comparable to the experience of living with paintings. And as his poetry grows in one's mind, the greater the abundance of comment which it seems to require. Clearly the primary comment must be the conviction that Stevens is a great poet, that his work as a whole is as important as that of Frost and Eliot. There are so many other things to be said about his work (naturally enough, since it is the fruit of fifty years) that, in a brief essay, one can hardly attempt to do more than name some of them. There is the complex neglected fact that Stevens is a New England poet, like Robinson and Frost, and like Emerson, Thoreau, and Emily Dickinson also. Exhibiting the strains of solitude, exoticism, and Puritanism, his poems are at times comparable to the precious and strange objects which Yankee skippers acquired in the China trade. Then there is Stevens' assimilation and mastery of the lessons of modern painting, *vers libre* and imagism, of the traditional norms of the blank verse style in Shakespeare and Milton, his inventive and original use of place names, of foreign and archaic words, and his witty coinages, his relationship to Whitman and to Baudelaire (two poets who almost never are a combined influence upon any modern poet). And then there is the triumph of his reputation, which like that of Marianne Moore and William Carlos Williams, has been slow but irresistible, and which must be credited solely to that literary sect which is almost wholly devoted to poetry and the criticism of poetry. It would be necessary to deal at length with these and other aspects of Stevens' work to define the important sense in which he is a profoundly modern and purely American poet.

If, however, it were necessary to define Stevens' poetry on the head of a pin, or in a word, perhaps the best word would be: interpretation (which is, I believe, an important part of the law). Interpretation is the key—and the glory—of Stevens' poetry: the power and richness of interpretation is made infinite by the poetic imagination. Uniting interpretation with imagination, Stevens arrives at a system of perspectives which makes or can make anything and everything poetic; everything which exists can be a rich instance of the poetic, once it is seen from the right bias, angle, or attitude of interpretation. If Molière's bourgeois gentleman had lived to read Stevens' poems, he might have been delighted to discover at last that he had been speaking poetry, not prose, all his life without knowing it.

The consummation is inconceivable, even among the modern children of the bourgeois gentleman, but this is only the negative side of the whole truth. It is true that the millions who heard the Elephant polka which Stravinsky composed for Ringling Bros. circus, and the millions of readers—or rather, viewers—of *Life* who saw Marianne Moore photographed on a visit to the zoo, among the animals who inspired some of her best poems, will never remember Stravinsky nor read Miss Moore's poems. But it is also true that millions who sit upon furniture which is what it is because of Picasso have never heard of Cubism. So too the poetry of Stevens will modify the speech and consciousness of many generations indirectly. His inventions, his discoveries, his long labor in the orchards of the imagination will directly affect other poets more and more in the future, giving a new, unintended and triumphant meaning to a pronouncement in his first book which was merely meant to be witty: "I am a man of fortune greeting heirs."

Wallace Stevens
An Appreciation

The death of Wallace Stevens concludes one of the most extraordinary of poetic careers. It is difficult to speak of the death of any human being without soon being overcome by the conviction that silence is the only appropriate speech. When it is the death of a great poet—a very great poet—comment seems inadequate and gratuitous. Perhaps it would be best to describe one of his rare public appearances.

In 1936 Stevens read his poems for the first time at Harvard—it was probably the first time he had ever read his poetry in public—and the occasion was at once an indescribable ordeal and a precious event: precious because he had been an undergraduate and a poet at Harvard some thirty-seven years before and had not returned since then, in his own person, although he had often gone to the Yale-Harvard games incognito. Before and after reading each poem, Stevens spoke of the nature of poetry, a subject which naturally obsessed him: the least sound counts, he said, the least sound and the least syllable. His illustration of this observation was wholly characteristic: he told of how he had wakened that week after midnight and heard the sounds made by a cat walking delicately and carefully on the crusted snow outside his house. He was listening, as in his lifelong vigil of awareness, for such phrases as this one, describing autumn leaves: "The skreak and skritter of evening gone"; no single one of thousands of such inventions is enough to suggest his genius for experience and language.

After his comment, Stevens returned to his typescript, prepared and bound for the occasion with a fabulous elegance which also was characteristic: but an old Cambridge lady, holding an ear trumpet aloft, and dressed in a style which must have been chic at Rutherford Hayes' inauguration, shouted out, hoarse and peremptory as crows, that she must ask Mr. Stevens to speak loudly and clearly, loudly and clearly, if you please. She might just as well have been shouting at President Hayes. Stevens continued in a very low voice, reading poems which were written in that bravura style, that extravagant, luxurious, misunderstood rhetoric which is as passionate as the most excited Elizabethan blank verse. And throughout the reading, although Stevens was extremely nervous and constrained, this showed only as a rigid impassivity which, since it might have expressed a very different state of mind, made his feelings invisible; nevertheless, as such readings became more frequent in recent years, it was impossible to persuade Stevens that no one save himself perceived his overwhelming nervousness, just as, when the first reading ended, Stevens said to the teacher who had introduced him: "I wonder what the boys at the office would think of this?" The office was the Hartford Accident and Indemnity Co., the boys were those who knew him as a vice-president, lawyer, and the most solid of citizens.

No one who thought a poet looked pale, distracted, unkempt and unbarbered was likely to recognize Stevens: he was a physical giant, robust, red-faced, and his large round head suggested not only a banker and judge, but Jupiter. He said then and after that the boys would hardly be more shocked to discover him the secret head of an opium ring—and although I would guess that in this instance he may have mistaken tact for ignorance—the important point is that he felt sure that this was how others regarded a poet. He had written poetry for many years as a kind of "secret vice," and he told many stories about himself of the same kind, resorting to that self-irony which often marks his poetic style.

It was this sense of what it was to be a poet in America which haunted Stevens and inspired his poems; yet if this sense was rooted in American life during his first youth in the 1890's and 1900's, Stevens also belonged to the great and tragic generation, in Europe, of Proust, Valery, and Kafka; for he was only four years younger than Rilke and three years older than Joyce whom he most resembled as a master and revolutionist of language. This temporal and spiritual kinship is often overlooked, probably because

[193]

his first book did not appear until he was 44, and then the critical comments disheartened him so much that he stopped writing for several years, so that his second book did not appear until he was 57. His intimate relationship with his own generation in Europe did not diminish but rather intensified the way in which he was a purely American poet.

The times have changed—and the more they change, the more, surely they are not the same—and it is easy to forget that when Stevens was a young man, the adult male who read a great deal was regarded as, at best, anti-social and probably literally addicted to secret vices: and the adult male, unless he was a foreigner, a gigolo, or a sissy, was supposed to suffer nausea or become co-matose when forced by his wife to go to the opera. You have only to see how often in the comics, the opera is a punishment, like the Black Hole of Calcutta; or you need merely read another great writer, Ring Lardner, making fun of *Carmen* to see how typical and how natural Stevens' feelings about being a poet were.

It is important to remember these matters, and to speak of the origins of Stevens' extreme shyness as a poet and about poetry, because it is so much a part of the quality of his work; and unless it is understood, this style is misunderstood as merely exquisite banter. This attitude and depth of feeling links Stevens with his forebears, with Poe, Whitman, Emily Dickinson, Melville, and all the others who, although they have known a spell of recognition and limelight, concluded in solitude, silence, obscurity or exile. Emily Dickinson made one pathetic attempt to publish her poems during her lifetime, and during the last 30 years of his life, Melville, having written the Great American Novel, hardly appeared in print at all. Thus one of the most wonderful things about Stevens is the new and astonishing ending which he gave to the old and tragic story. Stevens was neither reduced to silence nor compelled to exile; he transformed a limiting or wasting weakness into a powerful source of poetry and made solitude a mountain full of views denied to the valley.

It is clearly too soon to estimate the value of Stevens' poetry with justice, and nothing short of a detailed essay would make plausible what will surely seem personal and an over-estimation, my own conviction that the more than 500 pages of Stevens' *Collected*

Poems make a book as important as *Leaves of Grass*. The very charm and beauty of Stevens' language misleads the reader often: delighted with the tick and tock, the heigh ho of Hoon and Jocundus, "jubilating," "in the presto of the morning," the reader often missed the basic substance, the joy that for the moment at least the poet has grasped "the veritable *ding an sich* at last": for Stevens was essentially a philosophical poet, the rarest of all kinds, seeking always "in a good light for those who know the ultimate Plato," to see and possess "the nothing that is not there, and the nothing that is." It is natural enough not to recognize that a poem called *Le Monocle de Mon Oncle* is a serious discourse on the nature of love; a poem named *The Comedian As the Letter C,* may be a serious analysis of the perennial attitudes toward experience, but it is much longer than most poems that most readers of poetry read; and the title of *Thirteen Ways of Looking At a Blackbird* hardly makes clear the fact that its subject is everything involved in looking, loving, and living.

The primary philosophical motive leads to a major limitation— the meditative mode is a solitude which excludes the dramatic and narrative poet's human character and personality. But it also leads to a great access: Stevens, studying Picasso and Matisse, made the art of poetry visual in a way it has never been before, and made him the first poet to be influenced, very often in the same poem, by Shakespeare, Cubism, the Symbolist movement, and modern philosophy since Kant. And thus it is, that when John Crowe Ransom affirms Stevens' character as a philosophical poet, in the current issue of the *Kenyon Review,* he naturally adds that "surely no poet has written more verse about the understanding of poetry, unless it be Wordsworth." Just as Wordsworth mastered nature anew and made it more available to consciousness, so Stevens made the dimension of art open in a new way to consciousness.

Finally it would be wrong, in thus emphasizing his original genius, not to speak of how traditional his poetry is, how Stevens continues and renews the greatest rhetorical mode in English, the mode of blank verse in which Shakespeare and Milton wrote. Here, from the conclusion to *Academic Discourse in Havana,* is a passage which is representative at once of Stevens' eloquence, his possession of poetic tradition, his conception of the poet's role and

[195]

conviction that poetry may be "an infinite incantation of ourselves":

> Is the function of the poet here mere sound,
> Subtler than the ornatest prophecy,
> To stuff the ear? . . .
> As part of nature, he is part of us.
> His rarities are ours: may they be fit
> And reconcile us to our selves in those
> True reconcilings, dark pacific words . . .
> Close the cantina. Hood the chandelier.
> The moonlight is not yellow, but a white
> That silences the ever-faithful town.
> How pale and how possessed a night it is,
> How full of exhalations of the sea. . . .
> All this is older than the oldest hymn,
> Has no more meaning than tomorrow's bread
> But let the poet on his balcony
> Speak and the sleepers in their sleep shall move
> Waken, and watch the moonlight on their floors.
> This may be benediction, sepulcher,
> And epitaph. It may, however, be
> An incantation that the moon defines
> By mere example opulently clear.

How, reading such passages, which are a multitude, can we fail
to understand the poet's triumphant affirmation: "What more is
there to love than I have loved?" and lived? The Hoon—the
human alone—which he calls himself in a number of poems became in his recent work Jocundus; his poems became "the auroras
of Autumn"; Peter Quince "at the clavier" became "Professor
Eucalyptus," declaring that "the search for reality is as momentous
as the search for god," making continual "addresses to the
Academy of Fine Ideas," and once more reporting, in the last poem
of his collected volume, on "the thing itself"; a bird's "scrawny
cry," in the first morning, is that of "a chorister whose c preceded
the choir," it is a part of "the colossal sun's choral rings" and it is
truly "a new knowledge of reality": Prince of the realm and of
English, majestic voice, sovereign of the mind and of light, master
of reality.

The Cunning and the Craft of the Unconscious and the Preconscious

Words for the Wind, by Theodore Roethke

It is sufficiently clear by now that Theodore Roethke is a very important poet. It is also more than likely that his reputation among readers of poetry is based, for the most part, upon the extraordinary lyrics in his second and third volumes. These poems appear, at first glance, to be uncontrollable and subliminal outcries, the voices of roots, stones, leaves, logs, small birds; and they also resemble the songs in Shakespearean plays, Ophelia's songs perhaps most of all. This surface impression is genuine and ought not to be disregarded. But it is only the surface, however moving, and as such, it can be misleading or superficial. The reader who supposes that Roethke is really a primitive lyric poet loses or misses a great deal. Perhaps the best way to define the substance of Roethke's poetry is to quote Valéry's remarkable statement that the nervous system is the greatest of all poems.

The enchanted depths beneath the chanting surface become more recognizable when the reader goes through this new collection with care from beginning to end. Throughout his work, Roethke uses a variety of devices with the utmost cunning and craft to bring the unconscious to the surface of articulate expression. But he avoids the danger and the temptation—which is greater for him than for most poets—of letting this attentiveness to the depths of experience become glib and mechanical, a mere formula for lyricism, which, being willed as a formula, would lose its genuineness and spontaneity. Roethke's incantatory lyrics are not, as they may first seem, all alike; on the contrary, each of them has a uniqueness and individuality.

In a like way, when, in his latest poems, Roethke seems to be

imitating not only the manner but the subject-matter of Yeats—
and even the phrasing—this too may very well be misleading if it
is taken as *merely* imitation: for, first of all, it is paradoxical and
true that the most natural and frequent path to true originality, for
most good poets, is through imitating the style of a very great
poet; secondly, Roethke has begun to imitate Yeats in mid-career,
when he is at the height of his powers; and finally, since Yeats is
a very different kind of poet than Roethke, the imitation is itself
a feat of the imagination: Yeats discovered the concreteness and
colloquialism which made him a very great poet only after many
phases of vagueness, meandering through the long Celtic twilight;
while Roethke's mastery of concreteness of image and thing has
served him in good stead from the very start. It is likely enough
that the chief reason Roethke has followed Yeats's later style has
been to guard against the deadly habit of self-imitation which has
paralyzed some of the best poets in English—from Wordsworth to
Edwin Arlington Robinson—soon after they enjoyed—at long
last—the natural and longed-for recognition of the readers of
poetry, after decades of misunderstanding, abuse, and very often
the scorn of established critics.

If we compare one of Roethke's new, Yeatsian poems with the
kind of poem which it appears to echo and imitate, we can hardly
fail to discover not only the differences between the two writers, but
something about all of Roethke's poems and about Yeats also.

Here is Roethke in his most Yeatsian phase: this is a stanza from
a poem called *The Pure Fury:*

> The pure admire the pure and live alone;
> I love a woman with an empty face.
> Parmenides put nothingness in place;
> She tries to think and it flies loose again.
> How slow the changes of a golden mean:
> Great Boehme rooted all in yes and no;
> At times my darling squeaks in pure Plato.

And here is a stanza from *Among School Children,* one of the
best of all poems of the language, which I quote for close reading,
though it is or should be familiar to all readers of poetry:

> Plato thought nature but a spume that plays
> Upon a ghostly paradigm of things;

[198]

> Solider Aristotle played the taws
> Upon the bottom of a king of kings;
> World-famous golden-thighed Pythagoras
> Fingered upon a fiddle-stick or strings
> What a star sang and careless Muses heard:
> Old clothes upon old sticks to scare a bird.

The attitude and emotion in the latter poem is precisely the opposite of Roethke's; for Yeats, in this poem, as in so many of his later poems is full of a *contemptus mundi,* a scorn of nature, a detestation of history, which has left him an old man, however gifted: he too like the scarecrow face of the Leda-like beauty with whom he had been in love, has been by "the honey of generation betrayed." And this is why he ends his poem by saying: "How shall we know the dancer from the dance?", a Heraclitean statement that all is process and nothing is reality, except, as in other poems, the frozen artificial reality of Byzantium. And his poem is affirmative only in the sense of confronting despair and death: it is very close to Valéry's *La Cimitière Marin,* where existence itself and the mind of the poet seem the sole flaw in the pure diamond of being, so that Valéry's affirmation too is hardly more than "Il faut tenter de vivre" and he too is appalled by the reality of process and unable to believe in another reality.

Roethke is capable of far greater affirmation—which is not to say that he is, as yet, as good as Yeats and Valéry, but that he is original and important enough to be compared to both poets, and to be regarded as having his own uniqueness. Thus he concludes this, one of his most Yeatsian poems, with the stanza:

> Dream of a woman, and a dream of death;
> The light air takes my being's breath away;
> I look on white and it turns into gray—
> When will that creature give me back my breath?
> I live near the abyss, I hope to stay
> Until my eyes look at a brighter sun
> As the thick shade of the long night comes on.

And it is worth adding that the difficulty of affirmation and hope, and the reality of the abyss have become more and more clear, more and more appalling, for poets alive today, as for all of us, than they were for Yeats when he wrote *Among School Children,* and for Valéry when he wrote *La Cimitière Marin.*

[199]

On Fiction
·III·

The Duchess' Red Shoes

I

🦋 Good manners are very pleasant and literary criticism is often very inneresting, to be colloquial. When, however, manners become a major concept in literary criticism, that is something else again: it is an inneruption, to be colloquial again.

Just before manners came to the fore, the big word in literary criticism was myth: everything was myth; at the drop of a hat, or if anyone dropped a hat, that was a myth or at least had a mythical significance. And in a way it was true, of course, since any particular thing belongs to a general class of things which is part of the universe and the universal order of things; and by rapid generalizations, going from a particular hat to all hats, hatness and all hats as forms of dress, dress as a form of decoration, and decoration as a form of illusion, one soon arrives at the distinction between appearance and reality and is in the very heartland of myth. For everything in its very nature does have or can have or can be made to have a mythical meaning. The only trouble is this: the more lofty the generality, the more inclusive the myth, the more symbolic the symbol, the less attention one gives to the concreteness and particularity of things and literary works; and these qualities tend to be fairly important. Of this fact I was reminded recently while reading an essay by a Swiss critic on F. Scott Fitzgerald, in which the doctrines of Kant, Kierkegaard, Nietzsche, St. Augustine and Pascal were all made to apply to the life and work of Fitzgerald; and their doctrines did apply, since as philosophers they dealt with all men. The only thing wrong was that Fitzgerald might have lived all his life in Bulgaria, and it would not have made any difference or interfered with the Swiss critic's disquisitions.

The same or a like process of thought—broad, broader, and broadest generalizations—clouds the literary discussion of manners. Long before manners became fashionable in literary criticism, Yvor Winters, writing about Henry James's novels in *Maule's Curse,* said that the great novelist knew "next to nothing of the detail, the manners, of any single and reasonably representative class in its native environment." The result, said Mr. Winters, was that James tended to isolate the moral sense in his novels "from the manners which might have given it concreteness." Mr. Winters' thesis was at least understandable. It had never occurred to me in reading the novels of James, or, for that matter, in reading Racine and Sophocles, that the absence of the daily detail of life and of the observation of manners made the rendering of a moral sense any the less meaningful and intense. But, after all, I felt, Mr. Winters is a man of the world while I am virtually a recluse, so that perhaps I have no basis of judgment.

Some time after, a close friend of mine told me that at the age of 16 she had read Dostoevsky's *The Idiot* and liked it very much and thought that human beings were really what Dostoevsky portrayed them as being, but everyone she knew was engaged in covering up! This rather extreme conclusion made me remember Mr. Winters' dictum about the observation of manners as being necessary to the representation of a moral sense in works of fiction. My friend's remark suggested that one function of manners was to conceal morals and motives, which in turn illuminated Dostoevsky: *The Brothers Karamazov,* for example, was certainly about manners: it was about bad manners. *My snobbish error had been to assume that any reference to manners meant good manners!* Of course Dostoevsky's novel was really about something else, including an intense moral sense. But the bad manners of the characters were clearly necessary. The same was true of *Moby Dick*: it was about the bad manners of the White Whale when he met Captain Ahab and bit him. As for Captain Ahab, he was no gentleman, for he harbored a grudge, which is not good manners.

At this point I enjoyed that access of well-being which comes from the belief that one has succeeded in understanding something. But suddenly I dropped into a new bewilderment. For I remembered that, according to the prior school of literary thought, *Moby Dick*, like all great works of literature, was supposed to be a myth. If it was a myth essentially, could it be about manners superficially? Perhaps. But how about Shakespeare? What was the myth in *Othello*? What were the manners? Of course we might maintain that Iago was no gentleman, morally speaking, but he did seem to have good manners. And we might suppose that Iago created the myth of Desdemona's infidelity in Othello's mind, thus causing the sad tragedy. *Macbeth* also might be said to be about how rude a host and his wife can be to a guest, which was clearly bad manners again. These speculations were enough to make me wonder whether I had lost my mind.

II

I was sure that I would suffer such alarms when I reread Lionel Trilling's essay, "Manners, Morals and the Novel," in his book, *The Liberal Imagination*. For Mr. Trilling writes with much care, lucidity and solicitude for all sides of every question. His style is one of extreme tact and judiciousness. But beneath the surface of Mr. Trilling's style, a powerful point of view asserts itself.

In "Manners, Morals and the Novel," as elsewhere, Mr. Trilling pleads for moral realism. It is mere carping to observe that no one in his right mind will admit that he is against moral realism and in favor of moral unrealism. For by moral realism Mr. Trilling means a view of life which is critical of moral idealism, and its twin, social idealism. Of course no moral idealist and no social idealist will admit for a split second that he is not also a moral realist: he would claim of course that he is morally more realistic than most. Nevertheless I think Mr. Trilling's basic point is that we have too much moral and social idealism or have been too uncritical, particularly as social idealists and liberals, so that moral realism is now necessary to right the balance.

The novel, Mr. Trilling says, is one of the best ways in which we can achieve moral realism, for "the characteristic work of the novel is to record the illusion that snobbery generates and to try to penetrate to the truth which, as the novel assumes, lies hidden behind all false appearances. . . ." But to get the truth beneath false appearances, one must concentrate upon or possess a knowledge of false appearances, and here the novel excels and the observation

of manners becomes very important: "The novel then, is a perpetual quest for reality, the field of its research being always the
social world, the material of its analysis being always manners as
an indication of man's soul." This eloquent formulation is marred
by the double use of "always" and by the extremely ambiguous
reference, given the context, to manners. For Mr. Trilling began
his essay by saying that what he meant by manners was virtually
indefinable. He continued by making a series of assertions which
were intended to substitute a kind of circumscription for a definition: he did not mean "the rules of personal intercourse in our culture; and yet such rules were by no means irrelevant" nor did he
mean "manners in the sense of *mores*, customs," although that
meaning was also relevant. "What I understand by manners, then,
is a culture's hum and buzz of implication . . . that part of culture
which is made up of half-uttered or unuttered or unutterable expressions of value . . . the things that for good or bad draw the people of a culture together." This is Mr. Trilling's broad definition of
manners. Throughout his essay, however, he sometimes uses a
limited and very different definition of manners, namely, the manners of particular social classes and groups in a given social hierarchy. It is by moving back and forth between his broad (and
tentative) definition and his limited (and unexpressed) definition
that Mr. Trilling is able to hold forth *Don Quixote* as a true novel
(here the broad definition works) while *The Scarlet Letter* (here it
is the limited definition) suffers "from a lack of social texture" and
is, like almost all American novels, not concerned with society at
all.[1] How can one say, in terms of Mr. Trilling's broad definition,
that *The Scarlet Letter, Moby Dick*[2] and *Huckleberry Finn* lack
social texture? The equivalent would be to say that *Walden* is not
about society because it deals with a solitary individual. In the same
way, again, it is only by using his limited definition and ignoring
his broad one that Mr. Trilling can quote and agree with James

1. It is important to note, in passing, that unlike Yvor Winters, Mr. Trilling believes that James knew very well that to write novels, one had "to
use the ladder of social observation." Hawthorne did say, as Mr. Trilling
points out, that his books were "romances," and not "novels." But Hawthorne meant by a romance precisely such a book as *Don Quixote*.
2. As Irving Howe has observed, *Moby Dick* is, among other things, a
celebration of the manners of a free, open, democratic society in which
candor, friendship and equality are always desirable and necessary.

Fenimore Cooper and Henry James on "the thick social texture of English life and the English novel" in the nineteenth century as opposed to the thinness of American life and the American novel: for in terms of his broad definition there was just as much social texture in America as in England; it was a different social texture as it was a different society and it was not the kind of social texture that James was interested in; but it had just as much of "a culture's hum and buzz of implication," etc., which Mr. Trilling says he means by manners.

There was an adequate subject matter for some kinds of fiction in Hawthorne's and James's America, as we can see when we read the great historians, or a history of American politics, or the poems of Whitman and Emily Dickinson, or the biographies of Poe, Hawthorne, Melville, Aaron Burr, John Randolph of Roanoke, Daniel Webster, Henry Clay, Stephen Douglas, Abraham Lincoln, Mark Twain, Henry Adams, and others. It is true that Hawthorne and James did not know how to get into any full relationship with this rich subject matter. The reasons for their estrangement are complicated and have to do with personal disabilities as well as the literary and intellectual traditions which nurtured them. To say, however, that the thinness of American life caused the thinness of American fiction is an extreme oversimplification. It is not far from criticizing the Civil War as a war and as a subject for epic poetry because no major American poet has written an epic about it! And in this labyrinthine question, Mr. Trilling's intuition and insight are superior to James's, although he quotes James with approval. For Mr. Trilling sees, as James did not, that there is often something wrong in the relationship of the sensibility of the American writer to American society. It is Mr. Trilling's description of what is wrong which is extremely questionable: he says that Americans have the wrong idea of reality, but his conception of the right idea of reality, so far as I understand it, merely substitutes a new overemphasis and a new one-sidedness for an old one. If we are asked to choose between Jane Austen's and Henry James's idea of reality, on the one hand, and John Steinbeck's or Theodore Dreiser's on the other hand (Dreiser is Mr. Trilling's example), what can we answer but that we choose both and neither?

To continue, however, with Mr. Trilling's positive recommendations: "Now the novel as I have described it has never really established itself in America. Not that we have not had great novels, but that the novel in America diverges from its classic intention which, as I have said, is the investigation of reality beginning in the social field. The fact is that American writers of genius have not turned their minds to society." The latter sentence makes sense only if Mr. Trilling gives a very limited meaning to the word society. This becomes clear when Mr. Trilling explains why American writers have turned away from "society": "Americans have a kind of resistance to looking closely at society. They appear to believe that to touch upon a matter of class is somehow to demean ourselves." Which is to say that unless one is concerned with class and snobbery one is not really concerned with "society." One has turned one's mind away from "society" unless one is at least in part concerned with "high society" where, it is commonly believed, most snobbery begins or resides. And thus, since class, snobbery, and high society must be involved, the manners in question may after all be the good manners of so-called "polite society."

Recent American novelists have been concerned, Mr. Trilling says, with society in still another sense of the word, the sociological and political one. They have been concerned with social problems and social ideals, social conditions and broad human sympathies which educated Americans tend to think more important than the observation of manners. Hence "we have no books that raise questions in our minds not only about conditions, but about ourselves, that lead us to refine our motives and ask what might lie behind our impulses." The novel which is truly concerned with the social world and "society" has been "the literary form to which the motives of understanding and forgiveness were indigenous." Moreover, "so creative is the novelist's awareness of manners that we may say that it is a function of his love," and in neglecting the observation of manners, "we have lost something of our power of love."

What, it may well be asked, can be the reasonable objection to a critical doctrine which calls for moral realism, the observation of manners, the pursuit of reality, and the penetration of snobbery for the sake of understanding, forgiveness and love? Who can possibly be against understanding, forgiveness and love? Clearly we can never have too much of these qualities; we often have too little; and a vision of the novel which will increase our portion of charity certainly deserves the most passionate assent and allegiance.

The full force of what is difficult and troubling in Mr. Trilling's views cannot be made clear until we come to Mr. John Aldridge, who, by quoting Mr. Trilling, seems to make his views a starting-point and who prompted my rereading of Mr. Trilling's essay. Yet clearly Mr. Trilling is not wholly responsible for Mr. Aldridge's statements. It may be true that Mr. Aldridge has been brash and rash enough to make explicit some of the direct implications of Mr. Trilling's doctrine of manners in literature. Yet since all talk of implication risks the injustice of imputation, let me try to stick for a while longer to what Mr. Trilling says explicitly. He says that Shakespeare bears out his thesis and Dostoevsky does too: "The establishment of a person of low class in the privileges of a high class always suggested to Shakespeare's mind some radical instability of the senses and reason." Here Mr. Trilling is speaking of society in the sense of social status, and, unless I am entirely deceived, he is saying that we have the authority of the greatest of poets for the view that any change of social status is derangement and madness: is this Shakespeare's penetration of the illusion that snobbery generates? Is not Mr. Trilling saying that for Shakespeare, snobbery is no illusion; that for Shakespeare the illusion, delusion, and insanity, is to imagine a human being ever becoming somewhat free of his social status?[3]

As for Dostoevsky, he is cited by Mr. Trilling in an analogous manner: "The Russian novel, exploring the ultimate possibilities

3. It is impossible to make out what Mr. Trilling has in mind, concretely, in making this generalization about Shakespeare's social attitudes. He cites *Twelfth Night*, *A Midsummer Night's Dream*, *The Taming of the Shrew*, no other instances; and he does not explain how important, or unimportant, the madness of social climbing is to the theme and substance of each play. But surely *As You Like It*, in which a king and his followers prefer the equality of the forest to their place at the top of the social hierarchy, and *The Tempest*, in which Prospero makes a like choice with equal conviction, are but two important examples of how for Shakespeare to give up class status entirely, despite one's lofty or regal station, is not only *not* madness, but on the contrary is liberation, freedom, self-realization and a profound accession to superior individuality and magical existence.

of the human spirit, must start and end in class—every situation in Dostoevsky, no matter how spiritual, starts[4] with a point of social pride and a certain number of rubles." This may seem plausible enough at first glance, for it is not far from such comprehensive remarks as that every situation, no matter how spiritual, has its roots in physical reality, social reality, psychological reality, or the like. But as soon as one breaks with the suavity and the fluency of Mr. Trilling's prose style long enough to think of Dostoevsky's novels, the plausibility disappears: is the struggle between Dmitri Karamazov and his father for the favors of Grushenka a matter of *social* pride, even at the start? Only if we redefine social pride so broadly that it has to do with the Oedipus complex and the libido and hence is really not social pride at all. And the rubles which Grushenka wants: is it money that she wants, or love and revenge, which are a matter of *personal* pride; unless we want to stretch meanings again to make all personal pride inseparable from or derived from social pride? Do the arguments between Ivan and Alyosha Karamazov about the existence of God have anything to do, at the start or at any other time, with rubles or social pride? We know that in some circles, religious belief is connected with social pride in the form of social reaction, but surely Mr. Trilling would not accept so sophistical a version of social pride or so dishonest a version of religious belief. Could Mr. Trilling, without casuistical ingenuity, maintain that the poem of the Grand Inquisitor is a matter of social pride or rubles? Are rubles or social pride involved when Alyosha is revolted by the decaying corpse of the Elder Zossima? Of course, better embalming methods and a concern for personal hygiene might be by elaborate extension connected with social pride, but certainly this cannot be Mr. Trilling's meaning. And this is but one novel; the negative examples would make an interminable list. Only by an expandable and contractable definition of manners and of society can it be maintained that "every situation" or even most situations in Dostoevsky "start and end in class" or in "a point of social pride and a certain number of rubles," or are in any serious sense a question of manners at all.

4. "Starts" is a deceptive word. Mr. Trilling uses "begins" in a like way: "The greatness of *Great Expectations* begins in its title."

It is also difficult to see how there can have been great American novels, as Mr. Trilling says there have been, if the novel as he has described it "never really established itself in America." Here Mr. Trilling is operating again with several ambiguous definitions at the same time; the novel in its classic form which begins with the observation of manners and of the "social" world; the great American novels which are somehow great, although unconcerned with manners, lacking in social texture, and turned away from society; and lastly, some unformulated but all-reconciling conception of the novel which permits novels of classic intention and American novels to be, in the same sense, novels, and, in the same sense, great novels. The truth, I would guess, is that Mr. Trilling likes novels about society, and about the social world, better than other kinds of novels; and he makes it clear that he wants novelists to write about manners and the social world, presenting a thick social texture. There is no reason to question this as a personal preference; but it is erected by Mr. Trilling into a standard of judgment and a program for the novelist, and it leads Mr. Trilling to suggest, indeed almost to insist, that novels about society and the social world are the *best* vehicles of understanding, forgiveness, and love, while other novels are inferior vehicles, if indeed they are capable of supporting these qualities at all. But is it, after all, true that *The Scarlet Letter, Moby Dick* and *Huckleberry Finn* possess less understanding, forgiveness and love than the novels of Jane Austen (which are certainly concentrated on manners), or the novels of Dickens, Thackeray and Meredith (which are presumably part of what Mr. Trilling has in mind when he praises the nineteenth-century English novel as superior to the nineteenth-century American novel)?

The Brothers Karamazov is the best novel I ever read about understanding, forgiveness and love. It is not, to reiterate, in any literal sense about manners, society and the social world; nor, for that matter, are *The Idiot* or *Crime and Punishment,* which are almost as good, and which are of permanent interest to all human beings not because they present the observation of the manners of a given society (or make essential use of such observation), but because they are about the innermost depths of all human beings.

Mr. Trilling is often difficult to understand because he is so sensitive to all points of view, so conscious of others and of opposition, so active and ingenious at formulating his own view in such a way that it does not seem to disturb but rather to accommodate and assimilate itself to other points of views. And his critical method and style are an admirable expression of this sensitive attitude. Mr. Trilling is not using literature as a springboard toward sentiments and ideas about society. He is not using ideas about society in order to illuminate literature. Fundamentally (at least so far as I can make out), Mr. Trilling is interested in the ideas and attitudes and interests of the educated class, such as it is and such as it may become: it is of this class that he is, at heart, the guardian and the critic. Hence he cannot be criticized without bearing this intention in mind.

But given this intention, his use of the medium of literary criticism is misleading. He advocates literary opinions which would be immediately repugnant if he did not introduce them and connect them with a critique of social tendencies. And he entertains social views (and social misgivings) which would be intolerable if they were presented nakedly, as social criticism or a politcial program, instead of being united with literary considerations.

The best example of this process of mind, and one directly relavant to his essay on "Manners, Morals and the Novel," is the critique of liberalism throughout *The Liberal Imagination,* which he makes as one who is a professed liberal and a professional literary critic. He uses literary standards and values to establish the weaknesses and limitations of liberalism when he writes: "The modern European literature to which we can have an active, reciprocal relationship, which is the right relationship to have, has been written by men who are indifferent to, or even hostile to, the tradition of democratic liberalism. Yeats and Eliot, Proust and Joyce, Lawrence and Gide—these men do not seem to confirm us in the social and political ideals which we hold."

This is an inaccurate formulation and a false emphasis for a number of reasons. First, the great authors whom Mr. Trilling cites do not confirm any social and political group whatever in their social and political ideals: what group, political or social, has found in Joyce, Gide or Proust a genuine confirmation of their ideals? Second, there is the apparent fact, to which I will return, that Mr. Trilling does not admire these authors very much or with a great deal of conviction. And lastly, although these great authors are not democratic liberals, there is one important and essential element in their creative work which does literally support democratic liberalism, if indeed one has to ask whether democratic liberalism is being supported by any work of contemporary literature: Yeats was inspired by Irish nationalism, by folk poetry, and by the speech of the people; Eliot, on the surface the least sympathetic to liberalism, not only draws upon cockney speech and the music hall, but he presents a vision of modern life and modern human beings which, despite his avowed social allegiances, lends itself to a doctrine of social change and not to a doctrine of social conservatism, if again, the question must be raised; Proust's extensive and crucial use of the Dreyfus case is identical with democratic liberalism and would have been impossible without it; Lawrence's sexual heroes are lower class: they are game-keepers, and the like, and possess an emotional vitality lacking in the middle class and the aristocracy who are impotent or somewhat crippled sexually by their social station and by the tyranny of industrial capitalism; Joyce's sympathy for and concentration upon the common man (who is a Jew and a target of anti-Semitism), upon daily life, and upon the speech of the people, is the center of his work, and he is certainly neither indifferent nor hostile to the tradition of democratic liberalism; and finally Gide's justification and celebration of individualism, like his concern with social injustice, is one essential part of his work and genuinely "confirms" the tradition of democratic liberalism.

It is true that very often only *one* essential element in these authors supports the democratic liberal; other elements move in other directions; and all elements move in the direction of something which transcends all social and political ideals and is relevant to all of them, since the books in question are works of the imagination. And if we distinguish between the creative works of these authors, and their critical prose (in which, in an erratic and fey way, they sometimes praise a landed aristocracy as one might praise Shangri-La and Utopia), we cannot assert that their creative work is unequivocally indifferent to or hostile to democratic liberalism unless a merciless condemnation of French society in terms of the Dreyfus case can be interpreted as hostility and indifference to liberalism.

But though Mr. Trilling cites the greatness of these great authors, whenever he deals directly with literary values he is much more drawn to Forster, James, Howells and Keats, than to Joyce and Eliot; and he has the most serious misgivings about the extremism, the bias and the methods of all modernist authors.

But my emphasis upon Mr. Trilling's literary opinions also verges on exaggeration and falsehood. Mr. Trilling is neither a social liberal nor a social reactionary, neither a literary modernist nor a literary philistine. His literary allegiances depend upon the relationship of any author's work to Mr. Trilling's essential concern and anxiety, which is, to repeat, the welfare of the educated class: he is a guardian of its interests and a critic of its ideas. As the prestige and the problems of that class change, Mr. Trilling's literary opinions and social views also tend to change, and quite rightly, given his essential purpose.

To mention but one such change: In "Manners, Morals and the Novel" (1947), Mr. Trilling writes: "Howells never fulfilled himself because, although he saw the social subject clearly, he would never take it with full seriousness." In "The Roots of Modern Taste" (Partisan Review, Sept.-Oct. 1951), he praises Howells while virtually disregarding any failure to take the social subject with full seriousness. Among Howells' other virtues, "For Howells the center of reality was the family life of the middle class."

III

One thing usually leads to another, particularly in literary criticism. Last May, John Aldridge, who does not require as lengthy a scrutiny as Mr. Trilling, published in PARTISAN REVIEW a communication on "Manners and Values" in which he says that "it is through manners particularly as they take the form of what Lionel Trilling calls 'a conscious realization of social class,' that dramatic vitality and conflict have traditionally entered the world of fiction." He continues by stating that American writers have been increasingly unsuccessful because "in the last thirty or forty years the only contact American writers have had with manners has been with their disappearance." Mr. Aldridge then states that apart from Faulkner, Marquand and Robert Penn Warren, "we have had no considerable novelist of manners." This is because "there are only two cultural pockets [!] left in America, and they are in the deep South and that area of the northeastern United States whose moral [!] capital is Boston, Massachusetts." Everywhere else in America all other human beings inhabit a moral void, "a sort of infinite Middle West, and that means that they don't really live and that they don't really do anything," and certainly none of them have any manners whatever.

I think Mr. Aldridge must mean by manners, good manners. His charming conviction, which I would be overjoyed to possess, made me consult my own narrow experience. I had visited the deep South and found the manners there mighty pleasant; and the good manners certainly helped most folks very much in communicating with each other and being friendly. I had also lived in the "moral capital" of New England where everyone was always very polite, unless drunk. But neither in the deep South nor in the great moral capital was it possible for me to recognize how manners, good or bad, had the vital and fructifying connection with literature which Aldridge gets so excited about. In fact, almost all of the polite, well-mannered people were absolutely uninterested in literature at all. And one of the few exceptions, a person of exalted station, and also a Brahmin, once remarked to me that the only people in America he knew with good manners were Negroes. But probably he was just joking or being supercilious. However, T. S. Eliot was probably not joking when he said of Boston "society" that it was "quite uncivilized, but refined beyond the point of civilization." It is likely enough that Mr. Aldridge has spent more time in Boston in recent years than Mr. Eliot. Time is irrelevant, however. It does seem that one must choose between the views of the two critics; both cannot be right.

Nevertheless Mr. Aldridge does have some kind of point. Certainly the human beings in a subway rush are hardly to be considered well-mannered. This does not make them seem less worthy of being the subject of fiction than people in the deep South. But here Mr. Aldridge might invoke the illustrous word of Henry James who supposed that Emma Bovary was less worthy of attention than Anna Karenina because the latter was a member of the nobility, a statement which does not seem to jibe with the greatness of either *Madame Bovary* or *Anna Karenina* as works of fiction, and does seem, if I may make so bold as to say, to be a bit on the snobbish side. Snobbish also, perhaps, is James's belief that Flaubert really went too far in *Un Coeur Simple* by making a servant girl his heroine. But, after all, Flaubert is not alive today and does not know as Mr. Aldridge does how awful it is to live in the United States where almost no one has any manners whatever.

IV

Mr. Aldridge's communication drove me to a desperate resort, creating as it did the feeling that one had to find out what manners really are for the sake of deepening one's understanding of literature and literary criticism. Fortunately this fall a new book on good manners was published, Amy Vanderbilt's *Complete Book of Etiquette*. It is a work which should fascinate and educate most readers, if it is true, as Mr. Aldridge says, that most people in America have no maners at all. Mrs. Vanderbilt is kindly, clear, patient, democratic, liberal, tolerant: she tells one how to address dukes, ambassadors and rabbis, how to leave early without "elaborate and lengthy excuses," how to get rid of guests who won't go home: I doubt that Mrs. Vanderbilt's methods would work with some of my acquaintances, but Mrs. Vanderbilt might make a rather pointed remark in answer. She also takes up the question of what to do about guests and friends who are problem drinkers; before dinner, she says, give all guests two drinks, after dinner give them just one drink and no more: "The most agreeable solution, naturally, would be to omit from our guest list anyone who is a problem drinker. But as this is rarely [!] possible for business [!] or family [!] reasons, the only thing we can do, as hosts and hostesses, is to keep a sharp eye on the source of supply, keep track of each round, and lock up all the alcohol [!], including wine and beer, after a reasonable [!] amount has been dispensed."[5] This advice, unlike most of Mrs. Vanderbilt's counsel, seemed like madness to me. It also seemed impractical, since the problem drinkers

5. The exclamation points are mine.

would soon break off relations or would· arrive with their own liquor and stay until they had finished. Mad, impractical, and also rude, unpleasant and impractical. But by and large Mrs. Vanderbilt is illuminating as well as magnanimous; she tells one how often to have one's hair cut, how often to take a bath, how to brush one's teeth, how to feel about being bald (think nothing of it: "Satyrs are depicted as bald"), and how important it is to smell good, since human beings have more in common with the hound than is usually supposed, a reference which did seem a little indelicate and invidious.

My study of Mrs. Vanderbilt was suddenly halted and I was restored to literature abruptly when I read about the well-groomed man's attitude toward his shoes: "My grandfather often used to say that he judged a man by his shoes. Perhaps he was saying that our external effect is the only one most people see and judge us by." This left me thunderstruck. For I could not help but remember the heartbreaking scene in Marcel Proust's great novel when Swann goes with news to see his intimate friends, the Duc and Duchesse de Guermantes, who love him very much; his news is that he is dying. Since they are extremely fond of him, his death is hardly a matter of indifference to them. But these supreme products of an aristocracy—who would, moreover, consider Mr. Aldridge's gentle folk of the deep South and Boston as *parvenus* and *arrivistes*—can think of nothing to say![6] Until after much squirming, the Duke, overwhelmed with anxiety because his wife is wearing the wrong shoes for the dinner they are going to, hustles her away to get the right ones.

The passage is, of course, famous and has been cited many times. Edmund Wilson, in *Axel's Castle*, summing up Proust's attitude as a whole, says after remarking upon this and two other like episodes: "In each case, Proust has destroyed, and destroyed with ferocity, the social hierarchy he has just been expounding. Its values, he tells us, are an imposture; pretending to honor and distinction, it accepts all that is vulgar and base; its pride is nothing nobler than the instinct it shares with the woman who keeps the

6. They invented the words. The manners in Proust are never superior to those of Huck Finn and Jim, or Ishmael and Queequeg, at least in my opinion.

toilet and the elevator boy's sister to spit upon the person whom we happen to have at a disadvantage. And whatever the social world may say to the contrary, it either ignores or seeks to ignore those few impulses toward justice and beauty which make men admirable."

No matter what the social world may say! And no matter what literary critics may say! Mr. Trilling in his essay also refers to this passage; just after he has said that "it does not matter in what sense the word manners is taken" (but it does matter very much), he writes that "The Duchesse de Guermantes unable to delay her departure for the dinner party to receive properly from her friend Swann the news that he is dying but able to change the black slippers her husband objects to; Mr. Pickwick and Sam Weller; Priam and Achilles—they exit by reason of their observed manners. So true is this, indeed, so creative is the novelist's awareness of manners, that we may say that it is a function of his love."

Does Proust arrive at love, or at contempt and repudiation, by the observation of manners?

The entire episode in Proust's novel is far too long to be quoted in full but some direct presentation of it is necessary so that the reader can judge for himself the issues in question. The Duchesse de Guermantes has just asked Swann to go to Italy with her and her husband ten months hence. Swann pressed to say why he must refuse, hesitantly tells her that he is very ill, that he may die at any moment, that at most he will live only a few months more. But the footman has just announced the carriage which is to take the Duke and Duchess to dinner, and the Duke is quite impatient.

> "What's that you say?" cried the Duchess, stopping for a moment on her way to the carriage, and raising her fine eyes, their melancholy blue clouded by uncertainty. Placed for the first time in her life between two duties as incompatible as getting into her carriage and shewing pity for a man who was about to die, she could find nothing in the code of conventions that indicated the right line to follow, and not knowing which to choose, felt it better to make a show of not believing that the alternatives need be seriously considered, so as to follow the first, which demanded of her at the moment less effort, and thought that the best way of settling the conflict would be to deny that any existed. "You're joking," she said to Swann. "It would be a joke in charming

taste," replied he, ironically. "I don't know why I am telling you this; I have never said a word to you before about my illness. But as you asked me, and as I may die now at any moment . . . But whatever I do I mustn't make you late; you're dining out, remember," he added, because he knew that for other people their own social obligations took precedence of the death of a friend and could put himself in her place by dint of his instinctive politeness. But that of the Duchess enabled her to perceive in a vague way that the dinner to which she was going must count for less to Swann than his own death. And so, while continuing on her way to the carriage, she let her shoulders droop, saying: "Don't worry about our dinner. It's not of any importance." But this put the Duke in a bad humor.

The Duke has heard Swann's news, but he says to his wife: "You know very well that Mme. de Sainte-Euverte insists on sitting down to table at eight o'clock sharp." Obedient to her husband,

Mme. de Guermantes advanced resolutely towards the carriage and uttered a last farewell to Swann: "You know, we can talk about that another time; I don't believe a word you've been saying, but we must discuss it quietly". . . . She was just getting into her carriage when, seeing her foot exposed, the Duke cried out in a terrifying voice: "Oriane, what have you been thinking of, you wretch? You've kept on your black shoes."

The Duchess objects that they are late, the Duke answers that the proper shoes are more important than punctuality, and while she is changing her shoes, Swann, who is regarded as an expert by the Duchess in questions of dress, remarks that the black shoes did not seem unbecoming and did not offend him, and the Duke admits that the sartorial point is not beyond dispute. Then the Duke asks Swann to make his departure before the Duchess returns for she may wish to resume the conversation, and she is virtually dead of hunger, as he himself is:

". . . Besides, I tell you frankly I am dying of hunger. I had a wretched lunch this morning when I came from the train. There was the devil of a *béarnaise* sauce, I admit, but in spite of that I shan't be at all sorry to sit down to dinner. Five minutes to eight! O women, women! She'll give us both indigestion before tomorrow. She is not nearly as strong as people think." The Duke felt no compunction at speaking thus of his wife's ailments

[219]

and his own to a dying man, for the former interested him more, appeared to him more important. And so it was simply from good breeding and good fellowship that, after politely shewing us out, he cried from "off stage," in a stentorian voice to Swann, who was already in the courtyard: "You now, don't let yourself be taken in by the doctors' nonsense, damn them. They're jackasses. You're as strong as the Pont Neuf. You'll live to bury us all!"

Mr. Aldridge must also be quoted at length, for paraphrase may quickly become misinterpretation when one is unsympathetic:

To put value back where we found it is to do nothing more than put it where we always find it whenever we function as novelists and critics and not as surgeons. As novelists and critics we are aware of value only to the extent that we are able to discover it in the form it most characteristically takes in society; and that is in the form of social manners. Manners are the organized public manifestations of those dogmas, codes, myths, and moral idiosyncrasies which compose the value system of a culture. Manners stand to values precisely as religion stands to personal belief in God; and just as the question for the religionist is not whether we have beliefs but whether we believe; so the question for the literary mind is not whether we have values but whether we have manners. It is through manners, particularly as they take the form of what Lionel Trilling calls "a conscious realization of social class," that dramatic vitality and conflict have traditionally entered the world of fiction. Manners have been responsible for the presence in the great European novel of that prime virtue of Mr. Trilling's—"substantiality," the virtue, that is, of "intention, passion, thought" and profound character portrayal, "which is precisely a product of a class existence." It should follow, therefore, that if the contemporary novel in America has been increasingly characterized by moral vacuity and dramatic failure, it is because we have experienced a loss of our sense of social class, and, with it, of the convention of manners which alone can give it moral and dramatic life. . . . In the South and in New England there are still classes of people who live by a code and a vision of conduct which formulates and dramatizes their behavior. They have bias and idiosyncrasy as personalities because they are both restrained and liberated by the generally accepted dogmas of their class and place. The inhabitants of other areas belong to a society which is rapidly becoming completely classless and in which, therefore, behavior is deprived of the convention which would give it moral direction and vitality and the inhabitants dramatic personality.

The most appalling fact about the American way of life to-day, at least from the literary point of view, is not simply that people do nothing according to a prevailing conventional rule but that, because there is no conventional rule, they are losing their human personalities. Without dogma, we might say, there can be no personality; and without personality there can be no creation of character in fiction; and without character there can be no novel of manners; and without the novel of manners, we are left with nothing but the naked creative sensibility; and that, no matter how brilliant it may be, is never by itself enough.

Yes, we have no bananas. But all God's chillun got shoes.

Let me try to make myself as plain and clear as possible: good manners are obviously very important and very desirable. They are often necessary to the realization of kindness, goodness and sympathy, and to the avoidance of injury. But, as Proust shows, other matters are far more important, and good manners are sometimes merely a pleasant surface.

It is needless to say that Mr. Aldridge and Mr. Trilling would utterly and instinctively condemn the manners of the Duc de Guermantes when he hears that Swann is dying, and condemn and be disgusted by the equivalent behavior in actual life. And Mr. Aldridge can certainly argue that Proust had to be a great snob and great novelist of manners to pass beyond snobbery and see through the noble lords and ladies. Moreover, Proust has accomplished precisely what Mr. Trilling described as one of the prime virtues of the novel: the penetration of the illusion that snobbery generates. But the penetration becomes meaningless when anyone can write as Mr. Aldridge does, compounding snobbery by making it a necessary condition of serious literature. Mr. Aldridge makes me think of the critic who said to me, speaking of certain American authors: "How can the sons of tailors *know* enough to write well about human beings?" "Shakespeare was the son of a butcher," I answered. In a way, we were both wrong. But Mr. Aldridge cannot but be entirely wrong if Proust was right. For what Mr. Aldridge desires and praises is a social milieu and a literary situation which is, so to speak, prior to Proust: doubtless, as a literary man, Mr.

Aldridge wants the social milieu for the sake of the literary situation; that, at any rate, would be the kindest view of his statements. But to write and to think as Mr. Aldridge does is to cast away an important part of one's inheritance as a human being: it is a forgetting or a rejection of Proust, and of much else besides. Mr. Trilling's case is far more complicated and cannot be examined with complete justice here, for part of what Mr. Trilling is trying to do as a critic of literature and society is to salvage some of the lost or hurt pride of the middle class in its human inheritance, and his sensitivity reminds one of Swann. Nevertheless nothing that Mr. Trilling had to say prevented Mr. Aldridge from arriving at his views, even if we waive the question of whether Mr. Trilling has encouraged his views, or helped to support them.

Mr. Aldridge's tone, I think, is that of one who is trying to convince himself more than anyone else. Perhaps he has not truly made the choice which he declares with so much vigor. But the choice is real and inescapable in life and in literature: Mr. Aldridge, like all of us, must choose between Swann and the Duchess' red shoes.

Ring Lardner
Highbrow in Hiding

Ring Lardner's fame since his death in 1933 has been of the same character, essentially, as it was during his lifetime: He is regarded as a sports writer who wrote fiction in slang about baseball, a view that is at once accurate and inaccurate. Donald Elder's excellent full-length study of Lardner ought to help correct the neglect, one-sided understanding, and misunderstanding of Lardner's work.

Elder says that Lardner belongs "to a line of American originals, Thoreau, Hawthorne, Melville, Whitman, and Mark Twain," and it is obvious that he regards Lardner as a great writer of fiction and one of the greatest—possibly the greatest—of American humorists. But he does tend to take Lardner's importance for granted, like most devout admirers. This is perhaps largely because he is overly impressed by the tributes paid to Lardner during the last ten years of his life, when the highbrow literary acclaim he received involved comparisons with Shakespeare, Swift, and Chekhov, among others. It was a time when all authors were either major or worthless, and a critic who described an author as a good minor writer knew that he had dismissed him as a mediocrity.

The piece Scott Fitzgerald wrote on Lardner right after his death shows how quickly Lardner's literary reputation was dissipated. Fitzgerald, who should have known better, said that Lardner's mind had never gotten beyond the compass of the ball field. Although baseball is not only the national pastime but a national passion, and humor is a very important part of daily American

This essay is a review of Donald Elder, *Ring Lardner* (New York: Doubleday, 1956).

[223]

life, the tendency to think of writing about any sport and the work of any professional humorist as outside the realm of serious literature still persists fairly strongly.

Elder deals very well with the notion that Lardner's fiction is limited in meaning simply because he writes about baseball: "His preoccupation with sport reflected a longing for an ideal world where the rules, if observed, guaranteed the triumph of merit; it also reflected his acute sense of the disparity between the way people were supposed to behave and the way they did."

THE WISE FOOL

Lardner's wonderful nonsense plays show how easy it is to underestimate Lardner's work as merely amusing. Thus a stage direction in one nonsense play—"The curtain is lowered for seven days to denote the lapse of a week"—is very funny and is at the same time a concise definition of the limitations of naturalism in the theater, suggested probably by the later plays of Eugene O'Neill. This is true also of the wild list of characters with which each of the little plays begins. "Anne Nichols, a six day bicyclist," and "Herbert Swope, a nonentity," may be dated or topical, but to those who know something of Dreiser's life, "Theodore Dreiser, a former Follies girl," will mean more now than when Lardner wrote, and the present-day reader will surely recognize that "Walter Winchell, a nun" is something more than nonsense.

This is all the clearer in the dialogue of the nonsense plays, which abound in references to havoc, wedlock, marital discord, money, murder, and a good deal else that can be summarized in the time and place of one play, "a one way street in Jeopardy," and the acknowledgment on the title page of another: "translated from the Mastoid by Ring W. Lardner." The latter may or may not be evidence that the way English was used often affected Lardner like a serious disease, a pain in the ears, but there is sufficient evidence of the fact throughout his writing.

Lardner's hypersensitivity to language was a hypersensitivity to human suffering, a fact which becomes clear only when his fiction is related to his humor. His acute sense of the disparity between the way people should behave and the way they do is very often expressed in his stories by translations from the Mastoid, the use of English that dramatizes the disparity between the way English ought to be used and the way it is used. Since the comic style of his humor is identical with the narrative method of his fiction, where the characters often damn themselves by their own account of human behavior, it is natural enough to overlook the depth of satirical meaning that characterizes his fiction and a good deal of his humor also.

Lardner's work is, among other things, a serious criticism of American life, deeply rooted in the purely American and characteristically Midwestern belief that "the rules, if observed, guaranteed the triumph of merit," to quote Elder again. In some of Lardner's best stories the successful human beings are those who break all the rules continually. In other stories either the leading characters are entirely unaware of the quality of their behavior and of the possible existence of rules, in human relationships as well as in games, or the success gained by breaking the rules enables them to continue to break them with impunity. Lardner's insight went beyond any simple contrast of how those who broke the rules flourished and those who observed them found that they certainly did not guarantee the triumph of merit. The real points, again and again, is that the rules are irrelevant to success and failure.

In "Horseshoes" the hero is a ball-player who never gets credit for his feats on the playing field but is regarded as overwhelmingly lucky; his rival, who really is lucky, is regarded as very skillful. When the hero and his rival court the same girl, the hero wins out neither through skill nor luck, but by punching his rival in the nose. The unawareness of the small town is essentially the same as that of the big town, Broadway, Tin Pan Alley, and the expensive suburbs, whether it is a matter of playing practical jokes or that of playing golf and bridge. The characters are above all guilty of unawareness: They have no sense of the possibilities of existence, nor of the quality of their behavior when they are cruel and mean, or when they cheat and steal for trivial sums or a few golf balls.

At the center of Lardner's fiction, quite rightly, is the subject of marriage, since it is not only the inspiration and climax of romance and courtship, but presumably one of the chief reasons for desiring success. In one story after another, married life is a hideous disappointment, full of unbearable boredom for either the wife or the husband or both, a fact which is clearly articulated in Lardner's humor too. In "Marriage Made Easy," a parody of the columns of advice on the problems of life syndicated in the newspapers, Lardner provides ten rules—or commandments—for the realization of the "ideal married life" by "the two belligerents." Lardner's feeling about family life can be concisely summarized by quoting one exchange in "The Young Immigrunts," between four-year-old Ring, Jr., and his father during an automobile trip:

"Are you lost daddy I arsked tenderly.

"Shut up he explained?"

A BORN HATER?

When the stories that express this grim vision of life appeared in periodicals such as the *Saturday Evening Post*, it was natural enough to read them as merely amusing. But when, in 1929, *Round Up*, an omnibus collection of his short stories, was published, no competent critic could miss the consistent point of view which was at the heart of all of Lardner's writing. It remained possible, however, to mistake this point of view for simple misanthropy.

Clifton Fadiman's review is the best instance of this kind of judgment. Lardner's work had its source, Fadiman said, in the fact that ". . . he just doesn't like people." Lardner "hates himself . . . hates his characters; and . . . his characters hate each other." This was apparently one of the few occasions when critical comment impressed or distressed Lardner, who was sufficiently wounded to sign a letter, enclosing the comment, "A Born Hater." Lardner was actually, of course, a born lover.

When Lardner's friend Fitzgerald described one of his own heroes, Gatsby, as a human being who had an "extraordinary gift of hope" and "a heightened sensitivity to the promises of life," he was describing himself and also the idealism that was Lardner's underlying attitude. When another of Fitzgerald's characters, Nick Carraway, speaks of himself wryly as one of the few honest people he has ever known, he is expressing a more negative phase of the same attitude. In Lardner as in Fitzgerald, it is the decent who suffer nightmares while those who are free of scruples and any kind of sensitivity sleep very well.

Lardner successfully concealed himself beneath the lowbrow and deadpan mask of his comic style, which, like most American humor, was written "in character." Lardner's character was that of the wise boob, who is at once voluble and half illiterate, shrewd and gullible, cocky and quite insecure. Few readers of Lardner during his lifetime can have recognized that his work was the effort of one who had grown up with all the advantages of a prosperous family, including a tutor and a dancing master, in a family circle that was ardently devoted to literature and music. The letters Lardner wrote during his long and difficult courtship of his wife reveal the mark of the highbrow clearly when Lardner signs himself "Peer Gynt" and "The husband of Jane Eyre." And the reader of his humorous pieces might have suspected, without being sure, that the sports writer was really a highbrow in hiding when he came upon references to Henry (Peaches) Adams and to the hypothetical visit of Jane Austen to New York, where she met Texas Guinan, and to Hollywood, where *Pride and Prejudice* is made into a film called "The Bath in Champagne." It is indeed difficult to imagine how Lardner, at the height of his fame, managed to conceal his highbrow inclinations not only from the public but from his close friends. His characteristic silence must have helped —at one party, Mr. Elder says, he pretended to be a Pole who knew no English—but he seems also to have fooled Scott Fitzgerald, his next-door neighbor and constant drinking companion for years. The highbrow in hiding went so far as to pretend that he didn't understand the highbrow reviews of his books.

PURITAN IN SPEAKEASY

Although the major part of Mr. Elder's book illuminates Lardner's work by giving the readers a sense of the kind of human being Lardner really was, his account of the agony of the last seven years of Lardner's life raises a question which is either unanswerable or which perhaps can only be answered by studying his work.

The question is just why so successful and gifted a human being suffered so much and so helplessly. Lardner "was sometimes found asleep over his typewriter, his head bruised from having fallen on the machine." This kind of experience became more and more frequent during the years when Lardner was most successful and most admired—far more than he had ever expected or indeed wanted to be. Neither success nor admiration helped him very much or diminished the overwhelming anxiety that made him resort more and more to alcohol, morphine, and caffeine in an effort to cope with an insomnia that made it increasingly difficult for him to meet a daily or weekly dead line.

The anxiety often took the immediate form of financial insecurity, but this hardly accounts for a state of mind in which Lardner apparently thought seriously of suicide and which made him seem to others to be committing a kind of prolonged suicide. Lardner had been making $30,000 a year from his syndicated weekly column alone, which should have been sufficient even for the devoted husband and father of a growing family thirty years ago. Moreover, Lardner was close to acute alcoholism several times before he had a large family to support, and as his income increased, his desperation increased instead of diminishing. It seems likely that the need of money was a symbol rather than the real cause of whatever troubled him so much.

What troubled him so much is suggested strongly by the pieces which he wrote on radio programs for the *New Yorker* during the last year of his life. The savagery with which he attacked off-color songs is extreme, but not different in kind from the sentiments he expressed in previous writing. Lardner was genuinely horrified by the open and public mention of matters which he felt were proper subjects only for the private conversations of male adults. This latter attitude was certainly characteristic of the tough-talking newspaperman of Lardner's generation, including Westbrook Pegler and Harold Ross, and it is impossible to understand how, if Lardner had suffered from a total squeamishness, he could have frequented saloons, smoking cars, and speakeasies so fondly and assiduously. Whatever the kind and degree of his distaste, it is clear that there was a kind of Puritanism at the heart of his work—an innocent purity of heart and mind that was interminably appalled by the unfulfilled promises of life.

John Dos Passos and
the Whole Truth

➸ If we think for a moment of the newspaper as a representation of American life, we get some idea of the basis of John Dos Passos' enormous novel.[1] It is not merely that one of the devices of this novel is the "newsreel" and consists of an arrangement of quotations from newspapers of the past thirty years; nor that another device is the "camera eye," and still another consists of biographies of Americans who have for the most part been prominent in the newspaper. It is in its whole sense of American life and in its formal character—its omnibus, omnivorous span—that Dos Passos' novel seems to at least one reader to derive from the newspaper. The sense of the unknown lives behind the wedding announcements and the obituaries, the immense gap between private life and public events, and between the private experience of the individual and the public experience represented in the newspaper as being constituted by accident, violence, scandal, the speeches of politicians, and the deliberations of Congress—all this would seem to have a good deal to do with determining Dos Passos' vision and his intention. There were concerts, club meetings, and lectures in St. Petersburg on the night in October, 1917, when the Russian Revolution occurred—it is such a curious mixture of the private worlds and the public world that seems to obsess Dos Passos.

Another and related way of characterizing his novels is through the names he has given them: *Three Soldiers*, a "picture" of the World War (which, curiously enough, delighted Amy Lowell), *Manhattan Transfer*, a "picture" of New York City, *The 42nd*

1. *U. S. A.*, by John Dos Passos, Harcourt, Brace & Co.

Parallel, and *1919*. And thus it is interesting to remark that the name of *U. S. A.* apparently was chosen for Dos Passos by the reviewer in *Time* who said, when a part of the book appeared as a separate novel, that "Alone among U. S. writers, John Dos Passos has taken as his subject the whole U. S. A. and attempted to organize its chaotic high-pressure life into an understandable artistic pattern." The source of the title suggests that Dos Passos' way of grasping experience has a good deal, although not everything, in common not only with the triumvirate of *Time, Life,* and *Fortune,* but also with the whole tendency to get documents, to record facts, and to swallow the whole rich chaos of modern life. The motion picture called *The River,* with its mixture of lyricism and economic discourse, the picture-and-text books, the Federal theater plays about housing and the AAA, and even the poetry, in some of its aspects, of Mr. Horace Gregory and Miss Muriel Rukeyser are like examples of a distinct method of attempting to take hold of experience in its breathless and discorded contemporaneity. How widespread the sense of life exemplified in Dos Passos is, and what its basis is, can be seen in these words of a preface to a book of short stories edited by a wholly different kind of writer:

> We were in Austria at the beginning of a desperately eventful year—a year that was to be characterized by almost universal unrest, by civil war, revolution, by strikes and unemployment figures reaching monstrous proportions; a year which opened in France with the suicide or murder of Stavinsky, throwing that country into chaos, causing two governments to fall; a year which saw the February slaughter in Vienna and the eventual murder of the Austrian Chancellor; a year which in one part of the world brought the tragedy of the *Morro Castle* and the expansion of the unprecedented and hotly-disputed N.R.A., while another continent saw the King of Jugoslavia assassinated, the Blood Purge of Germany effected, and Hitler confirmed Leader-Chancellor of the Third Reich upon von Hindenburg's death; the year of a royal wedding in England, of Gandhi's retirement from politics, of civil strife in Spain, Austria, Bolivia; the year of the Chicago Fair, the devaluation of the dollar, the conclusion of the Holy Year at Vatican City, the year of the Great Drought—the year 1934.
>
> We decided then to compile a record in fiction form not only of that year's nationally or internationally important events but

as well of the ordinary individual's life as it was being lived on the five continents throughout that period of time.[2]

The poetic fashioned by this kind of awareness can perhaps be stated in this way: there are facts and things and processes continually going on in the world and the writer intends nothing so much as to provide portraits, even photographs, of them through the conventions of fiction—and sometimes without those conventions. Of Dos Passos we can say—and regard this as the best praise for anyone's intention—that his intention has been to tell the truth about the world in which he has had to exist. But more than that, he has apparently gone from one end of the world to the other in the effort to find the truth and not to permit the *Zeitgeist* to evade him. So, at any rate, his travel book[3] indicates, providing an image of the author as the sensitive, unassuming, anonymous observer who is intent upon seeing all that is to be seen—even when, as in Russia in 1928 and in Barcelona in 1937, he is compelled to see so much that will be contrary to his expectation and dearest hope.

At the conclusion of the last book of *U. S. A.* and after having written some 1400 pages, Dos Passos wrote a brief chapter to head the whole book and called the chapter *U. S. A.,* and here defined his intention, at the conclusion of his efforts, when he would know it best.

> The young man walks by himself through the crowd that thins into night streets. . . . eyes greedy for warm curves of faces. . . . mind a beehive of hopes . . . muscles ache for the knowledge of jobs. The young man walks by himself searching through the crowd with greedy eyes, greedy ears taut to hear, by himself, alone . . .
>
> The young man walks by himself, fast but not fast enough, far but not far enough (faces slide out of sight, talk trails into tattered scraps, ...) he must catch the last subway, the streetcar, the bus, run up the gangplank of all the steamboats, register at all the hotels, work in the cities, answer the want-ads, live in all the boardinghouses . . . one job is not enough, one life is not enough.

2. *365 Days,* Edited by Kay Boyle, Lawrence Vail, Nina Conarain. Harcourt, Brace & Co., 1936.

3. *Journey Between Two Wars,* by John Dos Passos, Harcourt, Brace & Co. This is a selection from Dos Passos' three previous travel books together with some very interesting additions having to do with Spain in 1937.

And the only link, we are told, between the young man walking alone and the life he wished to know so fully was in the speech of the people. U.S.A. meant and was many things—a part of a continent, a group of holding companies, the soldiers who died for the U.S.A., the letters on an address, a stack of newspapers on file— "but mostly U.S.A. is the speech of the people." And Dos Passos has told us this before, in the introduction written to *Three Soldiers*, in 1932, when that book was canonized by The Modern Library. Again what he says is worth quoting for its expression of the utter honesty and clarity of his intention.

> You wake up one morning and find that what was to have been a *springboard into reality* [*my italics*] is a profession. Making a living by selling daydreams is all right, but few men feel its much of a life for a man. . . . What I'm trying to get out is the difference in kind between the work of James Joyce, say, and that of any current dispenser of daydreams. . . . What do you write for, then? To convince people of something? That's preaching, and a part of the business of everyone who deals with words . . . . but outside of preaching I think there is such a thing as straight writing . . . The mind of a generation is its speech. A writer makes aspects of that speech enduring . . . makes of them forms to set the mind of tomorrow's generation. That's history. A writer who writes straight is the architect of history . . . Those of us who have lived through [these times] have seen the years strip the bunting off the great illusions of our time. We must deal with the raw structure of history now, we must deal with it quick, before it stamps us out.

One may regret the slanging tone, as of Mr. Otis Ferguson (as if Dos Passos too were afraid that if he used abstract terms and an unconversational diction, he would be considered a sissy), and one may feel that an "architect of history" is rather a fancy claim, but one cannot deny that Dos Passos knows very well what he wants to do in his novels.

Naturally such motives have infected his style and method in every aspect. In *U.S.A.*, Dos Passos uses four "forms" or "frames," each of them deriving directly from his representative intention, his desire to get at the truth about his time with any available instrument. Each of these forms needs to be considered in itself.

There is the camera eye, an intermittent sequence of prose poems in an impressionist style: "all week the fog clung to the sea and cliffs .... gray flakes green sea gray houses white fog lap of the waves against the wharf scream of gulls circling and swooping," or another brief example: "all over Tours you can smell the linden in bloom it's hot my uniform sticks the O.D. chafes me under the chin." Each impression is apparently autobiographical and dates from the childhood of the author to the 'twenties. The writing takes on the lyricism of a quasi-Joycean stream-of-consciousness and the emphasis is almost always upon the look and feel of things, mostly apart from any narrative context. At first glance the texture seems the crudity of an undergraduate determined to be modern, but upon examination this entirely disappears and one finds that all is based on faithful observation and is never pretentious, nor false. But these passages have no direct relation to the main story, although at times there is some link—just before a leading character goes to Havana, for example, the autobiographical impression is of a trip on a Spanish boat to Cuba.

Secondly, there are the newsreel passages which are inserted just as the camera eye panels are, between narratives. They consist of quotations from newspapers of a given time and period and also of its popular songs. Many amusing juxtapositions of headlines and stories are made by means of clever arrangements, and the lyrics are (where the present reader is able to judge) perfectly reminiscent. But the central intention of this form—to suggest the quality of various years and its public events—is not fulfilled for the most part. The newsreels are sometimes merely frivolous and trivial. One example may suffice to show this:

> the first thing the volunteer firefighters did was to open the windows to let the smoke out. This created a draft and the fire with a good thirty-mile wind from the ocean did the rest

RECORD TURNOVER IN INSURANCE SHARES

AS TRADING PROGRESSES

Change all of your grey skies
Turn them into blue skies
And keep sweeping the cobwebs off the moon.

[233]

learn new uses for concrete. How to develop profitable concrete business. How to judge materials. How to figure jobs.
How to reinforce concrete. How to build forms, roads, side-
walks, floors, culverts, cellars.

The time, one would suppose, is 1927 or 1928. The stock market
headlines indicate that time and are loosely relevant to the main
narrative. The first passage is a news story, however, and the last
is an advertisement. They are disjunct parts and they could with
no difficulty be transposed to any other of the fifty-eight newsreels
going back to the turn of the century.

A third form is the "Biography." Here we are provided with
concise recitatives in a Whitmanesque diction which is used at
times with power. Each biography concerns a great figure of the
period, and there are twenty-six of them. Four leaders of the working class, Eugene V. Debs, Joe Hill, Bill Haywood, and Wesley
Everest; seven capitalists, Andrew Carnegie, Henry Ford, William
Randolph Hearst, J. P. Morgan, Samuel Insull, and Minor C.
Keith; four politicians, Robert LaFollette (Sr.), Theodore Roosevelt, Woodrow Wilson, and William Jennings Bryan; four inventors, Luther Burbank, the Wright Brothers, Thomas Edison,
and Charles Steinmetz; three journalists, John Reed, Randolph
Bourne, and Paxton Hibben; an actor, Rudolph Valentino; a
dancer, Isadora Duncan; an efficiency expert, Frederick W. Taylor; an architect, Frank Lloyd Wright; and one genuine intellectual, Thorstein Veblen. One remarks that naturally enough
there are no musicians, musical life being what it is in America.
But one regrets the omission of poets, unless John Reed be considered one—Harriet Monroe, Vachel Lindsay, Amy Lowell, and
even Hart Crane suggest themselves. There is no characteristic
Broadway actor, such as Al Jolson. Professional sport, particularly
major league baseball, which in fact prepossesses at least two million American souls for six months a year, might also have been
represented, at least in the newsreels; and for biographies, one
thinks of Christy ·Matthewson, Connie Mack, Red Grange, and
Gertrude Ederle. But on the whole the biographies are as repre-

[234]

sentative as one could wish and are written with a fine power of generalization and concision—the gist abstracted from the life of a man and presented in four or five pages, concluding very well at times in the form of a simple contradiction, Henry Ford's nostalgic desire for the horse-and-buggy days, which his whole career, of course, worked to destroy, and Andrew Carnegie's bestowal of millions for world peace, the millions being acquired, of course, by the manufacture of steel used in munitions and battleships.

The major part of the novel, perhaps as much as 1200 pages, is, however, constituted by direct narratives of the lives of eleven leading characters and perhaps three times as many minor ones who are notable. In creating a mode in which to present the lives of these characters, Dos Passos has definitely extended the art of narration. It is difficult to describe what he has accomplished because it is so much a matter of the digestion of a great many details and the use of facts which rise from the historical scene—all caught into a smooth-running story which, taken in itself, cannot fail to hold the reader's attention. The narratives are always in the third person and yet have all the warm interior flow of a story presented through the medium of a stream-of-consciousness first-person. One remarkable achievement is the way in which the element of time is disposed. With no break or unevenness at all, the narrative passes quickly through several years of the character's life, presenting much that is essential briefly, and then contracts, without warning, without being noted, and focuses for several pages upon a single episode which is important. It is an ability which an apprentice writer can best appreciate and comes from the indispensable knowledge of how very much the writer can *omit* —Hemingway knows this very well also—and a knowledge of how each sentence can expand in the reader's mind to include a whole context of experience. Another feature to be noted is Dos Passos' immense command of details which seem to come from a thousand American places and to be invested with a kind of historical idiom at all times. There is, for example, the story of Eleanor Stoddard, which begins:

> When she was small she hated everything. She hated her father, a stout red haired man smelling of whiskers and stale pipe tobacco. He worked in an office in the stockyards . . . Nights

she used to dream she lived alone with her mother in a big clean white house in Oak Park in winter when there was snow on the ground and she'd been setting a white linen table cloth with bright white silver . . . When she was sixteen in highschool she and a girl named Isabelle swore together that if a boy ever touched them they'd kill themselves . . . The only other person Eleanor liked was Miss Oliphant, her English teacher . . . It was Miss Oliphant who induced Eleanor to take courses at the Art Institute. She had reproductions on her walls of pictures by Rossetti and Burne-Jones . . . She made Eleanor feel that Art was something ivory white and very pure and noble and distant and sad . . . She was reading through the complete works of George Eliot.

The whiskers and stale pipe smoke, the white house and the snow, the pictures of Rossetti and Burne-Jones, and the novels of George Eliot (as understood by such a person)—with such quantitative details a whole type of girlhood is summoned up and placed in time. The utterance, as if from the movement of the character's mind, is completely convincing and is achieved by a discreet use of speech diction and speech rhythms and words of direct feeling. Dos Passos has had to work for a long time to attain to this kind of mastery. In his earlier novels, the description was always thick, heavy, isolated, and the use of dialects at times approximated a vaudeville show. But these faults have been pursued to the point where they are magnificent virtues.

The thirteen leading characters who are presented through the medium of this kind of narrative are all members of the lower middle-class. The very rich and the working-class are not the subjects of direct attention, although they participate also in a variety of ways. It is true too that some of these characters are for all practical purposes reduced to the status of workers and most of them, on the other hand, desire to be rich, while three of them devote themselves to the cause of the working-class. But in the main, what we get is the typical life of the lower middle-class between 1900 and 1930. Typical indeed, for there is a constant "averaging," a constant effort to describe each character in terms which will reduce him to a type. The same motive seems to have dictated the kinds of character. There is an IWW typesetter, a Jewish radical leader, a movie star, an interior decorator, a publicity man, a stenographer, a Harvard aesthete, a sailor, an aviator, a social worker, a Red Cross nurse—all of them, I should add, might be characterized differently since they engage in other activities from time to time. Their chief values, which they do not examine or question in the least (except for the radicals), are "love" and "money." The accuracy of this presentation can be verified by examining a fair sample of advertising in order to see on what the advertisers are basing their appeals. And the fate of almost all the characters is defeat, inhuman, untragic defeat—either defeat of a violent death without meaning or the more complete degradation of "selling out"—selling one's friends, one's integrity, one's earnest ambition and hope, for nothing more than "the big money." By the conclusion of the book, every character with the exception of Ben Compton, the radical leader, has come to the point where self-respect is not remote, but a term as of a dead language. Compton has been thrown out of the Communist Party for being an "oppositionist" (a note which would indicate a change of heart in Dos Passos, a loss of faith in the radical movement, which has occurred since the writing of *U.S.A.* was begun). The conclusion, to repeat, is that of utter loss, degradation, and hopelessness, the suicide of one character, the killing of another, the disgusting lives of the others, and the final contrast of a vagabond who has not eaten for some time waiting for a lift on the highway while a plane passes overhead, containing the rich, one of whom "sickens and vomits into the carton container the steak and mushrooms he ate in New York."

Whatever else we may say of American life as represented in these narratives, there is one statement which we must make first: it is so, it is true; we have seen this with our own eyes and many of us have lived in this way. This is a true picture of the lives of many Americans, and anyone who doubts the fact can learn for himself very quickly how accurate Dos Passos is. But there is, on the other hand, a great deal more to be said about the truth which the novel as a form is capable of presenting.

To begin the attempt at a thorough judgment, the formal inadequacy of *U.S.A.*, taken as a whole, is the direct experience of every reader. There is no need to summon up abstract canons, nor to make that very interesting approach which can be summed up in the question: what would Henry James say? No reader can go from page one to page 1449 without feeling that the newsreels, camera eyes, and biographies, however good they may be in themselves, are interruptions which thwart his interest and break the novel into many isolated parts.[4] Even in the central narratives, where, as in the greatest pure prose (that of Stendhal and Tolstoy, where the word is transparent as glass), the reader passes without an awareness of style to the intense, ragged actuality presented, even here the novel falls into separate parts, even though there is an occasional interweaving of lives. The unity, the *felt* unity, is only the loose grab-bag of time and place, 1919 and the U.S.A. The binding together of lives (and thus of the reader's interest and gaze) into the progress of a plot—an element present even in a work of the scope of *War and Peace*—is wholly lacking. This heaping together of fragments of valuable perception is a characteristic of the best poetry of our time and the connection is interesting. *The Waste Land*, Pound's *Cantos*, *The Bridge*, and *The Orators* of Auden are all examples. And as there is a separation or gap between the sensibility of the camera eye and the narrative form in *U.S.A.*, so in the history of modern poetry we can remark the converse phenomenon, how, since Coleridge wrote marginal summaries of the narrative to "The Ancient Mariner," the capacity for a narrative framework has gradually disappeared from poetry of the first order: modern poetic style can bear the utmost strain of sensibility, but it cannot tell a story. In the medium of poetry, however, a unity of tone and mood and theme can substitute, although imperfectly, for other kinds of unity. *U.S.A.* cannot be considered a poem, however, and even if it could, Dos Passos does not rise to the level of the poets in question. As a narrative, it becomes a suite of narratives in which panels without direct relation to the subject are

4. In his essay on Dos Passos, Malcolm Cowley insists that there is a sufficient connection between the narratives and the other forms. There is, for example, a biography of Wilson when the fictional persons are concerned with the aftermath of the World War, a biography of Rudolph Valentino when one of the characters is a movie star. The connection is thus general, tangential, and wholly external, and occurs to the reader only as a passing afterthought, if at all. This kind of connection can be compared with the *internal* unity of any biography or narrative in the book, and then the difference between a unified whole and a loose collection will be clear in terms of the book itself.

inserted (one would suppose that Dos Passos in fact put the book together as a motion-picture director composes his film, by a procedure of cutting, arranging, and interposing parts). As a novel, it is not in any careful sense a novel, but rather an anthology of long stories and prose poems. And it is to be insisted that the unity and form in question are not the abstractions of the critic, but the generic traits of the actual experience of reading fiction.

But form is not, of course, applied to a novel as a press to a tennis racket. It is, on the contrary, the way in which the writer sees his subject, the very means of attempting to see. And thus it is obvious that the formal gaps in *U.S.A.* spring from Dos Passos' effort to see his world in conflicting ways. It has been observed that the stream-of-consciousness lyricism of the camera eye is an attempt to compensate for the flat naturalism of the narratives, and it is perhaps to this that Malcolm Cowley referred when he spoke of the remnants of "the Art Novel" in *U.S.A.* And T. K. Whipple, in his review of the book in *The Nation*, raises more serious questions and makes a much more negative judgment. Whipple remarks, with much insight, that there is an important contrast between the lives of the fictitious persons and the great persons in the biographies—the actual persons have "minds, consciousness, individuality, and personality" and especially the power to choose and to struggle, while these attributes are "reduced to a minimum" in the fictitious persons. This is very true, but, on the other hand, Dos Passos is not, as Whipple thinks, wrong and inaccurate—many American lives are of that quality and character.

And again, a like judgment, this time of *Manhattan Transfer* was made by the Hungarian Marxist critic, Georg Lukacs, in a remarkable article in *International Literature* (which Howard Baker has already cited in *The Southern Review*). Lukacs is engaged in showing that the best novels of the past have depended a great deal on their ability to give their characters "intellectual physiognomies," that is, have made the ideas and beliefs of their characters a very important element of the substance and method. Of Dos Passos, Lukacs says with precision:

he describes for example, a discussion of capitalism and socialism. The place in which the discussion takes place is excellently, vigorously described. We see the steaming Italian restaurant with the spots of tomato sauce on the tablecloth, the tricolored remains of melted ice cream on a plate, and the like. The individual tones of the various speakers are well described. But what they say is perfect banality, the commonplace for and against that can be heard at any time and at any place.

But here again it ought to be replied, at least to begin with, that in actual life such conversations are for the most part banal. Dos Passos is nothing if not accurate.

Both Whipple and Lukacs are excellent witnesses, but neither of them names what seems to me to be the root of the inadequacy which they have variously observed. Whipple attributes the lack to a conception of the individual which is "one-sided" and not "dialectical," nor "the whole man." Lukacs would say that what is lacking is a philosophy, most of all, that of dialectical materialism. A third standpoint would be that which attributed the inadequacy and formal lack to a technical misconception, Mr. Winters' "the fallacy of imitative form," the error of naturalism for which art is merely a mirror of the disorder and incompleteness of life itself.

It seems to me, however, that one must dig much deeper to get to the basic reason for this novel's character as a novel. The root of the inadequacy is, I think, an inadequate conception of what the truth, the whole truth about the U.S.A., for example, is. The term, truth, is used merely in its common-sensical meaning, of an accurate report of that which is. The truth about the whole of experience is precisely what is more than the truth about any actual standpoint. It is merely the truth about the life of an individual person, as it appeared to the person himself, that we get from Dos Passos. The truth about the whole of experience is more than the sum of many or all standpoints, of many blind and limited lives. The whole truth includes what might have been and what may be and what is not (as not being). It includes the whole scale of imaginative possibilities and the nameless assumptions and values by which a society lives. It is exactly because the whole truth is so complex and various that the imagination is a necessity. And this is the reason why fiction is full of the fictitious and the imaginative. It ought to be said, to forestall the reader, that however sophisticated we are about the nature of truth, this statement of its *extent* (its formal width, apart from insisting on any particular truth) is incontestable. It does not depend upon any view of life, as of Montgomery Belgion,[5] but is rather involved in all views and all viewing. It is, moreover, presupposed in the very nature of literature.

But furthermore the whole truth is involved in literature in what seems to me a still more basic way. One fundamental postulate of literature seems to me to be here in question. It too cannot be argued about because it is the assumption by means of which we are enabled to speak. One can merely point to examples—all literary judgment and analysis being, in the end, comparative—and as it happens, Dos Passos himself provides his own examples in this novel.

The unquestionable postulate—or presumption—of all literature is the individual of the fullest intelligence and sensibility—at least with respect to the circumstances of the work itself. Perhaps one can call this individual not the omniscient, but the multiscient individual. He is the one who in some one of many quite different fashions *transcends* the situation and the subject. Often the multiscient individual enters into the work only in the style of the author, and thus it is through the style that a mind of the fullest intelligence and sensibility is brought to bear on the subject. Another way of saying this is to observe that a story must have a hero and to say with Aristotle that the hero must be "superior"

5. The most recent issue of *The Southern Review* contains an article by Belgion which proposes a notion of fiction directly contradictory to the above one. Mr. Belgion argues, and has argued for ten years, as if unable to persuade even himself, that literature is never a representation or the truth of actual life because (1) "actual life is too various and vast to be brought as a whole within the compass of a novel," and because (2) the writer is attempting to impose his own view of life upon the reader, is, in fact, "the irresponsible propagandist" for his own view of life (in that he decides the consequences of his character's acts, for example), and hence, since, in the last analysis, the truth about life cannot be established by a rigorous logical demonstration, no novel can be said to be true to life.

In answer to the first point, one need merely observe that it is not a question of *either* all of life *or* none of it—merely the whole truth about a part of life will suffice—and moreover the part can stand for the whole, the symbol being of the very essence of literature. In answer to the second point, one need merely observe that the truth of much in any fiction does not rest upon ultimate metaphysical decisions, but is common to all mankind and verifiable by them, just as the sciences are thus independent of "views" of life. One proof of this is the fact that we can and do admire works based on views directly opposed to our own.

enough to make his fate significant—not as, for example, the death of a cow. Or again, one has to repeat with Aristotle that literature must concern itself not only with what men are, but with what they "ought" to be: ought is not used in its ethical sense (as of the didactic) for there is no Greek word equivalent to the ethical *ought;* but it is in the sense of the representation of the full scale of human potentialities that "what men ought to be" is meant. When literature concerns itself merely with what men are or have been, it is indistinguishable from history and journalism. But the multiscient individual takes other guises also: he is sometimes the ideas and beliefs by which a work is given its direction. Another method—the one which fulfills the need of transcending the subject best of all—is the use of the supernatural or the mythical, and this is perhaps the most characteristic convention of literature, occurring as it does not only in Shakespeare, when the ghosts or witches appear, and obviously in Dante and other descents into hell, but even in our time, in the hallucination scene of *Ulysses* and in such a play as *The Ascent of F6,* by Auden and Isherwood. The supernatural and the mythical tend to be the most obvious attributes of the imagination. In some form or other the subject is transcended by a superior standpoint, and the superior standpoint reduces itself to one thing, a human being of the greatest intelligence and sensibility, who views all that occurs and is involved in the action, and who is best able to grasp the whole truth of the subject.

What we want of literature is the truth, and the truth is the only intention of *U. S. A.* But, to repeat, the truth is not merely the way in which human beings behave and feel, nor is it wholly contained in their conscious experience. In Racine and in Henry James, to take extreme examples, many characters speak as no one has ever spoken, on land or sea. They speak so in order to contain many of the levels of truth present in any possible situation. The facts represented are always there, but a good many of them can never be consciously known by any actor involved up to his neck in the present moment, as the characters of *U.S.A.* usually are. Only through the focus of the imagination can the relevant facts be brought into the narrative. In Dos Passos, however, there is a beautiful imaginative sympathy which permits him to get under the skin of his characters, but there is no imagination, and no Don Quixote. Dos Passos testifies to all this by his use of newsreels, just as he seeks the full sensibility in the impressions of the camera eye and the heroic character in the biographies; but in his central narratives the standpoint is always narrowed to what the character himself knows as the quality of his existence, life as it appears to him. And this leveling drags with it and tends to make rather crude and sometimes commonplace the sensibility shown in the other panels. If Dos Passos were not so wholly successful in grasping this level of experience, then, undoubtedly, he would be less aware of the need to jump back to the other levels of truth, and his novel would not break into four "eyes" of uncoördinated vision. Or to shift the metaphor, his novel attempts to achieve the whole truth by going rapidly in two opposite directions—the direction of the known experience of his characters, in all their blindness and limitation, and on the other hand, the direction of the transcendent knowledge of experience, the full truth about it. And thus the formal breakdown was scarcely avoidable.

The view of literature, of the truth, and of the individual assumed by Dos Passos may be attributed to two sources. First to the tradition of naturalism, a none too precise term, of which one need here observe only a few aspects. Naturalism has engaged the efforts of writers of the greatest gifts, such as Flaubert and Joyce, but each has managed to smuggle into the method of strict recording certain elements which are radically different. In Flaubert, it is a style of the greatest sensitivity; in Joyce, it is the style too, in a manifold way which seems at first mere virtuosity. Moreover, in these writers, as in the lesser examples of naturalism, one finds a most curious method of work, which alone is sufficient to indicate that the conception of the nature of literature and of the truth it can contain has altered very much. They deliberately observe experience; they seek out experience with a literary intention. Flaubert visited Carthage to get material for "Salammbo" and instructed Maupassant to sit in the park and write down all that he saw. Let us try, on the other hand, to conceive of Shakespeare, Cervantes, Dante, or Aeschylus engaging in such activities in order to write down their works. They would say, one should suppose, that one writes from memory since one remembers what has deeply interested one, and one knows what has deeply interested one. And they would say that the imagination, with its compositional grasp, is the most important thing, the thing that one can get only from a work of art and nowhere else. The imagination which produces such figures as the Prince of Denmark and the Knight of the Doleful Countenance (apparently one of Dos Passos' favorite characters) is not derived from deliberate "research."

Moreover, we ought to remark that naturalism arose at the same time as the primacy of the physical sciences and industrialism; the intellectual and social relationship is this: the physical sciences and industrialism changed the conception of the nature of literature and truth in literature, and made writers of great genius attempt to compete with the scientist by adopting something of his special method. They thought, it would seem, that literature had changed or that its nature had been mistaken.

But naturalism and its external sources are merely effects of that society which has degraded the human being and his own conception of himself to the point where Dos Passos' presentation of him in his own terms is, in fact, perfectly true. One can only add that it is not the whole truth. The primary source of the formal breakdown of this novel is the U.S.A. It is only by distinguishing between the actual and the remotely potential that one can conceive of a different kind of life from that which Dos Passos accurately presents, on the part of most of the living. It is this mixture of the actual and the potential, however, which has made literature so precious to the human spirit.

One might, as a hypothesis, propose a brief theory of the relationship of the individual to the society as relevant to the contrast between Dos Passos' biographies and his narratives, and between the great imaginative figures of literature and the lives of most human beings as they are in any time and place. The elements, let us say, that constitute any person have their source in the society in which he lives and which produced him. The individual is always *in* the world and is inconceivable apart from it. But some individuals "prehend" these given, unavoidable elements in a new way—and this new way, new composition, alters the character of society. This individual, to refer only to Dos Passos' biographies, is usually the inventor, the artist, the intellectual—Socrates, St.

Francis, Lenin. Not only do his acts provide part of the basis of historical change, but, to return to the above consideration of the fundamental postulate of literature, he is the hero, he is the one whose fate as an individual is not merely an incident; and he is above all the type of the highest intelligence and sensibility. This view need not be mistaken for the romantic one of the poet against the world, nor for a stale individualism, nor for a class judgment: its validity here rests upon what, in actuality, literature has been (although certain of the other arts have obviously not). What happens to such an individual, as hero, or what he sees, believes and imagines, as author, is, in fact, one criterion by which all societies are judged. He is our utmost concern and the object of our genuine curiosity when we go to literature, for it is only in literature that we can be sure of finding him. The lives of most individuals are undoubtedly matters of much interest for the author, and the truth about those lives is important. But the whole truth of experience (if past literature is not wholly nonsense) is more than the quality of most lives. One is sure that Dos Passos knows this, since it is the reason for his four forms and his discontinuity. His novel is perhaps the greatest monument of naturalism because it betrays so fully the poverty and disintegration inherent in that method. Dos Passos is the gifted victim of his own extraordinary grasp of the truth. He is a victim of the truth and the whole truth.

The Fabulous Example
of André Gide

Gide himself wisely suggested that his play about Oedipus and his short novel about Theseus be published in one volume. The play was written in 1930, and the second work twelve years after. Thus the difference in time of composition is one of the fascinations of this volume, for the two works taken together make possible a comparison of two stages in Gide's long development as an artist and as a moralist.

Oedipus, at present the most famous of all literary characters, appears in both works, and his meeting with Theseus is an astonishing sequel to the view of him which Gide presents in his play. And the two works, in one book, made possible the kind of illuminating comparison which is one of the important reasons for the inexhaustible vitality and veritable immortality of classical mythology. We can hardly avoid comparing Gide's Oedipus with Sophocles' plays about the tragic hero, with the Freudian use of the myth, with Jean Cocteau's different modern interpretation of Oedipus in *The Infernal Machine,* and with his other manifestations. Then there is the extraordinary contrast between Gide's Theseus, and the Theseus of Euripides and Racine. Both the play and the novel make a rich use of these parallels and variations, and they are also full of sly hints, allusions and innuendoes directed at the reader who knows Gide's career. For example, Gide tells us that one of Oedipus' sons has written two books. These books

This essay is a review of André Gide, *Two Legends: Oedipus and Theseus,* tr. John Russell (New York: Knopf, 1951) and *The Journals of André Gide,* vol. 4, *1939–1949,* tr. Justin O'Brien (New York: Knopf, 1951).

have almost the same titles as two books by French disciples of
Gide. And both sons are accused by Oedipus of having misunderstood his teachings. This is a colossal joke, but a somewhat limited
and local one.

Yet neither work depends upon such tricks, nor need the reader
who does not recognize them be at a loss. Gide's Oedipus is very
interesting in himself, and the play is intelligible apart from any
external reference. Like so many of Gide's heroes, Oedipus is a
disciple of the author, a being who declares that he believes only
in himself, who wishes to discover some new form of unhappiness
to astonish the gods, and who takes pride in not knowing his
parents. When he finds out that his two sons wish to make love
to their sisters, he reproaches them not as immoral, but as lacking
in noble ambition, a view of incest which is not meant to shock the
reader but to illustrate the exalted and discriminating nature of
Gide's gospel of self-realization. In the same way, Gide's Oedipus
is not horrified to learn that he has committed parricide and incest,
for the gods have tricked him into committing these crimes. What
does horrify him, appall him, and make him say that he must
"awake from happiness" is the discovery of the abyss of his ignorance. This is an unbearable humiliation because he is a man who
has taken great pride in his knowledge, his self-knowledge above
all. He has delighted in himself as a self-made, self-reliant being
who conquered the Sphinx by knowing that Man, human nature,
and one's self were the passwords, the key and the answer to all
dangers and enigmas. Hence his tragedy is the recognition that
his happiness and success have been based on ignorance and self-
deception, and not, as he had supposed, on knowledge and independence. There is every reason to suppose that this interpretation of Oedipus is Gide's effort in old age to criticize the doctrines
of self-fulfillment on which his career had been based.

The weakness of the play, considered solely as a play, is that the
characters tend to talk about moral principles and ideas instead
of dramatizing them, a temptation to which most authors who are
interested in ideas succumb. Both Broadway and Henry James
warn of the danger, the former with the iron rule, "Don't tell 'em,
show 'em," and the latter by speaking of "the platitude of mere

statement." In Gide's case, as in Shaw's, however, the dramatic poverty does not matter too much because he knows how to make his ideas intensely interesting in themselves.

Gide's Theseus tells the story of his life in the first person, after his exploits have been accomplished. But the deeds which in the classic authors had been represented as heroic or noble now appear as the underhand tricks of a benign Machiavellian who takes nothing, not even himself, seriously, and who is cunning, cocky, sophisticated, and quite smug. He thinks everyone else is slightly ridiculous, particularly Daedalus and Icarus, who, it now turns out, wanted to have wings not to fly but to solve philosophical problems. And the labyrinth in which Theseus conquers the Minotaur is transformed by Gide into a charming garden: Theseus' heroism consists in refusing to permit pleasure itself, however enchanting, to distract him from what he regards as success. So too when an old friend argues with him about the founding of Athens and says: "Mankind isn't worth all this trouble," his characteristic reply is: "Well, what else is there to think about except mankind?"—which, however realistic, is hardly the answer and the tone of a devout humanist and democrat.

Of the two, Oedipus emerges as the truly noble hero who has surpassed himself. In Gide's novel the two characters meet after both have endured a great deal, and they exchange their studied views of existence. Oedipus declares that he has been trying to "break through to reality," and that he now believes in original sin, redemption through suffering, and the existence of an inner world compared to which the world of the living who are not blind is a deceitful illusion. Theseus congratulates Oedipus on having made "good use of his misfortunes," and then cynically congratulates himself on being other than Oedipus, shrewd enough to have other views, sensible enough to make practical and political use of Oedipus' religious beliefs.

In an interesting introduction to this volume, John Russell declares that Theseus resembles Goethe, Paul Valèry, and Gide himself. To the present reviewer, Theseus seems a complacent and hardened egotist quite unlike those great authors, whatever their shortcomings. But it may well be that a variety of interpretation is precisely Gide's ironic intention. Such an ironic intention can be too clever, and certainly there are passages where Gide indulges in cleverness for its own sake. The possible or probable meaningfulness of both interpretations may thus be Gide's acceptance, through the figure of Theseus, of limitations of humanity; or it may be a systematic ambiguity directed at the reader, as if Gide said: Sincere or hypocrite reader, you must judge Theseus in terms of what *you* are.

On the whole, and however we interpret the text, *Theseus* is a little masterpiece. And of both the play and the novel we must say what Gide's Antigone says of herself: "Not a word comes to my lips that has not first been in my heart." But of course we must never forget that it is Gide's complex heart.

The fourth volume of Gide's journals would not require attention in the pages of *Partisan Review* (its readers are certainly aware by now of how important this work in its entirety is), were it not for two distressing phenomena. One is the interpretation of passages in this new volume as a demonstration that Gide was a collaborationist or at least ambiguous for a time in his attitude toward the German occupation of France in 1940. The second phenomenon, which is linked with the first, is the use of Gide as a scapegoat whose sins and shortcomings are representative of the weakness and the wrongness of modern literature. In this way, by one of the curious and persistent logical leaps which are characteristic of the *rhetoric* of literary criticism, it is suggested that Gide shows how wrong, limited, and defective were Joyce, Mann, Proust, Kafka, T. S. Eliot, and practically every modernist author.

Now even if Gide had been a collaborationist, which he certainly was not, neither his creative work nor that of his compeers would be in the least impugned. Thomas Mann appears to be a misguided and well-meaning author who "collaborates" with Stalinism, while during the first World War he apparently was a confused reactionary or a German patriot, one or the other, depending on the reader's own bias, benevolence, or malevolence. The Joseph books and *The Magic Mountain* remain masterpieces, despite the author's foolish political opinions. It is unfortunately true that political insight does not coincide with literary genius; and although we may venture to think that, since the knowledge of reality which literature requires is in part a knowledge of politics, ultimately literature has serious political meanings, nevertheless this is not at all the same kind of knowledge of political reality which is necessary at the ballot-box or when France has just been occupied and conquered by Germany. Again, to use a second example, T. S. Eliot is a self-confessed reactionary and he is a very great poet and there is a good deal of political and social feeling in his poetry. But we can't conclude, as some have, that he is not a great poet because he is a reactionary any more than we can conclude, as others have, that since he is a great poet, political reaction is justified. It would be quite pleasant if life, literature, and politics were simple enough to allow for these easy judgments and connections, but they are not as simple as all that; they are clearly very complicated.

Gide was a very complicated human being, and his journal shows how for fifty years he wrestled with the labyrinthine complications of his being, self-doubting, self-questioning, self-tormented and above all honest. During the occupation of France, immediately after the Vichy régime had been installed, he was naturally despondent about the future of his country. But he had as always the courage of his confusion. On the 14th of June 1940 he wrote in his journal that Petain's speech was "admirable," because Petain praised effort and discipline, and condemned the arrogance of victory involved in the Treaty of Versailles. On the 24th of June 1940, his journal reads: "Yesterday evening we heard with amazement Petain's new speech on the radio. Can it be? Did Petain himself deliver it? Freely? One suspects some infamous deceit. How can one speak of France as 'intact' after handing over to the enemy over half of the country? How make these words fit those noble words he pronounced three days ago? How can one fail to approve Churchill? And not subscribe most heartily to General De Gaulle's declaration?"

During the following months, Gide continued to waver and grope in the darkness of the time. By the 8th of January 1941, he was writing in his journal of his own efforts at adjusting himself to the occupation and attempting as ever to explain himself to himself (the reader ought to bear in mind that anyone less honest than Gide would have felt free to suppress or conceal pages in which he reveals his own easily misinterpreted and painful sentiments). Seeking to explain how he came to contribute to a periodical which the Vichy régime permitted to appear, he wrote: "My contributing to the review, the *Feuillets* I gave to it, the very plan of resuming publication—all that goes back to the period of dejection immediately following the defeat. Not only was resistance not yet organized, but I did not even think it possible. To fight against the inescapable seemed to me useless, so that all my efforts at first tried to find wisdom in submission, and within my distress to right at least my thoughts." Ten months after the June 14, 1940, entry, on March 30, 1941, when the meaning of a passive submission to Vichy became clear to him (and long before military events in the least suggested that Germany would ultimately be defeated), he denounced a book by Jacques Chardonne[1] advocating collaboration, published an explicit and unequivocal attack on it, and wrote in his journal: "I am reading with amazement and dismay Chardonne's book . . . that sort of facile superiority . . . comes closer to revolting than enchanting me. . . . Yet I am grateful to Chardonne for having written this book which leaves everything in doubt except himself. . . . This book provides a reaction in me, for as I read it I feel clearly that this position is at the opposite pole from the one I must and will take; and it is important for me to declare it at once. My mind is only too inclined by nature to acceptance; but as soon as acceptance becomes advantageous or profitable, I am suspicious. An instinct warns me that I cannot accept being with them on 'the right side'; I am on the other."

These lengthy quotations are made necessary by the fact that one distinguished critic in a review of this volume of the journals has cited entries which, when isolated from the rest of the book, seem to justify the assertion that Gide was not really opposed to Nazism. This political deficiency is then connected with Gide's idea of culture and indeed his entire career, as if a few months' behavior were an adequate sample and trial of a lifetime's dedica-

---

1. In Justin O'Brien's glossary to this volume of the journals, we learn that Chardonne was elected to L'Academie Française in 1950. This is a beautiful example of having one's cake served up by whoever happens to be in power. It also casts a peculiar light on the political critics of Gide.

tion to culture, morality, and humanity. The process of using an author's political opinions as a criterion of his work ought to be left to those who are interested solely in politics: totalitarian politics.

There is much more to be said of Gide's journals and Gide's entire work as representative of all the virtues and limitations of modern literature. The limitations are real enough and nothing is gained by denying them or overlooking the necessary task of attempting to transcend them. But it is just as false to forget the virtues, and to overemphasize the limitations. There are always a sufficient number of philistines and middlebrows to remind us of the limitations while ignoring the virtues. And it is always tempting to listen to the sweet nothings of the *Zeitgeist* (that fickle, promiscuous, fancy lady who is so often getting married, divorced, and compromised). Any examination of Gide's work, his journals, and his idea of culture must include the valor with which he repudiated the Soviet Union, the strong and fruitful criticism he made of French colonial imperialism after visiting the Congo, his ceaseless effort to enlarge and extend the borders of sensibility and consciousness by learning foreign languages and studying foreign literatures. At the same time, bearing in mind these virtues, we ought to remember his weakness as a genuine novelist, the limitation involved in making sexual inversion the most important of moral problems or the symbol of moral freedom, and the errors in literary taste and sensibility which are at least in part the consequence of an omnivorous study of literature: such errors as his overestimation of Edmund Gosse, Pearl S. Buck, John Steinbeck, Dashiell Hammett, and many others.

When we think of Gide reading Milton in the moonlight in the French Congo, we must also think of how this literary pursuit in Africa was matched by his equal perception of the social injustice which prevailed about him and which he did much to make public. He was full of humility about his friend and peer, Paul Valèry; he was contrite, remorseful, and noble in acknowledging his failure, at first, to recognize Proust's genius; he was candid about and critical of his anti-Semitic emotions. He experienced to the full the attitude of the artist isolated from society and pursuing art for art's sake, just as he lived out and lived through the problem of the individual's moral freedom and moral justification; and just as he experienced with his whole being the burden and bewilderment of the author who attempts to find out what his social responsibilities are, as an author and as a human being.

If there are greater authors in the future, it will be partly the result of Gide's example and the knowledge of both his virtues and his shortcomings. There have been greater authors in our own era, but none can be said to be as fully and as adequately a witness to the truth about the apocalyptic period between 1870 and 1950: a living and marvelously articulate witness to the truth, despite enormous handicaps which would have silenced most men; despite fears, anxieties, and various other psychological disabilities; and most difficult of all, various social pressures, whether Catholic or Communist, which have made many another gifted author feel that it was not dishonest to be silent, indifferent, prudent, careful, and in the end incapable of distinguishing between patience and opportunism.

Gide is representative and he is a symbol. It is certainly fair enough that those who have serious doubts about modern literature as a whole should make his work the subject of the most careful examination. But the partial repudiation of modern literature which is now so fashionable would be more convincing if the critics and readers who participate in it were all devoutly reading and rereading Dostoevsky, Tolstoy, Balzac, Flaubert, Shakespeare and Sophocles; and drawing their standards of judgment from the great works which belong to a period prior to our own; and demonstrating that Proust's faults became clear when one had judged him in comparison with Tolstoy, Stendhal, and the author or editor of *The Iliad*.

Perhaps it is in the light of such studied comparisons—such a saturation in the experience of literature—that the authors of the twentieth century are being repudiated. But if this is the true reason, it has not been made explicit by the critics who declare that the time for a new revaluation and a partial rejection has arrived. Meanwhile in the great world itself many momentous cultural changes are occurring and perhaps this too has something to do with the new doubts about modern literature. If these cultural changes are troubling the doubtful readers and critics, one can only conclude that they are not troubled enough:[2] they are carping; they are cultivating subtle qualifications and reservations in the face of what may very well be an overwhelming change.

For it must be admitted that, in a way, after all, the classics are best sellers and hits right now. *Kiss Me Kate* has enjoyed a longer run than any other play by Shakespeare, with or without music, and we can certainly expect all of Shakespeare's plays to become musical comedies soon enough, a phenomenon which should make the Metro-Goldwyn-Mayer lion roar: *Ars gratia artis,* which, as everyone knows, means Art for the sake of the Almighty Dollar. Mr. W. Somerset Maugham has helped by editing Tolstoy, Dostoevsky, and others, so that the discursive and "uninteresting" passages in their masterpieces would not be present to irritate and bore the hurried reader. And the supreme dragon of television, which may transform motion-picture palaces into bare ruined choirs where late Bing Crosby sang, can very well make any doubts or hesitations about modern literature irrelevant or meaningless. Just as *Gulliver's Travels* became a children's book, *As You Like It, Hamlet, King Lear,* and *Oedipus Rex* may eventually appear as comic books. Sooner or later, moreover, no one will have to read anything at all: everything will be on the television screen. Television scripts will be written by those who have spent their happy childhoods looking at television performances, and then there will obviously be no need whatever any longer to discuss the virtues and the limitations of Gide and of modern literature.

2. It is certainly true that you can't fool all the readers all the time. But all the time is a long time to wait.

The Fiction of Ernest Hemingway
Moral Historian
of the American Dream

When Hemingway was awarded the Nobel Prize last year, *Time* magazine reported the honor under the rubric of *Heroes* instead of *Books*; and the summary of his career which followed spoke of Hemingway as "a globe-trotting expert on bullfights, booze, women, wars, big game hunting, deep sea fishing, and courage," adding that "his personality had made as deep an impression upon the public as his books." This excellent characterization may be misleading: it would be made more exact by asserting that the deep impression has been made upon the public by the personality encountered in Hemingway's books. This personality, which dominates all his writing, is a dramatized being combining the publicized public author with the typical heroes of his narratives.

The famous maxim, the style is the man, must become, to describe Hemingway's prose: the style is the personality. The leading characters in his novels are genuine and real but do not exist once and for all in the reader's mind as bywords and beings larger than life. The great characters of literature—Hamlet, Falstaff, Robinson Crusoe, Becky Sharp, Emma Bovary, Huck Finn, Leopold Bloom —possess that kind of reality; and it is the Hemingwayesque personality, more than his characters, which does also. This will be immediately recognized when Hemingway's narrative style is compared with his prose style when he writes in the first person, as in his books on bullfighting and big-game hunting. The style is exactly the same, whether it is fiction about an invented hero or the discourse of Hemingway himself, the most typical of his own heroes, when he speaks directly to the reader; it is not too much to say that he is then a heroic figment of his own narrative style, the robust, ebullient myth of a storyteller's imagination. It is because of this dramatized being that Hemingway has been the object of more publicity than any other American author, and the first to enjoy the kind of limelight accorded a Hollywood film star. For the majority of the reading public the distinction between the novelist and his books has become more and more a formality to be disregarded.

At the beginning of his career, it was the "wise guy" in Hemingway who made an impression: Hemingway seemed to be an extremely clever young man, possessing the special callous cleverness of the police reporter and the tough guy. To be a wise guy is to present an impudent, aggressive, knowing, and self-possessed face or "front" to the world. The most obvious mark of the wise guy is his sense of humor which expresses his scorn and his sense of independence; he exercises it as one of the best ways of controlling a situation and of demonstrating his superiority to all situations.

The mask of the wise guy is essential to Hemingway, the truly serious writer who is working, he has said, for a certain feeling of life and death. Once we remember how often such characteristic Americans as Lincoln and Mark Twain also wore a mask of humor, we can hardly help but recognize that in Hemingway, as in them, there is beneath the smiling mask a haunted mind and a heart so tender that it has been broken many times. This can be seen in the story *Homage to Switzerland*, when the Swiss waitress in a railroad café tells Mr. Johnson, an American writer, that she has learned English in a Berlitz school:

> "Tell me about it," Mr. Johnson said. "Were the Berlitz undergraduates a wild lot? What about all this necking and petting? Were there any smoothies? Did you ever run into Scott Fitzgerald? I mean were your college days the happiest days of your life? What sort of team did Berlitz have last fall?"

Mr. Johnson's remarks seem merely idle badinage, but they are not meant to be amusing at all, for soon after Mr. Johnson reveals that his wife has just decided to divorce him. His mockery is deadly serious and it has a poetic richness of meaning, since petting, necking, and being at college refer to the period of courtship when it seemed inconceivable that romance would conclude in divorce: hence this was the happiest time of life.

There is always a primary pattern at the heart of a serious writer's work, and it can be said that his style is the verbal realization of that pattern. It was the quality of Hemingway's style which attracted attention at the beginning of his career. It seemed the manifestation of a new point of view toward experience. His primary pattern can be seen in the clean, hard, bare, and clear-cut texture of the prose. The writing concentrates upon vivid sensation in the immediate present—and this is remarkable in a storyteller, since the art of fiction depends so much upon the present as arising from the past and moving toward the future. Perhaps Hemingway's human beings seek the immediacy and isolation of intense sensation because they have a profound need of being separate and alone, free of the past, history, the future, and hope, other human beings and all burdens.

In modern life, the experience of isolated enjoyment can be realized only under very special and privileged conditions. The most sensitive human beings feel a passionate devotion to sport because they find a fulfillment in it which they cannot attain in the serious pursuits by means of which they make a living. When Nick Adams, the first of Hemingway's heroes, tells a friend with whom he has gone skiing that his wife is going to have a child, his misgivings about fatherhood are painfully clear, and he clearly feels no such misgivings about skiing: "There's nothing that can really touch skiing, is there?" he says to his friend. The superiority of skiing to parenthood is typical of the criteria by means of which all experiences are judged. Skiing and activities like it give the self a sense of intense individuality, mastery, and freedom. In contrast, those activities which link the self with other human beings and are necessary to modern civilization not only fail to provide any such self-realization, but very often hinder it. The individual feels trapped in the identity assigned him by birth, social convention, economic necessity; he feels that this identity conceals his real self; and the sense that he is often only an anonymous part of the social mass makes him feel unreal. This is the reason that Hemingway's characters are so often drawn to the freedom of the holiday, are so often tourists, travelers, and expatriates, and so often appear at play and not at work. The desire for sensation is not the sensuality of the dilettante, but a striving for genuine individuality. The sensations of the immediate present have an authenticity which the senses make self-evident. Above all, those sensations which occur in the face of grave physical danger reveal the self's essential reality, since in the face of extreme threat, the self must depend wholly upon its own skill, strength, and courage.

Thus it is literally true that Hemingway's preoccupation with sensation is a preoccupation with genuine selfhood, moral character, and conduct. The holiday provides not only freedom, but good eating, good drinking, good landscapes, and good sexual intercourse under conditions which have the fairness of a game—so that drinking, making love, and most of the pursuits of the holiday become a trial of the self. Any concern with the self and its moral character requires a moral code, and the moral code in Hemingway is unmistakable. The rules of the code require honesty, sincerity, self-control, skill, and above all, personal courage. To be admirable is to play fairly and well; and to be a good loser when one has lost, acknowledging the victor and accepting defeat in silence. It is a sportsmanlike morality, which dictates a particular kind of carriage, good manners, and manner of speech: one must speak in clipped tones, condensing the most complex emotion into a few expletives or into the dignity of silence.

Perhaps Cohen, in *The Sun Also Rises,* is the best example of the character who repeatedly violates the Hemingway code. He is rich, gifted, and skillful; he has gone to Princeton, where he excelled in boxing, and he is a novelist and editor. Yet these advantages are unavailing, for he does not play the game according to the rules. He discusses his emotions in great detail, refuses to admit defeat when Brett, the lady with whom he is in love, rejects him, and, when he is hurt, he insists on telling everyone, instead of suffering in silence. Thus he is one of the damned. His damnation shows itself most explicitly when he struggles with Romero, the matador who has won Lady Brett's heart. Unlike several other rejected suitors, Cohen refuses to admit defeat, or the lady's right to choose. Instead he engages the matador in a first fight, knocks him down again and again, but cannot knock him out since the matador, a true Hemingway hero, takes interminable punishment, silently arising from the floor again and again until Cohen is finally defeated by the matador's fortitude and thus his moral superiority. In a like way, Lady Brett obeys the code and renounces the matador, when, coming to recognize that he fulfills an ideal of conduct as a human being and as a matador, she perceives that she is a threat to his purity: "It isn't the sort of thing one does," she says, adding that she does not want to be "one of those bitches who ruins children ... It makes one feel rather good deciding not to be a bitch ... It's sort of what we have instead of God."

Hemingway's style is the expression of the moral code at the heart of his writing. But it is neither primitive nor proletarian, as Mario Praz and Wyndham Lewis have suggested. It is sensitive to the whole range of difference between the speech of an aristocracy, the folk, the proletariat, the primitive, and the man in the street. Its devices include eloquent reticence, intensely emotional understatement, and above all the simplified speech which an American uses to a European ignorant of English. In fact what the American expatriate says and what he *hears* when he converses with a European are the very essence of Hemingway's style. The American, hearing the European speaking his own language, converts its idiom directly into a strange formalized English. When the Hemingway hero encounters the European, the dialogue which occurs intensifies the American hero's sense of his own attitudes and values to a remarkable degree, and results in a clear affirmation of Hemingway's moral code and his sense of the quality of modern life.

Hemingway's style is a poetic heightening of various forms of modern colloquial speech—among them, the idiom of the hard-boiled reporter, the foreign correspondent, and the sportswriter. It is masculine speech. Its reticence, understatement, and toughness derive from the American masculine ideal, which has a long history going back to the pioneer on the frontier and including the strong silent man of the Hollywood Western. The intense sensitivity to the way in which a European speaks broken English, echoing his own language's idioms, may also derive from the speech of the immigrants as well, perhaps, as from the special relationship of America to Europe which the fiction of Henry James first portrayed fully.

[259]

In the story called *The Gambler, the Nun and the Radio*, there is an example of the complexity of Hemingway's style which is as adequate as one illustration can be. A wounded Mexican gambler is being questioned by an American detective who tells him that he is going to die and wants to know who shot him:

> "Listen," the detective said, "this isn't Chicago. You're not a gangster. You don't have to act like a moving picture. It's all right to tell who shot you. That's all right to do."

Although the Mexican understands English perfectly, this colloquial American speech must be translated into a stylized foreign version for him by Mr. Frazer, an American writer, who is also a hospital patient:

> "Listen, amigo," said Mr. Frazer. "The policeman says that we are not in Chicago. You are not a bandit and this has nothing to do with the cinema."
> "I believe him," said Cayetano softly. *"Ya lo creo."*
> "One can with honor denounce one's assailant. Everyone does it here, he says."

It must be noted, for the sake of emphasis, that *the moving picture* becomes *the cinema* and *that's all right* becomes *one can with honor:* these and other parallel expressions show how completely and precisely the style is a realization of the moral code and two entirely antithetical attitudes toward it.

Hemingway's code has its Arcadias, where it is lived in spontaneous innocence—the Abruzzi of the priest in *A Farewell to Arms,* or the peasant Switzerland of the skiers. But Arcadia is very distant: the Abruzzi and Switzerland are at most tourist resorts for Hemingway's heroes; it is inconceivable that they should really live there. In the immediate background is the chaos and horror of modern war, or the mutilation, disillusion, and despair which marks those who survive the experience. Precisely this overwhelming experience or its aftermath distinguishes Hemingway's code from those it might seem to resemble—the codes of the gentleman, chivalry, and the profession of arms. For there is no reason rooted in existence itself, and no religious, social, or familial reason for obeying the code. To obey it is an act of desire, which sometimes gives one "good feelings," but remains essentially a mere preference, an arbitrary act justified by no future attainment or transformation. The matador is admirable, Cohen is detestable, but this is at most the brief concern of a few people, because existence is *nada*, a void. The community is not sustained by the individual's nobility or hurt by his wickedness. This is part of the hero's meaning in *A Farewell to Arms* when he silently asserts, during the First World War, in answer to another soldier who has said, "What has been done this summer cannot have been done in vain."

> I did not say anything. I was always embarrassed by the words sacred, glorious, and sacrifice and the expression in vain. We had heard them, sometimes standing in the rain almost out of ear-shot, so that only the shouted words came through, and had read them, on proclamations that were slapped up on billposters over other proclamations, now for a long time, and I had seen nothing sacred, and the things that were glorious had no glory and the sacrifices were like the stockyards at Chicago, if nothing was done with the meat except to bury it. There were many words that you could not stand to hear and finally only the names of places had dignity . . . Abstract words like glory, honor, courage and hallow were obscene beside the concrete names of villages.

And yet, although the hero deserts from the army, and although the abstract words have become obscene, it is nevertheless precisely glory, honor, courage, and sacrifice which are the true ideals and aims of conduct in all of Hemingway's writing. But most of his characters grasp these values, it must be repeated, by a fiat of will, as if they existed in a vacuum without any support or justification.

Yet at a great distance in the background there does exist a morality, utterly unlike that of modern life, where people do live as if human ideals did have an objective support in reality. When these characters appear, there is always the implication that they are naïve, old-fashioned, and do not know what has happened or that the world has changed; but in their naïveté and ignorance, they are nevertheless whole, noble, and integrated. Twice Catholicism provides the basis for these characters, and in nostalgic homage to their innocent superiority, the modern hero sometimes prays or is very courteous and friendly to a priest. Yet although the hero of *A Farewell to Arms* truly loved and admired the regimental priest, when the priest asked him to visit his own happy country, the Abruzzi, on his furlough, he promised that he would but went instead:

> . . . to the smoke of cafés and nights when the room whirled and you needed to look at the wall to make it stop, nights in bed drunk, when you knew that that was all there was, and then, in the morning, a sharp dispute about the cost.

And when he returned he said to himself that the priest "had always known what I did not know and what, when I learned, I was always able to forget. But I did not know that then though I learned it later."

This episode suggests the limitations of Hemingway's moral code and the style which is its articulation. On many levels of existence, the code is at most irrelevant. How meaningless, for example, Hemingway's morality becomes in relationship to a subject such as family life (as in Mann's *Buddenbrooks*), the way of life of an entire society (as in Proust), the struggle for religious belief (as in *The Brothers Karamazov*), the life of the city (as in *Ulysses*), or the span of all existence from birth to death in peace and war (as in Tolstoi). The great imaginative mode of death as such—which Shakespeare's dying heroes and his ghosts, the ghosts of Henry James, the supernatural beings in Dante, and the hero of Tolstoi's *The Death of Ivan Ilyitch* all illustrate, attaining a final, supreme, omniscient perspective on all existence—is far from Hemingway's limited interest in death. He says in *Death in the Afternoon*, that he went to bullfights "now that the wars were over" (a telltale phrase) because he wanted to see violent death, not "the complications of death by disease, or the death of a friend, or someone you have loved or have hated." Clearly it was not the vision of death but that of courage which Hemingway sought.

Eight years passed between the publication of *A Farewell to Arms* in October, 1929 and Hemingway's completion of a new novel. As it happened, aptly enough, October, 1929 was also the date of Hemingway's thirtieth birthday and of the stock market crash which began the Great Depression. Though the coincidence of dates is of course nothing more than accidental, it is nevertheless quite clear that the depression, as it continued, had a serious effect upon

Hemingway's creative powers. *Death in the Afternoon* (1932), and *The Green Hills of Africa* (1935) both had the appearance of books which were begun as works of fiction, and each of these books shows indirectly—and, at times, directly—how Hemingway was troubled more and more by the new attitude toward literature which took hold in literary circles soon after the beginning of the depression and became an overwhelming preoccupation as the economic crisis grew worse. All modern writing was judged by one criterion: its relationship to the social and economic crisis. The writer of fiction was told that he must make the social crisis the explicit subject of his work, and his fiction must arm the reader with attitudes which would lead to a just social order. It was assumed that postwar disillusion was the primary meaning of Hemingway's fiction; therefore his work was purely negative: he condemned war, but failed to show how it was to be prevented. His fiction was trivial because it dealt with expatriates, dilettantes, and idlers. It was the fiction of the lost generation, as Hemingway himself had acknowledged, and hence it was not the kind of fiction which could be regarded as important and valuable by a generation which did not want to be lost, but was resolved to determine the future and to create a society in which wars and depressions no longer occurred.

That Hemingway was disturbed by the new vogue we can see in one of the interludes of *Death in the Afternoon* in which he discusses the art of writing with an imaginary old lady: "Let those who want, save the world," he says to her, and to the social critics of the time, "the great thing is to last and get your work done and see and hear and learn and write; and write when there is something you know."

By April, 1933 the extent to which Hemingway was disturbed can clearly be seen as more acute in *The Gambler, the Nun and the Radio*. The leading character, Mr. Frazier, a writer, says at the conclusion:

> Religion is the opium of the people . . . Yes, and music is the opium of the people. Old mount-to-the-head [this is one of Mr. Frazer's scornful references to Karl Marx] hadn't thought of that. And now economics is the opium of the people; along with patriotism, the opium of the people in Italy and Germany.

Mr. Frazer adds drink, sexual intercourse, and ambition to this list of drugs and "the belief in any new form of government," and he says finally:

> What you wanted was the minimum of government . . . bread is the opium of the people . . . Education is the opium of the people . . . Why should the people be operated on without an anesthetic? . . . what do you want to do with the people? . . . But . . . revolution is no opium . . . Revolution is a katharsis which can only be prolonged by tyranny.

Other stories of the same period reveal that Hemingway was struggling with more than a powerful literary fashion: the despair in what is perhaps the best of all his stories, *A Clean Well-Lighted Place*, is at a great distance from the disillusion of the fiction of his early maturity. Everything is *nada*—nothing—the protagonist says, regretting that an old man has not been permitted to commit suicide and parodying the Lord's Prayer:

> What did he fear? It was not fear or dread . . . It was all a nothing and man was a nothing too . . . Our nada who art in nada, nada be thy name thy kingdom nada thy will be nada as it is in nada . . .

The final stage of the personal crisis had been reached by 1936, in *The Snows of Kilimanjaro*, a story about a dying writer, a self-indulgent failure who has written nothing good in years. Hemingway insists on the autobiographical intention of this story in several ways, above all in extended descriptions of the writer's early work which identify it with his own. As the writer lies dying of gangrene, convinced that he has wasted his powers beyond recovery, this is his own formulation of his failure:

> He had had his life and it was over . . . You were equipped with good insides so that you did not go to pieces the way most of them [most writers] had, and *you made an attitude that you did not care for the work that you used to do, now that you could no longer do it* . . . He had destroyed his talent himself . . . by not using it, by betrayals of himself and what he believed in, by drinking so much he had blunted the edge of his perceptions . . . There was so much to write. He had seen the world change; not just the events; though he had seen many of them and had watched the people, but he had seen the *subtler change and he*

could remember how the people were at different times . . . it was
his duty to write of it; but now he never would.

It is necessary to quote at length and to insert italics to show the
insight Hemingway discovered at the limits of desperation. The
world had changed inside of human beings; they were different:
not what they had been during the postwar period; hence it was
no longer possible to write about them and about the changed
world as he had in the fiction which made him famous before he
was thirty: "Not till we are lost," said Thoreau, "not till we have
lost the world, do we begin to find ourselves, and realize where we
are and the infinite extent of our relations."

Yet Hemingway's first attempts to find himself was a surrender
to the social consciousness he had scorned: *To Have and Have
Not* (1937) is a forced effort to repudiate his affirmation of the
isolated individual's heroism. The hero, Harry Morgan—Harry
is also the name of the dying writer in *The Snows of Kilimanjaro*
—declares as he lies dying:

> ". . . One man alone ain't got. No man alone now . . . No mat-
> ter how a man alone ain't got no . . . chance." He closed his eyes.
> It had taken him all his life to learn it . . .

But nothing in his experience gives this conclusion reality, and
though the novel contains passages of good writing, it is foolish,
disorganized, virtually hysterical and so entirely uncharacteristic
that its only interest, after eighteen years, is its relation to Hemingway's career as it moved forward from that point.

To Have and Have Not was written in great haste for a significant reason—the outbreak of the Spanish Civil War in 1936, and
Hemingway's eagerness to participate in it—and there is a curious
historical and literary irony in the fact that Hemingway should
have reached the extremity of desperation as a writer just at the
point when a new historical period, one of prolonged world war,
began. Once we recognize how superficial it was to regard Hemingway as an antiwar novelist, it becomes possible to see how his
eagerness to be in besieged Madrid must have been an intuition,
in part, that the new war and the new era might restore that intimate rapport between the modern world and the sense of existence
which had inspired his fiction at its best. The new war was a dif-

ferent war and not yet a world war. But it was from beginning to end a war against Fascism. It thus had a justification which the First World War lacked, since Fascism was a systematic denial of the freedom of the self in isolation.

The Fifth Column, Hemingway's only play, and the first product of his direct participation in the Spanish Civil War, is a poor work, but unlike *To Have and Have Not* it is not a falsification of his genius but a renewal of it. The very crudity of the plot is an ebullient and excited reaffirmation that the isolated individual's heroism is meaningful and important. And it prepares the way for Hemingway's most important novel, *For Whom the Bell Tolls*, in which the explicit theme and intention is to make the courage of the isolated hero inseparable from the fate of mankind and conversely to show that the fate of mankind depends upon the isolated hero. But what actually occurs gives the book a different meaning. During the major part of the story, the hero is engaged in guerrilla warfare for the Loyalists and he finds real self-fulfillment as a guerrilla soldier. But when toward the end the account of guerrilla warfare which makes the book successful is followed by an effort to satirize the Communists in the Loyalist regime who, by failing to respond to an appeal for help, cause the hero's death, the final meaning of the hero's experience is precisely the contrary of the author's intention: despite the reiteration that no man is an island unto himself, it is precisely and only as long as the hero in the isolation of guerrilla warfare defends his individuality that he triumphs. Immediately that his individuality is linked with, and his life depends upon, a large-scale social unit, such as an army or a political party, he is at the mercy of overwhelming powers which he cannot understand or control and upon which none of his heroic virtues has any influence.

For Whom the Bell Tolls appeared in 1940 and during the Second World War, it is reported, it was used as a textbook for guerrilla fighting by both the Americans and Russians. Hemingway took part in the Second World War also; professional soldiers who saw him in action as a correspondent in Spain and France said that he was the bravest human being they had ever seen. A long and ambitious novel about the Second World War was well under way when Hemingway, as the result of a hunting accident, had reason to suppose he was dying. It was then that he hurriedly wrote *Across the River and into the Trees*, which is revealing in a new way. There is in it an hysterical fury against modern war and modern generals: and it should be plain enough why Hemingway should feel thus about his experience in the Second World War. For in modern warfare more and more, apart from fighter pilots, the isolated individual has no part to play purely as an individual. His heroism is meaningless, since he is only an anonymous, expendable unit among millions. The book represents a total indulgence in romantic fantasy, the kind of surrender to every unlikely wish of the ego which is usually restricted to the reveries of adolescence. Yet though there is a complete failure of the novelist to be critical of the hero's attitudes and feelings, the novel is not wrong in the same sense as *To Have and Have Not*; it is not an attempt to repudiate the novelist's sense of existence, but on the contrary, it is a frantic and uncontrolled assertion and exaggeration of that sense of existence. Its bellicose, truculent, and intense bravado shows how, for Hemingway, the vision of life in all his fiction is identical with being alive.

The Old Man and the Sea, Hemingway's most recent novel (1952), is not so much a masterpiece in itself as a virtuoso performance, a new demonstration of the novelist's gifts far more than a new development of them. The experience of literature is always comparative; Hemingway's sixth novel has almost the same theme as *The Undefeated*, a story written twenty-five years before, and the old fisherman who has not made a catch for eighty-four days is in the same human situation as the aging matador of that story. Compared with that and other stories, and with the best episodes in Hemingway's previous novels, there is a certain thinness of characterization and situation.

Yet *The Old Man and the Sea* does give a new definition and meaning to Hemingway's work as a whole. It gives the reader an intensified awareness of how, for Hemingway, the kingdom of Heaven, which is within us, is moral stamina alone, and experience, stripped of illusion, is inexhaustible threat. It is completely clear in this novel, as it is not when his characters are expatriates in Europe, that Hemingway's primary sense of existence is the essential condition of the pioneer. It is above all the terror and isolation

[267]

of the pioneer in the forest that Hemingway seeks in his prize fighters, matadors, soldiers, and expatriate sportsmen. The old man's solitude is also meaningful: apart from the brief appearance of the young boy who is devoted to him, sorry for him, and has been told to avoid him, Santiago is the only human being in a narrative more than one hundred pages in length! The giant marlin is a sympathetic character for whom the old man develops a certain fondness and the sharks who destroy all but the marlin's skeleton are villains whom he detests: the astonishing fact remains that one human being is enough to make a genuine narrative. Moreover the old man is not only alone physically, but since he is old he will always be alone, cut off from youth, hope, friendship, love, and all the other relationships which sustain human beings. Hence, as the old man struggles with the sea—with time, nature, and death—he possesses a singular purity of will and emotion. The completeness of his solitude does much to relate the novel to all of Hemingway's work, making one more aware of how some form of solitude isolated every other leading character, giving a new clarity to Jake Barnes' mutilation, Frederick Henry's "separate peace," the solitude which the shell-shocked Nick Adams seeks on a fishing trip in *Big Two-Hearted River,* and the monologue of the dying writer in *The Snows of Kilimanjaro.* Thus, in a way, the old fisherman is the quintessential hero of Hemingway's fiction. Other human beings are simply absent now, and only the sharks are present to interfere with the naked confrontation of man and nature. It is the solitude which requires absolute courage and complete self-reliance.

With the old fisherman the pattern of Hemingway's fiction has come full circle. The hero as an old man stands in clear relation to the hero as a young boy and Nick Adams as a child in *Indian Camp*, the first story of Hemingway's first book. In that story Nick goes with his father, a doctor, to witness the mystery of birth: but he witnesses the horror of death also. The young Indian woman his father has come to help has been in labor for two days. "Daddy, can't you give her something to stop the screaming?" Nick asks his father. The doctor tells his son that despite her outcry the woman wants to be in labor and pain because she wants to have the baby and the baby too wants to be born. Then Dr. Adams performs a Caesarean using a jackknife. Dr. Adams feels exalted as he goes to tell the woman's husband the operation was successful—and finds him dead. His wife's screaming has made the Indian kill himself. This is hardly the initiation Dr. Adams had intended for his son. Yet, as father and son row home across the lake, Nick's reassurance grows as his father replies to his questions about suffering and death. As the sun rises over the lake Nick feels "sure that he would never die." This sentence illustrates the extreme illusion about existence which is native to the Hemingway hero and which makes disillusion, when it occurs, so astonishing and disastrous.

Just as the birth of a child causes the death of a man in *Indian Camp*, so in the last chapter of *A Farewell to Arms*, not only does the birth of a child cause the heroine's death, but before her death when she cries out in her agony, she speaks exactly like Nick Adams: "Can't they give me something?" and Frederick Henry says to himself: "She can't die," just as Nick was sure that he would not die. When the heroine dies, the burden of the hero's experience of birth, love, and death is a characterization of the nature of existence:

> So now they got her in the end. You never got away with anything . . . You did not know what it was about. They threw you in and told you the rules and the first time they caught you off base they killed you . . . They killed you in the end . . . You could count on that. Stay around and they would kill you.

The first illusion is that one will not die. The essential disillusion is death. Hence without exception every Hemingway hero suffers serious physical wounds, often as an initiation to the disillusion of reality and the ultimate wound of death.

The exact parallel of detail which links *Indian Camp* and the last chapter of *A Farewell to Arms* ought not to conceal an emotional difference which is quite important. Nick's primary illusion about existence in the first story, though it is shaken by his direct encounter with the reality of the agony of birth and suicide, is quickly restored: he concludes, as he began, with the same illusion that he will never die. Frederick Henry in *A Farewell to Arms* concludes in disillusion and despair. He has made a separate peace not only with war and love, but with life itself. Santiago in *The Old Man and the Sea* surpasses both prior characters. He suffers neither from illusion nor disillusion: he lives, as he says, by hope: "It is silly not to hope," he tells himself, and "besides, it is a sin." His kind of hope is clearly very different from Nick's return to illusion and Frederick Henry's surrender to disillusion. The passage from illusion through various phases of disillusion to the conclusion of sober hope represents the novelist's profound spiritual and emotional progress during the thirty years of his career.

The Capital of the World (1936) is perhaps one of Hemingway's most illuminating stories. The hero, a young waiter, gets killed in a pointless accident while practicing "the great media-veronica" of the matador. This is the author's comment and conclusion:

> He [the young waiter] died, as the Spanish phrase has it, full of illusions. He had not had any time in his life to lose any one of them, nor even, at the end, to complete an act of contrition . . . he had not even had time to be disappointed in the Garbo film which disappointed all Madrid for a week . . . The audience disliked the Garbo picture thoroughly . . . they were intensely disappointed to see the great star in miserable and low surroundings when they had been accustomed to her surrounded by great luxury and brilliance.

This is the most complete description of illusion in Hemingway and at the same time the most extreme statement of despair. Since the loss of illusion can only be prevented by early death, the only available anesthetic is the opium of death. This is as far as it is possible to travel from the belief that one will never die without believing in suicide. And it is a further indication of the immense experience of suffering which Hemingway's fiction encompasses. The vision of experience as pain, the imagination of suffering of every kind, requires a quality of compassion and sympathy on the author's part which seldom has been recognized.

Despair can only be known after the disappointment of hope; disillusion can only occur after the experience of illusion. The primary illusion in *The Capital of the World*—and the same illusion in all Hemingway's fiction—is illustrated by the reference to Greta Garbo in a Hollywood film. But the primary illusion and hope existed long before Hollywood, and it has often been called the American Dream. Hollywood has popularized and vulgarized the American Dream so widely that its true character and dignity has become somewhat obscured. It is formulated in the American Constitution as every human being's inalienable right to life, liberty, and the pursuit of happiness.

The American Dream is believed by many human beings who, like Hemingway's disillusioned characters, are unaware of their belief or convinced that they have awakened from it. The fact, which must be pointed out once more, that disillusion is inseparable from illusion and despair from hope, is disregarded. The right to happiness as the law of the land is the belief by which Hemingway's most desperate and unhappy characters live when they drink, travel, and play games. Like many more sanguine human beings, they have converted the legal right to life, liberty, and happiness into attitudes, emotions, an organized way of life which believes not only in the pursuit but the certainty of happiness. The American Dream converts the pursuit of happiness into the guarantee of a happy ending. For some this is promised by the nature of reality; for far more, it is supported by the nature of America as the New World where all are equal. And the American Dream is so primary and so important as a source of illusion and hope that the dream becomes insomnia when it is not fulfilled, or in a like way, courage is needed solely to cope with the unbearable pain of disappointment. Hemingway's fiction bears the same witness as the essential substance and avowed faith in the writings of Emerson, Thoreau, Whitman, and Melville.

The Hemingway hero's attitude toward himself and toward existence depends immediately upon the American Dream. Thus the first onset of disillusion is one in which the hero as a young man persuades the heroine to have an abortion: "We can have everything," the heroine says, "if we get married." "No, we can't," the hero answers, "it isn't ours anymore . . . Once they have taken it away, you never get it back." And when he adds this brief description of himself, "You know how I get when I worry," the heroine agrees to the abortion, thus: "If I do it you won't ever worry?" because never to worry is part of the dream. And when disillusion becomes despair, when the stock market crash begins a depression which seems unending, Hemingway, as his own hero, hunting big game in Africa feels that he is through with America since the American Dream has ended:

> A continent ages quickly once we come . . . The earth gets tired of being exploited . . . *A country was made to be as we found it.* Our people went to America because that was the place to go then. It had been a good country and we had made a bloody mess of it and I would go, now, somewhere else as *we always had the right to go somewhere else.* Let others come to America who did not know that it was too late . . . I knew a good country when I saw one. Here there was *game, plenty of birds . . . Here I could hunt and fish.*

Hemingway's sentences have been italicized to demonstrate that the pioneer and the immigrant and the hunter and fisherman are identical in the Hemingway hero whenever he thinks of how to regain the dream, and now how like Huck Finn he can always "light out for the frontier."

When the American Dream seems to have collapsed once and for all, the Hemingway hero (in *To Have and Have Not*) loses an arm smuggling to keep his family off the relief rolls, and decides that the heroic individual no longer has a chance by himself. And although the Hemingway hero has made a separate peace and said a farewell to arms years back, he goes to fight for the Loyalists in Spain because, as he says, he believes in life, liberty, and the pursuit of happiness, thus identifying the Spanish Civil War and the American Revolution: one man alone has a chance, after all, to save humanity and hence the hero, Robert Jordan, blows up a bridge as a way of firing a shot which will be heard around the world. Robert Jordan's father has killed himself because of the Wall Street stock market crash, just as Nick Adams' father has committed suicide because, being a sentimental man, he was always being betrayed. And every American of Hemingway's generation has known the most exalted expectations and the most desperate disasters. Living through the First World War, the great era of prosperity, the crash, the long depression, the Second World War, and a new era of prosperity, he has been subjected to the American Dream's giddy, unpredictable, magical, tragic, and fabulous juggernaut. It is thus natural enough that the Hemingway hero should always feel threatened, always in danger, always subject to what the sociologists call "status panic." A society committed to the American Dream is one which creates perpetual social mobility but also one in which the individual must suffer perpetual insecurity of status as the price of being free of fixed status. Hence the Hemingway hero is always afraid of failure, no matter how often he has succeeded, which is precisely what the old fisherman says: " 'I will show him what a man is and what he endures' ... The thousand times that he had proved it meant nothing. Now he was proving it again. Each time was a new time." This is the reason that the Hemingway hero must continually assert his masculinity: he may always lose it, as he may always lose his strength, his youth, his health, his skill, his success, and thus his sense of selfhood.

Of all the modern novelists it is Hemingway who has written the most complete moral history of the American Dream in the twentieth century: the greatest of human dreams is the beginning of heartbreaking hope and despair; its promise is the cause of overwhelming ambition and overwhelming anxiety: the anxiety and the hope make courage an obsession and an endless necessity in the face of endless fear and insecurity: but the dream, the hope, the anxiety, and the courage began with the discovery of America.

The Fiction of William Faulkner

Sanctuary was the novel which established William Faulkner as an author from the point of view of publishers. It even awakened the Hollywood version of consciousness. In an introduction written to the Modern Library edition of *Sanctuary*, Faulkner speaks of his work in the tough lingo many American authors appear to find necessary to any discussion of their work and their profession:

"I began to think of books in terms of possible money. I decided that I might just as well make some of it myself. I took a little time out, and speculated what a person in Mississippi would believe to be current trends, chose what I thought to be current trends, and invented the most horrific tale I could imagine and wrote it in about three weeks."

The effort was successful from several points of view. Now Faulkner has written eight books since the appearance of *Sanctuary*. These books have not only helped to dissipate the corncob immortality *Sanctuary* won for him; but for some time a quickly recognized quality has been defined and made various by the successive thunder-and-lightning of each book. It was an astonishing and just experience five years ago to attend a film named "Slave Ship," be struck by the Faulkneresque quality of the way in which the story was presented, and find later that Faulkner had written the scenario.

The consecutive sum of fourteen books read over a period of ten years and then brushed through again for the advantages of retrospect brings one the conviction that the Faulkneresque idiom is something of permanent interest. In reading these books and in bringing them freshly or fadedly to mind each time a new one

[274]

appears, one naturally cannot help but mark the recurrence and repetition of elements newly and differently. No more can one help interpreting these elements in their togetherness and seeing them as a kind of constellation. A constellation is an artificial order which helps one to see and to recognize the stars. If one keeps in mind the possibly artificial character, it is perfectly safe to look at the elements as such a constellation.

A MISSISSIPPI CONSTELLATION

There are many stars in the blackness of the sky. The star of the World War as a theme appears in *Soldier's Pay, Sartoris,* and several of the stories in *These Thirteen.* Two sub-themes are the return of the soldier and the soldier as an American in France or England during the World War.

Far more important, yet connected underground with the World War theme, is that of the Civil War. Often the soldier back from France behaves as if he had just lost the Civil War: this is the case with Bayard Sartoris, whose behavior is far in excess of the motive given for it, the death of his twin brother as an airman.

Obviously the Civil War theme cannot be separated from the White-Black theme which runs through almost all the books, but is especially prominent in *Light in August* and *Absalom, Absalom!*. In both these books the leading characters are trying to escape from having the stigma of Negro blood in themselves or in their families. Or this theme might better be named that of the Old South and its ruin.

Then there is the theme of the poor white and the peasant, seen most strikingly in the two books just mentioned: in both of them the poor white rises to a tragic dignity by simple tenacity and faithfulness. Wash Jones kills Colonel Sutpen, who has made his daughter pregnant, when Sutpen speaks with contempt of her; and in *Light in August,* Lena Grove follows her fugitive lover for hundreds of miles and hundreds of pages without a word of criticism or dismay; she is at least one reader's favorite character in the *dramatis personae* of all the books.

Then there is the theme, richest of all, of the primitive, the abnormal, and the virtually insane.

The primitives are the delightful Indians in *These Thirteen,* and

[275]

the Negroes when they are left to themselves, or when, as in one fine story, the Indians and the Negroes are together, and the white man's absence is a positive thing, like a sudden silence.

The abnormal has no better example than the celebrated Popeye, impotent like the hero of *The Sun Also Rises*, who rapes a co-ed with a corn cob and gains sexual satisfaction by regarding the sexual act and neighing by the bed like the horse who injured him. A number of other characters compete with Popeye, but without comparable success.

The insane figures occur many times also, in such an idiot as Benjy (in *The Sound and the Fury*), obsessed with a day in his childhood fifteen years back, or as Ike Snopes in *The Hamlet* who engages in sexual congress with a cow after a rapturous love affair: there are more novels which contain idiots than novels without them. But it is the peculiar use of them by Faulkner and the emphatic value placed upon their perceptions which make them most important elements.

The star of the obsessed lovers shines many times too, as in *The Wild Palms*, where the passionate pair are in flight from every aspect of society which weakens or intervenes or intermits their obsession with each other; or as in *The Hamlet* where a football player tackles the impassive schoolgirl he has been lusting after for months. In passing, it might be said that nowhere is Faulkner less successful than with this theme.

The star of the intellectual shines weakly. He is such a lawyer as Horace Benbow, who appears in several books, chiefly in *Sartoris* and *Sanctuary*, or he is such a minister as the Rev. Gail Hightower in *Light in August*. Both are ruined men and cuckolds. In dealing with the intellectual in himself, in attempting to present his states of mind, Faulkner does very poorly, almost as poorly as with his obsessed lovers, because of a failure of style, which then becomes literary in the worst sense.

But the intellectual is impressive and moving when, no longer alone and soliloquizing, he is caught into the story's movement. Then he expresses the failure of rationality, the failure of law and order and justice in an irrational world. This is what happens to Horace Benbow in *Sanctuary* when he tries to defend an innocent poor white accused of murder and in the course of his passion for justice in the abstract violates Southern mores by revealing publicly the shame of Temple Drake, a young lady of good family.

The brightest reddest star of all is that of violence and horror, the violent act and the violent man, and the emotion of horror conjured up by the forms of violence. This is what we see almost always, whether in the killing of Temple Drake's lover, the violence for generations of Thomas Sutpen, the murder and lynching in *Light in August*, the suicide in *The Sound and the Fury*, the desperate driving of a car in *Sartoris* and the equally desperate driving of a plane in *Pylon*, the cutting of a navel-cord with an empty jagged-edged tomato can during birth in *The Wild Palms*. The stage has not been so loaded with corpses since late Elizabethan tragedy.

Other themes, related and mixed with the mixture of those already mentioned, need only be marked: the city slicker theme and the village slicker theme: the latter is a trader and business man of one kind or another, best embodied in the many appearances of the Snopeses. And most successfully the comic theme, the immense and overwhelming comedy in which Faulkner too seldom engages his characters, as in the great Miss Reba of *Sanctuary*, the Indians already mentioned, and the tall tales of horse-trading in *The Hamlet*. Lastly there is the South as a region and landscape, described with strength and vividness by Faulkner, who rises to the truly poetic in his descriptions, as in his versions of the minds of intellectuals, he echoes the worst kind of poetry.

The constellation which gives these elements unity for at least one reader is that of obsession with the endless horror and irrationality of life. Again and again, violence ensues, horror triumphs, injustice is the victor, irrationality overcomes all, all human purpose and effort is vain, mistaken, and defeated. No author has more right than Faulkner to the much-used lines in *Macbeth* about the tale told by an idiot full of sound and fury, signifying nothing. In Shakespeare, however, this view of life is uttered by a murderer virtually at the end of his rope; not by the author. In Faulkner, signifying nothing signifies all, it is the ultimate revelation. Thus the critical question often becomes, does Faulkner's story bring itself to the point which Macbeth occupies when he makes his speech.

The conclusion of meaningless defeat can hardly be exaggerated. For in the end, Temple Drake is left hopeless and empty in the sanctuary of Paris, Joe Christmas is lynched, Popeye is hanged for a crime he did not commit, the righteous minister who would protect Joe Christmas is killed, the family mansion is burned down in *Absalom, Absalom!* and Thomas Sutpen's passion to found a landed white family ends in a halfbreed idiot son, Quentin Compson kills himself, and the aviators in *Pylon* are killed purposelessly.

The obsession with violence and evil is such that it is difficult to think of a crime not committed in the corpus of Faulkner's work. Simple murder is almost the least among such acts as incest, cannibalism, rape, various forms of sodomy, patricide, fratricide, and filicide, adultery, and castration.

The Style and Method of Horror

This vision of Life is delivered to the page by a variety of devices appropriate in their sum, but not always under the author's control, and often directed as much *against* the reader as upon the story to be told.

Most prominent is the deliberate *mystification* of style and method. The reader is deliberately kept from knowing the full significance of the action he is reading about and some of the characters are often kept in like ignorance. The mystification is achieved by the use of interior monologue, especially that of idiots; or it is achieved by a description of the action in the most detailed physical terms, terms so overwhelmingly physical that the motive of the action is not discernible and is purposely kept unknown. Frequently a related device is used, the narration of the action is separated from the narration of the motive by hundreds of pages. One reason for this is that the character responsible for the action conceals his motive, or his motive has its roots in the distant past, as in Popeye's rape of Temple Drake, or Sutpen's desire to found a landed white family because of the families he has seen in Virginia during his boyhood. Sometimes, however, the character himself does not know or is unsure of the motive for his action, and sometimes it appears that Faulkner himself does not know or does not care: thus the plot of *Absalom, Absalom!* is almost annihiliated by the conflict between Thomas Sutpen and his white son over the marriage of his daughter to the son who has colored blood: but this conflict directly contradicts Thomas Sutpen's initial and most important motive, to have a family free of colored blood: for his white son is the most important element in the fulfillment of this desire, and next to him, the marriage of a daughter to one with colored blood, though regrettable, is hardly sufficient cause for the conflict between father and son. This is an amazing example of forgetfulness on an author's part.

Frequently, too, a number of characters play a choric role. They stand by to be astonished, shocked, and enthralled by the action, as for example, the newspaper reporter in *Pylon*, Ratliff the sewing machine agent in *The Hamlet*, the friend of the obsessed lovers in *The Wild Palms*, the two students who ponder the story of *Absalom, Absalom!*, and various idiots here and there.

Sometimes these bystanders are normal human beings whose normality serves to define the shock of the abnormal action. Sometimes they are abnormal themselves and serve to heighten the fury. And sometimes they are so fascinated by the spectacle they regard that they are drawn into it: this is particularly the case with the reporter in *Pylon*.

These choric characters are present perhaps to instruct the reader, perhaps to help him discount his initial disbelief by admitting the cogency of his normal response.

But over and above all is the effort of the author to mystify his reader and to compel his characters to feel his vision of the horror and irrationality of life.

It is plain enough that there is a connection between a mystification of style—a deliberate effort to make the story difficult to apprehend—and a vision of Life's irrationality. That such a literary method is justified by such a vision is not plain.

Again, it is easy to see why the author attempts to compel his reader into the emotion of horror. But there is a serious distinction between compelling him by the story in itself, and compelling him by mystifying him or forcing a furious style upon him.

The same thing happens to the characters. The reader can quickly distinguish between occasions when the character's emotions are compelled by his situation, and occasions when they are compelled by the author's style. One sometimes see Faulkner shaking his characters to make them hysterical, jogging them up and down like a hysterical ventriloquist to gain the fury he wants.

This repeated distinction between what the subject makes available because of its nature and what the author attempts to compel in his subject, out of all reason, serves to define the primary cause for Faulkner's successes and failures.

When Faulkner has a subject extreme enough in its horror and abnormality, his style is measured, under control, and directed at the specific description of specific things. His writing is genuinely poetic and exact, his delaying obscuring method of presentation is matched and required by the nature of the story, and he has no need of the hysterical passion and the rapturous denunciation of Life in his style because the subject is sufficient unto the evil. The reader is left to respond to the subject without the author's obsessive coaching.

When the subject does not justify the author's horror, the devices of style become clumsiness and tricks, the writing is a stale version of the Swinburnian high poetic, and worst of all the style becomes purple, empty of specific objects, and sometimes insufferably periodic.

The distinction comes to the difference between boxing and shadow-boxing. Faulkner is able to get a subject to fight with about half the time. This would be good enough, were it not true that the boxing and shadow-boxing alternate in the same book: certainly this is the case in what seems to me to be Faulkner's best book, *Absalom, Absalom!*

Yet this is too pat and neat to explain everything. No doubt an irreducible factor is Faulkner's literary admirations. Another factor is an inveterate carelessness, as Mr. George Marion O'Donnell observed in his essay on Faulkner, a carelessness which results in contradictory motivation, repetitiousness, and undue prolongation of the story. The lush love of such words as *proud, gallant, subtle, myriad, richly,* especially in pairs, coupled with rare or polysyllabic words of Latin derivation—"a sound meaningless and profound, out of a suspirant and peaceful following silence"—is a more complex vice of style.

The forced intensity in the texture of the writing is often close to the excellence which results when Faulkner is content to seize

[280]

definite objects; here is an example where virtue and defect are an inseparable mixture:

> The sunny air was filled with competitive radios and phono- graphs in the doors of drug- and musicstores. Before these doors a throng stood all day, listening. The pieces which moved them were ballads simple in melody and theme, of bereavement and retribution and repentance metallically sung, blurred, empha- sized by static or needle—disembodied voices blaring from imita- tion wood cabinets or pebble-grain horn mouths above the rapt faces, the gnarled slow hands long shaped to the earth.

It is plain that "ballads simple in melody and theme . . ." is a characterization too general, too far from the concreteness of the other phrases. The "bereavement, repentance, and retribution" note is wrong in the same way and flows, though not as strikingly as many other passages in Faulkner, from the false sense of the highly poetic, just as "disembodied voices blaring from imitation wooden cabinets" is right because the word is seeking to define an object before compelling an emotion.

The carelessness suggests itself as that of an author who is in an immense hurry (impatience is a form of laziness, said Kafka) and who writes his books quickly, driving ahead without looking back at the previous pages. Malcolm Cowley has remarked that Faulk- ner, like few American writers, has a daemon: this seems to be true, but it is hardly the daemon of Socrates, who always said No. Faulkner's daemon is utterly positive.

Faulkner himself provides an image which seems most appro- priate in his introduction to *Sanctuary*. He describes how he wrote *As I Lay Dying* in the boiler room of a power plant all night long in the intermissions of loading a wheelbarrow with coal for the fireman to put into the boiler while nearby "a dynamo ran. It made a deep constant humming noise." The book was written in three weeks. Better books have been written in a shorter time and worse books have taken years. It is a question of one's attitude to one's art, rather than a question of time.

A further point is that Faulkner is one of the many American writers for whom writing and reading have no necessary relation- ship. He has profited by the example of such an author as Joyce, but beyond this there is little to show that he makes such a use of the reading of criticism and of other men's novels as a French author would make almost instinctively. One would never guess that America has had such writers as Hawthorne, Melville, and James, all of whom might have been of an immense usefulness to an author of Faulkner's character and uncontrollable gifts of sensibility.

The danger of imitation would not have been serious. The formal example of James might have kept Faulkner from such arbitrary, forced, superposed, and essentially pointless devices as the alternation of two stories in *The Wild Palms.*

But more than that, any serious reading might have kept Faulkner from being the victim of his own great gifts as well as the victim of the self-indulgence of his style. One comes finally to the guess that perhaps Faulkner does not even read his own books. This is one way to explain some of the superfluities and misorganizations which mar so fine a novel as *Light in August.*

In like manner, one has the sense that Faulkner has been the victim of his youthful reading in writers like Wilde, Symons, Pater, Dowson, and other writers of prose in the grand manner who may be responsible for the sudden occurrence, amid much good writing, of such a phrase as "her voice was proud and still as banners in the dust."

A final note on Faulkner's method rests on another guess. Faulkner's best writing almost invariably has to do with the locale he names Yoknapatawpha County, Mississippi, and the town of Jefferson. Many of the characters return through the successive novels. Sometimes they rise from the dead backward in time, like the redintegration of an explosion in a newsreel; for Quentin Compson kills himself in *The Sound and the Fury*, but returns in *Absalom, Absalom!* at a point six months earlier to tell a story four hundred pages in length, no doubt as much to the creator's surprise as to that of the reader of *The Sound and the Fury.* The Sartorises, the Compsons, the Sutpens, the Snopeses, and the Benbows suggest the guess that Faulkner has models of actuality to draw from. As soon as he goes from this region, as soon as he seems to invent *ex nihilo,* the forced quality becomes least tolerable and the characters become plainly incredible: this seems especially true of *The Wild Palm* and *Pylon.*

The suggestion is that for Faulkner, as for most authors, actuality is an inexhaustible well or mine; imagination and invention are bogus unless they are bound to actuality and inspired by it. This is one of the most important senses in which art is an imitation of life, beyond any assent to the doctrines of naturalism and realism. There are inconceivably more possibilities in Life for the author with gifts than anything his imagination can construct. As there is nothing in the mind not first in the senses, so there is no richness in the imagination which is not surpassed by the richness of Life when it works upon the imagination.

Genesis and Audience

On certain occasions, a literary critic feels that he ought to have call letters, like radio stations: followed by an announcement of the city from which the bodiless voice proceeds. It is obviously necessary to assume a common denominator between reader and writer. But in discussing so extraordinary an author as Faulkner, perhaps something ought to be said about the immense distance between the region of the critic and that of the author. Few readers of Faulkner or of this essay are likely to have heard of Washington Heights unless they have lived in New York City and even then they may be ignorant. But it should be said that a Washington Heights view of our time and our country may weaken or make wholly incorrect the following discussion of Faulkner as the product of a *milieu*, the agent of a body of fiction, and an author aware of his audience. The soul may be composed of the external world. Wallace Stevens has suggested: "I am what is around me."

If this seems to make too much of the bare region of it all, some prominent instances from the decade of the 'thirties are available. Is it conceivable that Steinbeck would have written *The Grapes of Wrath*, if his audience had not been yearning to hear about the dispossessed? if a certain section of the populace had not been dispossessed? Would James T. Farrell's Studs Lonigan trilogy or William Saroyan's endless happiness jag about how wonderful it is to be alive and on the WPA ("Aspirin is a member of the NRA" is the title of one of his early stories) have been possible in the 'twenties?

The issue is not in the least that of mechanical causation: the age strikes the author in the sensibility and the author strikes back with a book. If this meant anything, it would mean that authors of the same period would have to be very much alike. But the assumption here is merely that the age and the author's *living* are necessary conditions, among other necessary conditions, of the specific character of his work.

What, then, can be found in Faulkner's social background to satisfy the literary historian; also to make possible a nice discrimination between the *causes* of a work and the work itself and the audience at which it may be aimed and the mind of the audience which accepts or rejects the work?

Faulkner was an aviator during the World War. This probably explains the aviators in some of his stories and the World War theme of his earlier novels. The World War may also suggest a factor in the leading obsession with violence. It is matched by other authors of Faulkner's generation, though not of his region: Jeffers, O'Neill, and Hemingway. The Prohibition Era too (Popeye, for example, is a bootlegger) must have provided its violence for Faulkner's imagination.

It is evident enough, too, that the White-Black theme, the memory of the Civil War, and other like subjects begin in Faulkner's being a Southerner, making the critic with naturalist or realist assumptions look at Faulkner as the spokesman or literary representative of "decadent Southern families."

But the specific and dominant quality of his work is not explained by these general factors, which must have operated upon many other authors. What is it,—can we say what it is?—which compels Faulkner to be obsessed with the horror and irrationality of life, in his writing? Every period has such writers. But what has helped to make Faulkner such an author in our time and in our country?

The question will have to be answered with conviction by one who knows a great deal more about a number of things than the present critic.

But I would like to suggest a hypothesis (merely a hypothesis): the conflict between the idea of the Old South and the progressive actuality of the New South has brought Faulkner to the extreme where he can only seize his values, which are those of the idea of the Old South, by imagining them being violated by the most hideous crimes. Thus Temple Drake must be violated by a corn cob: mere rape is not enough.

What are the values of the *idea* of the Old South (I should say here that I know of these phrases only at second- and third-hand and may use them too inaccurately)? The emphasis on pride and gallantry, the attitude toward the Negro, the behavior of the decadent Southern families always remarked by reviewers, illustrate these values broadly. One of the best examples is in *Sartoris*.

Here one is greatly impressed by the story, told by one of the characters in the present, about a member of the Sartoris family in the Civil War who is an officer with Stuart. Stuart has captured a Northern officer during a raid made for the sole purpose of getting coffee. The captured officer is without a horse, much to Stuart's distress. Out of courtesy, Stuart determines to get his captive a horse by making another unnecessary raid. The Northern officer protests that this is foolish and rash behavior, especially for a mere prisoner. Stuart replies that it is not for a prisoner, but "for an officer suffering the fortunes of war. No gentleman would do less." The Northern officer answers that "no gentleman has any business in war. There is no place for him here. He is an anachronism, like anchovies. At least General Stuart did not capture our anchovies. Perhaps he will send Lee for them in person."

Bayard Sartoris, astride his mount nearby, hears the interchange, charges forward on his horse, though Stuart shouts a protest at him, attacks the commissary tent of the Northern company to get the anchovies, and is killed by a scared cook, as the captured Northern officer begs Stuart to go to his rescue, saying: "What is one man to a renewed belief in humanity?"

This story is told to illustrate the character of the Sartoris family. It is told in half-humor and not without a strong critical attitude. Yet despite the overtone of amusement and irony, there can be no doubt that this is where Faulkner's allegiances abide: his values are enacted and fulfilled in such an episode.

But enacted and fulfilled only in the Civil War, which has been over for a long time: the later Sartorises must exist in a society in which such behavior often seems meaningless: when the later Bayard Sartoris comes home from the World War, he has no way to express such values; consequently he expresses his frustration and despair by driving his car at hair-rising speeds.

So too with all the noble and heroic human beings who exist in the present: they have no medium in which to operate. They have carried forward inherited values to a period of time in which the dominant powers of the community do not so much oppose these values (opposition is obviously recognition, of a sort) as refuse to be aware of their existence.

Given those values, how can one experience them in modern life? How, except through the violence and abnormality which betrays them so brutally that, by a recognizable dialectic, their existence is recognized. The criminal helps one to remember the judge.

Moreover, from the point of view of those values, the irrationality of Life is seen in two ways: the alien environment is irrational because those values are foreign to it; and Life is irrational because those values fail to be embodied, are always frustrated and destroyed.

To repeat once more, this is merely a hypothesis: but many other examples might be cited to add to its persuasiveness.

The important point is that, though this state of being is responsible for Faulkner's defects as well as his virtues, the result is much more than a body of fiction representative of a *milieu*. For plainly, Faulkner's dominant situation, though extreme, is a permanent point on the compass of human fate, and Faulkner's effort for the most part is to see it in its generality, not as a piece of local color.

The local color appears, however, especially in the regional obsession with the White-Black theme. At the end of *Absalom, Absalom!* Quentin Compson, who has been telling a story of the Old South and a family as ridden by the Furies as the House of Atreus, is asked by his auditor, a Canadian student at Harvard, "Why do you hate the South?"

" 'I don't hate it,' Quentin said, quickly, at once, immediately; 'I don't hate it,' he said. *I don't hate it* he thought, panting in the cold air, the iron New England dark; I don't. *I don't! I don't hate it! I don't hate it!*' " This concludes the book.

A moment before, the Canadian boy has just made a prophecy about the interbreeding of whites and Negroes:

"I think that in time the Jim Bonds are going to conquer the Western hemisphere. Of course it won't quite be in our time and of course as they spread out towards the poles they will bleach out again like the rabbits and the birds do, so they won't show up so sharp against the snow. But it will still be Jim Bond; and so in a few thousand years, I who regard you will also have sprung from the loins of African kings."

This is the regional interest at its best. One must distinguish with the greatest care between what an author writes because of the life he has lived and known, and the objectives he sometimes gives his writing because of a sense of his audience. A Grosset & Dunlap reprint of *Sartoris* speaks on the jacket, in pure publishers' prose, of how "Every reader of *Sanctuary* and *Light in August* will want to read this other novel of life in the raw in the New South." This is rather raw, even for a publisher. But the worst thing is that Faulkner shows signs now and then of writing horror stories of the South for an urban audience. Certainly this is what his audience reads to look for. In *The Hamlet,* the sexual act of an idiot with a cow, regarded by the village people, makes one think that perhaps Faulkner has heard of the success of *Tobacco Road.*

But in the main, the body of his writing, both in its successes and its failures, seems to be engendered by an obsession with values which cannot be realized with sufficient intensity except through violation and perversion.

Judgment as Comparison

Is it not true that literary judgment in the end is literary comparison? One work is better than another work. If one did not think of better works, one might be satisfied with what is not good at all.

When we consider a body of work in itself, does not our past reading stand behind us and tug the hair on our heads, like the goddess Athena? Are not countless intuitive comparisons made when we recognize false notes or enjoy the rendering of actuality in language?

Considered in itself, the whole body of Faulkner's writing contains no work which seems completely successful. *Absalom, Absalom!, Light in August,* and several of the short stories in

[287]

These Thirteen come close to complete success. The first of these falls short because of a self-indulgence of style and a carelessness in the plot; *Light in August* suffers from an obscurity in Joe Christmas' motivation and poor organization at the end of the book; two of the novels are made difficult from the start by the fact that Faulkner has tried to work them up out of successful short stories, though unlike Hemingway, who does the same thing, Faulkner rewrites the short story which he is planting in his novel. But on the other hand, no volume of Faulkner's lacks pages and passages which are as remarkable as any American fiction of our time and worth all the expense of spirit which a reading of Faulkner requires.

There is a mixture of success and failure throughout and there need not have been such a mixture so often, with a little more active respect for literature as an art. But on the other hand, the mixture is a great deal better than nothing: it is a body of work which bears the marks of permanent interest.

When we look for comparisons outside the work, a considerable choice presents itself: one thinks of *Wuthering Heights*. One hardly thinks of Dostoievsky, as some critics have suggested; though Dostoievsky's Slavophilism is comparable to Faulkner's feeling about the South, the religious and intellectual motivations of Dostoievsky's novels are lacking in Faulkner.

But Faulkner's work is of sufficient ambition to suggest Shakespeare and of sufficient horror to bring to mind *King Lear*. Lear on the heath during the storm, calling on Nature to wipe out the works and the ungrateful heart of man is perhaps a suitable touchstone. What other better example of the horror and brutality of Life can we find? A fool the equal of Faulkner's idiots is present too.

Yet two important differences become plain. Shakespeare does not have to break down the framework of dramatic form in order to express his horror; he does not have to engage in the formal mystifications Faulkner uses; and most important of all, the genuine fool is matched by a rational man who makes believe he is a fool: rationality presides and triumphs over the scene, despite the irrationality of life.

Nevertheless, if the comparison shows how Faulkner falls short, it shows too that his work has the power and the seriousness to suggest the comparison. And with all its failures it is especially edifying in the winter after the year 1940, for as the true Fool so wisely remarks:

"This cold night will turn us all to fools and madmen"!

Faulkner's *A Fable*

Faulkner toiled over *A Fable* for more than nine years, a long time for most novelists, and particularly long for a writer of Faulkner's kind of inspiration which Malcolm Cowley has rightly compared to a state of demonic possession. The novelist's long labor suggests that the difficulty was one of conception, not of composition, and this should be enough in itself to indicate that the book must be read several times. This is true of much of Faulkner's fiction, but hitherto the reason has been the novelist's style and narrative method. In *A Fable* the same effort must be directed to style and method, but there is a greater difficulty in the theme itself. Within the literal story of a mutiny on the western front during the First World War, the Gospel account of Christ's passion emerges in a peculiar and unique way. The illiterate French corporal who leads the mutiny is the modern representative of Christ; his twelve followers are like the twelve apostles; one of them betrays him, another denies him thrice; he is tempted by the supreme commander of the Allied armies as Christ is tempted by Satan; and when, rejecting all temptation, he refuses to repudiate the mutiny, he is tied to a post and shot by a firing squad, his head, as he falls, caught in a barbed wire to make a modern crown of thorns. And there are a good many other genuine and powerful realizations of the Gospel pattern—a delightful modern version of the marriage in Cana of Galilee (which begins in a French village with American soldiers in a crap game), and a touching version of the Last Supper (in which the corporal who represents Christ simply urges his followers to eat more and talk less or afterward they will be hungry and sorry).

The peculiar way in which the Gospel pattern functions can perhaps best be suggested by a metaphor: it is as if, during a play, the actors were seen at recurrent, important moments, varying in length and meaning, in a lighting which like an X-ray machine showed their bone structure, brain, and heart in black, beneath and together with their ordinary visual appearance. This use of the Gospel story is quite unlike the prevailing mythical techniques of modern literature because it has only one purpose and meaning, the representation of supreme nobility, instead of the manifold meanings of contrast, simultaneity, irony, analogy, and the like, which other modern authors seek through mythical reference. Faulkner's sole purpose is to unite the theme of modern war with the theme of the appearance of Christ in the modern world (an aim which could be surpassed in daring and ambition only by the like one of the second coming of Christ as a Negro in the South) in order to give adequate actuality to the real subject of *A Fable*. The real subject is: are human beings worthy of supreme nobility? The wholesale impersonal brutality of modern war, intensified by the crisis of a mutiny, might by itself reduce this question to that of whether human beings are worth anything at all. By making the Gospel pattern emerge within the mutiny through the corporal who is its leader, the question is made to include the noble sacrifice which the corporal embodies, and at the same time it is strengthened by the most famous of precedents, the most vivid and tragic of all stories.

Hence this complexity of intention and meaning in *A Fable* (a complexity which is also, in part, a remarkable simplicity) makes two kinds of misunderstanding possible and even likely. The reader who is a devout Christian may misinterpret the novel as a hideous parody, pacifist and sacrilegious in intention. The reader without religious belief may mistake the book for a religious affirmation; so powerfully does the Gospel pattern assert itself, and with so much of a magical radiance, that one overlooks at first, the numerous points at which the Gospel pattern is ignored, avoided, contradicted, or modified. And the possibility of misunderstanding is increased by the style which, at first, seems bombastic and over-written when it is not hysterical or frenetic. Once the book is mastered, this first and false impression vanishes: Faulkner has

[291]

converted various extreme traits of his style into a systematic elevation and intensity, comparable to the mannerisms of opera, and perfect as a preparation and context for the simple directness of the illiterate corporal. Hence, although the complexity of conception in *A Fable* makes it the most difficult of all his books, the rewards, if one persists, are astonishing: *A Fable* is a masterpiece, a unique fulfillment of Faulkner's genius which gives a luminous new meaning to his works as a whole.

The extent to which *A Fable* is governed by a radically new attitude and point of view cannot be overemphasized. Throughout his career Faulkner has been concerned with the First World War; and he was directly concerned with the disillusioned or mutilated veteran of modern war in his first novel, *Soldier's Pay* (the same title might also serve for his latest book twenty-eight years after), in his third novel, *Sartoris* (which is, as Robert Cantwell has remarked, his first characteristic book and contains all his later work in embryo), and in many of his best stories, such as "Ad Astra" and "Victory." But in all this fiction the governing attitude which motivates the author, although it is that of the most intense disillusion, is the disillusion of one recently and severely deprived of important illusions. To use the stock phrase, it is the antiwar attitude of the lost generation to which Hemingway and Dos Passos also belonged. The point of view of *A Fable* is far beyond illusion and disillusion; there is no effort to show at the start that the mutiny has been provoked by the meaningless horror which common soldiers suffer; and from the beginning, it is taken for granted that the war is wrong so that antiwar sentiment is the starting point, and not the conclusion.

This is but one of the important and radical differences which distinguish *A Fable* from other fiction which deals with modern war: the degree of difference is so important that it must be characterized at length by comparing an episode in *A Fable* with an anecdote about the Civil War in *Sartoris*. The Civil War anecdote, set in deliberate contrast to the emotional paralysis of the modern Bayard Sartoris as a veteran of modern war, deals with his remarkable ancestor, the Bayard Sartoris of the Civil War. He is an officer of the famous Southern cavalry leader Jeb Stuart and with

Stuart he raids a Union encampment for the sole purpose of securing coffee, capturing, along with the coffee, a Northern officer, but not his horse. Stuart out of chivalry and courtesy determines to secure a mount by making another unnecessary raid, and when the Northern officer protests that this is heedless and foolish behavior, particularly for a mere prisoner's comfort, Stuart's haughty reply is that he is acting not for the prisoner but "for an officer suffering the fortunes of war. No gentleman would do less." The Union officer answers that "No gentleman has any business in this war . . . he is an anachronism, like anchovies. At least General Stuart did not capture our anchovies . . . Perhaps he will send General Lee for them in person." Bayard Sartoris, hearing the interchange, dashes off for the anchovies, and Stuart turns to follow him, as one of his own officers protests. But the captured Northern major, converted, cries out to Stuart: "Forward, sir . . . What is one man to a renewed belief in mankind?"

A good many episodes in *A Fable* provide an adequate comparison with this Civil War anecdote, since most of the important characters suffer from a loss of belief in mankind and seek some renewal of that belief. The best episode to cite for the purpose of characterizing the gulf between *Sartoris* and *A Fable* concerns the English battalion runner, who is not only one of the most important and moving characters in the new novel, but is as gallant a hero as Bayard Sartoris. When five months as an officer have made him hate himself and all other human beings, he feels that his loss of belief in mankind makes it necessary that he go to his company commander, resign his commission, and return to the ranks. The company commander advises him to shoot himself in the foot; in the same way, with the same useless advice, the battalion commander and finally the brigadier refuse his resignation. After three months, however, a simple method occurs to him, that of copulating with a girl in public. Since this jeopardizes the honor of the regiment, he is now permitted to resign and return to the ranks as a private: the request he has made with dignity as a human being is granted only after the performance of an obscene pantomine. When the girl hired to help him discovers that his true motive is not cowardice, as she supposed, but the extraordinary courage of an extraordinary protest, she then experiences the same immense renewal of belief in mankind as the captured Union major in *Sartoris*. The explicit meaning which Faulkner gives to the Civil War episode is so close to that of the episode in *A Fable* that the latter might almost be characterized as the former is, apart from irrelevant details: "what had been a harebrained prank of two heedless and reckless boys became a gallant and finely tragical point to which the [human] race had been raised from spiritual sloth . . . by two angels . . . purging the souls of men . . ." Yet although the meaning of both episodes is the same, in this sense of a renewed belief in man, the extreme difference in point of view is defined by comparing public copulation to a heedless prank, as the difference in attitude shows itself when an officer's greatest heroism becomes his effort to resign his commission as an officer.

The runner has convinced the girl that at least one human being is not worthless, but he cannot convince himself until he hears of the mutiny. Before it occurs, he visits an old Negro preacher, who, unlike himself and most other human beings of the book, is in serene possession of belief in God and man. Perceiving the runner's spiritual desperation, the old preacher tells him the story of a marvelous horse,[1] and although this episode has been dismissed by some critics as an interpolation, its function is quite clear and very important. Two years before the war, in the American South, this marvelous horse has broken a leg in a train wreck, and the old preacher and the horse's English groom have stolen him, knowing that otherwise, because of the accident, the horse's millionaire owner will use him only for breeding purposes instead of racing him. After stealing the marvelous horse, and patching up his leg, the preacher and the groom race him in small towns all over the country-side, and though he now must run three-legged, the horse continues to be a marvel of speed and wins most of the time. When the millionaire owner sets all the forces of the law in motion to regain the horse and arrest the thieves, the succession of officers who come in pursuit suppose like everyone else that the motive of the abduction is money, and that the horse must be winning enormous sums. But as each officer comes to

1. This story appeared in *Perspectives* 9 under the title "Notes on a Horse Thief."

recognize that the preacher and the groom are dedicated purely to the horse as a marvel of speed, they too experience a renewed belief in mankind: convinced that they have come upon a love and nobility which transcends the enforcement of the law, they are transformed into fanatical protectors of the horse's cause and his keepers' safety.

Hearing this story, the runner perceives that what he needs is the ability to believe in belief: "Maybe what I need is . . . To believe. Not in anything: just to believe." The horse is thus a stupendous narrative metaphor, since he is the cause of belief and nobility in other human beings just as the illiterate corporal is, an identification which does not become explicit until, after much mystery, the corporal's true nature is made clear.[2]

Several other characters in *A Fable* are comparable in interest and meaning to the runner, but perhaps most significant of all is the French general Gragnon, who commands the division in which the mutiny originates. Gragnon has lived by a belief in the army to the exclusion and scorn of all else; he has been the perfect soldier, making his way up the military hierarchy solely by virtue of a brilliant record of personal merit. But just before the mutiny he is ordered to launch an offensive the sole purpose of which, as he immediately perceives, is failure, a failure which will enable a superior officer to gain his marshal's baton but which will at the same time ruin Gragnon's career. The mutiny occurs at the moment the offensive is scheduled to begin, and when both Gragnon's troops and the enemy's fail to attack, Gragnon de-

2. Faulkner underscores the underlying meaning of the episode when the preacher and the groom share their religious beliefs during the period which must be called the passion of the horse: the groom makes the old Negro a mason, and the old preacher baptizes the groom into his own religious sect. There are further meaningful connections: the horse runs, though crippled; the runner "runs" toward belief; though crippled too, he is equally indomitable. One of the thieves who is shot with the corporal is named Horse and wants only to go to Paris, as the horse wants only to race. The groom, capable of complete self-sacrifice for the sake of the horse, is ruthless toward all human beings. And the preacher declares that he is a witness not to God, who needs none, but to man. Finally the horse is a natural symbol of the way in which the games and sports of American life provide objects of pure devotion and admiration: the chief reason is that in a country committed to a democratic ethos, the intrinsic skill of the individual attracts the greatest and most disinterested esteem and prestige.

mands successively of his immediate superior, the group commander for whose promotion he is being sacrificed, and finally of the supreme commander that, in accordance with military law, the mutinous regiment be shot. This request is refused as is his demand for a court-martial and lastly his resignation. "But to me? What will happen to me?" Gragnon asks when all his illusions have been exposed. "I don't know," a superior general answers, "but it will be glorious." What does happen to Gragnon is exactly what he has demanded for the mutinous regiment: instead of shooting the regiment, the high command decides that Gragnon had better be shot so that it can be maintained that he was killed in action, leading his troops against the enemy. The episode of his execution, which is written with a spectacular narrative power Faulkner has never surpassed, is one of the consummations of *A Fable's* extraordinary originality and insight. Most novelists of war are committed to the platitude that generals die in bed, which remains a literary platitude, no matter what the actual statistics may be. For Gragnon's agony of shocked disappointment would hardly be diminished if he had died in bed: the infamous manner of his death is the final dramatization of the fact that in modern war anything may happen to anyone, that a general may be just as expendable as a common soldier, and that most generals' hopes and ambitions are likely to be disappointed or rendered essentially meaningless by the very character of modern war, whether or not they die in bed. Since it is by hope that everyone, including generals, must live and die, Gragnon has suffered a death of the heart long before he is shot. He is, in fact, a martyr, like the illiterate corporal, for in an ironic symmetry which may not be immediately clear, he is crucified by three soldiers because of his dedicated belief in the army. The novelist's attitude toward him, combining compassion and contempt, is worthy of Dante who also felt compassion for the most arrogant and despicable of the damned.

Like Gragnon, other significant characters are overtaken by the mutiny in ways as various and meaningful. Within the limits of a review, one cannot be adequate to Gragnon, and certainly not to the complexity of characterization of the entire book. But it probably must be said, in view of some of the first reviews of *A Fable*, that until the reader is capable of a detailed synopsis of the novel, he has really not read it at all. This is also true as long as the reader suffers from the impression that some characters are melodramatic stereotypes: one review's instance is a German general's monocle! For once the characters are seen in full relation, not in isolation or out of focus, the reader will know that the melodrama is in his own mind or in the characters'. It can be regarded as a great novelist's triteness only if, with a great literary critic, the reader supposes that the cruel actions of cruel characters suffice to make a book cruel and prove that the author is a sadist.

The extreme complication of meaning throughout *A Fable* is typified in the climactic interview between the corporal and the supreme commander. The complication is justified and necessary; and its nature is such that the least diminution of attention or oversimplification of interpretation results not in perplexity but in what is worse, a false impression of understanding which occurs because part of the total meaning has been taken as the whole meaning of an episode. For example, the supreme commander's avowed purpose in the climactic interview is to persuade the corporal to repudiate the mutiny; and this, certainly, is one of his purposes; but he has a purpose more serious and important to himself, which is to reveal to the corporal that he is his father and that he has devoted his career to enigmatic and strange courses in order to gain a son worthy of his inheritance; the interview is thus also a trial of the success or failure of his own life. These and other motives are involved in the interview, and if any one is overstressed or entirely unnoticed, a systematic kind of misunderstanding is bound to occur.

There is a further and somewhat different difficulty in the fact that the interview also corresponds, up to a point, to Christ's temptation by Satan; after that point there are serious and remarkable developments which are missed unless the gospel analogy is disregarded. If Satan's temptation of Christ were the primary basis of the interview, and not merely one dimension of it, Satan, Caesar, Pontius Pilate, and God would have to be one and the same being. The chief reason that these oversimplifications lead to radical misunderstanding, instead of partial understanding, is that the

[297]

supreme commander is often misrepresenting his own point of view and the real issues. He affirms repeatedly at great rhetorical length that he believes in mankind and admires human beings, a claim which is quite false. Thus, offering the corporal the temptation of freedom, the general points out that one follower, the modern Peter, has denied him; one, the modern Judas, has betrayed him; and that all can soon be persuaded to the betrayal of the corporal. The corporal's simple answer is that for each human being who betrays him many more will spring up to follow him. Clearly the general's accusation is a denial of the admiration and belief which he claims that he has for humanity, as well as the "base under-estimation" of the corporal which he also disclaims, since he asks the corporal to be a traitor too. It is thus the way in which the general articulates each of the temptations that demonstrates his essential contempt for all human beings, including the corporal and himself. This fact is most marked in the offer of the temptation of recognition as the general's son which will mean, he says, the chance to be the first emperor of the world, a throne which would give the corporal the opportunity of providing human beings with "sweeter bread" and "bloodier circuses"; but the corporal, who has shown no interest in making circuses bloodier or bread sweeter, is in the position Gandhi would have occupied, had a British prime minister offered him the chance to be viceroy of India and to provide his fellow countrymen with superior tea-houses and cricket matches. Though the general is not a foolish man, he becomes foolish as the interview continues and he must contend with the corporal's simple desire to be faithful to his followers and to himself. The last, most subtle and damning of the general's temptations is another and still more ignorant appeal to the corporal to be treacherous: "I will be dead in a few years," the general says, "and you can use your inheritance to win the trick tomorrow which today my ace finessed."

Each of the corporal's answers is hardly a direct refusal, so little is he tempted, so strong and clear is his belief in human beings. Sometimes he says, "There are still ten [men]," and when he is offered the temptation of the kingship of the world, he says only: "Are you that afraid of me?" His final refusal is just as brief and bare, yet declares his own attitude toward existence and humanity.

[298]

"Don't be afraid," the corporal said. "There's nothing to be afraid of. Nothing's worth it."

This is the summit of the interview as of the book. Its negative phrasing may not reveal sufficiently that it is a supreme affirmation of what it is to be a human being, of how much depends upon courage if one is human. But in addition the corporal has said to the general that the general's entire view of existence is rooted in fear, an accusation all the more awful for being spoken with kindness, sympathy, and unemphatic directness. The immense sum of the corporal's moral triumph is thus that the supreme commander, seeking to tempt an illiterate corporal, has succeeded only in making himself pitiful!

Silenced for a time by the unbearable humiliation of the corporal's compassion, the general, when he regains self-possession, utters the most torrential and passionate of his perorations, denying that he suffers from fear and predicting man's catastrophic future to affirm once again that he really admires human beings. The future, he says, will be made inconceivably catastrophic by new instruments of warfare, but nevertheless man will survive and prevail over them even if he has to migrate to another planet as a result of war, the most perverse vice of man's deathless folly! His esteem for man is nothing more or less than the admiration reserved for successful criminals and homicidal maniacs. All that he has said to the corporal is based on the view that human beings are worthless, and this is illustrated perfectly when he calls himself "the champion of the mundane earth" and the corporal "the champion of man's baseless hopes": the one word, baseless, is sufficient to show his inexhaustible contempt of everything truly human.

The corporal for his part possesses hardly more than a belief that human beings are not worthless, and human hope and aspiration not baseless. He himself is the living proof that man has a unique worth: and all the complexity of the book moves toward the establishment and acceptance of the reality of the corporal as a simple illiterate noble human being: *Ecce Homo!* Behold the Corporal! The two phrases contain the simple ultimate meaning of *A Fable,* as if they were the plain nails or hooks from which the large and intricate tapestry depended.

The minimal character of the corporal's belief is the measure of Faulkner's ambition and daring: the corporal's belief in mankind can be neither helped nor hindered by coffee, anchovies, chivalry or cowardice, betrayal or loyalty. It is a belief which justifies itself and is independent of all else, including supernatural sources or sanctions. And it is a simple belief because it supposes that hope is necessary, fear is foolish, and life is only worth living if human beings are worth dying for.

It should be entirely clear that in the course of the interview the book has moved outside the gospel pattern, outside religious belief or disbelief, beyond the question of war or pacifism. There is no discussion of religion, apart from one scornful reference to immortality of the soul which the corporal ignores and to which the general does not return: there is almost as complete an absence of any argument about the mutiny as such.

It is in the light of this interview that everything else must be understood; and this fact makes it important to deny the comparison (which has been made twice in reviews and will doubtless be made often) of the climactic scene of *A Fable* to the legend of the grand inquisitor in Dostoevsky's *The Brothers Karamazov*, which is itself one of the most misinterpreted passages in the history of literature. The two scenes have a surface resemblance which makes the comparison worse than misleading: for Dostoevsky's scene is an imaginary poem composed by a leading character, Ivan Karamazov; its primary purpose is religious, as the whole of Dostoevsky's novel is also; its substance shows Ivan's character as an intellectual, as a human being in torment because he cannot believe in God's existence, nor disbelieve and ignore the question of God; and among Ivan's chief reasons for being unable to believe is his difficulty in believing in man because of that side of man revealed in the crimes which newspapers report. Faulkner's intention—and his triumph—is utterly unlike Dostoevsky's because he attempts to cut below the question of God's existence to a question which, for many modern human beings, is prior, the root conception of Man. The contrast is extreme and complete because Dostoevsky is intent upon asserting particular religious, doctrinal, and national meanings which Faulkner is equally determined to avoid. Dostoevsky's purpose is to show the true church of Christ as opposed by the church of the grand inquisitor, who is a cardinal and hence a symbol of Roman Catholicism. The true church belonged to the Russian people and to the czar, and gave men freedom to be good or evil, while the false church deprived man of freedom to prevent him from being evil. Faulkner's very different intention is to establish man as worthy of devotion, belief, and love, whatever his misdeeds and failings, and whether or not he is God's creature. Thus Dostoevsky sought to prove that without belief in God man is capable of every crime; but Faulkner seeks to show that man is capable of goodness purely because he is human. Dostoevsky's curious and wholly biased views linked the church with czarism; Faulkner is concerned with no particular church's claims, but writes from a point of view which is radically modern precisely because it seeks to avoid the question of God's existence so that a vision of humanity can be grasped which will be valid to readers of any and every shade of religious belief and disbelief. His attempt, it must be said again, depends only on the corporal's reality as a human being, almost as if the novelist said: If there is just one such human being, then it is possible for all human beings to be noble.

Another important reason for distinguishing between Dostoevsky's religious intention and Faulkner's intention as neither religious nor antireligious is illustrated by the scene, subsequent to the interview with the supreme commander and similar to it, in which a military chaplain, also seeking to persuade the corporal to repudiate the mutiny, claims that it is contrary to the doctrines of the church, and, through his arguments so perverts Christian doctrine and the character of Christ that, when he fails, he commits suicide. If *A Fable's* intention were religious, the priest's effort would be wholly false and without meaning; if the intention were essentially antireligious, then the priest's suicide, demonstrating his knowledge and guilt that he has betrayed the priesthood, would not have occurred, a point which seems worth making only because the episode has been thus interpreted as an attack on institutional Christianity and on all organized religion.

It is true, however, and it is important to note that throughout the book the question of whether or not the corporal has a supernatural status presents itself sharply. The most representative instance, typical in its systematic ambiguity, is the meeting summoned by the supreme commander at which the corporal is present (but silent except when he says that he knows only one language, French). Three officers, all stubborn in their certainty, testify that they have separately known the corporal at three different places and that he has died in 1914 and in 1917. The supreme commander queries the three officers scornfully, but each refuses to surrender his own certainty or to deny the conviction of the other two. The English officer, taunted by the supreme commander as to whether he has not also seen the ghosts of Agincourt above the trenches, replies: "I'm sorry, sir, I've got to believe in something," a new version of the runner's need to believe in something or anything. The supreme commander summarizes his own attitude and contempt thus: "one of our allies' officers . . . saw him slain . . . another buried him . . . so all that remains for us is to witness his resurrection." His irony is an assertion that he himself believes in nothing whatever, but that he expects others to assert foolish supernatural conviction with absolute certainty, now and henceforward. Here, as throughout, he speaks as one involved in a tragic masquerade of which he has foreknowledge, and in which, like an actor in a play he detests, he must play an assigned part conceived by another. In contrast to this nihilism, the officers' certainty that the corporal has died and returned among the living three times is their unwritting, intuitive expression of the necessity of such a being as Christ or the corporal every day, every week, every year. His perpetual death and return is a perpetual necessity.

But this need on the part of other human beings does not give the corporal a literal supernatural status, a point which Faulkner makes with the utmost emphasis in the last chapter, a year after the corporal's execution. The battalion runner has come to visit the corporal's sisters on their farm, and when the sister called Martha offers to show him the corporal's grave, the runner, refusing, says: "What for? He's finished." Martha is offended but Mary reassures her sister, telling her: "He didn't mean it that way. He just means that brother did the best he could and now he doesn't need to worry any more." This is a kind of credo which neither denies nor affirms a belief in Christianity. So too, in the penultimate episode, when the corporal's body by mischance becomes that of the Unknown Soldier, the apotheosis is the corporal's ironic failure and yet, in a sense, his triumph. And then there is the brutality of the final scene at the supreme commander's funeral, where the runner, kicked into unconsciousness by a French mob, recovers and laughs and says that he will never die: never. This affirmation is indomitable but desperate because he now has only one arm, leg, eye, and ear, and it inspires only tears in the one sympathetic character who is present.

The only true affirmation in the book is the corporal's "Don't be afraid." The only belief asserted without ambiguity is the belief that such a being as the corporal exists. But the reality of the corporal has endless implications. One important implication is that the test of any religious belief is such a person as the corporal, and no justifiable social or political movement can succeed without the help of such a person. Thus the chief reason for the gospel parallel and one of the reasons that it is so successful is that the gospel story represents the kind of being who must exist if any aspiration is to be worthy of realization.

The question of the worth of man has profoundly troubled such peers of Faulkner as Malraux and T. S. Eliot. After the Second World War, Malraux observed that the chief question of the nineteenth century, Is God dead? had now become, in the twentieth century: Is Man dead? In a poem written after the First World War, T. S. Eliot wrote, "After such knowledge, what forgiveness?" a comment on human history which, in its context, was compelled by the same fundamental anxiety as Malraux expressed. But Malraux sought salvation in political action and Eliot in religious belief; Faulkner, however, believes that it must be found in man first of all.

It may be that this view is caused by a new desperation far more than by a new hope and belief in man. Throughout *A Fable* and above all at the climax of the book, the supreme commander uses the same words as Faulkner himself in his Stockholm speech in 1950 to an extent which verges upon self-quotation and with an intention which admits of a variety of interpretations, including self-mockery, self-criticism, and the assumption that if the devil can quote scripture, a modern Satan can quote Faulkner. But whatever the intention, the speech itself rehearses the themes which have obsessed the novelist and inspired *A Fable*. The speech declares the novelist's belief that man will endure and prevail very much as the runner declares that he will never die, in a tone at once desperate and indomitable. In the same way, the novelist's speech asserts that other writers have been distracted from the themes of nobility, courage, pride, sacrifice, compassion and love by the terrifying question: "When will I be blown up?" Yet it is likely enough that the novelist's obsessed consciousness of this question (which is clearly an awareness of the atomic age) inspired the tormented hope and tragic recognition which make *A Fable* a masterpiece.

On Critics
·IV·

Our Literary Critics
An Appreciation

Since the war, literary criticism in America has become an active and flourishing industry to so great an extent that it has provoked an antagonism which I think ought to be examined and illustrated.

I remember a famous American poet, and a truly great one, beginning a reading of his poetry by speaking of the present state of criticism, poetry, and the criticism of poetry. Some poets, he said, write for other poets, some poets write for the critics, some critics write poetry because they are critics of poetry, some critics write poetry for other critics, and finally some critics write criticism for other critics. His audience was overjoyed. As they laughed, a flashlight photographer lighted the scene near the platform, directing his camera at the poet, who looked more guilty than startled. One cannot be sure, but he seemed to look as if he had been caught in the act of saying what he did say.

A literary critic expressed the same kind of antagonism when asked about a piece of abstract sculpture in his living room by the electrician who had come to repair the wiring in his apartment. "What does it mean?" the electrician wanted to know. "Do you like girls?" the critic replied. The electrician admitted that he did. "Do you ask what a pretty girl means?" the critic said then. The electrician made his departure. The important point is that he remained dissatisfied.

Then there is the antipathy which Randall Jarrell has expressed with characteristic eloquence in his recent book, *Poetry and Age*: this is, he says, an age of criticism: "there has never been an age

when so much good criticism was written—or so *much* bad." And
when you examine the leading literary reviews:

> Each of these contains several poems, and a piece of fiction—
> sometimes two pieces; the rest is criticism. . . . I am talking as a
> reader of the criticism of the last few years and am assuming its
> merits and services, which are great. . . . The magazines which
> enjoy attacking them are almost ludicrously inferior to them.
> But, I think, they print far too much criticism and far too much
> that is more attractive to critics and lovers of criticism than it is
> to poets and fiction-writers. . . . Some of this criticism is as good
> as anyone could wish; several of the best critics alive print most of
> their work in such magazines as these. Some more of this criti-
> cism is intelligent and useful—it sounds as if it had been writ-
> ten by a reader of readers, by a human being. But a great deal
> of this criticism might just as well have been written by a syndi-
> cate of encyclopedias for an International Business Machine. It is
> not only bad or mediocre, it is dull; it is, often, astonishingly
> graceless, joyless, humorless, long-winded, niggling, blinkered,
> methodical, self-important, cliché-ridden, prestige-obsessed, al-
> most autonomous criticism.

Mr. Jarrell's description is precise, or at any rate, my own feelings are so much akin to his that it seems precise to me. But perhaps
our own feelings are not important when measured against the
state of literacy in America and the endless necessity for the training of an educated class. The state of affairs which Mr. Jarrell
describes has come into being through the new union between
literary criticism and the teaching of English.

Some of the criticism to which Mr. Jarrell objects is known as
the New Criticism and is produced by overworked instructors who
must earn academic promotion by publication: in the past, most
of them would have published scholarly papers in the scholarly
journals; but now, although academic standards of scholarship remain unaltered, the teacher's worth is increased, from the point of
view of a university, if he functions as both a critic and a scholar.
Consequently there has been a rapprochement between scholarship and criticism instead of the senseless separation which existed
for far too long. The teacher has been drawn toward criticism and

the critic toward scholarship in a way which cannot but be good for both criticism and scholarship.

But more important by far, the practice of criticism has increased because of a definite social and cultural need. Much of the criticism which distresses Mr. Jarrell is given over almost entirely to an analysis and interpretation of the meanings of the literary object, which is certainly a one-sided and limited kind of criticism at best. But at worst it has helped to create and to keep alive a consciousness of literature at a higher and more serious level than at any time since the Civil War. The proof of this is that if it is an age of criticism, it is also an age of the reprint. For the ascendancy of the New Criticism has been accompanied by an important related phenomenon, the literary revival, which has restored the living as well as the dead. There have been valuable books and collections of essays about Faulkner, Fitzgerald, Hemingway, Eliot, Joyce, and Yeats, among others, a fact which must be connected with the state of affairs twenty years back when it was extremely difficult for a critic to get a book of criticism published at all.

The literary revival has resurrected James, and given the novels of Faulkner and Fitzgerald the attention of which they were deprived by the concerns of criticism during the depression; and classic American literature has established itself clearly and fully. We have only to think of Melville, Emily Dickinson, and Mark Twain to see there has been a real advance: the gulf between the present and the past which existed in virtually every other period has been greatly diminished, and this has come about chiefly because so many critics are teachers. Faulkner is perhaps the best example of how genuine the progress has been: in any other literary period, he might have suffered the fate of Melville after the writing of Moby Dick.

Nevertheless Mr. Jarrell's judgment is just in itself. It would certainly be very nice if all the critics in question wrote well, in a lucid style, free of cant, jargon, and preciosity; if their analysis of the meaning of poetry were balanced by a sense of the being of poetry, and a historical sense of literature; if they were more often able to recognize that a method which developed out of the analysis of lyric poetry cannot be directly translated to the criticism of fiction and the drama; and if more of them shared the social and moral values of Van Wyck Brooks and Edmund Wilson, instead of those of T. S. Eliot. It is easier to criticize the New Criticism than to shoot fish in a barrel; and it ought to be criticized; at the same time, in criticizing it, one ought to remember a fact which Mr. Jarrell cites elsewhere in his book, in his essay on the obscurity of the poet and the indifference to poetry in America: "One of our universities recently made a survey of the reading habits of the American public; it decided that forty-eight percent of all Americans read, during a year, no book at all." It is within this context, from the point of view of the sociology of literature, that the recent growth of criticism must be estimated. It is true enough that the most one can say, adopting this point of view, is: *better than nothing.*

It is better than nothing in this sense: if on the one hand it is now often necessary, because of the New Criticism, to insist that *Moby Dick* is about a white whale and whaling, whatever its more elevated and profound meanings may be, on the other hand *Moby Dick* was not mentioned at all during the first seventy years after it was published. In a like way, as the poems of Emily Dickinson were not published during her lifetime, so Edwin Arlington Robinson and Robert Frost suffered for twenty years from the lack of understanding and recognition which Emily Dickinson would have experienced if she had been published. For the time being at least, the New Criticism has diminished the kind of deafness and darkness with which these poets were confronted.

The consolations of a historical perspective can be overestimated. Yet, going back twenty-five years, one has only to read the pronouncements of H. L. Mencken on the art of poetry as a pack of lies, the avant-garde as a pack of poseurs and pretenders, the puerility of Thorstein Veblen and John Dewey and the nobility of war to see that the supposed glory of the first postwar period is mostly a nostalgia for exuberance. And if one goes back fifty years to the time of Howells, George Woodberry, Hamilton W. Mabie, Henry Van Dyke, and Barrett Wendell, one comes upon a literary scene which was an appealing gentleman's club inhabited by a host of genteel mediocrities most of whom were devoted to impersonating that familiar ghost who has haunted American literature since the time of Washington Irving, the imaginary Englishman.

Although in the ancient past, Sisyphus was condemned by the gods to roll a rock to the top of a mountain forever, today Sisyphus is a literary critic. Every time he finishes a book review, he has to begin a new one; his task being the task of criticism is endless and without reprieve. But now as the imaginary Englishman returning dressed in the guise of the new conservatism and as the howling Comanches of mass culture whoop it up on the TV screen, Sisyphus cannot help but see the new critic's love of literature in a redeeming light.

The Literary Dictatorship
of T. S. Eliot

I

When we think of the character of literary dictators in the past, it is easy to see that since 1922, at least, Eliot has occupied a position in the English-speaking world analogous to that occupied by Ben Jonson, Dryden, Pope, Samuel Johnson, Coleridge, and Matthew Arnold. It is noticeable that each of these dictators has been a critic as well as a poet, and we may infer from this the fact that it is necessary for them to practice both poetry and criticism.

Another characteristic is that each of these literary dictators has in some way reversed the judgments of his immediate predecessor. For example, Arnold denied that Pope and Dryden were really poets, declaring that they were merely "wit-writers." Eliot in the same way declared that Pope and Dryden were truly poets and that Keats and Shelley, two of Arnold's favorites, were really insufficient and inadequate as poets.

One can hardly use such a term as dictatorship without suggesting unfortunate political associations. A literary dictatorship, however, is quite unlike a political one because you cannot force people to like poets or poetry, although you can persuade them. The remarkable thing about most of the literary dictators I have mentioned is that they succeeded in persuading at least one generation of readers to accept their literary taste.

This essay is a shortened version of a lecture given at Columbia University on April 6, 1947. At the time, Delmore Schwartz did not know that Eliot had recently lectured on Milton to the British Academy and had publicly revised, if not reversed, his earlier attitude toward Milton ("Milton," 1936). Thus Schwartz was, in effect, predicting just such a revision.—Ed.

When we come to Eliot's reign, we find that something has really been added: we have virtually two dictatorships from one literary dictator. Between 1922 and 1933 Eliot, in a series of unprecedented essays which were initially disguised as book reviews, revaluated the history of English poetry in one set of terms; between 1933 and 1946 he gradually reversed his whole evaluation, so that, for example, Tennyson, whom he scorned in 1922, was the object of serious and elevated commendation in 1936. In the same way Yeats, who in 1922 was said to be outside of the tradition of English poetry merely because he was Irish, is praised in the highest terms in 1933 as someone who "by a great triumph of development began to write and is still writing some of the most beautiful poetry in the language, some of the clearest, simplest, most direct." Some of the poems that Eliot refers to were written long before 1922. Thus it is almost possible to say of Eliot, "The dictator has abdicated. Long live the dictator!" This is the only instance I know where anyone has abdicated and immediately succeeded to his own throne.

We can take 1922 as the approximate beginning of the first period, for in that year Eliot began to edit *The Criterion*, and "The Waste Land" was published in the first number, although it was in 1921 that Eliot published the reviews in the *London Times Literary Supplement* which were later collected as *Three Essays in Homage to John Dryden*. In the most famous of these essays, "Metaphysical Poets," Eliot declared that English poetry had not been the same since the death of John Donne. Dryden was a good poet, and Milton was a good poet, but their very virtues brought about a dissociation of sensibility in their successors. Since the time of Donne, according to this essay, there have been no poets in English who really enjoyed a unity of sensibility. What Eliot means by "unity of sensibility," a dubious psychological phrase, is difficult to make clear, but can perhaps best be stated by paraphrasing Eliot's remark that Donne felt his thoughts at the tips of his senses. All poets since Donne, with a few exceptional moments of unity, have permitted their thoughts and their emotions to be separated. "In the seventeenth century," says Eliot, "a dissociation of sensibility set in from which we have never recovered; this dissociation was not natural and was aggravated by the two most powerful poets of the century, Milton and Dryden. . . . The sentimental age began early in the eighteenth century and continued.

Poets revolted against the ratiocinative; they thought and felt by fits unbalanced. . . . In one or two passages of Shelley's 'Triumph of Life' and Keat's second 'Hyperion' there are traces of struggle toward unification of sensibility. But Keats and Shelley died, and Tennyson and Browning ruminated." The poets prior to Dryden and Milton, however, "are more mature . . . . and were better than later poets of certainly not less literary ability."

By 1934 Eliot had fruitfully contradicted, modified or qualified practically all the literary and critical judgments implicit in this essay. He had praised not only Tennyson and Yeats, but also Wordsworth and Coleridge, who were more or less beyond the pale of charity in 1921. In 1937, when questioned during a radio interview on the British Broadcasting Company about what he regarded as great poetry, he replied that Wordsworth's "Independence and Resolution" and Coleridge's "Ode on Dejection" were probably "touchstones of greatness." This is a far cry from what Eliot said in 1922 and what has been echoed a countless number of times by critics who have been influenced by Eliot.

And yet I do not mean to imply in the least that Eliot is merely contradictory. It is true that no one could have guessed, by reading his essay on the "Metaphysical Poets" in 1922, that by 1937 he would admire Wordsworth and Coleridge very much and cite them, rather than Donne, as "touchstones of greatness." Nor could any-one have guessed or suspected that he would praise Byron and Kipling, among other unlikely possibilities. But on the other hand, there is a real unity in back of all of these seemingly contradictory judgments. One basis of this unity is the admiration for Dante which obviously began when Eliot was still an undergraduate. If we understand Eliot's gradual and profound re-reading of Dante, then we can see how at one point, fascinated by one aspect of Dante, he would be likely to salute Donne, while at a later stage it would be natural for him to admire the characteristic directness and clarity of the poems by Wordsworth and Coleridge which he cited as touchstones of what is great in poetry. If we examine these poems carefully, we can see that in the most direct way they resemble the very beginning of *The Divine Comedy*.

And here, too, we can find at least one explanation of the distaste Eliot has expressed at various times for the poetry of Milton.

[314]

It was in 1933 here at Columbia that Eliot, by using what we may call the method of invidious comparison, compared Milton to Dante, although the two poets are not really comparable. Since Milton was a dedicated, self-conscious literary artist who decided to write an epic poem which would be like other epic poems and which would be a national epic, it seems clear to me that the true comparison would be to Virgil. How, then, are we to explain Eliot's dispraise of Milton?

We have as possibilities all sorts of unconvincing explanations: for example, it is said that Eliot depreciates Milton because Milton was anti-authoritarian in religious matters, while Eliot himself is nothing if not authoritarian—an explanation which might be based upon Eliot's remark that "Milton's celestial and infernal regions are large but insufficiently furnished apartments, filled by heavy conversation; and one remarks about the Puritan mythology its thinness." But this is clearly not a sufficient explanation, since we know that Ezra Pound expressed an equal dislike of Milton, and no one can suppose that Ezra Pound's literary opinions were influenced by Anglo-Catholicism.

Another possible explanation is that Milton is not the kind of poet that Eliot himself desired to be, and there is, as everyone knows, a natural tendency upon the part of a poet who writes criticism to try to justify and praise in his criticism what he attempts to accomplish in his poetry. Thus Eliot criticizes Milton and reduces his importance by saying that "the very greatest poets set you before real men talking, carry you on in real events, moving." In the same essay in which Eliot makes this remark he says, "There is a large class of persons, including some who appear in print as critics, who regard any censure upon a great poet as a breach of the peace, as an act of wanton iconoclasm, of even hoodlumism. The kind of derogatory criticism that I have to make upon Milton is not intended for such persons, who cannot understand that it is more important, in some vital respects, to be a good poet than to be a great poet." This sounds to me as if Mr. Eliot were protesting far too much.

Milton is a crucial instance, because Milton is the one poet for whom Eliot expresses a distaste in both his revaluations of English poetry. Let us take the sentence I have just quoted. In the same essay Eliot says, "It must be admitted that Milton is a very 'great' poet indeed." We have then to determine, if we can, the difference between being a "very great poet" and being "one of the very greatest," and since Eliot puts the term "great" in quotation marks as if it were a dubious one, it would not be strange if a man from Mars decided that some infinitesimal hairsplitting were involved, or that Eliot, like Milton, had found darkness visible, for surely there is a kind of darkness in distinguishing between "very great" and "the very greatest."

There are other possible explanations of Eliot's attitude to Milton, but they are all merely guesses which are easily punctured. Whatever the explanation may be, I should like to rush in where scientists fear to tread and, with complete foolhardiness, venture to predict that when Eliot next speaks of Milton, next month, he will praise him with more sympathy and justice than he ever has before. I should say that I have the advantage of knowing that Eliot has expressed a desire to lecture on Milton when he comes to America this spring. In saying this, I do not depend wholly upon a wish to indulge in predictions like a weather forecaster. There is real evidence in Eliot's recent poetry and criticism to suggest such a revision of judgment.

In *Four Quartets* there is not only a paraphrase of a famous passage in *Samson Agonistes*—

O dark, dark, dark. They all go into the dark.

but in addition, there are many indications that Eliot as a poet has found himself in an emotional situation which resembles Milton's when he was writing *Paradise Lost*, especially in the personal and autobiographical passages. The same kind of resemblances can be found between certain parts of *Samson Agonistes* and certain passages in the *Four Quartets*. For example, the justly famous passage in *Samson Agonistes*,

All is best, though we oft doubt
What the unsearchable dispose
Of highest Wisdom brings about,
And ever best found in the close.

This seems to me to be very close in feeling and attitude to one of the finest passages in the *Four Quartets*:

> Sin is Behovely, but
> All shall be well, and
> All manner of thing shall be well
> By the purification of motive
> In the ground of our beseeching.

And there are also other indications too detailed for my present purpose. However, the last quotation, and especially the line, "The purification of the motive," suggest a consideration of what standards were involved in Eliot's initial evaluation of the history of English poetry and his subsequent revaluation.

They can be named in a summary and incomplete way as follows: first, actuality; second, honesty (closely connected with actuality and with the "purification of motive" of which I have just spoken); third, the purification and maintenance of the English language; fourth, the dramatic sense, which I shall try to define in a moment; fifth, the quality of the versification.

Needless to say, this list is not by any means exhaustive and obviously each of these sought-for qualities overlaps and interconnects with the others. For example, the sense of the actual is necessary to a poet's being dramatic; a sensitivity to the manifold possibilities of versification cannot really be separated from a desire to purify, maintain and sustain the English language.

Let me now try briefly to define and illustrate each of these qualities as they manifest themselves in Eliot's criticism of English poetry. First, the sense of the actual, which is perhaps the most difficult of all to define, since whenever we attempt to define anything, we must do so by referring to the actual and perhaps by merely pointing to it.

An illustration, not from Eliot himself, but from James Joyce, who in so many ways is profoundly close to Eliot as an author, may be useful. A would-be novelist came to Joyce with a manuscript of a novel she had just finished, telling Joyce that she would like his opinion of the novel and saying that only one other person had read the book, the porter of the hotel in which she was living. "What did the porter say?" Joyce inquired. "He objected to only one episode," replied the female novelist. "The episode in which the lover finds the locket of his beloved while walking in the woods, picks it up, and kisses it passionately." "What was the porter's objection?" said Joyce. "He said," she replied, "that before kissing the locket passionately, the lover should have rubbed it against his coat to get the dirt off it." "Go back," said Joyce, "to that porter. There is nothing I can tell you that he does not already know." This too is not as complete a pointing to the actual as one might wish, since the actual might be misunderstood to mean only that which is sordid, only that which the muckraker concerns himself with, while Eliot has in mind the actuality of human emotion and human nobility as well.

Moreover, Eliot makes it clear that a sense of the actual is really incomplete and warped without a sense of the past, that sense of the past which, he says, is indispensable to "anyone who wants to continue to be a poet after his 25th year." But we must be careful not to misunderstand Eliot's concern with a sense of the past as mere nostalgia for the days when knighthood was in flower. It is the past as actual, as an actual part of the present, which concerns Eliot. And one must have a strong sense of actuality in order to know just what of the past is alive in the present and what is merely a monument or a souvenir. Without a sense of the past, one's sense of the actual is likely to be confused with an obsessive pursuit of what is degraded, or idiosyncratic, or transitory, or brand-new. This is the dead end of the naturalistic novelist who supposes that the slum is somehow more real than the library. Conversely, a sense of the actual enables one to understand the past itself as something which was not by any means Arcadian. Perhaps one can go so far as to say that one cannot have much of a sense of the past without a sense of the actual or much of a sense of the actual without a sense of the past. Thus, to use an example which can stand for much that is characteristic of Eliot, if one looks at a church, one does not really see very much of what one is looking at if one does not have both a sense of the actual, a sense of the past, and a sense of the past *as* actual in the present.

II

Let me turn now to a few instances of how Eliot uses the criterion of actuality in his criticism. Blake is praised because one of his poems expresses "the naked observation" and another "the naked insight":

But most through midnight streets I hear
How the youthful harlot's curse
Blasts the newborn infant's ear
And blights with plagues the marriage hearse.

In the same essay, which was written in 1920, Blake is praised because he possesses the peculiar honesty, which according to Eliot, is peculiar to all great poetry, an honesty which is to be found, Eliot says, in Homer, Aeschylus, and Dante, and an honesty which is, he adds, in a world too frightened to be honest, curiously terrifying, an honesty against which the whole world conspires because it is unpleasant. Here we can see how closely connected in Eliot's mind are the sense of the actual and the ability of a poet to be honest.

Now let us take a negative instance, that of Swinburne. Swinburne for Eliot is a poet whose real virtue was his verbalism, his use of words for their own sake. "In the verse of Swinburne the object (or we might say the actual) has ceased to exist. . . ." Swinburne, says Eliot, dwelt exclusively and consistently among words divorced from any reference to objects and actualities, and this kind of poetry is compared not only with that of Campion, which has both a beauty of language and a reference to actuality, but also to "the language which is more important to us . . . . the language which is struggling to digest new objects . . . new feelings, new aspects, as for instance the prose of James Joyce and Joseph Conrad."

There is another important negative instance. Eliot speaks of the images in the plays of Beaumont and Fletcher as "cut and slightly withered flowers stuck in the sand" in comparison with the images of Shakespeare, Donne, Webster, and Middleton, which have, he says, "tentacular roots" which reach down to "the deepest terrors and desires." In the same way, Tennyson is praised for his great technical skill but the quotations which Eliot cites, in 1936, when he reverses his judgment of Tennyson are praised because they are descriptions of a particular time and place. This could only be, Eliot says, an English street.[1]

1. The lines are:
> He is not there; but far away
> The noise of life begins again,
> And ghastly through the drizzling rain
> On the bald street breaks the blank day.

[319]

Now, to return for a moment to my general subject, we can see here the underlying unity which is involved in Eliot's revision of his first evaluation of English poetry. For in praising Blake as one who was unpleasantly honest and full of naked observations and insights, Eliot said that such honesty could not exist apart from great technical skill. In his first revaluation Eliot had praised Tennyson for his technical skill but dismissed him as one who merely ruminated. When Eliot came to revise his judgment of Tennyson in 1936, his revision was consequent upon a study of Tennyson's versification, which led him to see how that poet's great technical skill did in fact, at times, enable him to render the actual and not merely ruminate upon it. Thus, in a sense, Eliot is consistent throughout; the reason that a revision has been necessary is that Eliot was burdened by preconceptions which belonged to the period in which he was writing, and he had simply not read sufficiently in some of the poets he dismissed.

So too with the poetry of Milton, although I do not think that here it is a question of insufficient reading. When Eliot says in depreciation of some of Milton's poems that they are conventional, artificial, and enamelled, he is complaining again about the absence of the actual, as we see further in the same essay from which I have already quoted: "That the greatest poets set you before real men talking, carry you on in real events, moving." It seems to me likely enough that by now Eliot has perceived beneath the perhaps artificial and certainly grandiloquent surface of Milton's language precisely that peculiar honesty about the essential strength or sickness of the human soul, which he found in Dante, Shakespeare, Blake, and other of the very greatest poets. I should think that this desirable revision of opinion may also have come about as a result of the development of Eliot's own writing during recent years. When Eliot spoke of Milton here at Columbia in 1933, he said that *Samson Agonistes* is not really a dramatic poem but rather an extended lyric. In the *Four Quartets*, as I have already suggested, there are many indications that the kind of experience Milton deals with in *Samson Agonistes*—Samson, shorn, blind and chained to the wheel, and Milton himself blind and chained to old age—will be more understandable to the poet and critic who writes:

> The poetry does not matter.
> It was not to start again what one had expected,
> What was to be the value of the long looked forward to,
> Long hoped for calm, the autumnal serenity
> And the wisdom of age?

And who writes later in the same group of poems:

> Since our concern was speech, and speech impelled us
> To purify the dialect of the tribe
> And urge the mind to aftersight and foresight,
> Let me disclose the gifts reserved for age
> To set a crown upon your lifetime's effort.
> First, the cold friction of expiring sense
> Without enchantment, offering no promise,
> But bitter tastelessness of shadow fruit
> As body and soul begin to fall asunder.
> Second, the conscious impotence of rage
> At human folly, and the laceration
> Of laughter at what ceases to amuse.
> And last, the rending pain of re-enactment
> Of all that you have done and been; the shame
> Of motives late revealed, and the awareness
> Of things ill done and done to others' harm
> Which once we took for exercise of virtue.
> Then fools' approval stings and honor stains.

It seems to me that the poet who wrote these lines cannot fail to recognize at last both the spiritual grandeur of *Samson Agonistes* and also the concern with speech, the effort to purify the dialect of the tribe, and urge the mind to aftersight, which is characteristic of that great poem.

In thus supposing that Eliot's experience of the last decade will lead him to a new recognition and admiration of Milton, it seems to me that I am illustrating another aspect of the sense of the actual. It is actuality itself, the actuality of middle age approaching old age, which leads to a deeper understanding of Milton's major poetry, most of which, after all, was written in middle or old age.

III

Let us return now to the other touchstones, or criteria, of poetic genuineness.

Honesty is perhaps a shorthand term for a willingness to face the reality of one's emotions. Thomas Middleton is given what seems to me virtually fabulous praise by being said to have created in *The Changeling*, "an eternal tragedy, as permanent as *Oedipus* or *Antony and Cleopatra* . . . the tragedy of the unmoral nature suddenly trapped in the inexorable toils of morality. . . . A play which has a profound and permanent moral value and horror." Thus we can see how a poet's honesty is, in fact, very often a concern with morality, with the actuality of morality. Yet this moralism must be distinguished carefully from that overt didacticism which has spoiled the work of many great artists such as Tolstoy and resulted in the censorship of more than one masterpiece. Notice I have said the actuality of morality rather than simply morality as such. A further elucidation is to be found in Eliot's discussion of Hamlet, a character who suffered, says Eliot, from "the intense feeling, ecstatic or terrible, without an object or exceeding its object, which every person of sensibility has known. . . . The ordinary person puts such feelings to sleep, or trims down his feelings to fit the business world. The artist keeps them alive. . . ." In *Hamlet* Shakespeare "tackled a problem that proved too much for him. Why he attempted it at all, is an insoluble puzzle; under the compulsion of what experience he attempted to express the inexpressibly horrible, we cannot ever know." To conclude that *Hamlet* is a failure, as Eliot does, though it is the most read, performed, and studied of all plays, seems to me to have a curious notion of success. To inquire as to why he wrote the play at all is incomprehensible in view of the remarks Eliot makes about the artist's effort to deal with emotions which are ecstatic, terrible, and inexpressibly horrifying. But I am not concerned so much with the wrongness of Eliot's judgment in an essay written as early as 1919 as I am concerned with the relation of these remarks to the honesty of the poet and the actuality of moral existence, to which these remarks point. The poet's honesty, and thus his morality, consists in his ability to face the ecstasy and the terror of his emotions, his desires, his fears, his aspirations, and his failure to realize his and other human beings' moral allegiances. Thus the morality of the poet consists not in teaching other human beings how to behave, but in facing the deepest emotional and moral realities in his poems, and in this way making it possible for his readers to confront the total reality of their existence, physical, emotional, moral and religious.

As Eliot says in one of his poems, "Mankind cannot bear very much reality," and Eliot looks always for those qualities in a poem which are likely to help the reader to see reality, if not to bear it.

IV

Eliot's theory of the nature and history of English poetry as stated in this essay of 1921 can be summarized as follows: "The metaphysical poets possessed a mind and sensibility which could devour *any* kind of experience." (Here, in passing, we may question whether any poet can devour any or all kinds of experience, and further whether such a poet as Wordsworth was not capable of taking hold of certain kinds of experience which the metaphysical poets know little or nothing about.)

Eliot continues by saying that Milton and Dryden were so powerful—"performed certain poetic functions so magnificently that the magnitude of the effect conceals the absence of others." The language of poetry improved from that time forward, says Eliot, but "the feeling became more crude." In the metaphysical poets and their predecessors, "there is a direct sensuous apprehension of thought, or a recreation of thought into feeling," and there is also a kind of intellectual wit, as Eliot observes in his companion essay on Andrew Marvell. But in Collins, Gray, Wordsworth, Shelley, Tennyson, Browning, Hardy, Yeats, and practically every poet since the time of Donne, there is missing that capacity of the mind, that wholeness of sensibility which makes it possible to say of Donne that "a thought was to him an experience," while Tennyson and Browning "merely ruminated"—"they are poets and they think; but they do not feel their thoughts as immediately as the odor of a rose." When Eliot adds Hardy to this list because he was a modern Englishman and Yeats because he was Irish, it seems to me that we may justifiably say that seldom have so many poets been depreciated or dismissed in so few pages. Yet, extreme and sectarian as this view is, it depends nonetheless upon a profound sense of the nature of poetry. We can see what this sense comes to when Eliot says that "those critics who tell poets to look into their hearts and write do not tell them to look deep enough. . . . Racine and Donne looked into a great deal more than the heart. One must look into the cerebral cortex, the nervous system, and the digestive tracts."

V

The third of the standards with which Eliot has criticized poetry is language as such. This is connected, as we would expect, with the remarks I have just quoted, for Eliot says, that "in French poetry, for example, the two greatest masters of diction are also the two greatest psychologists, the most curious explorers of the soul." In English poetry, however, Eliot finds that two of the greatest masters of diction are Milton and Dryden and they triumph, he says, "by a dazzling disregard of the human soul." Here again there is an underlying consistency in the operation of Eliot's mind, for what he is saying of Dryden and Milton is close to what he had said in 1920 of Swinburne as being purely verbal, of using language really divorced from any reference to objects. And it should be noted that only by a very strong sense of the actual can we distinguish between poetry which explores the human soul and poetry which is largely verbal. There is an intermediate mode: poetry whose chief aim is that of incantation, of inducing a certain state of emotion. The two instances Eliot cites are Poe and Mallarmé in an essay written in French in 1926 and never translated into English.

The essence of Eliot's concern with language in itself is perhaps best formulated in the following quotation: "The poetry of a people takes its life from the people's speech and in turn gives life to it; it represents its highest point of consciousness, its greatest power, and its most delicate sensibility." If we take this concern with language in isolation it might seem that the chief purpose of poetry was to maintain and purify the language, and indeed Eliot's praise of Dryden often seems to be bestowed on that poet merely because he effected a reformation in the use of language, rather than for his intrinsic qualities. Throughout Eliot's own poetry there are references to the difficulties and trials of anyone who attempts to use language carefully. In "The Love Song of J. Alfred Prufrock," the protagonist resents the fact that he is formulated in a phrase; in "Sweeney Agonistes" one character says "I gotta use words when I talk to you," and it should be noted that the use of slang in this play witnesses an extraordinary sensitivity to colloquial language upon the part of one who in colloquial terms is known as a "highbrow." In "The Waste Land" each human being is said to be isolated from all other human beings, to be in a prison, the prison of the self, hearing only ethereal rumors of the external world. There are many other instances but perhaps a quotation from the *Four Quartets* is the most explicit of all:

> So here I am, in the middle way, having had twenty years—
> Twenty years largely wasted, the years of *l'entre deux guerres*—
> Trying to learn to use words, and every attempt
> Is a wholly new start, and different kind of failure
> Because one has only learned to get the better of words
> For the thing one no longer has to say, or the way in which
> One is no longer disposed to say it. . . .

Perhaps I should say at this point that I have quoted so often from the *Four Quartets* because they bear directly on Eliot's criticism, and not because I admire them very much; they seem to me one of his less successful works, although I confess that I have been unable to find anyone to agree with me. The main point is that throughout Eliot's criticism the quality of the poet's language and its effect upon the future of the English language has always concerned Eliot very much. I think we can say that never before has criticism been so conscious of all that can happen to language, how easily it can be debased, and how marvelously it can be elevated and made to illuminate the most difficult and delicate areas of experience.

VI

The fourth criterion is the dramatic sense, and Eliot maintains that all great poetry is dramatic. However, there is perhaps some confusion here, since Eliot means by dramatic the attitudes and emotions of a human being in a given situation. But when he comes to apply this broad definition, he is often influenced by his own love of Elizabethan drama, where the term, dramatic, narrows itself to the specific theatrical sense of the word, a sense in which it must be distinguished from meaning any human being's attitudes in any situation. This shift in meaning makes it possible for Eliot to say that Milton is not dramatic. For if we stick to the broad definition of the term, then, obviously, what could be more dramatic than the attitudes of Lucifer in *Paradise Lost,* or the attitudes of Samson in *Samson Agonistes?* Again, if we accept Eliot's broad definition, then perhaps we must say that the "Elegy in a Country Churchyard" is just as dramatic, qua dramatic, as *Hamlet, Prince of Denmark.* I do not mean to say that Eliot's emphasis upon the dramatic in poetry is not justified and fruitful to a certain extent; for example, there is a sense in which we can say that Gray's Elegy is less dramatic than, let us say, Donne's "The Funeral," which might be taken as a kind of elegy. My point is that Eliot sometimes uses this criterion of the dramatic to enforce prejudices about poetry which he does not like for other reasons.

We come, finally, to the question of versification. It is here that Eliot has been most influenced by his own poetic practice. For at one time or another he has enunciated practically every possible theory of what the nature of versification is. In a late essay on the poetry of Yeats he says that blank verse cannot be written in the 20th century because it still retains its period quality. The period presumably is the Elizabethan one, and such a statement is belied by the fact that not only has some of Eliot's best poetry been written in blank verse, but such a statement disregards the triumphs of blank verse, the inexhaustible variety of this form of versification to be found in Milton, Wordsworth, in Keats' "Hyperion," in certain poems of Tennyson which Eliot himself has praised precisely for their technical mastery of blank verse, and in Browning; many other instances could be mentioned. Eliot's fundamental concern has been, however, with what he calls the "auditory imagination," "the feeling for syllable and rhythm, penetrating far below the conscious levels of thought and feeling, invigorating every word; sinking to the most primitive and forgotten, returning to the origin and bringing something back; seeking the beginning and the end." This should suggest that underneath the contradictory statements about the possibilities of versification which run throughout Eliot's criticism, there is a powerful intuition of how various, unpredictable, and profound are the possibilities of language when it is versified. The quotation I have just cited should suggest certainly that Eliot has found versification a means of raising to the surface of consciousness much that is otherwise concealed. We ought to remember Goethe's remark about Wordsworth, which is quoted by Matthew Arnold in his essay on Wordsworth: that Wordsworth was deficient as a poet because he knew too well the reason he chose every word and line. This paradoxical remark is not based upon a belief that the poet ought to be irrational and spontaneous, but, I think, based upon the sense that through rhythm the poet drew upon depths of being which could not be deliberately or consciously tapped. And let us remember that Goethe and Arnold were in no sense exponents of surrealism.

If we examine Eliot's scrutiny of English versification from the time of Marlowe to the time of Hardy and Yeats, and are not seduced into glib and futile logic-chopping, we come upon a theory of the nature of versification which seems to do justice to the many different things that Eliot has said about it. Namely, the theory that the essence of metre and thus of versification is any repetitive pattern of words, and the endless arguments about versification from Campion to Amy Lowell and the free verse movement are caused by the curious feeling that some *one* repetitive pattern, or kind of pattern, is the only true method of versification.

It will doubtless have been obvious by now that in a summary and incomplete way I have been attempting to make systematic the work of a critic who far from proceeding in terms of system or of a priori conceptions or of philosophical theory as to the nature of poetry has, on the contrary, developed the body of his work in the course of writing book reviews, and essays inspired by a particular occasion. In fact, Eliot complains at one point that he often had to write criticism when he wanted to write poetry, and it is certainly true that he did not always choose the subjects of his criticism. Yet it is likely that, to proceed in this way, at the mercy of accident, editorial whim, and his own intuitive sense of what he really felt about poetry, was probably the only way in which much of Eliot's criticism could have come into being.

VII

Let me now try to place Eliot's criticism in terms of a classification which was first suggested by the late Irving Babbitt, and I believe misused by him. Babbitt speaks of impressionistic criticism, scientific criticism, neoclassical criticism, and a fourth kind to which he gives no name, except to quote Abraham Lincoln's epigram about how you can't fool all the people all the time: a kind of criticism which is sometimes called the test of time or the verdict of posterity. This fourth kind presents many difficulties, including the fact that the posterity of the past, the only posterity we know about, has changed its mind so often, at different times preferring Dryden's *All for Love* to Shakespeare's *Antony and Cleopatra,* not to dwell upon such sad and brutal facts as that most of Sophocles' ninety plays have disappeared, and thus evaded the test of time and the fickleness of posterity, or such another dismaying piece of information as the fact that the Romans thought Ennius, whose work has almost entirely disappeared, was a far better epic poet than Virgil. Or again, let us remember that when the Mohammedans burnt the great library at Alexandria, they destroyed survival in time as a literary criterion and a basis for literary criticism.

Babbitt's other three kinds of criticism are also, I think, inadequate classifications. For example, when Babbitt speaks of scientific criticism, what he really means is historical criticism, since he cites Taine as its leading exponent. What we ought to distinguish and emphasize is the purpose which each kind of critic has in mind when he takes hold of a literary work. The neoclassic critic looks in the new literary work for the specific characteristics which he has found in masterpieces of the past, and consequently he denounces Shakespeare because he did not write like Sophocles. Thus, Voltaire condemns Shakespeare as a barbarian because he does not write like Racine. The historical critic is interested in the causes, social and biographical, of the literary work rather than in the work itself. The impressionistic critic is interested in the effects of the literary work upon himself as a delicate and rare sensibility rather than in the work as an objective and social phenomenon. The historical critic goes in back of the work to its causes; the impressionistic critic is concerned with himself rather than with the work itself; to use Pater's unfortunately immortal phrase, he wants to burn with a hard gemlike flame before the work of art, usually neglecting, in his concern with being inflamed, to distinguish and discriminate carefully between the objects which excite him. Eliot's criticism fits none of these classifications, although it is to be regretted that there has not been more of the historical critic in him.

[328]

He has proceeded, as I have said, by intuition and by seeking out what most interested him from time to time. Yet, at his best he has been what I would like to call the classic kind of critic, the critic who is expert precisely because he depends upon the quality of his own experience, while, at the same time being aware that the more experience of literature he has, the more expert he becomes. There are no substitutes for experience, a platitude which is ignored invariably by the neoclassic critic, whose essential effort is to deduce from classics of the past a ready-made formula for judging any new work. Eliot's classicism at its best is illustrated when he says that if a truly classic work were written in our time, it would not be recognized as such by most of us. It would seem so monstrous, so queer and horrifying. This remark was made in 1933, when a good deal of James Joyce's *Finnegans Wake* had appeared and had been greeted by Eliot in the following terms, "We can't have much more of this sort of thing." Eliot has since changed his mind about this work, and though I do not know whether he considers it truly classical, certainly he admires it very much, and in this shift from dismay and perplexity to admiration we can see how the truly classical critic, the true expert, depends upon experience, and permits experience to correct his errors in appreciation. Experience is thus for the expert, or classical critic, not only the great teacher but the best textbook. Eliot, in revising his initial revaluation of English poetry, has permitted experience to teach him as no theory and no authority possibly could.

Having reviewed this long and complex critical career, we come finally to the question of what conclusions we can draw and what lessons we can gain from it. It seems to me that we have reached a point in our knowledge of the history of taste, the history of literary reputation, and literary judgment, where we can clearly mark out some of the most important dangers and pitfalls involved in any kind of literary criticism. Is it not clear that the kind of action and reaction which characterizes so good a critic as Eliot may very well be the expense of spirit in a waste of false discrimination? Is it necessary, in order to praise poets A, B, and C, to condemn poets D, E, F, G, H, and the rest of the alphabet? Perhaps it is necessary, but if we think concretely of the really shocking blunders in taste which prevail throughout literary history, then perhaps the very consciousness of these blunders can help us to arrive at a point of view in which there is no mere seesaw of praise and rejection. When Dr. Johnson declared that "Lycidas" was a worthless literary production, when Turgenev said that Dostoevsky was a "morbid mediocrity," and announced that he was very bored by the first volume of *War and Peace*, when Tolstoy ridiculed Shakespeare's *King Lear*, and asserted that his own masterpieces were worthless because they could not hold the attention of peasants; or when, for that matter, Shakespeare lost his popularity with Elizabethan audiences because Beaumont and Fletcher seemed to be able to turn out the same kind of thing in a slicker style—but it is unnecessary to continue with what might be an endless catalogue. The point is that the more we know about the history of literary reputation and literary opinion, the more conscious we are of how unjust and how stupid even the greatest critics can be, the more likely we are to avoid such errors in our own experience of literature. The matter is not merely a question of the reader's welfare; the creative writer himself is crucially involved, for just as we may suppose that Shakespeare turned to romantic comedy when his popularity declined, so too it seems likely enough that the failure of *Moby Dick* and *Pierre* reduced Melville to a silence and inactivity from which he emerged now and again for thirty years with short novels which suggest how much more he might have done, given his unquestionable genius, had his greatest work received the recognition it deserved at the time it appeared instead of some thirty years after Melville's death. Thus it does not seem to me to be claiming too much for literary criticism when one declares that upon the goodness, the consciousness, and the justice of literary criticism the very existence of great works sometimes depends, not to speak of the existence of great poets, nor to dwell too much upon mighty poets in their misery dead. I should add at this point that it is only by a knowledge of the literary past that contemporary critical practice can be of much use in preventing new neglect, stupidity, unjustified admiration, and unwarranted blindness. Two of the best poets of the nineteenth century, Gerard Manley Hopkins and Emily Dickinson, went to their graves with hardly any external recognition; it is quite possible that they did not really know that they had written good poetry. At present Hopkins and Emily Dickinson are much admired but only at the expense of Wordsworth and Hardy. By reviewing Eliot's critical career we can envisage a point of view which will free our scrutiny of literature from many of the sins of the past, while at the same time illuminating anew all that we have inherited from the past. And we can, I think, see how it might be desirable to have no literary dictators.

Primitivism and Decadence
by Yvor Winters

I

℘ Mr. Yvor Winters has written a book[1] which every serious American writer, and indeed everyone with the least pretense to serious interest in literature, ought to buy and ought to study. This is said by way of qualifying radically many of the difficulties which I wish to point out in his notions about the nature of poetry. And one ought also to say at the start that there are many remarkable insights in this book: Winters seems, for example, to have predicted, indirectly, Crane's death;[2] he has managed, apparently by a deliberate effort, to extend his taste from such writing as Joyce's to such an opposite extreme as Churchill and Gay, and in doing so he has provided us with the means of extending our tastes in like manner; and he is, I think, the first American critic of the present century to concern himself explicitly with meter. He is thus, in a way, more helpful than either of his only rivals in critical significance, for Mr. Tate would seem to be concerned, really, with moral, rather than specifically poetic, problems; and Mr. R. P. Blackmur depends, for the most part, upon the dictionary. Mr. Winters, however, is concerned throughout with the moral implications involved in structures and meters, with structure and meter, and with meaning, Mr. Blackmur's primary con-

1. *Primitivism and Decadence: A Study of American Experimental Poetry*, by Yvor Winters, Arrow Editions.
2. In his review of a book by Robinson Jeffers in *Poetry* for February, 1930, a review which is partly reprinted in this book, Winters pointed out that the logical consequence of Crane's and Jeffers' general feelings about nature was suicide.

cern. Indeed, Winters is the first critic, I should think, who has attempted to show the *specific* ways in which meter, morality, structure, and meaning are related, and, in a way, identical.

It would seem ungrateful, then, in view of all this extremely valuable work, to turn about and say that in section after section, Mr. Winters indulges himself in excess and exaggeration, displays prejudices which are wholly arbitrary, and is guilty either of misconstruction or ignorance. But each of these charges can be clearly demonstrated. What happens in each instance can be stated in several ways and it may be profitable to do so. One may use Mr. Tate's rather curious terms in his essay on "The Fallacy of Humanism" and point out how Winters is quantifying Quality before he gets to it (and it is interesting in this connection to note that he accepts the humanism of Babbitt, although with important reservations). Again, to use a concrete instance, when Winters proves to his own contentment that "Gerontion" is not a good poem, he is very much like Johnson when confronted with "Lycidas" (I do not mean to imply that the former is as good as the latter), or like Tolstoy, condemning *War and Peace*, and *Anna Karenina*. But in the most general terms, Winters' error is that of the reductive fallacy, which has many instances in the history of criticism: the critic, that is, decides to define Beauty (or aesthetic value, or worth, or whatever he calls it) and he decides that Beauty is unity in difference, or significant form, or the expression of the class struggle, or pleasure; and having decided this, he rules out all instances which do not conform to his definition or he attempts to reduce unlikely instances to the unique definition. The ruling definition for Winters is regularity of meter. This is a crude way of stating it; Winters has other criteria, which modify it; but I shall try to give a more adequate statement of this view later on.

II

Primitivism and Decadence divides itself into five parts, each of which reflects backward and forward upon the others; the subjects, in order, are: morality insofar as it is involved in poetry, structural methods of presenting the subject matter, poetic convention (a really illuminating discovery), ways of classifying types of poets, and finally, meter. All five refer to aspects of any given poem

[333]

which are, ultimately, identical: the moral insight exhibited in a poem is, for example, the same thing as its firmness and lucidity of structure, "the poet, in striving toward an ideal of poetic form ... is actually striving to perfect a moral attitude toward that range of experience of which he is aware." The range of his awareness is commensurate with the kind of meters he uses and the type of poet that he is and the way in which he presents his subject.

Beginning with the first and the most fundamental aspect of the poem with which Winters deals, one finds that the writing of a poem is a moral act because it is an attempt to order, control, and understand one's experiences. Each of the constituents of poetry is, in its very nature, an instrument of perception, so that poetry is "the last refinement of contemplation," "the richest and most perfect technique of contemplation."

Now the first difficulty is Mr. Winters' singular view of morality in general. Not only does he say that religion may be and philosophy can be a *preliminary* to poetry, but his whole view of what constitutes a moral act seems to be based upon a very narrow view of what the poet is involved in when he writes a poem. He thinks, for example, that social conditions and modern thought do not change the mode which moral responsibility will take and the mode which style and meter can take. Those who think these matters make the task of the modern poet different and more difficult suffer from "group hypochondria." This accusation when added to the different charges against various modern poets—Mr. Eliot's "spiritual limpness," for example—and when added to a good deal else which cannot be mentioned in a review, imply that Winters sees the poet operating in some kind of vacuum in which not only his act but the circumstances in which he acts depend upon his own choice. Winters, believing that he is "traditionalist" and concerned with the traditional wisdom, ought to remember that Aristotle, not Marx, asserted, in his *Ethics,* as well as his *Politics,* that man is a political animal literally, of course, an animal living in cities, in groups). Leaving this point in the air for a moment, it is worthwhile considering the moral preeminence which Winters gives to the act of writing a poem. He says that it is no substitute for action "in the face of a particular situation," but merely "a way of enriching one's awareness" and thus becoming more intelligent about the future; yet the emphasis betrays him: religion and philosophy are merely preliminary and the *richest* way of knowing is the act of writing a poem and the great poet has triumphed (in the terms of Mr. Richards' rhetoric) over life itself.

Thus an act of contemplation and a moral act are assumed to be in no way different, although Winters has seen that in particular situations they must be distinct. The consequences of blurring the distinction between what we know and what we do are well known: ignorance and evildoing become identical, and thus responsibility disappears, which is, one would suppose, the last thing which Winters would want to happen. This is also relevant to Winters' difficulty in explaining the sad and ugly lives of the poets, who, in his view, must nevertheless have been men of great character, since they wrote great poems. His explanation is that they were sometimes men of great character, sometimes and in relation to certain types of experience only, a view which can be entitled that of the intermissions of virtue. One would suppose, on the contrary, that the mastery of experience involved in a poem is a matter of perception, the mastery of language, and the poet's ability to bring to bear upon perception and within language his sense of values. The effort of the poet is thus representative, critical, and evaluative, but it is not a moral act, except in an indirect sense. The distinction becomes quite clear when we see that we regard writers as good poets, although their values, as operative in their poetry, are directly opposed to our own. The fact that perceptions, attitudes, and values have been adequately represented is enough. We do not, however, accept the thief because he himself regards his theft as justifiable.

As I will try to show in a moment, Winters is involved in the same difficulty when it is a question of the beliefs of the poet. But it is worthwhile considering, before going on, what seems to be the root of Winters' critical method. This is to be found, I think, mainly in the little book by I. A. Richards called *Science and Poetry*, and also in his *Principles of Literary Criticism* and certain pages on the "sincerity ritual" in *Practical Criticism*. The ideas of Richards are well-known and may be rapidly summed up. He

[335]

thinks the poet is, in the poem, engaged in organizing his impulses—his appetencies and aversions: the good poem is the one in which a psychological balance or harmony—synaesthesis is Richards' term—has been achieved. And this view flows from the belief that nature has been "neutralized," that most of the values of the past have been unmasked and repudiated, and that poetry alone is left to the human being as a means of integrating his life. Richards attacks Yeats, De la Mare and Lawrence as poets who refuse to face the modern situation, the neutrality and meaninglessness of nature, and who attempt to provide elaborate fictions to belie the truth. Winters duplicates this attack in some of his statements about Yeats and Crane. The difficulty here is that Winters has obviously changed his mind: he no longer accepts the crude naturalism of Richards—which Richards in *Coleridge on the Imagination* turns upside down into a kind of subjective idealism, and which was initially derived from doctrines which Lord Russell has long since abandoned—and Winters has taken upon himself beliefs and values of a neohumanist variety. One is permitted to change one's mind, but a certain thoroughness is preferable. Winters, however, still drags along Richards' psychological-moral notion of the substance of a poem. The mixture is indeed curious. Winters is perhaps as sensitive as anyone could be to the concrete poem, and he must know that a poem is not primarily a balance of appetencies and aversions, but an effort at perception and evaluation. But the former belief remains, transformed into the idea that the creative act itself, with all the absorption and effort it necessitates, makes the writing of the poem a moral act. One can only observe that the criminal may also exhibit a like devotion and concentration.

It would be worthwhile, in another context, to consider fully the other consequences of Winters' views of morality. In passing, one can note that once poetry involves the moral act to so full an extent there is no answer to the demand that poetry aid directly in the transformation of society.

Before continuing, it may be useful also to refer to the philosophy-mongering in which Winters and so many other poets and critics indulge. It is of course partly unavoidable in a time like the present. But there is also the possibility of availing oneself to a greater extent of the discipline of philosophical method.

Winters refers repeatedly to such matters as the nature of definition, the nature of moral intelligence, etc., and his remarks are
unfailingly inexact. Mr. Eliot is, as usual, to the point about this
practice: "My objection is . . . to Mr. Foerster . . . for playing
the games of philosophy and theology without knowing the rules.
One may consider the study of philosophy vain, but then one
should not philosophise." One ought to add, in justice to Mr.
Winters, that Mr. Eliot is himself not without sin in this respect,
nor is R. P. Blackmur (with his fantastic comparison of Charles
S. Peirce and Kenneth Burke), nor is Allen Tate (who considers
Mr. Blackmur a master of ideas), nor Kenneth Burke, Howard
Baker, Edmund Wilson, and James T. Farrell. The only writer
of this kind who does not, at one time or another, seem foolish and
half educated when touching on these things is John Crowe
Ransom, and even he has taken the name of Plato in vain and
forced a metaphysical interpretation of the nature of meter. The
pity is obviously that Winters and these other writers are sometimes trying to formulate intuitions of no mean value.

Mr. Winters makes a good many of his judgments on the basis of
the metrical character of a poem. From the meter of the poem he
infers the spiritual or moral character of the poem.

There is, to begin with, the statement that "the limp versification of Mr. Eliot is inseparable from the spiritual limpness that one
feels behind the poems." What spiritual limpness is, one can only
guess, and even limp versification is a term which is fairly vague;
the statement is made, morever, rather tentatively ("one feels").
Still, it will serve as an example of Mr. Winters' method. Suppose,
however, two instances are used to test this method. Quoting from
Bridges, one of Mr. Winters' touchstones,

> Though thou, I know not why,
> Didst kill my childish trust,
> That breach with toil did I
> Repair because I must:
>   And spite of frighting schemes,
> With which the fiends of Hell
> Blaspheme thee in my dreams,
> So far I have hoped well.

Suppose I say that this is spiritually stiff, or frivolous, or superficial
(I do not believe that it is), and that one of Mr. Eliot's magi—

All this was a long time ago, I remember,
And I would do it again, but set down
This set down
This: were we led all that way for
Birth or Death?—

is far more aware of spiritual reality. Mr. Winters would justify his praise of the one and contempt of the other by reference to his theory of meter, for meter turns out to be the same thing as spiritual awareness. The poem of Bridges is according to Winters (in *The American Review* for January, 1937) the "experience of the intellectual who has progressed beyond the disillusionment of 'Dover Beach.' " So, I think, is the poem by Eliot.

The point here is not merely a difference in taste. Mr. Winters exhibits prejudice and a lack of tact and exactness in judging the meters of Eliot, although elsewhere in the book, in writing of "The Subway," by Allen Tate, he has provided a brilliant elucidation of the relationship of meter and feeling, meter and attitude, meter and meaning. If you abstract the meter of the poem from its statements and base your judgment upon the meter alone, then you conclude that Mr. Eliot is spiritually limp, or that Bridges is spiritually stiff, frivolous, and superficial. But there is a different situation in the concrete poem. One does not start with the meter, nor with the explicit statements, but with both, taken together. Their relationship is one of reciprocal modification; each "characterizes" the other, and they cannot be separated, a fact upon which Winters himself insists. This fact is often forgotten. One is offered examples of sublime verse and nonsense rhymes with the same vowels or in the same meter, in order to show that meter is not expressive. This is the error correlative to that of Winters. Mr. Eliot himself was once guilty of it, in a lecture. He read several verses of Tennyson, and then lines with the same meter and rhyme-scheme from a nonsense ballad by Lear. The audience giggled; Mr. Eliot concluded that here was indeed a problem, and then passed hurriedly on to another subject.

But there is a good deal more than a metrical basis for Winters' dislike of Eliot's poetry, which recently, he says, has been a kind of "psychic impressionism, a formless curiosity concerning queer feelings related to odds and ends of more or less profound thought."

Here again Winters' beliefs are intruded upon his literary judgment. Ultimately Winters would have to say that he just does not like Mr. Eliot's religion. Winters thinks that such poems as "Ash Wednesday," "Animula," and "Journey of the Magi," from which I have just quoted, are the products of psychic impressionism and a formless curiosity only because of his own beliefs, which, so far as they are available, seem to relate mainly to a conception of nature as full of sensuous temptation, which must be resisted—and perhaps also to a view of rationality and consciousness as the supreme goods. One would scarcely wish to deny the importance of these concerns, but the point at issue is the way in which they distort his literary judgments. As a literary critic, Winters is justified in judging the *representation* of a belief, not the belief itself. This does not imply a purely formal approach to literature because the representation in question is a matter of understanding and evaluation as well as the use of language. It is difficult in literary criticism to avoid moral, political, and even theological judgments, not to speak of the tendency to praise our friends' poems, but one can with effort separate literary judgment from all these and thus avoid confusion. A model for such separation is to be found in F. O. Matthiessen's book on Eliot, and precisely in the example of Eliot's religious and political beliefs.

We have to insist that the poem is not a mere prolongation of experience upon the verbal level, but experience grasped, understood, and evaluated. Yet we cannot, as literary critics, dictate the terms of such understanding and evaluation. We cannot reject Homer because his deities are mythical. The criterion is thus the simple truth of representation, or if Mr. Winters prefers the classical word, *verisimilitude*. Such truth is self-sufficient; and it may also serve the moral purposes which Winters requires of a poem. But I will have to deal with this more explicitly later on.

The more general point which follows from this one refers us again to the void in which Mr. Winters' poet is writing. Mr. Eliot wrote his poem in a definite period in history; he was trying, as he says of others in his essay on Swinburne, to use language which would have something to do with his *whole* experience: "the language which is more important to us is that which is struggling to digest and express new objects, new groups of objects, new

[339]

feelings, new aspects, as, for instance, the prose of Mr. James Joyce." The emphasis on newness is unfortunate but the point remains. It can be reinforced by Mr. Tate's remark, "It is probable that there is an intimate relation between a generally accepted 'picture of the world' and the general acceptance of a metrical system." Mr. Winters may regard this merely as a confirmation of his own view; if he does, let him ask himself if it is merely arbitrary whim on the part of individual poets that good dramatic blank verse, *in a play performed in a theater,* has not been written since 1640 or so.[3] In general, then, it seems much more likely that the faults of modern poetry result at least partly from an effort to take up, reflect, record, and represent experiences of unheard-of complexity and difficulty, occurring in a world in which the rate of social change has accelerated to an unprecedented degree.

But Mr. Winters will say that this involves the "fallacy of imitative form," a notion which will have to be dealt with in due course.

III

Mr. Winters' next subject is structural methods of presenting the subject matter and we are presented with what is, for the most part, an extremely valuable analysis of different forms, repetitive, narrative, and logical; pseudo-reference, of which seven varities are elucidated; qualitative progression; alternation of method; double mood. Some of these structures, Mr. Winters claims, are better than others, and it would be foolish to deny it. But they are used as weapons in the continuous polemic which Winters is carrying on throughout the book against Laforgue, Eliot, Crane, Pound, and others; and in his application of these structures, Mr. Winters seems to force himself to misconstrue specific quotations. He illustrates one type of what he calls pseudo-reference, the type which he explains as "Grammatical coherence in excess of, or in absence of, rational coherence," by quoting the following lines of Hart Crane

3. Mr. Winters might consider the following statistical contrast as another and more brutal fact bearing upon the relation of society to what the individual can do and cannot do: there have been more good female poets in the last one hundred years than in the previous five thousand. Mr. Winters cannot say that the whole sex was affected with "group hypochondria."

The mind is brushed by sparrow wings;
Numbers, rebuffed by asphalt, crowd
The margins of the day, accent the curbs
Conveying divers dawns on every corner
To druggist, barber and tobacconist,
Until the graduate opacities of evening
Take them away as suddenly to somewhere
Virginal, perhaps, less fragmentary, cool.

Mr. Winters comments as follows: "The activities of the 'numbers,'
if the entire sentence is surveyed, appear wholly obscure . . . If one
suppose the numbers to be the mathematical abstractions of modern life, structural, temporal, financial, and others similar, there is
greater clarity; but the first five lines are so precious and indirect
as to be somewhat obscure, and the last three lines are perfectly
obscure." If, however, the whole poem had been quoted, or at least
a few of the preceding lines, Winters' accusation would clearly
have no basis. The first stanza of "For the Marriage of Faustus
and Helen" reads:

The mind has shown itself at times
Too much the baked and labeled dough
Divided by accepted multitudes.
Across the stacked partitions of the day—
Across the memoranda, baseball scores,
The stenographic smiles and stock quotations
Smutty wings flash out equivocations.

Obviously, the numbers in question are the baseball scores and
stock quotations, especially the latter, as conveying divers dawns
of success and money. As to the somewhere which is virginal, etc.,
this is partly defined by the later mention of aspiration to Helen—
"suppose some evening I got by that way . . . then I might find your
eyes across an aisle"—and it is partly vague, as in the minds of
barber, druggist, etc.; but the vagueness is fixed, deliberate, and
controlled, a device which Winters justifies in the case of a poem
by Williams when he is thinking of something else: "more feeling
is *assumed,* or *claimed,* by the poet . . . than is justified by his
language . . . But . . . the strain is deliberately sought and exactly
rendered."

Again, Eliot is accused of pseudo-reference in the following
lines:

[341]

> Burbank crossed a little bridge,
> Descending at a small hotel;
> Princess Volupine arrived,
> They were together, and he fell.

"What is the significance of the facts in the first two lines? They have no real value as perception . . . no bearing on what follows." To this we need only answer with Winters' own words: "When I speak of *conventional language,* I shall mean language in which the perceptual content is slight. A conventional passage . . . is poetic, however, in so far as it is necessary to the entire poetic intention." The reader need only examine the poem in question, "Burbank with a Baedeker; Bleistein with a Cigar," to see whether the tone and attitude, as well as the location, of the poem are not set off by the lines in question.

There are several other passages which are also treated in this way; but the crux of our objection turns out to be the same as when Winters' morality was in question. He is using his own views of God, freedom, and immortality when he attacks a passage of Crane in "The Bridge" by saying, "What myths have we in mind here? None. Or none unless it be the myth of Pocahontas, which, as we have seen is irreducible to any idea." Winters has other objections to this passage also. The point involved here, however, is the exclusion of Crane's beliefs because Winters cannot accept them. If it were mainly a matter of not being able to find the poet's assertions *in* his actual words, the canon which R. P. Blackmur uses so ably, then the objection would be just. But this is not the objection and Winters a little later accepts the "reference to a purely private symbolic value," which is what this is. If, however, we begin to reject the poetry based upon beliefs which are different from our own (despite the fact that such poetry presents most objectively what-it-is-to-hold-such-beliefs in actual experience), then Winters knows very well that few great poets will be left to us.

And again, Winters objects to what he calls qualitative progression, a setting forth of the subject matter in which the "sole principle of unity is mood" . . . so that one "proceeds from image to image wholly through a coherence of feeling." The trouble with such a method is that "the principle of selection being less definite, the selection of details is presumably less rigid . . . the symbolic range is . . . reduced . . . the movement is proportionately slow and wavering." None of these qualitative adjectives are made very much more exact in the context and in the illustrations, but Winters does not mean that such "poetry cannot refer to a great many types of actions and persons"—"but it can find in them little variety of value," a remark elucidated in what Winters says about the perceptual and expressive value of meter. But in passing, Winters has pointed out the reason why the method of qualitative progression is used: it can refer to a great deal. And at the end of the book, Winters, in discussing a carryall form, compares a poem by Mr. Tate with one by Churchill and admits that the former "is in a sense more serious . . . has wider implications . . . rests upon wider and more careful thought." The question is once more, then, one of finding forms and structures which will be adequate to very difficult types of experience. Mr. Winters answers this in advance and by oversimplification when he says: "To say that a poet is justified in employing a disintegrated form in order to express a feeling of disintegration, is merely a sophistical justification of bad poetry." This is what Winters means by the fallacy of imitative form. But no claim is made for a disintegrating form; merely, I think, a form which will digest the subject matter without annihilating it is what is required, and this will be a different problem in every case. And thus when Winters accuses Joyce in *Ulysses* of being guilty of imitative form, he reduces his fallacy to absurdity.

Such an example as *Ulysses* betrays the mechanical way in which Mr. Winters uses his criterion of form. There is perhaps a page and a half in Joyce's novel—pages 252 and 253, beginning "Bronze by gold heard the hoofirons, steelyringing"—where the form is actually broken down to express a breakdown, or rather, relaxation, of consciousness. Elsewhere in the book the most daring modulations occur, but the narrative framework is merely extended and strengthened by them. Mr. Winters' fallacy applies to Studs Lonigan, not to Stephen Dedalus. It is limited in its application to writing in which the effort is merely to reproduce experience —in the case of James T. Farrell it is a heroic effort—and to exclude most of the elements by means of which the writer penetrates the experience in question with understanding and judgment. What Winters seems to forget, especially with regard to Joyce, is that such understanding and judgment is very often not explicit, but is given in the quality of the style. In a short story by Ring Lardner, for example, the irony of the writer, his almost absolute disgust with human beings, is never expressed through any character, or any explicit judgment, but it is there sometimes in the form of a grammatical error and pun, such as "the world serious," sometimes in a brief exaggeration of tone.

But there is a further modern complication which Winters neglects. We know that in order to tell a story, in order to join one perception to another, ideas, beliefs and values are necessary as a means of ordering, if nothing else. If one's heroine commits adultery, or if one is describing the sea, it is necessary to bring some attitude to bear on the situation in order to go on with the story or the poem and bring it to a genuine conclusion. Indeed, it seems as if this fusion of value and perception were a primary motive of writing. But the predicament of the modern writer is exactly the fact that there is a gap, a distance, between the writer's perceptions and his beliefs or values. This is, I think, at least in part what Allen Tate meant in saying (in his introduction to Hart Crane's *White Buildings*) that Crane could not find a theme adequate to his vision. Crane's obscurity was explained by this, and Tate pointed out previous examples of it in the history of poetry, beginning with Blake. It is thus sometimes this gulf between what the writer sees and what he believes which accounts for a certain disorder, strain, and obscurity in his work. It is not the most fortunate of situations, but in order to escape from it, it would be necessary to sacrifice either one's perceptions or one's beliefs.

The fallacy of imitative form is relevant to the documentary novelist on the one hand and to the *transition* group on the other, but most of the writers whom Winters is considering fall outside of both groups. Since these writers are struggling to express the complexities of modern life, and their discontinuous values, their efforts tend to exert a pressure on normal modes of syntax and arrangement: there is an omission of transition and explanation. In time, of course, the new method of presentation becomes as familiar as the old. It is difficult in 1937 to understand why *Ulysses*

[344]

seemed obscure in 1921; and the obscurity of Keats is almost inconceivable. But Winters tends to regard an omission of punctuation as an abandonment of rationality. How else are his strictures on Joyce, Eliot, and Perse, to be understood when it is a question of their literary method? Winters thinks that a "classicist" cannot "with perfect taste" admire these writers. Mr. Eliot has said that if there were a classical writer in our time, one would not recognize him, so monstrous would he seem. Mr. Winters, however, has no trouble in recognizing classicists. Amid these extremists, there is no need to restrain oneself: it seems perfectly obvious to me that in *Ulysses* James Joyce has produced a work of which Aristotle and Dante would approve.

IV

There are according to Mr. Winters four different systems of measuring rhythm in a poem, the quantitative, the syllabic, the accentual, and the accentual-syllabic. The first two, except for Bridges' experiments, have almost no relevance to verse in English. Winters is mainly interested in showing how free verse can be analyzed out into accentual verse, and how accentual-syllabic verse is superior to it. The analysis of both types of verse will probably be very useful to poets, and the whole theory of meter is elucidated with both lucidity and subtlety. A concise summary of the thory is to be had by quoting Winters' own words in the foreword to his pamphlet of verse, *Before Disaster:*

> There has been a marked tendency of late years, a tendency fostered by the purely accentual systems of free verse and neo-Websterian movements, and of the verse of Hopkins, to extremely free substitution within accentual-syllabic forms, and particularly to the very free use of extra-syllabic feet. I believe accentual-syllabic verse superior in principle to accentual, since it provides a norm which accounts for the conformity or deviation of every syllable, renders it possible to perceive every detail in relation to a perfect norm, and hence makes for the greatest precision of movement, the most sensitive shades of perception, that is, of variation. The finest sensitivity is the product of the clearest form; the abandonment or weakening of form in the interests of greater fluidity can lead only in the direction of imperception. Accentual verse, on the other hand, as distinct from

accentual-syllabic, tends to substitute perpetual variety for exact variation; change exists for its own sake and is only imperfectly a form of perception. Furthermore, the vogue of accentual verse, as I have already suggested, has broken down the vogue of minimum variation in accentual-syllabic forms; namely, that the source of variation to be most extensively employed is quantity, that (in iambic verse) substitution should be restricted as far as possible to inversion of accent, and that in tri-syllabic feet the two light syllables should be as light and as short as possible.

To generalize crudely, what Winters wants in any meter is strict regularity, so that every divergence from regularity can be used to express or imitate the feelings or perceptions which are being referred to by the words. Now the requirement of a norm, strict regularity, cannot be denied. But from this, Winters' argument makes two rapid jumps. The best norm, it is claimed then, is the accentual-syllabic one just mentioned. And then the nature of this norm is generalized from the practice (but certainly not the theory) of Bridges, T. Sturge Moore, Pope, and Dryden. What would happen, however, if Winters looked for the norm in *The Winter's Tale,* or *Samson Agonistes?* What, furthermore, would happen if Winters examined the free verse in the English Bible? In passing, Mr. Winters refers to the meters of *Samson Agonistes* as in part a failure, in part a *tour de force,* but he mentions neither the *Psalms* nor Shakespearean blank verse. If these types of writing were examined, it would be clear that several norms are possible, and each type of subject matter would imply a special modification of existing meters. I cannot here illustrate this fact at length, but I can refer to the Bible[4] (which Winters will not be able to cry

4. If he wishes, the reader may compare Milton's translations of the Psalms to the King James' versions in order to see whether or not the accentual-syllabic norm is not, for some purposes, inadequate, or at least replaceable. Milton's translation of Psalm VIII reads in part:

> O Jehovah our Lord, how wondrous great
>> And glorious is thy name through all the earth?
> So as above the Heavens thy praise to set
>> Out of the tender mouths of latest bearth,

> Out of the mouths of babes and sucklings thou
>> Hast founded strength because of all thy foes
> To stint th'enemy and slack th'avengers brow
>> That bends his rage thy providence to oppose.

down, like the free verse of William Carlos Williams, as limited in its possibilities), and I can offer one example of a metrical device which Winters ignores and which illustrates the fact that the rhythm of verse can be expressive in ways other than the variation of accentual or accentual-syllabic norm. This is the familiar device of foreshortening the length of a line. Shakespeare uses it again and again, Milton uses it in "Lycidas" and *Samson Agonistes,* and it is used by Collins with obvious expressiveness in "Ode to Evening":

> If aught of oaten stop or pastoral song,
> May hope, chaste eve, to soothe thy modest ear
>   Like thy own solemn springs,
>   Thy springs and solemn gales,
>
>   .   .   .   .   .   .
>
> Now air is hushed, save where the weak-eyed bat
> With short, shrill shreik, flits by on leathern wing;
>   Or where the beetle winds
>   His small but sullen horn,

or, to use another instance to show the variety of effect possible:

> Those who sharpen the tooth of the dog, meaning
> Death
> Those who glitter with the glory of the humming bird, meaning
> Death
> Those who sit in the stye of contentment, meaning
> Death
> Those who suffer the ecstasy of animals, meaning
> Death

And a dozen other like usages, which not only have nothing to do with an accentual-syllabic norm, but which make it impossible, could be elaborated, if there were sufficient room in a review.

When Winters comes to illustrate specifically what he means by an expressive variation of a norm, he betrays a literalism which is

---

while the free verse of the King James' version reads:

> O Lord our Lord, how excellent is thy name in all the earth! who hast set thy glory above the heavens.
>   Out of the mouths of babes and sucklings hast thou ordained strength because of thine enemies, that thou mightest still the enemy and the avenger.

hard to fathom and which reflects back upon the so-called fallacy of imitative form. He quotes the following lines by Williams:

> All along the road the reddish
> purplish, forked, upstanding, twiggy
> stuff of bushes and small trees

and says that the beat in these lines "has perceptual value, as indicating the 'twiggy' appearance of the landscape." On the other hand, one would suppose that Winters would condemn the following lines from *The Waste Land* (since he rejects Eliot almost wholly):

> when the human engine waits
> Like a taxi throbbing waiting

The expressive effect is gained by the participles, rather than by the variation of an accentual-syllabic norm. Indeed the whole of *The Waste Land* is full of imitative or expressive form which is not in the least as faint as the one which Winters finds in the lines from Williams. And the absence of the norm which Winters thinks is best does not involve the author of *The Waste Land* in any abandonment of rationality, in any attempt to submerge himself in his experience, rather than the attempt to grasp it, represent it, and evaluate it.

At times Winters writes of the use of the accentual-syllabic norm in a way so extreme that the use which Winters most emphasizes seems a fiction. It is as if the poet deliberately ticked off deviations from the norm on suitable occasions. Perhaps some poets do. But it is obvious that taken in metrical abstraction such deviations are more or less limited in number, unequal to the variety of perception, and insufficiently precise. One may substitute a trochee for an iamb at the beginning of a line in order to have a perceptive variation for anger: "Scoundrel!"—or the same substitution to express affection: "Darling!" The substitution as merely metrical is largely indeterminate.

But if we take meter and meaning together, as I suggested above, the way in which meter is expressive becomes a much more complicated matter than the deviation from a metrical norm. In the great sonnets of Milton, as Mr. Winters must be perfectly aware, the expressive effect of firmness of character and indomitable spirit is gained by the latinity of the diction as it conflicts with the meter, with the sonnet form, and with the normal sentence order of English. This results in certain metrical variations, but none equal to the expressive effect: the primary means of expressiveness is Milton's diction. And in general one must suppose that the meter plays a passive, although essential, role in the poem. It provides a kind of substratum whose evenness and regularity are, so to speak, cut into by the modulations of style and diction and meaning. The fusion of style and meter, meaning and meter, provides the expressiveness of the poem, and carries its tone and attitude. The deviations from the norm are for the most part minor aspects or consequences of this fusion. And it seems to me that one can say that the style *is* the poem. The quality of the style is the verbal and aural realization of the poet's sensibility. The style is, in fact, the poet's values, focused upon his perceptions and revealed in all their purity. No poet can escape from this style, although he may change his meters. The poem apart from its style is not a poem but something which belongs to psychology or biography or politics or history. Meter is a necessary element in style, but it is far from being the only one.

One concludes, then, by supposing that the nature of structure and meter is not as simple, nor as exclusive as Mr. Winters has made it out to be; nor are their *specific* modes established for future experience and future writing (although the *principles* involved are so established: such a principle as Mr. Blackmur uses, that the poem be *contained* in the words, or such another one as Mr. Winters makes us more aware of, that there be a norm of regularity in the rhythm). One must be grateful, too, for the extension of taste to such poets as Churchill, Gay, Rochester, and T. Sturge Moore. If there is no meaning, on the one hand, in making this extension of taste, for the purposes of convincing others or oneself, negative to the extent that T. S. Eliot becomes a bad poet, on the other hand Mr. Winters' judgments are sometimes illuminating even when his reasons are unacceptable. The defects in Pound and MacLeish, for example, are not a mere willful departure from accentual-syllabic verse, nor merely a deliberate blindness to experience. Pound can see only surfaces and his favorite periods in history, and MacLeish can get no further, at

[349]

any time, than a catalogue of objects and a reverie, but the reasons for this, whatever they may be, are not simple, as we see more clearly in the instance of Crane, a poet in search of objects of devotion in an age when there were no devotional objects. If, then, we permit religion and philosophy and the society in which we live to be somewhat more than preliminary to the act of writing poetry, perhaps "the clear understanding of motive, and a just evaluation of feeling," which Mr. Winters asks for on his last page, will be less difficult and rare. This much, however, is certain: when good poetry is written, Mr. Winters will recognize it (although he may later change his mind because of some preconception), and meanwhile he will be writing his own extremely fine verse.

The Critical Method of
R. P. Blackmur

In *The Double Agent,* R. P. Blackmur characterizes his method as primarily technical, and states, with a humility which is insistent, that this method "does not tell the whole story either. The reader is conscientiously left with the real work to do." This qualification is to be accepted only when we have clear in mind what that real work is. Blackmur uses his method upon many of the best contemporary writers of verse and the results are usually such that aspects of the text have been opened up, illuminated, and even augmented by the critic. But, this being said, one must also observe the serious abstraction, incompleteness, and omission involved in Blackmur's whole method. Such an attempt at correction is given point by the fact that Blackmur's method is spreading (one's hope is that this will continue), his method is likely to be a model for both poets and critics, and his criticism (without exaggeration and so far as one can judge of such matters at an early date) will surely be of lasting value.

There is little need to look for Blackmur's sources as a critic. One would guess, merely guess, that whether or not he studied at Harvard, the textual and philological approach to Chaucer and earlier poets by leading teachers at that school may have suggested a good deal to Blackmur. At any rate, his method is original in the extreme to which he has extended it; and it is, in fact, instructive to analyze Wallace Stevens as if he were a Scotch Chaucerian

This note is concerned only with Mr. Blackmur's essays on poetry, adding to those in his volume of criticism the two later essays on Yeats and Emily Dickinson which have appeared in *The Southern Review,* and several reviews of volumes of verse.—ED.

of the 15th century. There is also the influence of Henry James as critic, the possible influence of I. A. Richards in his concern with meaning, and the impossible influence but significant relation of this method to the philosophy of logical positivism.

There is a brief need to rehearse some of the specific results of Blackmur's use of his instrument: Cummings is found wanting because he uses language "privately." Pound is attacked for three not wholly consistent faults—that he is only able to make a surface for a poem whose substance is already digested (and thus is best as translator), (2) that he uses the method of free association, (3) that he uses the ideographic method of the Chinese language, the sum of these faults being only that a good deal of information is needed to read Pound. Stevens' use of unfamiliar words is shown to be a justifiable and necessary poetic device. Hart Crane is shown as engaged in a similar technique. D. H. Lawrence is displayed as failing to use the formal resources of poetry in bringing to light his vision (perhaps it should be called: ethic), and Marianne Moore is shown as using those formal resources. Emily Dickinson is displayed as, in much of her verse, using words privately, and Yeats and Eliot are displayed as compelled to the usage of religious and mystical beliefs in order to make available on the page their perceptions and emotions. I will have to refer to this hurried and unjust summary in a moment.

Specifically and primarily, the method can be described as that of taking hold of the words of the poem and asking two very important questions: (1) Do these words represent a genuine fact, condition, or feeling? (2) Does the combining of these words result in "an access of knowledge"? Knowledge in the full sense, one must add, for something must be made known "publicly," "objectively," in terms which any intelligent reader, with the proper effort, can grasp; as distinct from terms and language used "privately," "personally," "subjectively." Now of these two questions, it is the first that Blackmur emphasizes and the second which he often neglects. The discrete parts—sentences, phrases, single words (which are sometimes counted)—are the main object of his attention. The way in which they combine is sometimes an afterthought (though this is less so in the more

[352]

recent essays). In the essay on Lawrence, Blackmur lists some of the formal resources which Lawrence did not use:

> The ordering of words in component rhythms, the array of rhymes for prediction, contrast, transition, and suspense, the delay of ornament, the anticipation of an exactly situated dramatic trope, the development of image and observation to an inevitable end—the devices which make a poem cohere, move, and shine apart.

The significant thing to note is that Blackmur does not especially concentrate on these devices in his specific acts of criticism, nor does his scrutiny attend to the large forms of composition. The list, too, is otherwise inadequate (perhaps necessarily so as merely a passage in an essay). In his concern about how the equivocal character of words is used, meter, for example, is entirely ignored. This is not a too great omission when a poet like Stevens is the subject, but it would seem a serious one when not only writers like Shakespeare and Milton are in question, but also in a comprehensive judgment of Eliot in whose verse the rhythm is so important a part of the meaning. The list which Blackmur gives could be increased a hundredfold. Let one example stand for a good many. The couplet form of rhyme is sometimes used by Shakespeare in his sonnets and his plays to suggest, in fact, to carry the *tone* of resolution and conclusiveness, and Shakespeare seems to have developed this device further by adding a foreshortened line to the couplet, a familiar example being the close of *Hamlet*.

> Take up the bodies.—Such a sight as this
> Becomes the field, but here shows much amiss.
> Go, bid the soldiers shoot.

This occurs so often that one cannot doubt that Shakespeare was very much aware of what he was doing. My point here is the assertion that the main formal devices of poetry are of this character, while the use of the multiple meanings of words is relatively subsidiary (though hardly to be disregarded). It is with this in mind that one can maintain that Blackmur's use of technique is too limited, granting however that it may be adequate to certain poets.

The primary burden of Blackmur's method, however, is much

[353]

more central to the art of poetry and is provides him with an unquestionable canon for deciding whether a poem is "successful"
or not. To repeat what cannot be repeated too often, a poem is
successful when its words represent its substance. A complicated, if
crude, metaphor is desirable so that what is meant by this (at least
what seems to me to be meant) will be absolutely clear: a poet
has feelings, observations, attitudes which are *in* him, speaking
crudely once more, in their full qualitative uniqueness. The poet
wishes to establish these observations, feelings, etc., *outside* himself once and for all, in the full light, in a stadium from which
the crowd never goes home. The only way in which to get his
private possessions into that public place is by using words in
certain formal ways, meter, metaphor, rhymes, etc. and by otherwise drawing upon what is the common property of all who can
read the language. All of this and more is involved in the notion
of representing a substance.

This seems to me to be Blackmur's essential canon, however
differently he might wish to see it stated, and it is a canon which
I accept. But an important difficulty infects it as it is used by
Blackmur, for it does, it seems to me, involve a separation of form
and content, technique and substance. That form and content are
inseparable is a dogma which all modern critics accept, contradict
in practice, and never elucidate. Let me not risk my luck where so
many angels have feared, faltered, stumbled and fallen down,
except to make a brief note for the sake of the present subject. I
repeat the dogma: form and content are inseparable; and explain
only by adding that form is the way in which a poet sees anything: if he looks at a thing in a different way, with a different
form (from a different point of view, for example), he sees something proportionately different. What bearing does this have on
concrete criticism? For obviously we can, by abstraction, discuss
the sonnet form apart from any particular content. This insep-
arability means that we ought never, in specific analysis of given
poems, to permit either technique or substance to preoccupy our
attention apart from one another. Each is relative to the other and
could not exist, in its particular quality, without the others. Ignore
one and the other begins to look unlike what it is in the poem
itself.

This question relates to Blackmur in that Blackmur is most often training his gaze on the form and quickly summarizing the substance in a general statement. In writing of Hart Crane, it is only in passing that Blackmur says anything of Crane's effort to express a religious emotion. The same passing glance at the substance limits the essays on Lawrence, Pound, Yeats and Emily Dickinson. It is not wholly true of the essay on Stevens, but we are told almost nothing of the extraordinary affirmation of this world and rejection of Christianity which marks *Sunday Morning* and must have motivated that remarkable poem. In his analysis of *Sunday Morning*, Blackmur gives us just so much about Stevens' substance as will justify and elucidate Stevens' use of certain words and images. And these examples could be quickly multiplied.

One exception to this emphasis on technique is the essay on Marianne Moore. Here technique and substance are shown throughout in their concrete interweaving. The result is instructive, for at the end of the essay, a question is raised which is infrequent in Blackmur's explicit discourse, namely, is Miss Moore a major or minor poet? Such a question cannot be answered in purely technical terms, as Blackmur admits at this juncture: "Method ought never, in the consideration of a poet, be kept long separate from sensibility." Nevertheless Blackmur concludes on technical grounds that Miss Moore, good as she is, is a minor poet: "Major themes are not susceptible of expression through a method of which it is the virtue to produce the idiosyncratic in the fine and strict sense of that word." On what basis one can distinguish major and minor themes we are never told.

Again with respect to the essay on Cummings, the vast machinery brought forward to blow down that poet seems excessive (though good in itself as helping to establish Blackmur's method). It would, one should suppose, have been more significant to note at every formal point the adolescent sensibility abusing the form (I would except much of *The Enormous Room,* and *Eimi* from this concurrence with Blackmur's judgment). In actuality poets use language as Cummings does because they suffer from an immature sensibility, and not because they have a theory about language.

[355]

Reinforcement to this point is to be found in the examples where Blackmur does covertly accept a poet because of a liking for his substance. The high praise which Blackmur has given to the later poetry of Conrad Aiken (and which I do not mean to question) flows from Blackmur's interest in psychological-epistemological subjects, and the isolation of the individual sensibility. And this explains the occasional praise Blackmur has given to poets who, unlike Aiken, are simply worthless. A similar shift to judgment of substance occurs in his condemnation of A. E. Housman.

Suppose that now we widen the range of examples and consider further criticism and poetry which Blackmur admires. In the famous essays in which T. S. Eliot analyzes the verse of Dryden, Andrew Marvell, and the metaphysical poets, what we find from sentence to sentence is a discussion of the all-devouring sensibility of the poets in question, with brief indications of formal usages. If anything, it is technique which is neglected. To reverse the emphasis, consider a classic mistake in the history of literature, Johnson's condemnation of *Lycidas* because, being an elegy (the form) and full of remote allusions (the form again), it cannot be said to be the expression of sincere grief, since grief "runs not" to remote allusions. Here we have a great critic becoming completely stupid because he has separated form and content, instead of starting with the specific substance-in-a-form of a very great poem as it presents itself for the reader. Blackmur never errs in this sense, of course, but rather gives us a one-sided emphasis which, if we stop with it, is a distortion.

And again, consider two lines from Eliot which Blackmur cites and surely admires:

> The awful daring of a moment's surrender
> Which an age of prudence can never retract

The greatness of these lines rests upon their insight into a whole realm of human experience. It is true that one of the conditions necessary to the writing of these lines was Eliot's interest in iambic pentameter as it is varied in late Elizabethan tragedy. This is a formal influence in part: the insight however is into an actual fact (and the interest in the blank verse of Webster was in turn bound up with certain attitudes toward experience). One cannot keep form and substance apart, no matter what abstraction one commits: like a loving couple they find their way together again. Furthermore, facts drag the whole world along with them and thus it is that the critic's appreciation of Eliot's lines depends very much upon his sense of facts and of the whole world together with his sense for blank verse. It is in terms of the significance of facts, too, that we distinguish between major and minor poetry.

Technique and substance are, to repeat once more, inseparable. We need Blackmur's method as well as similar instruments in order to get at the inseparable form and content, but, once we are in possession, all depends upon our sense of fact and our ear for rhythm. I say *fact* in an effort to curve about the problem of poetry and belief, and say of that difficult question only this: that beliefs in most poetry are only a means, a framework to help the poet represent the ragged, unwieldy facts of experience. Proof of this assertion is seen in that we do not reject a poet because of his beliefs (*quâ* beliefs), although we can condemn the *effect* of his beliefs on his knowledge of facts and his representation of them—of course that some people have certain beliefs is itself a fact worth representing and this explains the authenticity of *The Divine Comedy* in its doctrinal portions to those who are not Roman Catholics. Ultimately we judge a poem genuine because by means of words it discovers the truth of a fact for us, and we reject a poem as bogus because it is foisting some falsity upon us or it is not making the truth adequately available in its words.[1] As Blackmur has noted, there is a good deal of poetry in which the explicit statement is commonplace, and the quality of language and style constitute the worth of the poem. This too flows from the in-

1. This assertion may perplex the reader who believes that poetry is full of "pseudostatements" and also the reader who is inclined to think that facts are questions of one's "point of view." The first reader misunderstands metaphorical devices: when the poet says that his love is a red rose, he is stating an actual likeness in shorthand; when the symbolist poet says that the sky is green and loud, he is attempting to render with exactness the quality of an experience. As for the second reader, he ought to remember that each moment of our lives verifies many facts, and any point of view is a window upon certain facts. Given the point of view, we can verify what is seen from it, and a point of view is itself a fact.

[357]

separability of form and substance, for a style may often mean a whole set of attitudes and feelings.

But the reader will have noted that in attempting to judge Blackmur's extreme, I have leaned the other way and emphasized substance. One excess begets another, as philosophers have observed many times, and keeping one's attention on the concrete marriage of form and substance is like walking on a tightrope between Scylla and Charybdis. The dangers of going to the extreme which is opposite to Blackmur's and forgetting form in one's interest in substance are even greater. When that is done, we get the various and familiar forms of literary, biographical, social and doctrinal distortion. The poet is explained away in terms of his eventful life, rejected because of the vague political or social effects of his poetry, or accepted because his beliefs are pleasant. Meanwhile the poem itself remains untouched. It is here that we can see the legitimate basis for the abstraction and isolation of the critic. He separates the poem from its personal, psychological, and social basis, so that he can see what it is apart from its origins and its ulterior motives. Once this separation is done, the social critic, for example, can enter and be sure that he is discussing the actual poem.

Blackmur's prepossession with words as words leads, as one would expect, to certain defects of critical style. There is a constant punning which is scarcely warranted in expository prose: "Criticism," he says, "is the formal discourse of an amateur", where he means to emphasize the love of the professional. And sometimes the syntactical arrangement of the sentence or the formal succession of the argument becomes so slippery that it requires several readings; and critical prose, unlike poetry, ought not to require several readings. To balance this, however, Blackmur's writing is sometimes of a fine freshness, invention, and genuine beauty.

Lastly, as one final complaint which I do not have room to discuss adequately, there are sometimes errors of a logical-philosophical sort which seem to come from uneven reading in those fields, too much reading of Santayana, and again the special approach to words. One pardonable example is the startling phrase "a variable constant"; another simple contradiction (from a review) is the statement that a poem "is a tautology on the plane of dramatic entelechy", which is less excusable because it mixes a logical term with one from ancient biology. In addition, merely to note and not justly discuss, there are passages in which the nature of knowledge is spoken of in an unnecessarily metaphorical and emotional way as "bottomless" etc.; a peculiar separation of criticism and aesthetics; inexact remarks about Aristotle's *Poetics*, the nature of epistemology, and the psychological basis of the doctrines of I. A. Richards; and what seems to be a misrepresentation of Eliot's conception of the organic nature of literary tradition, which Blackmur calls a mathematical idea.

These defects are by no means inconsistent with the assertion that the body of Blackmur's criticism is certainly of permanent worth. It is a curious notion of the very good critic which supposes that he has no defects, nor serious limitations. It would be a still more curious thing not to point them out because of one's admiration for what is positive in the critic. Nothing could promise more for the future of poetry than the likelihood of many critics of Blackmur's ability, and few prospects are less likely of fulfillment.

The Writing of Edmund Wilson

🐝 Readers of Edmund Wilson's latest collection of essays ought to go back to his novel, *I Thought of Daisy* (1929). The view of the artist and of the genesis of literary works which has become a method for Wilson in *The Wound and the Bow* is stated there in terms of personal experience. It is not perfectly clear that *I Thought of Daisy* is a novel—its success depends too much upon two long meditations on the hero's part, and not on any dramatic action— but, in any case, it is a good book, better now, perhaps, than when published, for it can be seen as defining a period (as a photograph gains new qualities with the passage of time), but most of all because it makes clear Wilson's basic attitudes as an author.

The Wound and the Bow rests upon the thesis that the artist is strong and weak at the same time; his great virtue as an artist inseparable from his weakness; his weakness perhaps (Wilson is not too clear on this point) the cause or one of the causes of his strength; or, to use Wilson's sentence, the artist is "the victim of a malodorous disease which renders him abhorrent to society and periodically degrades him and makes him helpless; but is also the master of a superhuman art which everybody has to respect and which the normal man finds he needs."

Just this conception of the artist upsets the unnamed hero of *I Thought of Daisy*. Of this unnamed "I," one gets a most touching image in the course of the novel. He is a modest and humble young man who wants to write verse and to know the interesting intellectual and artistic people in the New York of the Twenties. But this is not the right way to state his complex attitude, for it seems at times that what he wants most of all is to know Life, to break out of his own personal isolation and limitation into Life at its best; and Life at its best he takes to be the literary life in the best sense of the phrase. He does not draw a sharp distinction between literary people and literary works. He admires the literary people of his acquaintance—among them, the famous poetess and the famous novelist—and is willing to stand for a great deal from them. But they often disgust him: there is a gap between the nobility of their writing, and the stupidity, viciousness, weakness, and self-absorption of their lives. What good is literature, after all, he asks himself, if it must arise from such lives? This question is inspired by a disagreeable, utterly pointless Greenwich Village drinking party, but it leads the hero to a feeling of doubt about the worth of literature and the literary life in which he turns on Dostoyevsky and Sophocles (both cited in *The Wound and the Bow*) and rejects them also because their great works seem to have been generated by lives which are equally offensive. In the end, this emotion is transcended by a new attitude, an attitude of critical and reasonable acceptance, on the part of the hero, of the people he knows. He accepts them as inextricable mixtures of good and evil. How this attitude is arrived at in the novel is not relevant right now; the point here is the way in which the resolution of shifting attitudes in *I Thought of Daisy* can be seen as the keynote of all of Wilson's writing. Some of the hero's concluding thoughts might well serve as quotations for the title pages of the critic's later books:

> So, by the way of literature itself, I should break through into the real world. . . . On that very day when she [the famous poetess] had filled my imagination with the splendor of her genius and her beauty, when she had seemed to me a goddess or a muse—on that day, her own mind had been haunted by visions of imbecility and deformity.

These phrases and thoughts echo through *Axel's Castle*, the critical work which established Wilson's position. Amid a careful, reflective, judicious analysis of Yeats, Joyce, Proust, and Valéry, one can hear again and again the reproaches of the unnamed hero of *I Thought of Daisy*. Valéry, for instance, is reproached for his condemnation of Anatole France on an occasion—his election to the French Academy to take France's seat—when the customary thing was to compose an eulogy. This is, says Wilson, pretentiousness and snobbery; and one feels that the reproach is directed not against literary taste or opinion, but against *a person*. It is as a person, too, that Proust seems to be reproached as engaged in "self-coddling, chronic complaining, over-cultivated sensibility"—Wilson quotes a French critic's remark that there was much of the spoiled child in Proust. And yet Wilson says also that these elements were important factors in the making of Proust's great work. And the whole movement of which *Axel's Castle* is a proposed history is accused of "over-cultivated sensibility" and of not being at the center of life, even as Joyce is scolded, in passing, because he did not make the reading of his work easier for the common reader by providing introductions. As a history, *Axel's Castle* suffers from the virtue of being addressed—how deliberately one does not know—to an audience which is vague in extent, but is certainly constituted for the most part of readers who would like to be helped to read the difficult new authors. The essays are good introductions for such readers (*Axel's Castle* ran first as a serial in the *New Republic*); but for the reader who has mastered Proust and Joyce, there is little which he really needs. To define the point further, the book is not the kind of criticism which helps to germinate new writing; it is not a book for writers. The definition of Symbolism intended to unify the book is so general and so loose that it permits the inclusion of authors who are really apart from Symbolism, such as Yeats. "To intimate things rather than to state them plainly was thus one of the primary aims of the symbolists," to compete with the suggestiveness of music, "to communicate unique personal feelings by a complicated association of ideas represented by a medley of metaphors"—this is the closest Wilson can come to a literary definition, although he is excellent on the social and intellectual background of Symbolism.

Actually Symbolism was a prolonged cultivation of the power of language for its own sake which eventuated in an emphasis upon the connotative usages of language to an exclusion, varying from author to author, of the denotative usages. The purest and completest example is Mallarmé. Wilson knows very well and paints with sure strokes the isolation of the artist from the rest of society which brought about the desire and the need to cultivate language in this way. He knows the Life in back of the work. But when it

becomes a point of describing the technical working, the craftsman-
ship and the unique forms, which are an essential part of Symbolism, and the authors who were greatly influenced by the Symbolists, Wilson is impatient and hurried. He is not actually interested
in the formal working which delivers the subject-matter to the
reader (as the rhyme-scheme of a limerick delivers its wit). It is
for him the wrapping-paper which covers the gift; it is necessary
to spend some time taking off the wrapping-paper and undoing
the difficult knots of the cord tied about it, but the main thing is
the gift inside, the subject-matter, which always turns out to be an
intimate life: in *Ulysses*, we "possess Dublin seen, smelt, heard,
and felt, brooded over, imagined, and remembered." So, by way
of literature, one can break through into the real world. It is Life
that matters; books are a way of getting into Life; we forget the
formal character of the book as we forget the door through which
we came into the house. *Axel's Castle* concludes by suggesting that,
important as the authors in question are and unique and valuable
though their discoveries may be in the future, literature must return to wholesome objectivity—not, however, without remembering and using the discoveries of these authors.

Axel's Castle appeared in 1931, two years after *I Thought of
Daisy*. By this time, Life had broken in on every private life, however isolated and limited. The social decade of American literature
had begun, showing itself first in the intellectual uneasiness of the
Neo-Humanist controversy, and then, as the Depression continued,
in the explicit affirmations and denials of the importance of social
consciousness and class allegiances in literature.

The effect upon Wilson was profound; and partly, it would
seem, because he had already felt, before the Depression and before
almost any other author of his generation, the relevance of social
criticism, and the intimate relationship between the individual and
the society which gave him life and kept him alive. Most authors
of the Twenties had been able to express their criticism and rejection of our business civilization merely in some version of the attitudes made popular and colorful by H. L. Mencken. The phrase,
"the civilized minority," expresses and virtually exhausts the insight which these authors depended upon. The curious resemblances one can find between H. L. Mencken and Edna St. Vincent

Millay, so far as their leading attitudes and sentiments go, sum up the period. Wilson admired both these authors—in later years, he seems unable to forget to be loyal to these admirations, as if loyalty were actually relevant, as if it were once more friendship and not literature that was in question—but in his going from an editorship of *Vanity Fair* to the literary editorship of the *New Republic*, the development of his interests, before the Depression, is clear. It is clear too in his admiration of John Dos Passos, the one important author of the Twenties who really depended upon an explicit social consciousness.

The result was that Wilson was prepared for the Thirties, and the three books he wrote after *Axel's Castle* are a direct and a strong product of the impress of the Depression upon him. *The American Jitters, Travels in Two Democracies*, and *To the Finland Station* are all efforts inspired by an interest in the Depression and in Socialism. The first two works are on the surface merely superior notebooks; but the sensibility and the honesty of the traveller are so great that these works are far more than journalism. Both contain chapters which, with hardly a change, might have been part of *I Thought of Daisy*. The last chapter of *The American Jitters* presents "The Case of the Author": after declaring his rejection of American capitalism and the life it made possible, and after affirming his acceptance of Marxism as a correct analysis of society and of the necessity of socialism, Wilson goes on to apply the Marxist formula to himself:

> My family have on both sides belonged for several generations to what used to be called the learned professions. . . . My father's and uncles' generation were obviously alienated by their old-fashioned education from the world of the great American money-making period. . . . My father, for example, was a lawyer in New Jersey and at one time Attorney-General of the state; but his love of independence and his distrust of big business were so great that he stuck all his life to his miscellaneous local practice and resisted all temptations to become a corporation lawyer in a state governed by corporations. He even refused to invest in the corporations. . . . One of the results of this [family background] has been that I have grown up in modern prosperous America with a slightly outside point of view, due not merely to the professional tradition in the family . . . but also

to the fact that my family have never really departed very far from the old American life of the countryside and the provincial cities. . . . . It began to dawn on me that the best people were usually satisfied with a very thin grade of culture, that when you tried to go into the adventures of creation or the exploration of the causes of things they didn't follow or approve of you. . . . . My life had seemed to me both false and dull. . . . I have tried at one time or another all the attitudes with which thoughtful Americans have attempted to reconcile themselves to the brokers' world . . . they were all ways of compromising with the broker.

These sentences point to a depth of feeling and attitude on Wilson's part which is not stated in theory but which is made perfectly clear in its applications and concrete instances. The right phrase is difficult to find: "fundamental decency" will have to do, and it will do very well if it reminds the reader of the heroes of Henry James. This sense of a fundamental decency, a living remnant perhaps of Christianity, operates in the hero of *I Thought of Daisy* when he resents the excesses and weaknesses of literary people, even though he is much more appalled by the business civilization against which they are rebelling. He is thinking of the dignified and self-contained *person* of "the old American life" when he is dismayed by the anger and hatred in Dante, the weakness and viciousness in the life of Dostoyevsky, the savagery and madness in the life of Sophocles, or when he reproves Valéry for priggishness and Proust for coddling himself, or when he speaks of "rather childish" rages of Greek heroes, actual and imaginary.

The picture can be rounded out, perhaps too patly, if we jump ahead to the moment in *Travels in Two Democracies* when the traveller, disappointed and dismayed by the squalor, drabness, and narrowness of the brave new world of Soviet Russia, turns with immense pleasure to the poetry of Elinor Wylie, a pure although dead product of "the old American life": "I had never before felt so vividly the rarity and value of people who could do something fine very well."

Travels in Two Democracies continues the excellent reporting, the clear, sensitive descriptive prose, of *The American Jitters*. One remarkable chapter, "The Old Stone House," describes a place where "the old American life" was lived; and the book concludes, after the traveller's fundamental decency has been shocked any number of times in America and the Soviet Union, with an almost lyrical return to the individual who determines his own existence with strength of character—"accuracy of insight," "courage of judgment" independent of "obsolete authorities," "invisible forces," and "all the names in all the books."

This disillusion and return corresponds not only to the disillusion with the literary life in *I Thought of Daisy*, but also and more importantly with a breaking of the spell of Marxism, a spell which had never been complete. It apparently stopped and modified the writing of Wilson's next and most ambitious book, *To the Finland Station*. The same thing happened in the writing of John Dos Passos's *U.S.A.*, in between the second and third novels. Both instances are very interesting examples of Life breaking in on the author.

To the Finland Station is an important work in itself, apart from its connection with, and the light it sheds upon, all of Wilson's writing. What is relevant here is the continued and indeed the augmented interest in persons. Although he is writing about men who made or wrote history, it is to personal traits that he returns again and again, dwelling, for example, upon Karl Marx's family life (and with especial love upon the Sunday picnics of the Marx family), Lenin's asceticism, and Trotsky's pride of intellect. This process of mind arrives sometimes at absurdity, as when Wilson suggests that Bakunin's politics had their real origin in the conspirational games he played with his sister when he was a boy; and it keeps the book from complete success by suggesting that the failure of the Russian Revolution was a failure of Trotsky and Lenin as persons; or perhaps one should say the embodiment of their personal defects in political and social policies. Or again, Marx's personal traits and failings are suggested as causes of the inadequacy of Marxism. On the other hand, the book justifies itself precisely because it contains so many good portraits of persons. The same excellence of portraiture is to be found in *The Triple Thinkers*, published before *To the Finland Station*. The essays on A. E. Housman and Paul Elmer More are actually concerned with these two men as inadequate human beings, and again we are presented with—and gratified by—the reproofs Wilson administers to them.

[366]

It is perhaps because Housman and More are in so many ways inferior to Valéry and Proust as authors that the personal emphasis and judgment seem just and worth bringing to the forefront of attention. Elsewhere in the book is an essay on Flaubert's politics, in which, by the additional device of quoting from two letters of Flaubert, the novelist is used as a figure of the proper attitude of the artist toward the social problems and the social claims of his time, and towards life as a whole. And then there is what is perhaps Wilson's best essay, on Pushkin, in which the feats of introduction which marked *Axel's Castle* are repeated, but this time with an author not otherwise available to most readers, and with more concern, perhaps as a consequence, with *placing* his literary quality, an act performed by citing Byron and Keats.

In the same essay, Wilson resumes the habit of breaking through to the subject-matter: he provides the reader with a very interesting synopsis of the plot of *Evgeni Onegin*. This is mentioned particularly because in another essay of this book, "Is Verse a Dying Technique?," it is just this conception of the relationship of form to subject-matter and just this habit of wanting to get as quickly as possible to the subject-matter in itself that leads Wilson to suppose that versification is finished, at least for the modern author. This is far from being the first time that Wilson has felt this is to be so. In an essay published in 1926, Wilson reviewed American writing and in passing spoke of Marianne Moore, asking whether or not it was actually possible to consider her verse poetry. In *Axel's Castle*, Wilson makes the point that Joyce is really a poet. But in this essay of *The Triple Thinkers*, Wilson is prepared to go much further and to suppose the devices of versification are no longer necessary to the ambitious modern author.

Wilson's reasons are mixed. It would seem that one reason for this view is the fact that William Butler Yeats and Edna St. Vincent Millay, taken together and providing a common denominator, appear to serve Wilson as a touchstone for what verse, as verse, ought to be, so that as a consequence he views with much suspicion such a poet as Auden, who seems to be using too many of the devices of prose and whose verse-writing seems to sound too much like prose. But a more important and less limited reason is the fact, which Wilson cites at length, that the major literary works of the

[367]

last one hundred years have been in prose and not in verse. But most of all, I think, Wilson is prepared to regard versification as a dying technique because the formal character of the work is for him merely the wrapping of the package. It does not seem to be necessary to the representation of the subject-matter, which is what we really want.

This is not the place to discuss this view at length. It should be enough, so far as this essay goes, to point out that what we really want is the formal character of the literary work penetrating, illuminating, and uniting with the subject-matter. Moreover, the major prose authors who, for Wilson, have succeeded the major poets not only learned a great deal from versification as a technique, but in their prose works reveal a dependence upon rhythm and metaphor which would be impossible without a thriving school of versifiers and body of versification: Baudelaire and Hugo influenced Flaubert, just as the poets of the Nineties and the early Yeats influenced Joyce. But it is Wilson's attitude toward literary technique which I want to underline once more, in this instance.[1]

The Wound and the Bow represents the next, the latest, and one should think the last step in Wilson's interest in the author as a person and in the literary work as a means of getting to know the person. About two-thirds of the book is devoted to Dickens and to Kipling; the rest is made up of fairly short essays on Casanova, Edith Wharton, Hemingway, *Finnegans Wake*, and the *Philoctetes* of Sophocles, (this last serving to explain in the form of fable the inseparable weakness and strength of the artist). In each author some weakness, pain, or sorrow—such as blindness in Joyce, a nervous breakdown in Edith Wharton, childhood unhappiness and marital difficulty in Dickens and Kipling, old age and cruel

---

1. *The Boys in the Back Room* represents another aspect of the same fundamental attitude toward literature. In this small book, published last year by the Colt Press, Wilson writes of authors who, apart from Steinbeck and Saroyan, are what circulating libraries call "good rentals." His remarks are as usual penetrating, and what he has to say about Steinbeck is especially revealing; but it is perfectly clear that what makes these authors interesting to Wilson is the fact that they are significant products of Hollywood and California. Hollywood and California and Life are what make him pay so much serious attention to such authors, whose lack of literary distinction he is aware of. The boys in the back room have always been very interesting to one intent on breaking into the real world, and this may also be why Wilson has long been fascinated by Hemingway.

sons for Sophocles—seems to Wilson to be one of the prime factors in the creation of the literary work. I say *one* of the prime factors, although at times Wilson writes as if it were *the* prime factor; indeed, he goes so far as to say of one of Dickens' novels that it cannot be understood without reference to his personal life—so that there is the inevitable suggestion that perhaps all of these authors were mistaken in their method: what they should have done first of all, even if they did nothing else, was to provide a full *dossier* of their childhood and their married life. This is to press Wilson's view to an absurd extreme, of course; but the suggestion is there, and it renews itself whenever the personal connection is forced, or overburdened, as an explanation of the genesis and the *interest* of the work.

In the long essay on Dickens, it is quite evident that Wilson has not forgotten all that he learned from Marxism. There is an effort throughout to see the social aspect as well as the purely personal aspect of the trauma which is to mean so much in the writing of Dickens. The six-month period spent by Dickens at the age of twelve in a blacking bottle factory is seen as a fall in the social scale as well as a shocking episode in the life of a boy who is in despair because he has been taken out of school. But the union of Freud and Marx is incomplete, and the Freudian emphasis wins out. Thus in writing of the very poor books which Edith Wharton produced during the last twelve years of her life, Wilson suggests, although without conviction, that it is mainly the fading of the shock of the nervous breakdown which made her begin to write— this fading of the trauma together with a lack of a professional sense of authorship—which explains the poor writing. Yet there is a much better explanation in the work itself, and particularly in the shift in subject-matter. We can see how Mrs. Wharton lost most of her fine power every time she abandoned her genuine subject-matter, the conflict between a rising plutocracy and the morality of the old merchant society of her forbears; and we can see how she made a perfect recovery each time she went back to this subject-matter by returning to the periods in which it was best located, first in *The Age of Innocence* (which Wilson underestimates) and the four small novels about *Old New York*, and later in her last and unfinished book, *The Buccaneers*.

The same thing is true of what Wilson has to say, in general, of

Kipling: the personal situation is emphasized to the extreme where one almost forgets, critic and reader both, that a much simpler and much more persuasive explanation of Kipling's decline is to be found in the difficulty of maintaining and nourishing the view of the British Empire which inspired him to write at the very start. I do not want to press forward the claims of social criticism beyond a certain point. The difficulty in *The Wound and the Bow* is the converse of this, the over-emphasis of the personal event, and the personal situation. And even if the Freudian analysis is taken as a primary explanation, it is clear that Wilson does not want to adopt it with any degree of fullness. Thus Dickens' childhood exile in the blacking factory, which was to become so important a factor, brought about a renewal of nervous fits Dickens had known in earlier childhood. But of course, for the true and thoroughgoing Freudian, the important thing is the cause of these nervous fits in earlier childhood and not their recurrence at the age of twelve, a very late date in the psyche from the Freudian standpoint.

Yet one of Wilson's virtues as an author has always been to avoid giving himself to any systematic view of Life, to see how Life is more than any systematic view of it, but at the same time to see how systematic views are useful instruments. This *roundedness* of feeling and interest was apparent in the books Wilson wrote in the Thirties, when Marxism was uppermost in his mind, and it is clear in *The Wound and the Bow*, too. If the long essays on Dickens and Kipling press an amateur Freudianism too far, they nevertheless contain notes on much else, and they carry forward the old concern with authors as human beings: Kipling is reproached for snobbery and for excessive anger, as Housman and More were condemned for similar faults. If we try to take these factors as causes of the work, we are bound to be dissatisfied; there is too much complication in the genesis of any literary work, despite the *Philoctetes*.[2] But if we see this interest in the human being in the

2. It is interesting and pleasant to have a critic in America feel the need to refer to Sophocles. But not only does the *Philoctetes* suggest a number of other interpretations quite different from the one Wilson gives it, but we cannot help thinking of the many other classical stories, from Pegasus and Orpheus to Oedipus, which express aspects of the creative situation. Thus, the poet can be viewed in these legends as depending upon a great exaltation, a kind of madness, and ecstasy; or he can be regarded as one who goes down

context of such books as *I Thought of Daisy* and *Travels in Two Democracies*, if we remember the tone and lucidity of Wilson's prose throughout, then it is easy to understand and to accept not only the thoughts and observations in this new work, but the whole body of Wilson's writing.

Is it not true, I mean to say, that literary history and literary criticism have always been merely pretexts for Wilson? For we do not get from his ostensibly critical essays the strict formal analysis,

---

into Hell to regain from death or oblivion that which he loves; or he can be seen as the man who kills his father and marries his mother and whose crime must be revealed and expiated in order that sickness may depart from the city. The latter interpretation is the richest, for it contains the strict Freudian view and yet emphasizes the necessity of revelation, discovery, and knowledge.

Each of these stories is illuminating. There seems to be no reason to insist on one to the exclusion of the others. Various authors seem to be moved to write for a variety of reasons. But there is one thing they have in common, however different they may be, a *mastery of language*; if Wilson were able to show that such a mastery was always traumatic in origin, there might be more reason to emphasize as he does the necessary union of strength and weakness in the creative artist.

Or, to examine Wilson's view in reverse, a number of women in Edith Wharton's time must have suffered from a nervous breakdown consequent upon an unsuccessful marriage. The difference between them and Mrs. Wharton, so far as literary criticism is concerned, is in Mrs. Wharton's literary powers. No doubt such an event as a nervous breakdown had something to do with her becoming an author, but the all-important factor is precisely the grasp of literary devices and forms which Wilson, despite his sensitivity to it, is always brushing aside in his actual scrutiny of his authors. I do not mean to say that a gift for literary expression is itself a simple and irreducible fact; it obviously springs from a complex of conditions; but it is the gift for expression and the expression as such which separates authors from other human beings, whether they suffer from childhood unhappiness, marital failure, psychological disorders, or are beautifully normal. A further possibility is that the unhappiness and disorder of creative lives is the *effect* and not the cause of creative effort, which does, after all, tend to make a human being more sensitive, more easily disturbed, and, last but not least, less able to make a living and be a devoted husband and friend.

Or lastly, to return to the *Philoctetes*, it is clear in the story itself that Philoctetes not only has his matchless bow (it is given him by Heracles) before he suffers his wound, but the wound is in no way connected with the power of the bow. One might contract wounds as a result of having and using a bow, but it seems much less likely that one would gain a bow as a result of being wounded.

[371]

which is one kind of traditional literary criticism; we do not get the reformation, correction, and extension of taste, which is another important kind; nor do we get the propagation of the leading ideas of an age, which is a third kind and which also tends to forget the literary work as such. Coleridge, Matthew Arnold, and T. S. Eliot illustrate in different aspects of their work each of these kinds, for good or for evil as the case may be, and we can see how Coleridge's criticism helped to bring about the poetry of Wordsworth, how Arnold created the consciousness of Neo-Humanism, and how Eliot reformed taste. But if we look for literary judgment in Wilson, we find a singular weakness and lack of critical pioneering. There is a curious tenderness for such authors as Thornton Wilder, Edna St. Vincent Millay, the later Van Wyck Brooks, Max Eastman, and Henry Miller, an author who merely turns Céline upside-down with a stale optimism. On the other hand, there is an equally curious indifference or aversion to such authors as Gide, Kafka, Thomas Mann, Rilke, Wallace Stevens (who really extends the Symbolist movement as much as any of the authors discussed in *Axel's Castle*), and Céline. Thus Wilson speaks in the same sentence of Proust and Dorothy Parker, and compares Max Eastman favorably with Gide. And there are equivalent defects, as I have tried to point out, in Wilson as a literary historian.

But it does not matter, because the whole of Wilson's work actually represents something else and something just as important as literary history and literary criticism. Once we have seen both history and criticism as a device or pretext or convenient form, we can see how Wilson has provided a history of the American of "fundamental decency," who has come from "the old American life," and has borne this feeling about Life throughout the America of his time, Princeton, the First World War, the Greenwich Village and the New York of the Twenties, the social ferment and the moral disillusion of the Thirties. The actuality of this experience is to be found nowhere else in the writing of our time. It is as if we were provided, to vary an earlier reference, with a history of one of the sons of a hero of Henry James; but this character has not only gone to Europe to bring back the art treasures of the Old World in *Axel's Castle*—he has had his moral experience in the Soviet Union, rather than in the Italy of Milly Theale, or the France of Lambert Strether, who also wanted to break into the real world. Another comparison worth taking with the utmost literalness is to *The Education of Henry Adams,* for in Wilson we have another and later and more difficult education under circumstances which Adams foresaw but did not live to experience. It is an education without conclusion, but fruitful and illuminating in the concreteness of its experience: the Soviet Union, for example, is grasped as something lived through by one kind of American.

And the actuality of the experience, the education, and the American background is rendered by the lucidity and the sensitivity of the prose style. Wilson's prose is above all a *friendly* and a *reasonable* prose; the phrase, "Isn't it true," recurs at crucial moments to express the reasonableness, the judiciousness, and the "fundamental decency" of attitude. It is because this attitude and this tone ring true and carry conviction that we can accept the characteristic act of taking hold of the literary work in order to find the human being, break into the real world, and know Life concretely and fully. The attitude and the assumption at work throughout can be seen perhaps most explicitly by quoting from a passage in *Axel's Castle.*

> It is at the death of Bergotte that Proust's narrator, in what is perhaps the noblest passage of the book, affirms the reality of those obligations, culminating in the obligation of the writer to do his work as it ought to be done, which seem to be derived from some other world, 'based on goodness, scrupulousness, sacrifice,' so little sanction can we recognize them as having in the uncertain and selfish world of humanity—those 'laws which we have obeyed because we have carried their precepts within us without knowing who inscribed them there—those laws to which we are brought by every profound exercise of the intelligence, and which are invisible only—and are they really?—to fools.'

Miscellaneous Pieces
Reviews and Comments
·V·

The Grapes of Crisis

From knowledge comes suffering.
From suffering comes knowledge.

Generalizations are notoriously easy, false, dangerous, and necessary. It was Oliver Wendell Holmes who declared that "no generalization is entirely true, not even this one," a remark which, like so many witticisms, can be quite misleading, since some generalizations are entirely false, some are false to a large extent, some are true except for a few exceptions, and some are entirely true (for example, the generalization that human beings postpone and procrastinate about tasks which they do not like, or perform these tasks with too much haste and impatience). The few generalizations which I intend to propose are, I think, neither entirely true nor entirely false; and I can only guess about the extent to which they are true. But apart from their truth, they seem to me to be worth examining for the sake of the examples which have suggested them and the further or opposed generalizations which they may suggest to the reader.

Tragedy with a Happy Ending

The happy ending is no longer fashionable and certainly it is no longer one of the iron laws of the box office. When Edith Wharton's novel, *The Age of Innocence*, was made into a play and produced on Broadway and soon proved to be a failure, William Dean Howells told Mrs. Wharton that what the American pubilc wanted was a tragedy with a happy ending. It is not even perfectly clear that the public wanted a tragedy at all—melodrama probably was as far as the dramatist was supposed to go in the direction of *King Lear* (which was itself revised in the nineteenth century, thus delighting no lesser person than Leo Tolstoy no end). And

[377]

the hundreds of motion pictures which have had a happy ending as hasty, distasteful, and forced as a shot-gun marriage illustrate the obvious truth that the American public as a whole did not like the idea that existence ever arrived at a conclusion which was not full of lasting happiness for everyone except the maiden who has not preserved her virginity for her husband, and the scoundrel·who has betrayed everyone, beginning with his mother.

But something has happened—the explicit beginning was probably some time during the second World War—and an unhappy ending has now become a howling success. And it is often also more than an unhappy ending, it is a catastrophe: the sympathetic character with whom the audience or the reader should identify himself concludes in frustration, failure, and whimpering death. This is not at all like the classic conclusion of tragedy, for the death of the hero is not heroic, it does not declare a triumph of the nature of existence over the overweening pride of man, and it is not what Hegel said tragedy was (thinking probably most of all of the *Antigone*), the conflict between two rights (in which one or the other must be violated). The new doom is degrading and disgraceful and humiliating. In Tennessee Williams' *A Streetcar Named Desire*, the Southern belle, so often until now a blushing bride at the finish, is dragged away to an insane asylum. In Paul Bowles' *The Sheltering Sky*, the heroine becomes a nymphomaniac in a harem and also concludes as a lunatic. Arthur Miller's *Death of a Salesman* is an even more pertinent instance because in American life salesmen are not supposed to fail and die, they are supposed to be quite successful, provided, of course, that they are honest and hard working. And then there is the very different example of T. S. Eliot's *The Cocktail Party* in which the only two grim possibilities of existence are a loveless marriage or a martyrdom the very point of which is that the other characters feel that to them it must seem pointless.

That these works should be very successful might be less significant—for of course there have been works which ended in tragedy and were successful—were it not that Hollywood too has sought out the unhappy ending. In one motion picture two representative and popular symbols of the heroic American, Spencer Tracy, for long the rough and ready mechanic, cab driver, and champion of virtue, and James Stewart, the incorruptible Princeton man and Arrow-collar ad, are shot down and die at the end. It is true that they die for the sake of getting rubber from the Japanese in the midst of the war in the Pacific. And Spencer Tracy has been guilty of grave crimes and imprisoned in Alcatraz before being given a chance to sacrifice his life for his country. But in the past, death was unnecessary in Hollywood and the hero who saved his country was decorated at the end of the picture by the President of the United States, while the lovable and heroic gangster was sometimes permitted to reform and become a junior executive.

So too in John Ford's film, *When Johnny Comes Marching Home*, the hero is prevented from being heroic by his excellence as a teacher of aerial gunnery in a training camp. He succeeds in escaping the bondage and penalty of his pedagogic talent only because another soldier has suddenly had an attack of acute appendicitis, and he performs heroic exploits—which, it is loudly implied, have done much to defeat Nazi Germany—largely through a series of accidents and weaknesses, such as falling asleep at the wrong time and getting drunk when he did not want to drink. He is rewarded for his feats by being sent to a psychiatric ward: all his efforts to explain himself are frustrated by high-ranking generals who insist on forcing him to drink more alcohol so that he will regain his senses, and when he escapes from the psychiatric ward, he has to climb back into his own home in the early morning like a burglar, which is what his father supposes him to be, clouting his son into unconsciousness with a monkey wrench as he comes through the kitchen window and refusing to believe any part of his son's account of his heroism except for the visit to the psychiatric ward. At the very end of the picture, there occurs the traditional decoration of the hero by high-ranking officials, but only after many reels in which the most holy sanctions and mores of America have been made the butts of scorn, slapstick, satire, and in short the most merciless comic rejection.

From Hollywood to modern poetry is an enormous jump, but since we are all involved with one another and in the same endangered boat, poetry can also be a good index of the climate of society. As R. P. Blackmur remarked in *Partisan Review's* symposium on the state of American writing, Robert Lowell called his book of poems *Lord Weary's Castle*, Randall Jarrell his, *Losses*, and John Berryman his, *The Dispossessed* (Saul Bellow's second novel is named *The Victim*, Isaac Rosenfeld's first novel *Passage From Home*, and Hemingway's latest novel derives its title from Stonewall Jackson's dying words). A quotation from Berryman's book will show one basis in reality for the attitudes which these authors bring forward as keys to their work:

> The approaching television of baseball.
> The King approaching Quebec. Cotton down.
> Skirts up. Four persons shot. Advertisements.
> Twenty-six policemen are decorated.
> Mother's Day repercussions. A film star
> Hopes marriage will preserve him from his fans.
>
> News of one day, one afternoon, one time.
> If it were possible to take these things
> Quite seriously, I believe they might
> Curry disorder in the strongest brain,
> Immobilize the most resilient will,
> Stop trains, break up the city's food supply,
> And perfectly demoralize the nation.

Berryman's poem was written in 1939, which means that his lines were prophetic: F. Scott Fitzgerald's description of his nervous breakdown in *The Crack Up* has just gone into a new edition and Budd Schulberg's novel about him, *The Disenchanted*, is a best seller which contains such remarks as "Nothing fails like success" and "You never get a second chance. There is only one chance."

Daisy Miller Has Become Cynical

The beautiful innocence and goodness of the American girl which fascinated Henry James so much and inspired the creation of such characters as Daisy Miller and Isabel Archer has always been an important part of the American credo. It is embodied in the legal principle that everyone is innocent until proven guilty— which does not hold in Mediterranean nations—and it may have much to do with the disbelief, before and after two trials, in the guilt of Alger Hiss. But the truly glamorous modern heroine begins with cynicism and self-doubt as we can see in the fiction of Mary McCarthy, Carson McCullers, and Jean Stafford. Starting with the habit of distrust, she rapidly arrives at a seduction on a

Pullman, a desire to know all the four-letter words, or a marriage which is contracted with the reservation that it can be terminated by divorce. Daisy Miller was a misunderstood virgin, and her modern granddaughter is a self-confessed nymphomaniac who insists that promiscuity is a civil liberty, or perhaps one of the rights secured through woman's suffrage. And if she is reproached for being suspicious of men and of existence, she answers that she is really being "realistic," or motivated by honesty, candor, and intelligence.

One reason for the character of the modern heroine is obviously the revolution in sexual mores which has occurred and continued since the first World War. Another reason is the natural delight a woman may enjoy in undressing and the equal pleasure of the reader in looking at her as she takes off all her clothes. It was possible for the hero of F. Scott Fitzgerald's first novel to feel damned forever because he had slept with a chorus girl, and the popular success of Fitzgerald's early work was partly based on curiosity, to the point of fascination, in reading about necking parties. But the radical shift in sexual morality and the ubiquity of the peeping Tom are hardly the whole story.

The Psychiatrist as Hero

T. S. Eliot in *The Waste Land* invoked Tiresias, the priest and seer, to judge the act of making love. Twenty-six years after, in *The Cocktail Party*, his priest and seer must play the part, or use the methods of a psychiatrist, in order to judge three love affairs and an unhappy marriage. There are two more Broadway plays and innumerable films in which the psychiatrist is a supreme judge and healer. At the same time the vocabulary of psychoanalysis dominates ordinary conversation. People are now "neurotic," not unhappy, personal relationships are full of "tensions," "resentments," and "insecurity"; an intimate friendship is interpreted as the result of "identification" with a father image or a mother image when it is not suspected of being "repressed homosexuality." Human beings are not said to be evil and immoral, but "destructive," "narcissistic," "infantile" or "regressive," while being good is described as being "normal," "functioning well," "being mature," or "adjusted." Guilt and self-accusation are more popular and more voluble than they have ever been except in Dostoevsky's fiction.

[381]

This fondness for a medical terminology may have begun merely as another manifestation of the love of new jargons, and it is probably true that Clara Bow's sexual allure was called "It" because scenario writers had heard about Freud's concept of the Id. But it is no longer merely a vogue, it is a vision, however distorted and poorly understood, of human nature and human relationships, which reached a hilarious peak at that moment in a film when Betty Grable, Clara Bow's apostolic successor, successfully explained her husband's trials and difficulties as caused by the fact that her father-in-law was her husband's Super-Ego!

THE MOUNTING AND ENDLESS CRISIS

Clearly the social origins of the sense of crisis which shows itself in so many ways must include the depression, the two World Wars and the fear of a third war with Russia. If one has expected pie or at least manna in the sky, the dropping of atom bombs becomes an apocalyptic transformation of the blue. And if one expected to be rich and successful, two luxurious promises of the American Dream, one can hardly help but be terrified when riches and success bring greater conflict and unhappiness, instead of gratification and peace. To have hopes which may be disappointed is a possibility which one naturally envisages and for which one has braced oneself. But to find that the overwhelming fulfillment of hope and desire leave one in disillusion or despair is one of the most demoralizing of experiences. It is unexpected, and one cannot be prepared for it. The fact is that one has been prepared against it in the sense that virtue was always supposed to triumph, wickedness was to be punished, and after the struggle against the powers of evil concluded in an inevitable victory, one was supposed to be happy in this life and even more happy in the next one. The first World War was supposed to end all wars; the second World War was viewed with more skepticism, but still it was supposed to secure peace for a long period of time, and victory was supposed to bring with it the annihilation of totalitarian regimes.[1] But the postwar

1. "We are all the last generation," Adolf Hitler might have remarked to Gertrude Stein or Pablo Picasso in Paris in May, 1940. Gertrude Stein said to Hemingway after the first World War: "You are all a lost generation."

period quickly assumed the appearance and generated the atmosphere of a new pre-war period.

The international crisis affects the life of the individual in a hundred thousand ways, whether through housing shortages, inflation, or uncertainty and fear of the future. And this was true even before many people understood Russia's foreign policy (it is not wholly clear that anyone really understands it, not even the Politburo), for the crowds in Times Square on V-J day looked lost, instead of jubilant; they looked as if they were not sure what emotion would be appropriate to victory, or certain that they were victorious. In the same way it was natural and naive to suppose that the defeat of Hitler would end or reduce the infamy of racial discrimination, instead of intensifying it and bringing a greater consciousness and self-consciousness of it, so that, for example, New York Jews are accused by Jews elsewhere of being the cause of anti-Semitism. And the phenomenon of racial discrimination has itself become a leading theme of novels and films.

"THE COLD MEDUSA-FACE OF LIFE"[2]

It is a truism that the great problems of an age are reflected in works of literature, and that the authors of fiction may be inspired by a desire to cope with them or to identify their personal problems with the immediate problems of society. What is less likely and what requires explanation is a profound modification in the ways of attempting to deal with contemporary problems through the medium of creative works. The unhappy ending can serve as a symbol of the radical change which has occurred since William Dean Howells remarked upon the kind of tragedy which Americans wanted. Eugene O'Neill's plays were full of unhappiness and they were successful, but a fair proportion of the audience felt that there was something strange in enjoying the spectacle of agony,

2. This phrase of Henry James, and its significant context, is quoted in F. W. Dupee's forthcoming book on James, and there the context can be examined in detail. James as an author is an important witness of the thesis of this essay. He was the first victim of mass-culture for he tried harder and harder to become popular and the harder he tried, the more unpopular, and the better, he became; and some thirty years after his death he has become the most popular and the most famous of classic American authors, as the dramatization of *The Ambassadors* on television demonstrates.

and one representative comment about any such play was: "Life is awful enough; when I go to the theater I want to forget about all that is awful, I don't want to be reminded of it." No one now makes such remarks about Arthur Miller's *Death of a Salesman* or Williams' *A Streetcar Named Desire.*

The new technique consists in a confrontation of all that may be wrong, where in the past escape from evil or the denial of evil prevailed. There were exceptions, of course, and of course the literature of Europe always depended upon the resolutions of tragedy. But in America since the Gilded Age, happiness was required, as if, one must suppose, the mere imaginative declaration of the happy ending would help to make life itself a more successful affair. It was wrong to be pessimistic, disillusioned, or even gloomy, and it was right and American to be optimistic, to be a booster, and to have fabulous expectations. The shift is not a complete one, nor is it a mechanical shift from affirmation to despair, and we can only speculate, we are still too much in the midst of it, about the nature of the change, its permanence, and its essential quality. We can guess hopefully that perhaps Americans no longer want to be children and they no longer want to be told fairy tales: they are mature enough to want the confrontation of reality which tragedy provides. Or we can suppose that there is so much disruption about us and the sense of crisis is so intense that an unhappy ending makes possible purgation and relief. Misery loves company and desperation is reduced by a scrutiny of how much more terrifying the situation of other human beings may be when compared to one's own situation. In a period of depression, the image of a Utopia is welcome; but when civilization itself seems capable of destroying itself and when the end of the crisis does not seem likely tomorrow, it is a genuine relief and blessing to be able to comtemplate images of the worst that may happen.

Whatever the explanation of the change, and there are of course other possible explanations, it is certainly true that the conditions under which a serious literature can thrive have been advanced in this one important respect. In other important ways there has been a deterioration, but the sole repeal of the dogma that the attitudes of the author must be optimistic, cheerful, and affirmative, at all costs, creates the possibility of a genuine tragic art. Nobility is quickened by tragedy and nurtured by necessity. Once the mind is capable of regarding the future with a sense of tragedy and a sense of comedy, instead of requiring the forced smiles (and the whistling in the dark) of dogmatic optimism, the awakened consciousness is prepared to respond to existence with courage and intelligence.

F. Scott Fitzgerald was a hero and nothing less than everything can have been the cause of his tragic suffering. He embraced the myths of American life with a love, a daring, and a gaiety which now make his own life a tragic myth, a fate which he himself must have sensed when he said: "Show me a hero and I'll show you a tragedy." The elegy which John Peale Bishop wrote about Fitzgerald's death declares his tragic heroism:

> None had such promise then, and none
> Your scapegrace wit or your disarming grace;
> For you were bold as was Danaë's son,
> Conceived like Perseus in a dream of gold.
> And there was none when you were young, not one,
> So prompt in the reflecting shield to trace
> The glittering aspect of a Gorgon age.

To think of the future is to think of a myth, a myth in which we can all believe. And the past is spellbound by myths like bad dreams, myths which link a modern American novelist with the inexhaustible stories of the ancients. When the author of *The Great Gatsby* and *The Last Tycoon* is compared to Perseus, we remember that Perseus was commanded to be a hero and to prove himself one by destroying the Gorgon, Medusa. Anyone who looked at the face of the Medusa was instantly turned to stone. But with his curved sword, with the brazen shield Hermes had given him and guided by Athena, Perseus stood with his back to the monstrous being, caught her image in his shining shield and cut off her head, immediately after which a winged horse, Pegasus, sprang from her headless body. If Perseus had not succeeded in beheading the Medusa, he would have failed to be a hero. If he had not gazed at her indirectly, he would have turned to stone. It is still necessary to stare at the Medusa before we turn to stone.

Novels and the News

📖 During the past generation, literary essays and critical comments announcing the imminent death of the novel have appeared with increasing frequency. The obsolescence of the novel is, in literary circles, as perennial a subject as the weather among most human beings. The very fact that the subject recurs so often should be sufficient to indicate that there is something wrong, something misleading and deceptive about the pronouncements. Surely anything which has been overtaken by death so often is immortal and has never suffered death at all. It is like the phoenix of the literary and mythological imagination. But the death of the phoenix is inseparable from its resurrection. In direct contrast, it is difficult to think of an instance in which a critic declared that the novel had been reborn, or that it had survived a severe illness. In fact, it is characteristic of most statements of the decline of the novel that all prior statements of the same nature are ignored, and almost as often the imminence of mortality is set down in a tone which suggests relief rather than sorrow.

Yet the very terms which have been used to express the novel's state of decline or impending death suggest that the critic is moved by matters which concerned him more profoundly than the art of the novel. Seldom, if ever, does the critic speak of the death of *fiction*—or, to emphasize the self-deceptive trick of formulation further—the critic never says that the telling of *stories* has come to an end; nor does he say that the human imagination will soon cease inventing imaginary situations and events. Fiction, story-telling, and imagination are terms which are naturally avoided, since the end of story-telling is inconceivable, apart from the annihilation of mankind. Human beings are seldom with one another for more than a few minutes, at the most, without telling stories about what has been happening. This inclination is obviously so universal and so constant that a human being who remains silent under ordinary circumstances is regarded as a remarkable eccentric, even when, like Calvin Coolidge, he is the President of the United States.

It is true, as Gertrude Stein told Hemingway, that remarks are not literature; if they were, there would be more good and many more bad novelists. Her statement clearly implies that anecdotes are not novels, and that a love of conversation is not in itself a love of literature. The pessimistic critics of the novel are often well-informed and sophisticated readers who point out the variety of evidence which justifies their negative predictions. They point out, for example, that a literary genre, however popular, does sometimes vanish: the short and brilliant life of the poetic drama during the Elizabethan and Jacobean period is a powerful instance, since all subsequent efforts to revive the poetic drama, despite the excellence of isolated plays in verse by first-rate poets, have failed. At first glance, this example may be quite impressive. It is entirely unconvincing, however, because the drama or any art which depends upon the theatre and upon performance is invariably as precarious as it is popular: it requires so much collaboration upon the part of so many different people: there are so many interests, risks, and contingencies involved in the theatre and all the performing arts that any production is at the mercy of uncontrollable factors; the mood and taste of the public at one extreme, and pure accident or good luck at the other.

The art of the novel does not depend at all upon many external agents and it does not need so much collaboration in order to exist, and perhaps this is one reason that modern American fiction has always existed on a level far superior to modern American drama: if there were nothing else involved, the fact, simple, coarse and crass, that it costs far less to publish a novel than to produce a play would be enough to cause the difference between the novel and the drama.

The negative evidence that the novel as a literary structure is, as Louis MacNeice wrote, "stale and plethoric," includes a good deal more which is relevant to the novel itself. Thus it is said, and it will be said time and again that it is the realistic novel of the past 150 years which has exhausted its possibilities and which cannot be renewed as a major form of literature. Hence the argument that the novel has a rich and indeed boundless future based upon the permanent desire for conversation, story-telling, and the inventions of the imagination cuts both ways.

The sanguine critic may point out how deeply-rooted fiction is in daily experience, in fish stories and tall tales of conversation, in revery, day dream and dreams at night: any comprehensive characterization of fiction would have to recognize the fantasies which occur during sleep and the revery of waking consciousness as a primitive kind of fiction common to all human beings. The pessimistic critic can use this fact as negative evidence, pointing out how during recent generations more and more important novelists have tried to go beyond the ordinary limits of the novel as a literary structure and as "a slice of life." Joyce, Mann, Proust, Kafka and Virginia Woolf, all, in one or another way, introduce material and use devices which the realistic novel as such seemed to exclude. They draw upon fantasy, stream of consciousness, nightmare, hallucination and above all they make use of the methods of poetry and depend upon the power of style to an extent which indicates how inadequate they found the traditional realistic novel as a structure.

Thus Mann often uses the essay as a form in his novels, and in *Dr. Faustus* he uses the biography as the structure of his novel; Joyce's extreme modifications of ordinary language in *Finnegans Wake* and the fact that Proust's great novel uses the structure of the autobiographical essay and memoir are but two among many examples which might very well be cited to demonstrate that it is precisely the depths of the imagination, the complexity of human experience, in the middle of the 20th Century, which makes it impossible to suppose that the novel will flourish in the future as it has during the past 150 years and continue to be the most comprehensive and popular form of literature. So the argument goes.

The best answer and the best basis for a belief in the richness of the future of the novel is suggested by the origins of the very word, novel, which derive from *nouvelle* and *novella*, the French and Italian words for news. The novel from the very start—or at whatever starting-point we choose—has always, whatever its other traits, been characterized by a direct relationship to the news, to what is new, to new experiences of mankind. There is always something new under the sun: this assumption, whether or not it is explicit, has always united the novelist and the reader of novels. And it is this direct relationship to recent history and to the news which explains the comparative eclipse of the novel during the past decade. Recent history and the news have been so spectacular that only the writer of science fiction appears to be able to keep from being as outmoded as the bow and arrow. This is the reason too for the greatly increased popularity of books about recent history whether they take the form of memoirs or of biography. The novelist has had to compete with the sensational reality of the Second World War, the atomic bomb, and worldwide revolution: he has also had to compete with the almost equally sensational and dramatic events which appear in the daily newspapers. In the past, the resources for securing the latest news about reality did not include the press, radio, and TV, to say almost nothing of the fact that events were not as continuously and increasingly spectacular and astonishing as they have come to be during the past twenty years.

The writer of fiction has always, as a matter of instinct, attempted to compete with the reality of the news and the news of reality—Defoe's *Robinson Crusoe* is perhaps the most familiar example—and this instinct can be seen at work in those who write the fictional scenarios for TV. An overwhelming number of TV plays tend, week by week, to use as their subject-matter the headlines in the newspapers of two or three weeks before: a murder, a kidnapping, an outbreak of juvenile delinquency or the uncovering of drug addiction will invariably inspire the fiction writers of TV within the weeks immediately following.

This and other related facts may seem to indicate even more strongly that the future of the novel has become more limited and restricted, that its possibilities of development have indeed declined. The contrary is true, insofar as one can speak with assurance about anything in the future. However spectacular the news may be, however interesting the first-hand account of a historical event, however fascinating the attractions on the TV screen, however quick and comprehensive the news about the present which the newspaper makes available, there is no substitute for the particular ways in which the reader of novels encounters experience, or for particular satisfactions which only the art of the novel makes possible. The very nature of fiction makes it possible to enter a complete world of reality as if one lived in it oneself: it makes it possible to grasp experience from the *inside*, looking out, by means of the immediate and natural identification with characters and experiences which occurs the moment one finds a novel "interesting." The reader inhabits the interior of another being in a way which no other art makes possible.

This is of course the reason that fiction is so often merely a form of vicarious experience and what is more important it is the reason for the degree of hypnotic absorption which the reading of a novel provides. It is precisely because the reading of a novel gratifies a primary human need and provides a unique and invaluable experience of reality that its future possibilities have continually increased, along with the possibilities of human experience. It is worth bearing in mind that *Don Quixote*, one of the first and perhaps the greatest of novels, took as its starting part the foolishness and the foibles of a human being who was a devout reader of fiction. An obsessed reader of one kind of fiction, the chivalric romance which was no longer fashionable and had come to be regarded as ridiculous. Thus at the very birth or beginning of the history of the novel, a great work of fiction announced the impending death of another genre of fiction, once in vogue, mocking the declining genre and expressing satirical delight in its passing.

French Taste in American Writing

Some erroneous attitudes are so persistent and recurrent that often the less said about them, the less the confusion increases. The attitude expressed by R. L. Bruckbecker, a French Dominican priest in "French Fiction and American Reality" (in the *New York Times* Book Review, for July 31, 1955) has been manifest many times in many forms: Socrates was condemned for corrupting Athenian youth and the plays of Euripedes were attacked for a like offense. And one might make an interminable list of the instances where the same attitude since the time of Socrates resulted in disastrous consequences: when the Puritans closed the London stage in 1640, they terminated the greatest period in English literature and the drama has never entirely recovered. No matter where we turn, the same attitude appears: in Russia the Czarist police read novels with a care police have never shown before or since and censored them inspired by the same principle as the Vatican, the Nazi and the Soviet governments. And if the attitude does not always lead to the burning of books, it certainly must have made many writers afraid or silent far more often than anyone knows. In detail: Thomas Hardy stopped writing novels at the height of his powers, just as Boris Pasternak, the best, probably, of modern Russian poets, stopped writing poems and took to the prudent activity of translating Shakespeare. The reason for citing these scattered instances is to point to the fact that the most antithetical powers and institutions, the Puritans and the Catholics, the Czarist and the Soviet regime, the autocratic state in Europe and the democratic censors of America since the time of Poe, have all agreed on one doctrine alone amid a disagreement to the point of war and death otherwise: the view that the pen is mightier than the sword; they have demonstrated how true this is by using the sword to destroy the pen whenever they possessed the power.

Father Bruckbecker's version of this persistent and pernicious attitude is comparatively mild; but his version has a subtle and systematic confusion within it which his avowed motives make all the more insidious. For he speaks in friendship and good will, seeking to promote international understanding, and particularly to diminish anti-American sentiment in France. And it is this sympathy and fondness for America and for the modern American novels which makes his essay remarkable: Instead of the obvious antagonism and ruthless detestation of literature of most proponents of his views, his admiration of America and devotion to literature are repeatedly affirmed. To state his attitude in his own words, "The French find in their own literature a terribly denunciatory image of America . . . some of the great American novelists widely read in France have accentuated the impression instead of correcting it."

This and other like statements seem so simple and direct that their confusion is not immediately apparent, and it is further concealed, in the entire essay, by contradictory professions of what Father Bruckbecker asserts to be his view of the nature of literature:

> The honor of a true literature lies in that it never allows itself to be domesticated to the level of propaganda. The mission of a true literature has always been to sustain a great quarrel within the national conscience.

Who would believe that, having stated this important truth, Father Bruckbecker would then propose that the American novelist domesticate his work to propaganda, and cease to sustain the great quarrel within the national conscience? Who would believe that soon after saying "Don't misunderstand me. I do not reproach American novelists" (No?) "for having written books that sometimes give a cruel vision of America," he engages in what is nothing if not a reproach: "Perhaps American novelists are right from a purely literary standpoint . . . but their foreign public, which reads them assiduously, remains, by *their neglect of responsibility* [italics ours] in the same errors ... prejudices ... calumnies against America, at a time when it is extremely important that America should be known and loved for what she is."

Let us overlook the fact that all the American novels to which Father Bruckbecker refers were written a decade or a generation ago when there was, first of all, no such need to deal with anti-American sentiment in Europe and, second, no sign that the modern American novel was going to be translated and read widely. But it is pertinent to ask how one can maintain that one is not reproaching modern American novelists and at the same time accuse them of "their neglect of responsibility." It would be interesting to know what Father Bruckbecker regards as genuine reproach, particularly since the hydrogen bomb becomes involved in his argument at one point, as one more horror which American novelists for all their prescience, fail to take into account when they write their novels.

Some American writers, antagonized by Father Bruckbecker's argument have answered by saying that there are instances of modern American fiction which show America in a far more becoming light. This is true enough and it points to Father Bruckbecker's most extreme error, the fact that these works have not been translated precisely because the French reading public, avid as it is for modern American fiction, has no desire to read that kind of fiction. But to answer Father Bruckbecker's argument by such assertions is pointless. Worse, it concedes his primary assumption about the essential purposes of literature. To say only that there are in existence novels which present a favorable image of America is to admit that only such books should be written and further that the fiction critical of American life is, as such, deplorable, since it may help to increase anti-American sentiment in France and elsewhere.

Much might be said about both this attack on literature and any such effort to defend literature; but I must concentrate upon what is less obvious. Father Bruckbecker's profound misrepresentation of the French reading public and the French novelist. Father Bruckbecker says, "I am merely pointing out a fact" when he asserts that American fiction has "accentuated" "the terrible denunciatory image of America" in France. But this is not a fact at all.

The French public are delighted by the image of America which they find in modern American fiction: in fact, it is not too much to say that they adore it—otherwise modern American novels would not be best-sellers in France. For the novels which are translated and admired present a picture of American life which complements, supplements, illustrates and exacerbates that picture which Hollywood films were the first to present. This would be clear enough without the collateral evidence of their evaluation of American novelists. They admire Faulkner, Caldwell, Raymond Chandler, James M. Cain and Dashiell Hammett as equally great writers, and even Gide, free of most popular tendencies, seriously asks whether Dashiell Hammett is or is not a better writer than Faulkner! The novelists I've named and others like them—some, in fact, hardly known at all in America, like Horace McCoy—have as the common denominator of their fiction the subject of violence and as typical hero, the strong, silent gunman, gangster or mindless man of action. This is what makes American fiction so attractive to the French: their own literature and culture, dominated by traditional reason, clarity, lucidity and analysis, contains nothing comparable to the typical American hero who turns to his gun or to violent action with the same spontaneity as the French hero turns to introspective analysis.

Not only do the French delight in the picture of American life which they find in modern American novels, but they read it for reasons which, in misrepresenting their attitudes, Father Bruckbecker ignores: they read it for pro-American reasons as undesirable as anti-Americanism. This is one of the facts which Father Bruckbecker points out and then ignores when he says:

> Unfortunately, novelists in France have an unequalled power over opinion. In the time of Stendhal and Balzac, Tocqueville was writing his admirable book on America. Stendhal is still a best seller, as is Balzac.

Let us disregard the misfortune of having great novelists exercise great power over opinion. What cannot be emphasized too much is the statement that Tocqueville remains unread while French and American novelists are best sellers. Why do the French ignore Tocqueville, or so many other writers who deal with the nature of American life directly, such as Henry Adams, whose autobiography was a best seller in America, and Thorstein Veblen, who provides as unfavorable a picture of America as any anti-American ideologue could desire? The answer is one of those self-evident disregarded truisms: the French reader reads novels for fun, naturally enough, and the fun in this instance is the image of heroism so unlike the most heroic protagonist in French fiction (for even such men of action as Stendhal's Julian Sorel and Fabrizio, however active they were, were equally analytic and intellectual). This is the reason that the French read Dashiell Hammett, and not Henry Adams, or for that matter, Hawthorne and Henry James.

And Father Bruckbecker's instance conceals another complicated misrepresentation in the allusion to Tocqueville as unread: here as throughout his essay he combines fiction and non-fiction with a wrongness made worse by citing the non-fiction of writers famous as novelists. He mentions Bernanos and Duhamel as modern French novelists who have intensified greatly the unfavorable image of America, but he fails to say that this occurs not in their novels but in single works dealing directly with America, like Tocqueville's. In a like way he cites Henry Miller's *The Air-Conditioned Nightmare*, along with *The Grapes of Wrath* as if it were a novel too, and not a book of essays by an expatriate who first became famous for fiction describing the degradation of life in Paris!

It may be naïve and superficial to examine Father Bruckbecker's argument thus in detail; and in any case, the following instances and points, which are both literary and unliterary, have a bearing upon the entire subject of literature and international misunderstanding. I present them separate, unconnected and with the minimum of comment:

1. Shortly after the war, I told a French professor—of American literature—how Scott Fitzgerald's novels were much more representative of American life, at its best and worst, in addition to their intrinsic excellence and superiority to most of the American fiction which the French avidly devoured. He asked for a list of Fitzgerald's books and as I went from *The Great Gatsby* to *The Last Tycoon*, I thought of how difficult it would be for a French reader to understand the emotional meaning attached to a Senior Prom or a Yale-Harvard game. But the word "tycoon" was itself a prob-

lem and not merely one of language: the closest equivalent in French was "mogul," which fell quite short of Fitzgerald's meaning: to write of the last multi-millionaire, maharajah or mogul does not at all communicate the real meaning, which derived directly from the American dream, of a meteoric ascent from poverty to wealth, from obscurity to the limelight which Fitzgerald dramatized in the figures of Jay Gatsby and Monroe Stahr: and this was far more than a problem of language or information, it was a matter of the ethos and mythos of America and that of France: to inherit wealth or to acquire it rapidly are admirable or undesirable in each nation in ways which are opposite.

2. There is a further illustration in a different incident, which I have at third hand: the French have finally translated Dreiser's *An American Tragedy*, possibly because the supply of novels of the hard-boiled school has begun to run low. One French reader inquired in great perplexity about the nature of the conflict which made Clyde Griffiths murder his sweetheart: why instead did this young man not marry the rich girl and use a portion of the *dot* he acquired in this manner to establish the poor girl in a domicile agreeable and in accord with her taste!

To have tried to tell this sympathetic inquirer that in America, a young man does not receive a *dot* even when he marries a young lady whose papa is of great riches would have been madness: the reason for marrying the rich girl would then disappear, since in that case Clyde Griffiths might as well marry the poor girl whom he loved, or better still remain unmarried until someone had a *dot* or more dough. No amount of patient explication would do more than bring forth new enigmas while the extreme irrationality of murdering the poor girl merely became more and more of an aberration. This difference between tribal marital customs is the reason that the French have been unable to read the most French of American novelists, Henry James, who wrote so often about the problems of marriage in the Anglo-Saxon world.

3. It is easy to forget that international misunderstanding is prior to all international understanding. During the First World War, the German Press proved how barbarous the English were in news stories about how English girls were beheading their sweethearts, demonstrating that this was not mere propaganda by quoting per-

sonals in the *London Times* in which English girls warned their young men that they would cut them dead unless they enlisted immediately. I choose this instance among many because it was probably not a deliberate distortion, at least at the outset.

4. The understanding between nations as between any two human beings is often rooted in an extreme difference of point of view; there is often a gulf to cross; it is not as simple to understand another point of view as those who recommend this program seem to think. Thus Cleveland Amory quotes John Jacob Astor's remark, which seems to have been made in kindness and fellow-feeling: "Anyone who has a million dollars is just as well off as if he were rich." Again, to move from one to another extreme of the economic ladder, I was once invited by a gifted young musician to dinner at his home with his mother, brother and sister-in-law. I said that I was in that kind of poor humor in which it is painful to meet strangers. "There are no strangers here," he said in bewilderment.

5. The misunderstanding and ignorance of nations and human beings are often proof against the advantage of a common language. The Shorter Oxford English Dictionary, until the most recent revision, defined a cocktail as "spirits, bitters, sugar, etc." The etc. is stupendous, and this is, in fact, an old-fashioned definition of an old-fashioned cocktail, "without the garbage," as the Duchess of Windsor is said to have said. If this seems trivial and relevant only to drunkards who understand all things and misunderstand everything, here is a more impressive and incredible example from the O. E. D., a definition which was only noted as false and deleted after the second World War had instructed the scholar or editor: anti-Semitism was defined as objection to "the excessive participation of Jews in politics!"

I forbear to add many other instances, which become more abundant as Fulbright professors return and report on their problems in teaching American literature abroad. There remains something which must be said about Father Bruckbecker's practical proposal to American novelists, which he reinforces by citing the example of the modern French novelists "who clearly understand that they have a responsibility toward their country. Bernanos, Montherlant, Mauriac, Malraux, Sartre, Camus have all taken political posi-

[397]

tions and have supported them in their books." The novelists mentioned certainly have taken political positions, several have taken a good many such positions so that they have been accused of being collaborationists, renegades, agents of the Kremlin, the Vatican, the American State Department, Nazi Germany and perfidious Albion, whenever they were not being attacked as neutralists or merely irresponsible.

Mauriac, the one Catholic novelist among them, is, to be sure, an exception, since he writes sexual melodrama with the avowed purpose of making the reader more aware of original sin, but which makes the unbelieving reader far more aware of sex, and thus, like Colette's fiction and that of innumerable others, helps to create and sustain the image of a France obsessed with sex on the farms and in the chateaux as well as gay Paree.

Solicitude begins at home: these novelists are almost all excellent critics of fiction. If they studied American literature thoroughly and adequately along with other French critics, they might do much to direct the French reader to the vast undiscovered important regions of American literature and thought which when understood are quite as fascinating as the fiction they cherish so much.

This really is a practical proposal, since the French critic influences the French publisher a good ideal; it is clearly the kind of practical proposal which has no chance of being adopted. Father Bruckbecker's proposal is both practical and impractical: if, conceivably, modern American novelists wrote the edifying kind of fiction he requests, the reviewers paid to read it would characterize it, often enough, as American propaganda, like Coca-Cola; or two professors would write learned studies in two volumes: Tome I: *Grandeur du roman americain, 1919–1939;* Tome II: *Decadence du roman americain, 1955—*: or: *Pangloss, ou La Trahison et le chauvinism du romancier americain, 1919–1955.* As for the French reading public, whom Father Bruckbecker regards as having a mind which is a *tabula rasa* on which the novelist inscribes impressions freely, yet also diseased with the tumor of anti-Americanism, one can categorically predict that these readers would merely shrug, and go to the cinema to see the latest film of Hollywood; in short, they would just stop reading American fiction.

[398]

Our Country and Our Culture

During the worst part of the depression, a well-known and very gifted critic, having just arrived at the home of a Southern friend for a visit, had hardly put down his suitcase when he asked his host: "Where are the share-croppers?"

If we take this incident as a representative caricature of intellectual consciousness between 1929 and 1939, the present is equally typified in a recent argument between two literary critics. The subject of the argument does not matter except that it involved fundamental assumptions. When one critic had said all he had to say in condemnation of a point of view he abhorred, the other said: "I agree with you entirely, but how do I know I am right?"

The two incidents show clearly to what a desperate extent the intellectual is a prisoner and a creature of the *Zeitgeist*. Yet by comparing these incidents and by like comparisons, we can achieve a little historical objectivity. The reply of the second critic—"How do I know I am right?"—expresses perfectly the uncertainty and the groping which dominate the present. And the certainty implicit in the first incident, the conviction that sociological categories reveal the inner essence of existence, has vanished as if it had never existed. The present which confronts us in 1952 was inconceivable in 1935. We knew then that the future would be different, but we expected it to be a continuation and devolopment, not a complete breach with the social consciousness which preoccupied intellectuals then.

Although we know very well now in 1952 that the present period will come to an end, our knowledge of this truth is isolated from most of our thinking, just as our knowledge of mortality is put aside in daily life. Yet it is very important to remember how different 1952 is from 1935, and to summon to consciousness the fact that the present, and the way in which we think about it, is temporary, limited, or wrong. The more we reflect upon the changes of past and present, the clearer it becomes that the present, whatever else it may be, is essentially an intermediate period, a period of both *after* and *before*, a time of waiting in darkness before what may be a new beginning and morning, or a catastrophic degradation of civilization. The only certainty is that overwhelming and radical modifications in the nature of society have begun. For example, the peoples of Asia have entered into the destiny of Western civilization, and an enormous mass audience has begun to assert itself in the theater of Western culture. But these instances give us only knowledge of our ignorance.

It is in the light of this darkness that the will of conformism, which is now the chief prevailing fashion among intellectuals, reveals its true nature: it is a flight from the flux, chaos and uncertainty of the present, a forced and false affirmation of stability in the face of immense and continually mounting instability. The desire for stability is understandable, particularly in the midst of an earthquake, or its social and spiritual equivalent. What is difficult to understand is the illusion that genuine stability is gained by denying the earthquake and by pretending, after two world wars and a great worldwide depression, that nothing has changed and that there is no crisis apart from the cultivated desperation of certain poets and painters. The intellectual will to conformism is formulated in terms of the startling discovery that the middle class is not entirely depraved, that liberalism does not provide an answer to all social questions, and that a state of perpetual revolution in literature and art is neither an end in itself nor the chief purpose of either literature or revolution. Who, apart from the intellectuals who make these extraordinary revelations, is helped, comforted and illuminated? During a period of economic prosperity, the middle class has no more need of intellectuals to defend it than the editors of *The Saturday Evening Post* need James Joyce as a novelist, Pablo Picasso as an illustrator, and T. S. Eliot as an editor.

I make an especial point of the uselessness of an intellectualized

[400]

conformism because of the crucial and growing need of a critical nonconformism. Mass culture and the New Criticism, different as they are, both make more acute the need of the intellectual as a critical nonconformist. It is obvious enough that the intellectual is necessary to sustain the traditional forms of culture amid the rank and overpowering growth of mass culture. It is perhaps less clear that the New Criticism naturally tends to attach literature to the university, so only a critical nonconformist intelligentsia, inside and outside the university, can right the balance and keep serious literature from becoming merely a set of courses in the departments of English and comparative literature. To this actual situation, in which the vested reality of mass culture, formal education, and the New Criticism prevail, we must add the pious hope of a possibility, the fulfillment of which also requires a critical nonconformist intelligentsia. It is the possibility that universal education, in combination with the very mechanical agencies which make mass culture profitable, may create and sustain a genuine educated class partly by the mere increase in the number of intelligent readers. The reasonable and logical basis of this hope is modest indeed, as modest as any assumption can be: the hopeful, modest assumption is that as the number of human beings who can read increases, the number of intelligent readers will also increase, though certainly not in the same proportion. Thus if the so-called reading public of fiction rose to twenty million readers there might be fifty thousand readers interested in serious fiction; a like thing has certainly come to pass in music where the radio, for all its infamy, has certainly enlarged the audience for good music by making it available for a small fraction of each week. But any such realization and fulfillment cannot come about or last through a mere quantitative increase: it requires the existence of a critical, non-conformist minority, conscious of itself, articulate, and capable of resisting the temptation and the insidiousness of the most powerful social and psychological pressures.

Critical nonconformism is an unfortunate but unavoidable term. It suggests the village atheist, the urban crackpot, and the parlor socialist. It is less likely to suggest Socrates, who whatever else he may have been, was certainly a critical nonconformist, and in a

[401]

systematic, committed, quintessential way. So, to use the rhetoric of citation, among other critical nonconformists are Montaigne, Pascal, Voltaire, Kant, Kierkegaard, Tolstoy, and Freud; and in America, whether we think of Emerson and Thoreau, or Veblen and Mencken, there is hardly a name to invoke in whom critical non-conformism is not central and essential. Apart from names, if we think of the human situation in any time, how can we conceive of the functioning of the intelligence apart from the possibility of criticism and dissent? The intelligence is in its very nature critical; to be an intellectual is to be committed to the intelligence and to be a critic and to raise endlessly the question of acceptance and rejection. It is true that there is always the danger of dissent as automatic, and criticism for its own sake, but surely this is far less of a danger to civilized existence than the barbarism which prevails whenever the intelligence is absent and often enough when it is present.

Whether this description of the intelligence as critical and nonconformist seems just for all human situations, it certainly cannot be overemphasized or overestimated in our own situation: we live in a mass society and in an industrial economy. As things are and as they are likely to be in any near future, the highest values of art, thought and the spirit are not only not supported by the majority of human beings nor by the dominant ways of modern society, but they are attacked, denied or ignored by society as a mass.

Hence each of the questions of the symposium must be answered by reference to the existence and the functioning of a critical, nonconformist minority.

It is true that American intellectuals have changed their attitude toward America and its institutions. But the change has occurred because only America can any longer guarantee the survival of that critical nonconformism without which the very term intellectual— and the reality of the intelligence—is meaningless. However, to believe that America provides the real basis for such a survival is precisely the opposite of believing in America right or wrong.

It is only as part of a critical nonconformist minority that the intellectual can make any adaptation to mass culture; although for the creative artist other forms of adaptation are possible.

[402]

Again, whatever other sources of strength, recognition, and renewal may exist, surely the chief one is in the community of a critical nonconformist minority. The intelligence and the intellectual can only exist where the actuality of critical nonconformism also exists. In the past, there was a genuine choice between exile in Europe, which was a kind of nonconformism, and the attitude exemplified in America in every period and in a variety of ways from Emerson to Mencken. Now that there is no longer a choice, the tradition and the vitality of critical nonconformism is more important than ever.

The Meaningfulness of Absurdity

Camus' doctrines have already been described so clearly by Hannah Arendt in *The Nation* for February 23 that a quotation from her essay will save time and space:

> For Camus man is essentially a stranger because the world in general and man as man are not fitted for each other; that they are together makes the human condition an absurdity. Man is essentially alone with his "revolt" and his "clairvoyance," that is, with his reason, which makes him ridiculous because the gift of reason was bestowed upon him in a world "where everything is given and nothing ever explained."

The temptation to split hairs and indulge in logic-chopping about such doctrines is obvious. The important question is: what is the full significance of Camus' doctrines and how do they enter into his plays? The usual pitfall of the author who makes an explicit use of ideas or who is inspired to composition by ideas is what Henry James called "the platitude of mere statement," the direct declaration of the meanings involved in his subject. The result at its most extreme is the morality play, the allegory or the fable. When characters are given names like Prudence or Vice, the texture of the work and the particulars of time, place, and action are diminished, thin, or unreal. In his two plays Camus shows that he is well aware of this difficulty, although he does not always escape it. And in his essay, *The Myth of Sisyphus*, after saying that "the great novelists are philosophical novelists," he adds, "philosophical novelists, that is to say, exactly the contrary of writers with a thesis," the authors of problem-plays.

However, if for the most part Camus' plays do not resemble

[404]

as drama the products of such a problem-playwright as Bernard Shaw, the influence of his ideas upon his drama takes another more peculiar form: he allows the ideas in which he is interested to determine the nature of his subject-matter, where most authors can be said to let the subject-matter which has taken hold of their sensibility determine the ideas which their works contain. Balzac, cited by Camus as a philosophical novelist, was a Catholic, but he did not write Catholic novels; the ideas of *The Human Comedy* do not in the least resemble those of *The Divine Comedy*. And no one has ever been sure of just what ideas Shakespeare believed, among the many he used. Camus, however, chooses as his subjects the murder of a son by his mother and his sister, a murder the absurdity of which is heightened because the murderers do not know whom they are killing; and in *Caligula* he deals with the monstrous crimes of an emperor who is determined to commit every kind of crime in order to prove that he is superior to the gods and that there is no good and evil. Does this not suggest a lack of conviction in the absurdity of existence, or a desire to prove its absurdity by fastening upon the monstrous, the extraordinary, and the accidental? It is true enough that there are monstrous rulers and that a mother may from time to time murder her son without knowing that he is her son. But surely the absurdity of existence, if it is in essence absurd, makes itself manifest in *any* kind of situation. And thus an ordinary story of love and marriage ought to have more literary persuasiveness than any theme in which aberration, in the usual sense of the word, is the substance of the plot. If the world is one in which everything is given and nothing is ever explained, in which the very fact that man has the gift of reason and is thrown into a world of unreasoning things constitutes the absurdity of existence, then surely what is daily, usual, ordinary and never celebrated in newspaper headlines ought to be the proper subject-matter of the absurd or existential author.

I emphasize this point not because I think that the literary critic can get very far by discussing what *should* have been an author's proper subject-matter, but for the sake of showing that Camus is superior to his ideas; and the truth of his ideas, insofar as they are true, is temporal and not metaphysical. At the start of *Sisyphus,* Camus declares "Il n'y a qu'un problème philosophique vraiment sérieux: le suicide." It would follow that much of the history of philosophy has concerned itself with what is not serious, what is trivial, and perhaps pointless. "Juger que la vie vaut ou ne vaut pas la peine d'être vécue, c'est repondre à la question fondamentale philosophique," he continues, "Le reste, si le monde a trois dimensions, si l'esprit a neuf ou douze catègories, vient ensuite." But there are other serious and fundamental philosophical questions, and the very way in which Camus states what he considers the subordinate or auxiliary problems of philosophy is rhetorical and inaccurate. The question of whether the world has three dimensions may not be a philosophical problem at all; and no one seriously inquires as to whether the mind has nine or twelve categories. What is the good life? What is the good state? What am I? What can I know? What ought I to do? Does God exist? These are serious and fundamental philosophical problems. And insofar as the problem of suicide is not a psychological one, it is a question settled when these prior problems are settled. In *The Myth of Sisyphus,* Camus quotes Dostoevsky's description of *The Brothers Karamazov*: "The principal question which will be pursued in every part of this book is the very one from which I have suffered consciously or unconsciously throughout my life: the existence of God." Faced with this serious and fundamental problem of a great philosophical novelist, Camus attempts to transform Dostoevsky's question into something consistent with his own views by saying that the Russian author did not write "une oeuvre absurde," but a work "qui pose le problème absurde." But the best he can do to make Dostoevsky say what he himself is trying to say is to cite a critic who declared that Dostoevsky identified himself with Ivan Karamazov. And then, as further evidence, Camus adds that the religious passages in *The Brothers Karamazov* required three months of effort while the blasphemous portions were written in three weeks and in a state of exaltation! As if it were a question of time or exaltation! Camus himself appears to be unconvinced by his argument, for he concludes by maintaining that in *The Possessed,* where the problem of suicide is posed, Dostoevsky failed to recognize the essential absurdity of existence because he raised the problem of immortality: "ce qui contredit l'absurde dans cette oeuvre, ce n'est pas son caractère chrétien, c'est l'annonce qu'elle fait de la vie future." The dissociation of Christianity and immortality is interesting, original, and false; and the reader will remember that one remarkable character in *The Possessed*, Kirillov, finds the problems of God, immortality, and suicide inseparable; he decides to commit suicide because he had *previously* decided that God and immortality are merely the "pain of the fear of death."

Dostoevsky wrote in Czarist Russia. Camus has lived through the German occupation of France. That is why the problem of suicide—of resisting the Gestapo, or collaborating with the Germans, or joining the underground—seems to be the only serious problem. And when, at the end of his essay, he singles out the myth of Sisyphus (let us remember that the Greeks esteemed quite different myths) and salutes Sisyphus as the absurd hero, the man who endlessly rolls a rock up a hill only to have it roll down endlessly, he is saluting the heroes of the French underground who struggled against the Germans when it seemed that the struggle was endless, hopeless, and absurd, absurd in Camus' new sense that it was a matter of human pride to resist the Germans, god-like in power, even though the struggle seemed to have no chance of success. But the struggle, as it turns out, was not hopeless; and if God exists and there is a future life, then human life, since it does not terminate with death, may not be absurd. There are also other reasons for maintaining that it is not without meaning. In any case, it should be clear that one fundamental question, the question which Camus begs, is the problem: Is existence absurd or is it meaningful? Does God exist or is he an illusion? Camus has merely formulated a modern version of Stoicism, inspired by his age just as the Stoics were inspired by the conditions of their own period. Camus' ideas are valuable not as a description of existence, but as a description of certain states of existence; and they are valuable above all as a means necessary to the interpretation of an extremely gifted playwright's experience.

This is not the first nor the last time that the truth or falsity of an author's ideas are less important than the fact that his ideas make possible a grasp of experience and the composition of first-rate literary works.

[407]

Does Existentialism Still Exist?

Let me explain this question. Is it not true that the discussion of the meaning of existentialism has been dying down? or at any rate is being taken more and more for granted, like cynicism, optimism, surrealism, alcoholism, and practically all the other well-known topics of conversation?

If so, this is a dangerous state of affairs. For as soon as a philosophy is taken for granted, as soon as its meaning is assumed, then it begins to be misunderstood and misinterpreted. Philosophical idealism is a good example. It was once just as fashionable as existentialism and is now generally thought to have to do with those impractical people who believe in ideals and never amount to anything.

I propose a revival of interest in the meaning of existentialism because when everyone asks what something means, the possibilities of misunderstanding are, if not lessened, more controllable. Having studied existentialism in an off-hand way since 1935, I become more and more convinced that its meaning can be reduced to the following formulation: *Existentialism means that no one else can take a bath for you.*

This example is suggested by Heidegger, who points out that no one else can die for you. You must die your own death. But the same is true of taking a bath. And I prefer the bath as an example to death because, as Heidegger further observes, no one likes to think very much about death, except indigent undertakers perhaps. Death is for most a distant event, however unpleasant and inevitable.

A bath, however, is a daily affair, at least in America. Thus it is something you have to think about somewhat everyday, and while you are thinking about it, and while, perforce, you are taking a bath, you might just as well be thinking about what existentialism means. Otherwise you will probably just be thinking about yourself, which is narcissism; or about other human beings, which is likely to be malicious, unless you are feeling very good; or worst of all, you may not be thinking at all, which is senseless and a waste of time.

Of course, there are other acts which each human being must perform for himself, such as eating, breathing, sleeping, making love, etc. But taking a bath seems to me the best of the lot because it involves the vital existentialist emphasis on choice: you can choose *not* to take a bath, you can waver in your choice, you can finally decide to take a bath, the whole drama of human freedom can become quite hectic or for that matter quite boring. But eating is hardly a matter of choice, except for the menu itself, nor is breathing which can be done not only without taking thought but while one is quite unconscious. As for making love, taking a bath is a better example because you can keep it clean, simple, free of fixations, perversions, inhibitions, and an overpowering sense of guilt.

Now despite the fact that most of the bathtubs which exist are in America, some Americans are not in the habit of taking baths for granted. I know of one American (formerly an existentialist, by the way) who avoids taking frequent baths because he feels that the taking of a bath is an *extreme situation*. (He is not averse to using existentialist arguments when it suits his purpose, though in company he attacks existentialism.) He says that taking a bath is an extreme situation because God knows what may occur to you when you are in the tub, you may decide to drown yourself because existence, as existentialists say, is essentially *absurd;* you may decide to become a narcissist because of the pleasures of the warm and loving water; you may decide to join the Roman Catholic Church because it too is quite comforting and comfortable. But there's no use listing all the catastrophes this fellow thinks may occur to anyone in the extreme situation of taking a bath.

So too with the bathtaking of a close friend of mine, who finds the taking of baths a matter of no little thought. He takes two baths a day, but he has to force himself to do so because there are so many other more important things to do (so it seems to him!) or which he feels he ought to do during the time occupied in taking a bath (note how the question of moral value enters at this point). It is a matter for much thought also because he has to decide whether to take a bath or a shower. He is afraid that sooner or later he will break his neck slipping on a cake of soap while taking a shower (which he prefers to a bath), although, on the other hand, he feels that in some ways it is better to take a shower than a bath because then he does not have to wash out the tub for others (*the others* are always important, as Sartre has observed), and in short the taking of baths is not a simple matter for him. Once I visited him while he was taking a shower, and while I was conversing with his wife in their handsome living-room, he kept crying out through the downpour of the shower: "Say, you know it's mighty lonesome in here." He wanted me to visit with him and keep him company (note the *aloneness* of the human situation as depicted by the existentialists), to converse with him. Consequently, after he had shouted his fourth appeal for my company, I had to go in and point out to him that we would have to shout at each other because of the noise of the shower and we shouted at each other often enough for more justifiable reasons.

In the upper class, as is well known, it is customary (I am told by friends who have soared to these circles at times ho, ho!) to take at least two baths a day, while in the lower middle class and working class this is less true, an observation I bring forward to show how important social and economic factors are, or, as the existentialists say, how all being is being-in-the-world, although they seem to think that the social and economic aspects of being-in-the-world are not so important as I am forced to think they are. Of course, some of the existentialists may have changed their minds during the second World War and the recent so-called peace.

The real difficulty in explaining what existentialism means flows from the basis of this philosophy, a basis which can be summarized in the following proposition: *Human beings exist.* They have an existence which is human and thus different from that of stones, trees, animals, cigar store Indians, and numerous human beings who are trying their best not to exist or not to be human.

If you are really human, if you really exist as a human being, you have no need of any explanation of existence or existentialism. In the meantime, the best thing to do is to keep on reading explanations of existentialism and existence.

Smile and Grin, Relax and Collapse

It is easy to make fun of *The New Yorker*, especially since *The New Yorker* has taught us how to make fun of anything and everything. At the same time it is just as easy and just as wrong to dismiss *The New Yorker* as merely a weekly periodical which pretends to be nothing more than amusing, and intends to divert the reader, while he glances and grins at the cartoons, and becomes acquisitive, looking at the luscious or luxurious advertisements. *The New Yorker* propagates a definite set of values, it has an enormous influence, and it certainly stands for something important and full of consequences. For most of its devoted readers, it provides a weekly lesson in how to be sophisticated and civilized in one's thoughts, in one's conversation, and in one's attitudes toward all of the possibilities and actualities of existence. Although *The New Yorker* obviously has no political views, its pages are paved with good intentions, the good intentions of that kind of well-meaning liberalism which cannot tell the difference between a Socialist and a Stalinist, or between a genuine defense of civil liberties and a conspiratorial exploitation of democratic rights.

However, its politics do not matter very much since no one seems to be dissuaded or persuaded, but merely confirmed in his views, or indifferent or oblivious. It is the effect of *The New Yorker* upon literature (of which the present selection of short stories published between 1940 and 1950 is a good sample), which is powerful and pernicious. The effect can be overestimated, no doubt, but perhaps overestimation would be preferable to underestimation, an underestimation based on the misleading truth that the deliberate intention of *The New Yorker* is solely to be amusing.

[412]

Thus there can be no doubt that *The New Yorker* does set up a model of what the short story ought to be and just what a good prose style is. The fact that writers cooperate and collaborate with editorial standards does not lessen but rather illustrates the extent of *The New Yorker's* power. There are exceptions, but as usual they merely probe the rule and prove the tendency, just as the book reviews of Edmund Wilson, by their very appearance, make clear the philistine uneasiness, ignorance, and arrogance which prevail in most of the other efforts at literary criticism. The chief recent tendency, so far as fiction goes, has been to break down the short story as such into some form of memoir, reminiscence, or anecdote, especially about childhood or about one's dear, foolish, pathetic, and comical elders, a genre which was probably initiated by *Life With Father*, the interminable Broadway success which first appeared (as prose revery, nostalgia, and reminiscence) in *The New Yorker*. And in fact, Mary McCarthy makes the most of this transformation or confusion of genres in her story, anecdote, or whatever it is, "Yonder Peasant, Who Is He?" declaring joyously: "Luckily, I am writing a memoir and not a work of fiction, and therefore do not have to account for my grandmother's unpleasant character and look for the Oedipal fixation or the traumatic experience which would give her that clinical authenticity that is nowadays so desirable in portraiture." Miss McCarthy is not as lucky as she thinks she is, for she takes her assumed freedom from fiction's requirements as an excuse for seeking no authenticity whatever; and her irony is misplaced, for she assumes that in memoirs, in literary portraits, and in biographical writing there is no need for reasons, explanations (clinical or some other kind), and an effort to connect effect and cause. Miss McCarthy is also an excellent illustration of the fact that when good writers write for *The New Yorker*, they adopt attitudes and mannerisms which are absent from their serious writing elsewhere. And this is also true of such different and gifted writers as Robert Gorham Davis, Peter Taylor, Niccolo Tucci, Christine Weston, Kay Boyle, Jean Stafford, Vladimir Nabokov, Carson McCullers, Mark Schorer, and probably true of others with whose work elsewhere I am unfamiliar. Most of these writers are striving in one guise or another—or none at all—to write their memoirs, although they are authors who in

[413]

their writings elsewhere manage to distinguish very well between fiction and personal history, as if they knew by heart and believed Aristotle's distinction between poetry and history, and never forgot Gertrude Stein's remark that anecdotes are not literature.

These writers must be distinguished from other kinds of authors whom *The New Yorker* also bring forward as masters of the short story. One kind is the genuine *New Yorker* author such as James Thurber and Ludwig Bemelmans, who are comic geniuses: but who are humorists, and not storytellers. The distinction is a real one, but *The New Yorker* ignores or blurs it. Probably *The New Yorker* made possible or helped to foster their kind of humor, and if all the writing in its pages were like theirs, there could be no reasonable objection to it. But then there is another kind of writer who also engages in false impersonation, the engaging reporter or journalist who never disguises himself as an author of fiction except in *The New Yorker*: A. J. Liebling and Russell Maloney are two typical instances, and they seem to write short stories merely because they are writing for *The New Yorker*. Thus two other tendencies become clear, the process of making the short story into a joke because one is a humorist, and the process of converting a genuine piece of journalism into a half-hearted short story. It is probably needless to say that personal experience, memory, and conversation are often the beginning of fiction. But in *The New Yorker* it is swiftly becoming the end of fiction, in more ways than one.

A third kind of short story is also worth noticing, and with wonder, astonishment, sorrow, and perplexity; the writer who, having appeared in various kinds of publications, appears only in *The New Yorker,* and then finally disappears! Where is Morley Callaghan? Perhaps I should explain that for some time he seemed to be just as gifted a writer of fiction as Ernest Hemingway and Katherine Anne Porter. But this impression diminished as he began to appear in *The New Yorker,* and by now no one seems to have heard of him.

At the other extreme is John O'Hara who certainly belongs in *The New Yorker* and who in his fiction accomplishes what most of the other *New Yorker* authors merely seem to parody; compared with O'Hara, most of the others often seem like girls trying to play baseball. But O'Hara is the real McCoy. He has a rich gift for social observation, for knowing how people are, what they are because of their background, and he has an acute, accurate ear which makes it possible for his characters to possess reality when they converse. But best of all O'Hara is a snob (in the fundamental attitudes with which he regards his characters); he is as sensitive to social distinctions as any *arriviste* ever was, and his snob-sensitivity provides him with inexhaustible energy for the trans-formation of observation into fiction. It was probably neither accident nor intention which made O'Hara call the scapegoat hero of his first novel, Julian English; for English is an Anglo-Saxon, he resents the Irish, he belongs to what is supposed to be the upper class, and the tragic action which leads to his suicide is his throw-ing a drink in the face of a man with the choice name of Harry Reilly. It might as well have been Murphy, O'Mara, or Parnell. So too in the story by O'Hara in the present collection, the hero is named Francis Townsend, he comes of a good family and a rich one, he smokes cigars in an Irish bar "as though William Howard Taft or Harry Truman had just asked his advice on whom to appoint to the Court of St. James"; and he certainly is the end of the town or at least that part of the town, since he is drinking himself to death, having been told that he could not hope to practice medicine because his mother and father had gone insane. An author like O'Hara is perfect in *The New Yorker* because *The New Yorker* is in the most thorough-going way devoted to a sense of the social milieu, the hopes, resentments, frustrations, and fears which the American scene creates or compels. And if there is a persistent nastiness and contempt for human beings in much of O'Hara's writing, that is valuable too, because many people feel like that without admitting it. O'Hara's explicitness is desir-able, just as candor is more desirable than hypocrisy, although one might well prefer the compassion of Dostoevsky, or at least Scott Fitzgerald, but let us not be Utopian, difficult to satisfy, and worst of all, *high-brow*.

If the literary influence of *The New Yorker* is pernicious, it is not because O'Hara flourishes in its pages, but rather because there does seem to be a kind of periodical style at work in it from week to week, a style pervasive, intensive, comprehensive, and one that gets stronger and stronger all the time. It we take prose style merely as a matter of the choice of words, phrases, tones, and references, it is clear that in *The New Yorker* you are supposed to be chatty, relaxed, not very serious, and certainly never (God forbid!) intellectual. There is no reason that anyone should not write in such a style, for whatever reason, to earn an honest dollar, or to seem elegant, charming, sophisticated, full of good manners and good taste. And it would soon become unbearable if everyone wrote in the style of Djuna Barnes, or Virginia Woolf, or in the careful and composed prose which helps to make the short stories of Joyce a succession of masterpieces. But the periodical style which now characterizes *The New Yorker* excludes or dismisses various important kinds of perceptions, attitudes, and values, no matter how great the good will of the editors. And apart from writers like O'Hara, Thurber, S. J. Perelman, Philip Hamburger, and Bemelmans, the prose style of most of the fiction becomes increasingly nondescript and anonymous. When everyone begins to try to write in a style imposed from without (imposed, whether or not it is true that the editors rewrite sentences which seem inappropriate to them), then everyone sees and feels, after a time, only those sights which can be expressed in the periodical style; and in the end the readers, too, see, feel, hear, and think of things in the same way. As it is common by now to say of something funny that it is just like a *New Yorker* cartoon, so we may conclude by finding all existence *New Yorker*ish. Perhaps this is one reason for the disappearance of some authors: what's the sense of having a mind and sensibility of your own, if you have to use someone else's, which is, moreover, not his, but a kind of consensus of opinion, deadly average, and readers' plebiscite?

These remarks may seem severe, especially since the work in question is obviously not the product of a deliberate conspiracy, but the result of a profound and intuitive collaboration between the taste of numerous readers and hard-pressed editors who do the best they can, according to their lights. Nevertheless, whatever the compulsion of public taste may be, *The New Yorker* is rich and free. If it can afford the luxury of the criticism of Edmund Wilson, it ought to be able to encourage in its gifted authors a greater cultivation of their own originality. Proust appeared in the French equivalent of *The New Yorker,* and Chekhov wrote a story every week for Russian equivalents. It is true that James Thurber, as good an index as any, does not seem to like Proust very much (he once wrote with pleasure that some likeable person had made Proust more clear to him and less important than anyone else had succeeded in doing, an indubitable yet ambiguous feat); but Thurber is fascinated by Henry James, a fondness which may lead to God knows what, and anyway, as everyone knows, you get used to anything, you can even get used to writing governed by the motives which inspired fiction in the past.

Masterpieces as Cartoons

Recently I have been trying hard to watch television and read comic books. I do not know whether this is an effort to keep in touch with the rest of the American population or an attempt to win the esteem and keep up with my brother-in-law, aged twelve, who regards me as a hideous highbrow and thinks that I am probably a defrocked high school English teacher. The effort is, at any rate, one which permits me moments of self-congratulation. I feel that no one can say that I have not tried my best to keep open the lines of communication between myself and others, and to share the intellectual interests of the entire community.

The bottom of the pit has been reached, I think, in the cartoon books which are called *Classics Illustrated,* a series of picture-and-text versions of the masterpieces of literature. Seventy-eight of them have been published, but so far I have only been able to obtain six of them, and they have been so exciting and fascinating and distracting that I have only been able to read three of them with any care: Dostoevsky's *Crime and Punishment,* Shakespeare's *A Midsummer Night's Dream*, and *Gulliver's Travels*. The intentions of the publishers and the editors of these illustrated classics are either good, or they feel guilty, or perhaps both, since at the end of *A Midsummer Night's Dream* there is a striking and entirely capitalized sentence: "NOW THAT YOU HAVE READ THE CLASSICS ILLUSTRATED EDITION, DON'T MISS THE ADDED ENJOYMENT OF READING THE ORIGINAL, OBTAINABLE AT YOUR SCHOOL OR PUBLIC LIBRARY." Notice how it is assumed that the reader has not read the original version of these works and it is taken for granted that he will not buy, he will only borrow, the original version from school or the public library. An interesting and significant fact to discover would be: just how many readers who first encounter Shakespeare, Dostoevsky, or Jonathan Swift in their comic strip garb are moved by this encounter to read the original. It would take a good detective or a good pollster to find out. When one feels optimistic, it seems possible that some quality of the masterpiece may bring some readers to the original; but when one feels pessimistic, one remembers an analogous phenomenon: even when a reader goes from James M. Cain to William Faulkner and James Joyce because they are all available in pocket book form for twenty-five cents, most readers who come to Faulkner and Joyce by means of pocket books do not know the difference between James M. Cain and James Joyce or Dashiell Hammett and William Faulkner; and some of the time they do not remember the names of the authors, no matter how many of their works they read.

The good intentions, or the guilty conscience of the publishers of *Classics Illustrated* show clearly at the end of the cartoon version of *Crime and Punishment*, where again, as with Shakespeare, they write sentences of bold apology and excellent advice: "BECAUSE OF SPACE LIMITATIONS, WE REGRETFULLY OMITTED SOME OF THE ORIGINAL CHARACTERS AND SUB-PLOTS OF THIS BRILLIANTLY WRITTEN NOVEL. NEVERTHELESS, WE HAVE RETAINED ITS MAIN THEME AND MOOD. WE STRONGLY URGE YOU TO READ THE ORIGINAL." This explanation is more interesting and more inaccurate, the more one thinks about it and the more one remembers the novel which Dostoevsky wrote. For one of the characters who is omitted is Sonia, the heroine. She may have been omitted because of space limitations but it is just as likely that her prostitution had something to do with her absence from the illustrated version. What remains after the deletion of some of the original characters and sub-plots is the thin line of a detective story in which a murderer is tracked down; as the publishers explain, at the end of the last slot in which Raskolnikov confesses his crime: "This then was the story of the intelligent young man who committed a premeditated 'perfect crime.' His conscience and the efforts of a brilliant police attorney brought about the dramatic confession and a just punishment. Raskolnikov was sentenced to serve a long term at hard labor in a Siberian prison." Not much is left of the profound affirmation of Christianity with which the original work concludes, although there are cartoon book versions of the Old and New testaments.

The miracle, or perhaps one should say the triumph of Dostoevsky's genius, is that despite all the cuts and mutilations of the original, there are gleams and glitters throughout the illustrated version of the psychological insight which Dostoevsky possessed to so powerful a degree and which made so stern a judge as Freud declare that only Shakespeare surpassed him as an author and as a literary psychologist. The brilliance and the originality of Dostoevsky's psychologizing come through mainly in the exchanges between Raskolnikov and Porfiry the detective as the latter gradually traps the murderer into confessing his crime. There are also numerous movements in the illustrated edition which are unknowingly comic and probably the expression of deep unconscious attitudes upon the part of the illustrator and the editor. For example, Raskolnikov at times looks very much like a Russian delegate to the UN who is afraid that the NKVD is after him. At other times Raskolnikov has an unquestionable resemblance to Peter Lorre, the film star who has so often been a villain. At other moments the illustrations—but not the text—suggest a detestation of all intellectuals, not only Raskolnikov, and in general there is the sharp implication throughout that most Russians·are either criminals or police agents, and all Russians are somehow fundamentally evil.

I tried to check on this impression which seemed possibly an overinterpretation by examining another cartoon series called *Crime Does NOT Pay* (an immortal aphorism which is not going to hold much weight when the readers and the children find out about Frank Costello); a series about true crimes in the United States. The results of the comparison are incontestable: American crimes and criminals do not resemble Russia's or Dostoevsky's in the least.

The illustrated "edition" of *A Midsummer Night's Dream* is much less of a distortion of the original work. There are none of the serious cuts and omissions which virtually reduce the cartoon version of *Crime and Punishment* to a trite detective story. And the reason is clear enough: Shakespeare's play was intended for an audience which was very much like the juvenile readers of *Classics Illustrated*, and *A Midsummer Night's Dream* is one of the most playful and child-like of plays. Nevertheless here too the medium of the cartoon tends to make this version misleading. For one thing, the title page presents the (juvenile) reader with boxed and oval portraits of four of the leading characters. Under them is a landscape—a lake, a grove of trees, a distant temple, and Puck flying through the air in front of an enormous rising moon—and at the foot of the page there is a scroll-like band of words which announces the leading elements of the plot: "A dark forest . . . An angry fairy king . . . His mischievous messenger . . . A magic flower . . . Four thwarted lovers . . . And a troupe of wretched actors make a merry mix-up on a midsummer night . . . ," all of which is fair enough as a brief overture. The illustrated edition begins at the very beginning of the play (something which is certainly far from being the case in all cartoon versions of the classics) and it is at this point that the most important kind of distortion takes place. For, first, there is a slot which explains to the youthful reader the purpose of the scene: "In his palace, Theseus, Duke of Athens, and Hippolyta, Queen of the Amazons, discuss their coming wedding . . . ," an explanation which interferes with the natural dramatic unfolding, although the intention, I suppose, is to help the reader as much as possible and keep him from being in the least perplexed or from feeling that he has to make any serious exertion beyond keeping his eyes open.

Second, and more important, by far, the opening speeches, which are in blank verse, are printed as if they were prose. This occurs from beginning to end. There is no conceivable way in which the juvenile reader can find out from the illustrated edition itself that he is reading poetry and not prose, although one would guess that some sense of the movement of language in blank verse rhythms certainly must impinge upon every reader. This failure to make it clear that the speeches are often poetry and not prose may not seem as serious, at first glance, as in actuality it is. For the speeches are bound to be read incorrectly; and worse still, when

[421]

the juvenile reader does at some later date encounter poetry printed as poetry he is likely to be annoyed, if not irritated to the point where he refuses to read whatever is printed as poetry at all. His illustrated edition will have given him an easy and pleasant experience which becomes an obstacle to the more laborious and unfamiliar effort involved in reading poetry straight, that is to say, as it was written and as it was meant to be read.

Perhaps it is not as important as I think it is that there should be a certain number of readers of poetry. But the fear that disturbs me can be exemplified by what occurred in a class of freshmen at one of the best universities in the world. The instructor, who was teaching English composition, asked the students to define blank verse. No student volunteered an answer. The instructor expressed his dismay and asked his class if they had not studied Shakespeare and other poets in high school. The students admitted that they had, and finally one student, perhaps feeling sympathy for the clearly distressed teacher, raised his hand and attempted a definition of blank verse: "Sir," he said, hesitantly, tentatively, and unsurely, "isn't blank verse something which looks like poetry, but is not poetry?" It turned out that the well-meaning student supposed that unless there were rhymes at the end of each line, he was not reading poetry. Now this class of students represented what was probably the most intensively and expensively educated young men in America. And as I have said, the incident and others like it occurred at one of the best schools in the world. If such a systematic misunderstanding of the nature of literature and poetry can exist among such young men, what, after all, can be expected of a population which first comes upon great literature in the guise of cartoon editions? One can well imagine a student insisting to his instructor that *A Midsummer Night's Dream* cannot be a play in blank verse, since the student has seen with his own eyes that it was printed as prose. And it is certainly not fanciful to suppose that the day is swiftly approaching when one human being says to another: "Have you read *Hamlet?*" and is answered: "No, but I seen the comic book edition."

Yet certainly there is a good side to everything, however infamous. There always is. And the good side to Shakespeare's plays as cartoon strips might be that some juvenile readers who are oppressed and biased by the way in which Shakespeare is for the most part taught in high schools all over America will now come upon Shakespeare first of all as a cartoon and see that he is really a great deal of fun, he is not a painful assignment in homework and a difficult, outmoded, canonized ancient author who wrote strange plays which provide the teachers of English with inexhaustible and eminently respectable reasons for boring their students. But there must be other and less misleading ways of demonstrating the pleasures of poetry to juvenile readers.

It is true that to encounter a literary masterpiece in a dramatic or cinematic form sometimes gives the reader, juvenile or adult, a new view and a new interest in the work. The French films of Dostoevsky's *The Idiot* and *Crime and Punishment* not only gave me a new and clarified understanding of both novels, but it seemed to me that the changes that were made in the original text were often improvements. The same was true of the German film version of *The Brothers Karamazov*, even though the character of Alyosha and the fable of the Grand Inquisitor were omitted, probably for theatrical reasons. And it is even more true that when a Shakespearean film is made well, as *A Midsummer Night's Dream* and *Henry V* were, there is a great gain for the common reader of Shakespeare who is used to reading him in a book rather than grasping his plays as visual experiences.

The fundamental question, whether it is a matter of the filmed Shakespeare or the cartoon book Shakespeare, seems to me to be: will the juvenile reader ever arrive at the point where he wants to see the original as it was intended to be, in its full actuality as a work? And the answer which suggests itself is a depressing one. If you get used to getting literature with illustrations— "visualized" is the phrase, I think—then you are likely to feel deprived when there are no illustrations and you have to do all the work yourself, depending upon the book itself. Moreover, the vice of having your visualizing done for you is all too likely to make you unused if not unwilling to read books which have no pictures in them. The Chinese proverb, "A picture is worth a thousand words," is often quoted by American advertisers. But the Chinese meant something very different from what the advertisers are trying to say. The Chinese meant that the visual experience

[423]

of an object was more likely to give the full concreteness of that object than many of the words about it, which are for the most part abstract, generalized, colorless, and the like. The advertisers mean that human beings are more interested in looking at things (and find it easier) than in reading about them, so that the pictures in an ad are more efficacious in increasing sales than the words that accompany the pictures.

This fact is relevant to *Classics Illustrated* in the most direct way: the reader finds it easy and pleasant to look at words-with-pictures, he finds it more difficult and less pleasant to look at words which have no pictures to make them clear and visual. There is a tendency among some readers to read so much that their capacity to look at the visual world is spoiled. But far worse and far more prevalent is the tendency (of which masterpieces in cartoon form are an apt example) to read as little as possible and to prefer a thousand pictures to a single paragraph of intelligent reading matter. The over-all picture of the state of literacy was formulated two years ago by Gilbert Seldes in *The Great Audience*, a book which did not receive the attention it deserved: "In fourteen million homes equipped with radios, *no* magazines are read; families with television sets read fewer magazines than those who do not have them; half the adults in America never buy books." It is simple to transpose this statement to the great juvenile audience and to their reading of comic books and of the classics in cartoon form.

When we turn to the cartoon book version of *Gulliver's Travels*, other aspects of juvenile literacy (I was about to write, delinquency!) become clear. Of course *Gulliver's Travels* has been a children's classic for a long time as well as one of the greatest works of English literature for those who have reached the age of reason and consent. In the past, however, it is unquestionably true that the children's version of Swift's best work did not become a barrier to the interest of the same children in that work when they were old enough to want to enjoy the master-works of their native language. The cartoon book version, unlike the older children's editions of *Gulliver's Travels,* goes much further in mutilation. At the end of the cartoon version, there is no plea by the publisher, as there was in *Crime and Punishment,* and in

A Midsummer Night's Dream, telling the reader that he ought to read this work in its original form. There is, however, as in all the *Classics Illustrated,* a biography of the author (these biographies vary in inaccuracy, but they are all inaccurate to some degree). Swift's cartoon biography contains a number of trivial errors—such as the statement that he began to write in 1704—but the important distortion is a truth which is stated in such a way that it is likely to mislead and deceive anyone who wants to find out the truth and is limited in the resources and skills necessary to finding out what the truth is (as, obviously, most juvenile readers are, whether they are quiz kids or not). The truth which is stated in such a way as to be entirely misleading is set forth in the cartoon biography of Swift as follows: *"Gulliver's Travels* was written by Swift as a savage commentary on the European world Swift knew, as a condemnation of the laws and customs of his own and other countries that led one of the characters in the story to describe the inhabitants of Europe as 'the most pernicious race of little odious vermin that nature ever suffered to crawl upon the surface of the earth.' In later years Swift's satire became more and more violently bitter, possibly the result of mental disease which, by 1736, caused him to become insane."

Whoever wrote the cartoon biography may not have a chance to read the cartoon version. For there is very little in the cartoon version to suggest that the original is a "savage commentary" in which human beings are condemned as "odious little vermin." Moreover, the cartoon biography suggests that Swift was commenting on the state of human nature in his own time, and not in all times and places which he knew about. There is also the suggestion that the bitterness and violence of his satire were probably due to the onset of mental disease. All of this apology is unnecessary, however, for the reader who only knows of Swift through the cartoon edition. And what the biography states is literally true and as true, deceptive. Swift did suffer from mental disease and the disappointment of his political ambition did inspire in part the savage indignation which makes *Gulliver's Travels* a masterpiece. But the juvenile reader has no need of reassurance as to the benign character of human nature and the one-sidedness of Swift's point of view. In the cartoon version Gulliver returns to England

and we last see and hear of him as he stands at the wheel of the ship which is coming into an English harbor. The captain of the ship, who is standing next to him says: "There she is! Good old Britannia!" and Gulliver expresses his own pleasure in returning to civilized Europe and merry England by saying: "I certainly am happy to be back . . . but it will take me weeks to get used to moving among people my own size!" He has had strange and interesting adventures and now he is delighted to be home.

Surely no explanation that Swift was a disappointed man of genius who concluded in insanity is necessary if all the reader has read is the cartoon edition. If he reads the original, he is certainly bound to be disturbed. For the original concludes in a way which is very different from *Classics Illustrated*. Gulliver explains to the "Courteous Readers," on the next to the last page, that having lived among horses and among human beings, he still prefers horses to human beings. When he has just come back to his own house in England, his wife's kiss makes him faint: "My Wife took me in her Arms, and kissed me; at which, having not been used to the touch of that odious Animal for so many years, I fell in a Swoon for almost an Hour," and he feels disgusted with himself at the thought that he has become the father of human beings: the fact strikes him "with the utmost Shame, Confusion, and Horror." For the first year after his return to England "I could not endure my Wife or Children in my Presence, the Smell of them was intolerable." (I am quoting at length because anyone who has not read *Gulliver's Travels* recently will probably think any synopsis or paraphrase an exaggeration of Swift's satire.) As to the purpose of the work, Gulliver declares that "I write for the noblest End, to inform and instruct Mankind, over whom I may, without Breach of Modesty, pretend to some superiority, from the Advantages I received by conversing among the most accomplished Houyhnhnms. I write without any View toward Profit or Praise," which is to say that, having dwelt with horses, Gulliver feels superior to mankind and capable of instructing human beings in how to improve. At the very end, having been back among civilized human beings for five years, Gulliver declares that he is now able to sit at the same dinner table with his wife, although since the smell of any civilized being is still offensive to him, he has to keep applying rue, lavender, or tobacco to his nose. And he adds that he would be able to accept human nature as it is in most of its follies and vices except for one unbearable trait, the vice of pride, which causes more viciousness than any other human trait. It is the viciousness of pride and vanity which make civilized existence insupportable.

Clearly, there is little likelihood that the juvenile reader of the cartoon version of *Gulliver's Travels* will be corrupted by Swift's cynicism and nihilism (which was inspired, we ought to remember, by an intense idealism and an intense purity as well as by the disappointment of ambition and the distortion of growing neurosis). But the important point here is not the juvenile reader himself or herself, but the adult publisher and editor who has exhibited a well-meaning solicitude for the juvenile reader's tender sensibility. For whoever is responsible for the cartoon version is very much aware of the true character of *Gulliver's Travels* and wishes to spare the feelings and the minds of the juvenile audience. But where does this solicitude stop?

I must turn to personal experience to show how far the solicitude and the censorship can go. When I taught composition to freshmen and coeds ten years ago along with some twenty-five other instructors, a crisis occurred as a result of the modern novels which the students had been assigned to read. One of the coeds had been reading late at night at her English assignment, which was John Dos Passos' *U.S.A.* Dos Passos' savage indignation, which resembles Swifts's, and his explicit account of the sexual experiences of his characters, terrified the young lady to the point where she had to waken her father (not her mother!) and tell him that she had been scared and shocked by her reading assignment in English. The unhappy father conferred with the head of the English staff, who in turn discussed the entire issue with the entire staff. The head of the staff was very much aware of both sides of the problem and he tried to be just to the interests and rights of his instructors as well as to the problems of adolescents who are in the first year of their undergraduate careers. But in such a situation, judiciousness and compromise can accomplish very little. Most of

[427]

the instructors felt, whether rightly or wrongly, that they had been told not to assign Dos Passos, or Joyce, or Thomas Mann, or Proust, or Gide or Céline to their students. They felt that they probably would be fulfilling their duty as teachers of English composition and literature better if they went no further than such authors as Dickens, Thackeray, George Eliot, and George Meredith. Thomas Hardy was an ambiguous and questionable author, given the point of view which a shocked coed had brought to the fore, since *Jude the Obscure* and *Tess of the D'Urbervilles* were both books which might very well be shocking again as they had been when they first appeared (as a result of which scandal, the heartsick Hardy ceased to write novels).

The juvenile and adolescent reader certainly ought not to be scared and shocked. But he ought not to be cut off from the reality of great literature and of modern literature (the latter being, because of its contemporaneity, the best way of getting the ordinary adolescent reader interested in literature of any kind). And it is essential and necessary to remember that if a human being does not become interested in literature when he is an undergraduate, it is quite unlikely that he will become a devoted reader at any other time of life.

The teaching of English has a direct and continuous relationship to the kind of books which juvenile, adolescent, and adult readers are likely to desire to read. The cartoon version of *Gulliver's Travels* suggests still another incident in the teaching of English literature. The text in this instance was Swift's *A Modest Proposal,* in which Swift proposes among other things that the economic problem of Ireland might be solved if the Irish bred children and then butchered them for food. In the seven years during which, at some point during the year, I had to assign this little classic of satire to freshmen students, I naturally encountered a variety of impressions on their part. But the most frequent and representative comment was exemplified by a student of Armenian parents (he must have heard of the Turks) and a boy who was Irish (and who must have heard of the English in Ireland). Both students announced that Swift was "morbid." I was tempted to embark upon a self-indulgent excursion when I heard this comment and to say

[428]

that I would not permit the greatest prose writer in English, except for Shakespeare, perhaps, to be called "morbid," and to recall to the students what they had heard about the Turks in Armenia, the English in Ireland, to say nothing of Buchenwald and Dachau. But I felt that the students would merely have concluded that I too was morbid. By questioning them with some degree of patience, I found out that after they had read comic books, listened to soap operas, and witnessed the sweetness and light of the motion pictures, they were inclined to regard anything which is serious satire as morbid sensationalism.

To return directly to the cartoon versions of the classics: it is customary and habitual, when one has expressed the point of view I have suggested here, to be asked, *What is to be done?* I do not suffer from the delusion that I know what is to be done. But I confess that I sometimes entertain modest guesses, the practicality of which I cannot determine. The reading of comic books, and cartoon versions of the classics (and listening to the radio, looking at the motion pictures and listening and looking at television programs) cannot be stopped. Mass culture is here to stay: it is a major industry and a very profitable one, and one can no more banish it than one can banish the use of automobiles because thirty-four thousand people are killed by cars every year. And even if the reading of cartoon books might be stopped, it is probable that prohibition and censorship would have the usual boomerang effect.

What can be done, I think (or rather, I guess), is to set a good example, or perhaps I should say an example which is the least of all the possible evil examples, namely: each adult and literate human being who feels that literature is one of the necessary conditions of civilized existence can set the example of reading *both* the original classics and the cartoon versions. By doing both, he is keeping his hold on literature at its best and at the same time he is remaining aware of the experience and thus the consciousness of any other reader: children, juveniles, adolescents, housewives, aged relatives, farmers, mechanics, taxi-drivers—in fact, everyone! For the products of mass culture preoccupy the minds of most human beings in America, whether they know it or not. And in setting the good or least evil example of maintaining his hold on great literature in the midst of forcing himself to be aware of the debased versions and mutilations and dilutions of it, he may make some other readers imitative enough to come or return to the classics in their full actuality. This proposal may seem very much like one of the labors of Hercules. But it is also a lot of fun, at least some of the time. Besides, Hercules was a hero, and as practically everyone knows, all human beings want to be heroic heroes and heroines, at least once in a while.

On Movie People
and Movies
·VI·

The Genius of W. C. Fields

W. C. Fields was a very funny man, but it does not follow that his biography has to be funny too. He was a wonderful comedian and a purely American one, and a good biography of him might illuminate much more than Fields alone. Unfortunately Robert Lewis Taylor—working under conditions, probably, in which discretion and good taste prevented the use of much that was personal—has written a book[1] which is chiefly a collection of anecdotes tied together by biographical data. The result is a kind of W. C. Fields film, and an inferior one at that. On numerous occasions Mr. Taylor comes close to aspects of Fields which may have been the mainsprings of his profound comic powers, but he hardly ever does more than touch on these things briefly, perhaps because of an admirable sense of the feelings of living people who were connected with Fields, but also because his conception of a biography derives from the Profiles in the *New Yorker*, which are all very well in a setting of cartoons and advertisements but which are naturally remote from the questions that biographical writing ought to try to answer. Mr. Taylor's attempt to be entertaining is itself a form of irrelevance, for in Fields's life there was really little that was humorous—except in the old sense of the word. Hence Mr. Taylor's relentless succession of hilarious incidents becomes quite trying when one is teased by such problems as why Fields, like many other comedians, was so anxious, and so unhappy, and why he had to drink as much as he did.

Humor is of course a very important part of American life, and

1. *W. C. Fields: His Follies and Fortunes.* New York: Doubleday and Company, 1949.

Fields's version and extension of American humor are sufficiently representative to raise other natural questions which Mr. Taylor's method eliminates. For example, Fields's father was a cockney Englishman. At one point in his career Fields met King Edward VII—like Nana and other theatrical personages—and this meeting became a matter of great pride to Fields, who afterward referred very fondly to "Eddie." Mr. Taylor does not try to connect these facts, or to interpret them, although the array of facts, here as in other matters, is full of suggestions of significance, and there may well have been some connection between Fields's cockney antecedents, his attitude toward the English, his use of the comedy of names, and his rich feeling for the comic possibilities of pompous, pretentious, or hypocritical language. This too is related to American humor as a whole, especially that traditional vein which makes the most of educated speech, illiterate speech, mispronunciation, jargon, the feelings of a nation which is partly immigrant in origin and afraid of book learning, resentful of the mother country, and at once afraid and scornful of Europe.

Fields continued the great tradition of Artemus Ward, Mark Twain, and the matchless Ring Lardner—who is not mentioned by Mr. Taylor but who probably influenced and was influenced by Fields. There is much in Fields that corresponds with or extends those aspects of Lardner which are manifest when he refers to the Atlantic as "the big pond" (by way of disparagement) and in his detestation of Amy Lowell, free verse, and grand opera. The common ground shared by Fields and Lardner shows itself in another obvious connection—the extent to which they both hated Florenz Ziegfeld, for whom they toiled to be funny.

In some passages Mr. Taylor is guilty of more than the sin of omission, for he engages in a sedulous defense of Hollywood and Hollywood executives, who were the objects of Fields's wrath and satire not only in life but in his pictures. Although Fields's genius was a source of great profit to those who employed him, Mr. Taylor feels that those Hollywood figures who found Fields impossible were justified because he caused these unfortunate men considerable discomfiture. This is not to say that Mr. Taylor is at all unsympathetic to Fields. But his sympathy and his sense of Fields's suffering and unhappiness, particularly during the last ten years of his life, are at times superficial or patronizing. Gene Fowler, a friend of Fields to whom Mr. Taylor has dedicated his book and who probably suggested the idea that a biography is a vaudeville show, is far more sensitive in his life of John Barrymore, perhaps because on the surface Barrymore seemed a more serious subject. The lives of Barrymore and Fields resemble each other in ways which may be coincidental; yet so many accidental resemblances may be as symptomatic and as essential as the accidents which occur on a Fourth of July week-end.

Mr. Taylor compares Fields to Charlie Chaplin, and he thinks that Fields was the superior comedian. The question of who was better is not important, but a comparison of the two styles of comedy, their origins, motives, basic attitudes, and the like, might make a fascinating study if it were sufficiently detailed. Chaplin is innocent or naive, oppressed and downhearted, pathetic and threadbare, and yet deft, quick to escape from the tyrant and the cop, and to make the most of the worst; and he is profoundly silent. Fields is an out-and-out scoundrel with no reservations—he frankly hates children most of all—and he is overwhelmingly articulate, not to say verbose (redundant is one of his favorite words), in the best tradition of that key character in American life and humor, the suave and fluent swindler. Where Charlie skids around the corner rapidly enough to escape the falling lamp post or to make the cop the victim of his own cruel night stick, Fields envelops every situation of superior force in elaborate schemes, alarming and mystifying reformulations, beautifully self-righteous attitudes, and a sophisticated cynicism about everyone, including himself—which is very different from Chaplin's melancholy, pathos, and hurried evasions but which is at the same time a response to the very same world and social set-up. Chaplin makes desperate and downcast efforts to behave with decorum, although the ceiling is falling down or the law is after him. Fields, faced with a bank examiner who will discover a robbery in which he is involved, lures this official gentleman to a bar and orders a drink for him, instructing the bartender by asking him if he has seen his friend Michael Finn lately. The two comic strategies are recognizable and pervasive: you can respond to a threat by being crushed or by being a crook, by running or by making a speech, by pleading or by bluffing, by making faces or by becoming as oratorical as a barker.

There are clear personal reasons for the contrast. Chaplin is a little man in fact and as a symbol. Fields tended to plumpness and looked a bit grandiose in appearance and dress—he had a distinct resemblance, and a perplexing one, to Herbert Hoover and Henry James. But the contrast may be significant of much that is more than personal. Chaplin is willing to make some kind of adjustment, genteel in aspiration very often, to all that is overbearing, pompous, or unjust. But Fields is openly committed to non-adjustment, to the principle that although you can't cheat an honest man, there are so few honest men that one must be pretty tricky, at the very least, to keep from being destroyed. There are few honest men, and the chief distinction is between different kinds of crooks, so that, since it is difficult to become a banker, one must become some other kind of crook in order to cope with the chilly and respectable infamy of bankers.

So too with ladies and with liquor, two leading comic subjects. Chaplin is shy, hesitant, and fearful of rejection by members of the fair sex. He really adores them. And alcohol—one source perhaps of the Al of Lardner's "You Know Me Al"—is ticklish, titillating, special, and disconcerting, and likely to conclude in weaving and hangovers. For Fields drink is an incessant and acute daily necessity without which a man can hardly function. And the only way to deal with a hangover is to have one more or four more of what he called "depth bombs," which are often used as panaceas, for existence itself is somewhat of a hangover. As for the other sex, the ladies are also depth bombs, sometimes to be approached cautiously, but certainly shyness and adoration are irrelevant, except as pretense. And if Chaplin often has to tiptoe past his landlady, Fields is in a more desperate case by far, for his landlady is usually his wife or his mother-in-law. (His encounter with Mae West in "My Little Chickadee" is, however, another story.)

There is much more to be said about these two comedians and about American comedy in general, and if Mr. Taylor's book is inadequate as a whole, it does suggest several fruitful approaches.

[436]

Certainly the whole subject is an important one, if only because one real if not decisive reason why Truman was preferred to Dewey as a personality was that he toured the country during the campaign of 1948 giving an unmistakable impersonation not of Franklin D. Roosevelt but of Will Rogers, one of the first Americans to understand Russia.

Mary Pickford
The Little Girl in Curls

   Mary Pickford's autobiography, *Sunshine and Shadow,* is fascinating and valuable in a variety of important ways. It is full of material for the historian, the sociologist, the psychologist, and the student of American civilization and popular culture. And in another kind of review it would be possible to deal at length with Miss Pickford's friendships, her travels, her relationships with David Belasco, Mack Sennett, Samuel Goldwyn, D. W. Griffith, Ernst Lubitsch, her meetings with Rudolph Valentino, Woodrow Wilson, Einstein, George Bernard Shaw, Eisenstein and particularly her friendship with Charlie Chaplin. What Miss Pickford omits is at times almost as important as what she includes: she says nothing of having written a novel, and almost nothing about her two books of personal philosophy which indicated how little fulfillment she found in fame. She scarcely speaks of other female stars, except for Pearl White and a passing reference to Clare Boothe, whom she identifies in a characteristic way as "later to become a famous playwright and ambassador"; and it is equally characteristic that when she tells of her meeting with Shaw she should remember two objects on his desk: a bust of Shakespeare and an Academy Award Oscar. So, too, a paragraph about how "I raised $5,000,000 in one afternoon and evening in Pittsburgh during the Liberty Bond Drive," is immediately followed by "another child's role that I played when I was an adult was Sarah Crew of *The Little Princess.*" There is an unintended precision here, for in both instances Miss Pickford was playing a starring part before an enthralled audience.

   What is most valuable for the purpose of understanding the

motion pictures is Miss Pickford's experience of stardom and its overwhelming effect upon her attitude toward herself. The fabulous identity of the star continues to be the most powerful and tyrannical of influences in determining the quality of a film; as Miss Pickford shows, the star's identity intervenes not only in her private life, but in the choice of scripts, the character of the direction, the camera work, the acting and the attention given to other players until, sooner or later, the star becomes the prisoner of her own stardom forever.

Miss Pickford had to continue to play the part of America's sweetheart through most of her career, as Greta Garbo had to play the part, in all her films, of an imaginary being named Greta Garbo, and as Marilyn Monroe will be Marilyn Monroe in all her films. In fact, at one point Miss Pickford says: "If reincarnation should prove to be true and I had to come back as one of my roles, I suppose that some avenging fate would return me to earth as Pollyanna, 'the glad girl'," and this is only one instance of Miss Pickford's strong sense of stardom as destiny.

Cecil B. deMille's foreword to Miss Pickford's book shows a like attitude. Mr. deMille either failed to read Miss Pickford's book to the end or forgot what he read: but it does not matter at all; the meaningfulness of his remarks remains important enough to quote at length:

> I do not know who first called Mary Pickford America's sweetheart [Miss Pickford provides a detailed account], but whoever it was put in two words the most remarkable personal achievement in the history of motion pictures . . . Mary Pickford [has] on the screen the absolutely unique position which no actress can challenge . . . she was one of the . . . handful in any generation who fire the imagination of millions because, somehow, they respond to something very deep in the hearts of their contemporaries . . . the explanation of her enduring career [is that she] typified, more than anyone else in motion pictures, the kind of person we all want to love.

This suggests what the scripts of Miss Pickford's films bear out, that the kind of a person we all want to love is out of reach, except upon the screen. And Mr. de Mille's sensitivity is such that, fearing his reference to Miss Pickford on the screen may be misunderstood or understood in a privative sense, he immediately hastens to add that those who have known Miss Pickford personally know that "the public's image of her is a true one." And then Mr. de Mille speaks of an occasion in 1953, twenty years after Miss Pickford's last film was released, when he appeared with Miss Pickford on radio and TV and he spoke of how long he had been a friend of hers:

> She seemed a little dismayed . . . perhaps it was ungallant of me not to explain to the vast audience that when Mary and I first played together on the New York stage, Mary had the part of my very much younger sister. But Mary should not be worried about anyone's counting the years. It will be a good many years before she is as old as I am now: but even then she will still be the image of childhood.

Thus Mr. de Mille's attitude matches Miss Pickford's view of reincarnation: both ascertain the notion that the universe may be casting the stars their parts for eternity. Whatever Mr. de Mille's literal belief, it is unimportant compared with his desire to say what he does say and his sense that what he asserts is desirable. For it is not immortality, but an immortal childhood which he confers upon Miss Pickford. It is possible to identify his sentiment with the mode of being which Keats praises in *Ode on A Grecian Urn*; but it is also possible to see its kinship with the timeless, changeless and deathless existence of human beings in comic strips; his distressing assumption that an immortal childhood is entirely desirable is unquestionable, and there is the implication, which Mr. de Mille naturally disregards, that if America's sweetheart must always be a child who never reaches puberty, then she may also be America's spiritual jailbait or something worse.

Exaggeration: unless one looks at the photographs which throng Miss Pickford's book, this will seem an unjustified interpretation of the extent to which Miss Pickford concentrated upon being the image of a child on the screen and in person. The photographs drawn from Miss Pickford's films show her becoming younger and younger from 1914 to 1922, and some of the photographs drawn from private life intensify this impression by suggesting that Miss Pickford's screen identity was devouring the rest of her being: there is one photograph taken in 1926 of Miss Pickford with her husband Douglas Fairbanks in which the latter looks 23 years of age and his wife looks like his nine-year-old kid sister. The image of America's sweetheart is that of a child before puberty, it is a vivid, visual and physical image of a dear cunning child who is presexual, asexual and even at times unbiological: to judge by the choice of attire this effect can hardly have been wholly unconscious or unwilled: but it was the public, not the star, who was guilty of morbidity of some sort.

The degree to which some powerful sexual undercurrent and identification made Miss Pickford powerful shows itself most clearly in the tendencies which came to the fore when her popularity began to decline in 1922: for example, Miss Pickford's immediate successor was Clara Bow. Clearly the It girl could hardly have supplanted America's sweetheart without the collaboration of many things which go far beyond the compass of Hollywood. Yet at the same time this exhibits Hollywood's sensitivity to national moods and the quickness with which it responds. Hollywood responded to the advent of the flapper and the Jazz Age by making films in which sex became comparatively respectable, and the new vogue was introduced by none other than Cecil de Mille, who remarked at the time that "the ruined woman is as out of style as the Victorian who used to faint." Miss Pickford, bewildered, attempted after a time to gain a new identity, and by playing the part of a flirtatious grown woman to establish a more overt connection with that Id whence, with the help of Elinor Glyn and Freud, Miss Bow's It derived its strength. But Miss Pickford's effort was wholly in vain. She remained as much a captive of her own image upon the screen as she had been when her films were most successful.

It was at the height of her fame that she enjoyed, she says in retrospect, her happiest years as America's sweetheart; she was one of Adolph Zukor's Four Famous Players, and she is certain that the happiness of those years depended upon her relationship with Mr. Zukor. She became, in her own words, one of his three children —the other two were begotten in marriage—and if it was as a father that he supervised her public and private life, it was as a daughter that she obeyed. This is illustrated very well by the occasion when Mr. Zukor, Miss Pickford and her mother journeyed by train to Boston. As they boarded the train, Miss Pickford caught a glimpse of Pearl White in the club car, looking like an empress in a large picture hat, surrounded by admirers, lighting a cigarette and lifting a highball to her lips "in the presence of all those men." "I requested permission to sit in the club car," to which Mr. Zukor answered, "Mary, are you out of your mind?" and then departed for the club car himself.

The peril of Pearl White should indicate what a prolonged and soul-searching ordeal Miss Pickford's desire to divorce her first husband and marry Douglas Fairbanks must have been. It was not only the club car which Miss Pickford had to renounce as America's sweetheart, but also the large sums offered her to lend her name to advertisements of evening gowns and cosmetics; and "with complete sincerity" she solemnly promised newspaper reporters that she would not marry for a year after she secured her divorce. Now, some thirty-five years after, she still feels the necessity of justifying the breach of her promise to the press, which occurred, after much hesitation, as a result of Fairbank's pleading. And she feels, still, some guilt about the divorce itself as her characterization of her first husband shows; and she also feels some consolation in the fact that when she went with her mother and her attorney to Nevada to get the divorce, everyone seemed to think that it was either her mother or her attorney who was getting the divorce: "They never suspected that this creature with the flat-heeled shoes and the blond curls hanging down her back was married." Her pleasure in the visual image can hardly be dismissed; and it involves her blond curls and freedom from the stigma of marriage. A sweetheart is not a wife, nor does she look like one; in most films, romance ends with marriage; hence, a married woman can come no closer to being a real sweetheart than adultery.

Fairbanks and Miss Pickford were warned that "our pictures might be total failures at the box office, that our hard won prestige would be buried under an avalanche of malignant gossip and denunciation," and Miss Pickford felt strongly an obligation to the public "to sustain the special picture which the roles portrayed on the screen built up in the world's eyes." The result was a period of severe tension and anxiety; Miss Pickford was troubled enough to ask Fairbanks if their love could survive the loss of their screen careers. His answer, which is in subtitles like much of the dialogue reported by Miss Pickford, was: "I can't speak for you, Mary, but my feeling for you is not of the moment. It has nothing to do with your career or your fame, or how other people feel about you. I love you for yourself."

Miss Pickford disregards or is unaware that this avowal says nothing of Fairbanks' loss of his own career. As it happened, both careers declined but survived their love. And Miss Pickford's account disregards also the unexpected outcome; after a period of unfortunate publicity, the possibility that Miss Pickford's divorce would be invalidated transformed the newly wedded couple from sinners to victims in the mind of the public.

This very real drama is literally no more intense nor important, in Miss Pickford's account, than the occasion, years after, when she decided to cut the curls to which, she has referred again and again. It was an event comparable only to the cutting of the Gordian knot: Miss Pickford describes the hairdresser as "a pathetic picture of stifled rebellion and indecision" and "as he gripped the shears I had the feeling he needed aromatic spirits of ammonia more than I did. I closed my eyes when he applied the scissors." Elsewhere Miss Pickford has described her feelings before the event as a nightmare in which she believed she would become "almost as Samson after his unfortunate meeting with Delilah." And the consumation itself requires italics: *"it was the first time scissors had ever touched my head!"*

The piety of the hairdresser left six curls intact: "two of these are now in the Museum of San Diego, two in Los Angeles," and Miss Pickford kept two for herself. When she returned home shorn with all six, Douglas Fairbanks turned pale, fell into a chair and cried " 'O no, no, no!' " as great tears came into his eyes. Seeing how upset she herself was, he expressed the hope that it was for the best and was silent as she placed the curls "gently side by side." But soon after "an avalanche of criticism overwhelmed me. You would have thought that I had murdered someone and perhaps I had . . . but it was very sad to be made to feel that my success depended solely or at least in large part, on a head of hair." Yet Miss Pickford did not resent this dependence until her popularity had

[443]

diminished a great deal. She felt misgivings about "how as the years went by and I continued to play child's roles it would worry me that I was becoming a personality instead of an actress. I would suddenly resent the fact that I had allowed myself to be hypnotized by the public into remaining a little girl." But Miss Pickford neither made her irrevocable visit to the hairdresser, nor, save for two instances, attempted any other kind of role until the public was no longer hypnotized. Yet she is right to make as much as she does of her curls, for they were essential to the visual image which made her America's sweetheart.

It is not until her last chapter that Miss Pickford deals directly with the title which identified her, and before describing its origin, she tells of how, on a sleepless night, she made an inventory of all her nicknames and titles, "appalled by their number." The number is large to begin with, and it becomes even larger because the names she was called in private life and the names of the characters she played in films are equally real. Hence it may not be their quantity that is appalling, but their passing: "I wonder whether with the going of each name there had also gone the particular identity." This is a recognition of what is implicit throughout. Miss Pickford's intense feeling that the reality of selfhood was given to her by the parts she played: appearance is the supreme reality and the actuality of the individual merely the nondescript soil out of which it has grown. Miss Pickford was born Gladys Smith—which displeased her even in childhood—and it was David Belasco who bestowed Mary Pickford upon her, a name which, she rejoices to think, has been used by only two others, a great aunt killed by a train in London at the age of seven, and an Eskimo boy, aged three. Among other nicknames, she mentions with pride and pleasure one which is not literally a title or a nickname at all: "Marion Davies always introduces me as 'my illegitimate daughter by Calvin Coolidge,' a title which she first bestowed on me when that blameless gentleman was still in the White House."

Miss Davies may or may not have been thinking of Warren G. Harding. But given Miss Pickford's intense and persistent solicitude about moral propriety in every other connection, and above all her indignation that the newspapers voiced "cowardly and disgusting" suggestions that Miss Pickford had married Fairbanks in haste because a baby, who might be illegitimate, was on the way, her willingness to accept the title of the President's daughter is extraordinary and becoming; the stigma of the bar sinister is clearly annulled by the radiance of the White House: this is the attitude of a queen, and precisely the attitude communicated by King Alfonso of Spain when they met and he inquired about Fatty Arbuckle and on being told of the scandal that had overtaken Arbuckle expressed sympathy and sent regards. It was again with the dignity of a queen that Miss Pickford responded when a Hollywood producer asked her to "relinquish the title of America's sweetheart in favor of a young protegée of his": "I answered that the title was not mine to give, that, in fact, I had never accepted it, but that, such as it was, it had been conferred on me as a gesture of love by an old and honored friend."

The drama of this incident and the perfection of Miss Pickford's reply permit no comment. It should be said, however, that the old friend was not Uncle Sam; it was Pop Grauman who first used the phrase in 1914, on the marquee of a theater, spelled out in electric lights.

Miss Pickford's final paragraph is an overwhelming coda:

> Almost twenty-five years later I was back in Toronto as guest of honor to 800 young World War II aviation cadets. Everything was all right until they began singing "Let Me Call You Sweetheart," . . . It was more than I could bear. Despite my firm resolution and the overgenerous mascara the tears started rolling down my cheeks. . . . I can only say in all humility that it is good to have lived to know that after so many years off the screen these young men, soldiers soon to embark, perhaps on their last voyage, could still pay me the sweetest most gallant compliment of all, to ask to be called their collective sweetheart.

The stills of her most famous films make one certain that Miss Pickford will live forever in the hush, the darkness, and the immortality of her silent pictures, worthy of Keats's words:

> Bold lover, never, never can'st thou
>   kiss,
> Though winning near the goal—yet do
>   not grieve
> She cannot fade, though thou hast not
>   thy bliss,
> Forever wilt thou love and she be fair
> . . . Forever panting and forever young.

[445]

Some Movie Reviews

Henry V (1946)

One thing about Shakespeare as a photoplay, you can hear the speeches better than in most productions. In Laurence Olivier's *Henry V,* the blank verse is spoken very well. But otherwise this production is marked by a host of mixed intentions, a mixture fascinating in itself, but hardly faithful to the play or dedicated to a genuine version or paraphrase. For example, the intention of showing what Elizabethan stage conditions were joins with the effort to show what it may have been like to be seated in an Elizabethan audience. This is good in itself—the self-consciousness and the historical sense of modern literature and art has at last infected the makers of films—but it is not done with any system or, so far as I was able to make out, in relation to any coherent conception of the play. It is natural, then, that the rendering of stage conditions should become slapstick, as when the actor who plays the Archbishop of Canterbury slaps the boy actor for stuffing oranges in his false bosom. And it becomes a kind of period-slumming, for the applause of the Elizabethan audience is often naive, occurring at moments when the modern audience can feel superior and amused.

The sets are also the same kind of mixture. The camera moves back and forth between actual shots of a real countryside and contrived stage-sets vague as fogs and in the prevailing style of Christmas cards and calendar art. There are brilliant moments of straight photography, and the imitation of great art, as when one shot of the battle scene resembles Breughel's "The Road to Calvary." But at other times the background is crude as a vaudeville backdrop or it is just plain Technicolor.

The mixed intentions are most incompatible when the Chorus,

introduced by Shakespeare *precisely because* the stage was inadequate to large-scale events, is illustrated gratuitously by the camera.
This would not matter, were it not for the contrast between the
descriptive power of the poetry and the triteness of the camera's
description. The moral is perhaps that in a Shakespearean film,
one ought not to try to help the best poet in English when he has
chosen and used very well his own method for helping himself.
Furthermore, the illustration as such is inconsistent too, for at
times it attempts to render the Elizabethan production's make-
shift methods and at other times it ranges all over like any true
film.

From beginning to end, the medium of the film is irresistible
to the director. And the medium's triumph becomes thrilling when
the battle scene occurs and looks very much like the climax of a
Western: the cavalry charge of the French becomes an Indian
charge against embattled pioneers, and for a moment Olivier
on his horse bears a clear resemblance to William S. Hart. So too
toward the end the use of closeups, which is very effective, shows
what an overwhelming power the medium of the film exerts upon
the imagination of anyone who makes a film, however great the
interest in Shakespeare and the Elizabethan period. Once this tendency is noted, the most interesting aspect of the film is the struggle
between Shakespeare's play and the medium of the screen. Sometimes Shakespearean passages are so profound that the film as such
is disregarded, but sometimes the great set-pieces of movie-making
—the firing of artillery (like the classic newsreel shot of a dread-
naught's salvoes) or the movement of large bodies of men and animals (like covered wagons lumbering on file toward the horizon)
—transform Shakespeare into something which has nothing to do
with his play; into passages which are digressions, however good,
instead of extensions of the text. Yet the camera and the text collaborate very well in one important scene, the scene in which the
king moves anonymously among his men on the night before
Agincourt, listening to their emotions about the war and arguing
with them about his responsibility for their lives and deaths. Here
the camera, by submitting itself to the drama, performs like the
accompanist of a great singer, and achieves more through the close-
up than would have been possible on the stage.

For the most part, however, the conflicts between the nature of the text and the nature of the medium are such that the review in *Time* is difficult to understand. *Time's* review was full of remarkable perceptions but also full of an exalted over-estimation, as if the reviewer had just discovered Shakespeare, or found out that he was as good as he was supposed to be. How can it be said that the entire conception of the film is anti-naturalistic when the camera, more naturalistic than any other medium, attempts literal exactitude so often? Moreover, the very effort to represent Elizabethan stage conditions is a form of naturalism.

Certainly this production does much to clarify the problems of translating Shakespeare to the screen. I should guess that one rich possibility might be cartoons in black-and-white, where attention would be fixed upon the dramatic poetry as such and a true anti-naturalism would be the starting-point. The underlying attitudes of the producers are also worth guessing about. Made during the war, the film displays a pride and love of England and the English countryside (although the actual countryside filmed by the camera is Ireland!), and the exultant patriotism of the invasion of France suggests D-Day more than Agincourt. But above all, the pride and love in the possession of Shakespeare ought to induce reflections about the fate of prestige in our society, for Shakespeare is not really a money-maker at present, but many people think well of him.

Animal Farm (1955)

It is a serious pity that one can only praise the film version of George Orwell's *Animal Farm* as a valuable beginning or experiment, and hardly more than that. For the project, under the sponsorship of Louis de Rochemont, was clearly given the benefit of a great deal of intelligence, devotion and skill, to say almost nothing of the amount of money involved. The reviews in the daily newspaper have already pronounced the damnation of faint praise upon the film with a genuine kindness which will serve no purpose and certainly will not help at the box office. One can only hope that Mr. de Rochemont, and others of like mind and intention, will not draw premature and discouraging conclusions on the basis of one effort. For despite Disney, the medium of the animated film is largely a *terra incognita* in which an enormous number of possibilities wait to be discovered, unearthed or invented. The heights and depths of these possibilities will be recognized as soon as one remembers the rich actuality of the literary masterpieces which virtually plead for the vivid translation of visual animation. Everyone will think of *Gulliver's Travels*; but there is a great deal else, beginning with the inexhaustible El Dorado of the great folklores and mythologies and concluding with certain of Kafka's best stories and some of the most inspired passages in *Finnegan's Wake*. There is also the more distant and difficult possibility, which the makers of the film of *Animal Farm* have previously attempted, of using the animated film for visual versions of some kinds of lyric poetry; the most valuable augmentation, interpretation and orchestration seems possible, a veritable new dimension in which the folk ballad becomes a little opera.

The animated film of *Animal Farm*, considered in itself and apart from its close connection with Orwell's text, mostly lacks that characteristic verve and *brio* which is the most enchanting immediate quality of film cartoons at their best. The resources of style and stylization which Disney drew upon in his best films—in the *Silly Symphonies* perhaps most of all—are present in the film of *Animal Farm* only briefly and erratically in a few passages.

The essential dynamism of the animated film (which apparently requires, of necessity, the framework and support of a musical score) has its source in the ancient supernaturalism or magic realism which is at the heart of all poetry: metaphor and metamorphosis, metaphor and miracle, transition as transformation, incident as epiphany, action as advent must continually occur and emerge as if the universe were being created anew, a fact which may have made Disney attempt to depict the first morning of the world in one of his most ambitious, unfortunate undertakings. In Disney, as in all masters of the film cartoon, a locomotive lunches on railroad tracks like celery, a dog's ears revolve like electric fans, automobiles waltz, tango and do the Charleston, pigs play the piano, roosters chant Wagner, dogs skate on ice rinks, trees applaud and boo, curtsey and snicker. However this be formulated, as metaphor, miracle or Ovidean metamorphosis, the crucial process, which the medium itself demands, is the delightful, triumphant transcendence of the laws of nature and the probabilities of experience; the film cartoon must be a supernatural ballet. Yet there is only one moment in *Animal Farm* when anything of the sort occurs, the point, towards the end, at which the faces of the pig dictators who have betrayed the revolution on the farm fade into the visage of the drunken and brutal farmer. But this effect is trite in itself, rendered with timidity, and so unlike the prevailing idiom of the entire film that it is at once ineffective and gratuitous.

Some sense of what may have gone wrong suggests itself when one returns to Orwell's text, which is used abundantly as a verbal accompaniment and followed with an unnecessary literal fidelity. Orwell's fable is the penultimate expression of a complex social and moral pilgrimage, the kind of journey which few human beings and fewer writers have either the courage or the opportunity to make. The dry tone and spare style of Orwell's text is implicit with the disillusion and heartbroken disappointment of a desperately honest human being who had lived to see the greatest and best social hope of human beings converted into a cynical despotism which equalled that of Fascism, or perhaps exceeded it, in the very real sense that its leaders and supporters were for the most part not gangsters and careerists, but dedicated martyred heroes and millions of men of good will. *Animal Farm* was written with a sense of ultimate disappointment in the historical process as such, and perhaps also a hopelessness about the gullibility of human beings as an organized political mass. Orwell's state of mind was as painful as it was rare, being the product of sophistication, innocence, hope and suffering combined. Little of this sense of things gets into the animation of *Animal Farm*, despite the abundant quotation from the text. What is characteristic and, in a way, effective is the episode when the faithful, hardworking horse, Boxer, collapses and is shipped with pure callousness to the glue factory. But this has the quality of an instance of cruelty to animals, not a betrayal of a social ideal or political injustice. It is true that heretofore the animated film has for the most part avoided direct social satire and devoted itself to pure comedy, and most of all to the purely poetic comedy of which Disney is the most eminent master. But political cartoons show—and the example of *Gulliver's Travels* suggests—how the methods and resources of the animated medium are naturally satirical.

[450]

It is hard to be sure what a person unacquainted with Orwell's little book or ignorant of the history of the Soviet Union would make of the images of the film. For one thing, the boars and pigs who become the totalitarian tyrants of the animal politburo resemble, at times, British politicians of the past generation—Ernest Bevin most of all; although at one point there is a gleam of resemblance to Churchill's plump baby face, there is, on the other hand, no suggestion of Stalin, Molotov, or Malenkov. This strange impression is increased by speeches uttered in a strong British accent and it is intensified by parliamentary mannerisms and procedures. Although the effect occurs only in passing, it is but one among many aspects of the film which tend to make one think that to a Rip Van Winkle or a Martian man the film might seem to be an attack on the British Labour Party or a parable of the vanity and foolishness of all political and social reform.

Purely as a matter of method, there is certainly too much of a reliance upon literal transposition and Orwell's text just as there is certainly too little effort to respond to the animated strip as a playground for the visual imagination. Whatever doubts one might have about this judgment disappear when one reads the description of how the film was produced in *The Animated Film*, by Roger Manvell, who reports that the makers of the film "before they began their work, had to prepare themselves to recreate the life of an English farm . . ." and hence "they had spent much time on farms observing animal movement and behavior." That this is misplaced conscientiousness is a fact disregarded by Mr. Manvell, although when he comes to speak of the entire medium, he says:

> . . . the master of the animated film is complete master of the way in which he presents his artificial world to the audience . . . he can reproduce actuality with [a] final degree of representationalism. But he would be ill-advised to do so. Representationalism is better left to the action film, to which it belongs by nature.

It is unfortunate that this principle has so little influence upon the making of the film. But on the other hand, it is quite foolish to forget how difficult, under any circumstances, it would have been to be adequate to the parable of an author who wrote with the feeling that he no longer wanted nor had any reason to live.

To Catch a Thief (1955)

To Catch A Thief is supposed to be a mystery having to do with the exertions Cary Grant must make as a famous jewel thief who has retired and is unjustly suspected of having resumed his vocation. The real mystery is how the product of Hitchcock's direction, given such care, toil and intelligence, could be so poor. Jessie Royce Landis gives a remarkable performance as the heroine's mother, and Danielle Lamar is more than remarkable, when the script permits her to be. As the incomparably sophisticated teen age rival of Grace Kelly for Cary Grant's heart, Miss Lamar delivers several remarks with a leer which suggests Mona Lisa elucidating Freud's theory of her enigmatic smile to Krafft-Ebing. In fact, all the actors are excellent, except Cary Grant. He wears a pained grin almost throughout the film and the sneakers or tennis shoes he wears are the only remnant of his usual aplomb. For although he is being pursued by Miss Kelly, Miss Lamar, the police and a set of hardened criminals he seems to be disturbed by something else, it is impossible to say just what, unless the clue is buried in the moment when he steps into a bus and finds himself seated next to Hitchcock himself (the director resembles, in this new version of his Old Master signature, both Humpty Dumpty and Buddha), and looks at him in a most peculiar way which, since it may mean anything, may very well mean: let's go back to America, get a new script and start all over again.

These remarks are misleading if they suggest that the film is anything but a dud. Nevertheless it is a significant dud, and Grace Kelly's role has the virtue of making clearer the quality which excited so much attention in previous roles—her sexual allure; and this in turn has a significance in relation to Hitchcock's career in America.

Miss Kelly's screen image is that of purity, chastity and modesty. She looks "aristocratic," which is of course not an American word and perhaps for that reason an American obsession. And it is not too much to suppose that one of the flashes of Hitchcock's original genius in *To Catch a Thief* is the contrast between her aristocratic look and her actual status as *noveau riche*, a contrast which Jessie Royce Landis as her mother continually makes explicit. The image of "class" is sustained just long enough to give the maximum effect to that moment when Miss Kelly suddenly, abruptly and yet with naturalness and a sly, faint smile takes the sexual initiative and keeps it without in the least diminishing the impression of lady-like respectability.

It was remarked that in *Mogambo* Miss Kelly had restored the wife as a sexual being, and her performance as a meek housewife in that film certainly left Ava Gardner looking quite old-fashioned and uninteresting. But this, like most of the expressions of admiration excited by Miss Kelly, is inadequate because it suggests that the cause of the excitement is merely her image upon the screen. The image is necessary, of course, but it would be ineffective without the most supple powers of an actress, the extreme imagination and intelligence which an absolute mastery of the illusion of spontaneity requires.

There is a good deal more to say, since Miss Kelly has a particular and fabulous significance which is not limited to the screen but illuminates the suburbs and thus American life in general; but here I must restrict myself to the bearing which her emergence as a star has upon Hitchcock's career as a director in relation to Hollywood. At one point in *To Catch A Thief* Miss Kelly tells Cary Grant that his impersonation of an American is wholly unconvincing; he is, she says, as bogus as the Americans encountered in British mystery films. This remark, unimportant in itself, is hilarious and sad when related to Hitchcock as the director of the film and the director of such masterpieces among British mystery films as *The Thirty-Nine Steps* and *The Lady Vanishes*. Hitchcock obviously knows that something is wrong and has been wrong since he came to America some 15 years ago. His awareness was evident in his remark last spring that the trouble with film melodrama at present is that all the spies have to be Communists. Some of his American films have certainly been good enough and most of them have been marked to one or another degree by the originality of his style. But he has never come closer than self-imitation to the sustained brilliance and invention to his best English films, which not only made him famous but have exercised an overwhelming influence upon the making of English films in general. Like a great realistic novelist, Hitchcock depended upon a milieu which he knew with the utmost intimacy. But this explanation can hardly be the whole story, for then it would only be necessary for Hitchcock to make films with an English background in America, as, in fact, he did, in *Rebecca*. Too many other gifted directors and actors have lost their magic or dissipated it in Hollywood.

To say that Hollywood is responsible for anyone's partial failure would be a far too familiar accusation and one which resembles the tendency to attribute the outbreak of a particular war to the sinfulness of human nature. But in *To Catch A Thief*, Grace Kelly's performance, and that of Jessie Royce Landis as well, provides concrete evidence of the ways in which Hollywood may be guilty and Hitchcock innocent. For just as Colette was responsible for Audrey Hepburn's start, so Hitchcock either discovered Grace Kelly or directed her far better than anyone else has. The emergence of both new stars, both genuine actresses, is a triumph of personality which would not have occurred if Hollywood's conception of what the public wants always prevailed, as it certainly does most of the time.

The real trouble is that Hollywood thinks that it knows what the public wants, which is inseparable from the view that you can fool all the people all the time and if you don't, the reason is that you yourself are a fool. This view is also implicit in the practice of the Svengalis of Madison Avenue, but they at least have the excuse, peculiar though it is, that they must persuade the public that it wants and needs what it neither needs nor wants, or something far more difficult, that one shaving cream is better than another, which is a falsehood.

Hollywood, by contrast, exists in relation to a genuine need of the public which it attempts to gratify by mere repetition or mere novelty. A successful film is imitated until it is an unbearable stereotype. And the slow panic caused by the competition of TV leads to one novelty after another. First the mechanical exploitation of depth made the public slightly cockeyed while the size of the screen grew until no further increase could occur without razing most of the motion picture houses in America. The latest bid for popularity is what may be termed tourism, as if the real rival were not TV, but the inexpensive cost of a subscription to the *National Geographic Magazine*.

The implications of Miss Kelley's success are various. But at least one implication is that Hollywood's surprise at her success shows that it does not know what the public wants. And Hitchcock very well *may* know. And now that Stephen, the Metro-Goldwyn-Mayer lion, has just died in Dublin, perhaps his roar, *ars gratia artis*, ought to be reinterpreted. The phrase means, as every Latinist knows. Art for the sake of the Almighty Dollar, or *vox populi* box office. But perhaps it also means that when you judge all things by the gate, you bore others as you bore yourself. What the public may want (and what Hitchcock can give) is vividness and vitality of personality, genuineness of experience, a renewal of the excitement of curiosity and wonder.

The Court Jester (1956)

As everyone knows, or ought to know, Danny Kaye is wonderfully funny, given any chance at all. But he only has a chance now and then in *The Court Jester*. This time Danny goes all the way back to medieval England, taking the American Legion Zouaves of Detroit, Michigan, along with him. Neither the Detroit Zouaves nor medieval England interfere much because wherever Danny is is Brooklyn, and he is far more at home in merry old England than Sir Lancelot or Sir Galahad would ever have been at Ebbets Field. Nevertheless Danny is wasted and the film is very poor, perhaps precisely because it has practically everything in it, all mixed up, and perhaps also because it cost four million dollars and is, therefore, the most expensive comedy ever produced.

Danny himself declares at one point, "Plot we've got a lot," and a lot of other things which Danny names, including Danny's split personality, knights in armor and beautiful heroines at a Royal court; a king who has usurped the British throne and an amiable infant who is the rightful heir and bears a purple pimpernel "on his royal backside" as proof of his authentic claims; a princess who thinks that Danny is the cat's pajamas; a noble rebel leading a noble rebellion to regain the throne; a tricky witch who practices hypnotism among her other charms and powers; several concurrent conspiracies which run parallel to one another; Basil Rathbone's best British accent and villainy and most contemptuous sneer; and lyrics in which Danny sings of himself as "the maladjusted jester" while rhyming "derring-do" with "herring too." Hardly anything is left out, and very little is included which deserves the slightest attention.

It must require a good deal of calculated and misguided effort to make so little use of genuine comic genius. Danny would be funny anywhere at any time—on top of the Parthenon, under a pyramid, in the Academie Française or in an academy for the deaf and dumb; he is capable of transforming a funeral into a colossal joke. But even his comic genius fails to overcome, save for a few moments, the plentitude of embarrassed riches which confront him in *The Court Jester*.

Just as Chaplin is first of all the comedian of shyness and meek, shabby aspiration, so Danny always starts out as the comedian of pure nervousness, expecting the worst at all times and not at all surprised that it is even worse than he expected and feared. The plot of *The Court Jester* provides Danny with more than enough occasions for nervousness, but deprives him of them so quickly that he has no time to make the most of them. Thus when he goes through the rites and trials which initiate him into knighthood, the speed increases continually, until when he is dubbed a knight so that he can be killed in a knightly tournament by one of his enemies, his pants begin to fall down because his entire being from the knees up is shaken by mounting terror. But before his pants fall down, the plot rushes ahead at full speed, into the mortal combat itself, where again, every time he gets nervous enough to be truly himself, the story goes serious on him, and he emerges unscathed and lost as a comedian. The succession of his knightly victories comes so quickly that Danny has no time to be thunderstruck—one of his favorite emotions and second only to the gaping, open-mouthed, bug-eyed face with which he responds to appalling danger.

Although one can hardly escape the impression that Danny himself sometimes feels he needs the plot of *The Court Jester* like he needs a hole in the head, one possibility, and a truly new one, is opened up but not developed very much by the episodes in which the witch's spells and charms transform Danny from the nervous wreck which is his innermost self into the most dauntless of heroes, the most daring young man of all time. In one episode, he does, in fact, swing on a kind of trapeze above the castle, the cliff and the sea, and as long as the hypnotic spell lasts, he has the matchless courage of a chain-smoker of marijuana cigarettes. The spell which makes him an absolutely nonchalant hero can be broken off in the split-second by anyone snapping his fingers, but however often and quickly broken, it is equally restored by another snapping of the fingers.

The result is that Danny commutes, as in a taxi or a roller coaster, between pure nervousness and fearless aplomb, a comic possibility which has the promise of that great silent film in which Buster Keaton, expressionless from the first reel to the last, was the railroad engineer on an empty train which continually crossed the Mason-Dixon line during the Civil War and had to change from an Abolitionist to a Secessionist at a moment's notice again and again. But this opportunity is slighted and passed over, as are the characteristic moments of the old Kaye style: perhaps the best instance is Danny's courtship of his true love during which he admires the beauty of her face and hears her remark, as his glance lights upon her teeth, that "My father made me everything I am." "Your father does beautiful work," Danny says in adoration, but he is whisked back in so much haste to the era when knighthood, and not dentistry, was in flower that the quality of the remark is almost unnoticed.

It may very well be that *The Court Jester* has so much of everything—and so little as well—because of Hollywood's desire, which is more intense than it has ever been, to please everyone by providing everything, no matter what the disorder and weakening of the entire effect. There is a clear desire in the film to please the small shots of the kindergarten set far more than the adolescents who have come to neck in the darkness of the balcony and who were supposed to be a major part of the film audience, the age group to which, for the past 10 years, Hollywood has decided to direct its efforts. The theatre was certainly full of young children when I saw the film, and they all seemed to be gurgling with pleasure. But this is the way they always seem at all the pictures: they are always delighted by everything on the screen. The adults were far less amused, but perhaps they are not important, if the children can drag them to the theatre. Apart from the children or others who are always pleased, it just goes to show that the more you try to please everyone, the less you are likely to please anyone very much, which is something we have known all along, for all the good it does us.

MARILYN MONROE AND *The Seven Year Itch* (1955)

The film version of *The Seven Year Itch*, George Axelrod's Broadway hit, has carried over enough of the play's sophisticated brightness to indicate the reasons for the play's success: the perfect fulfillment of the well-known Broadway genre of gag, gag, punch-line, epigram, and paradox, crackling like machine-gun fire for three acts until everyone is exhausted, and everything but the next wisecrack is unreal. Certainly some very funny things get said, as when a vegetarian waitress in an offhand way presents the first serious argument for nudism: pacifism. The soldiers, lacking uniforms, will be unable to tell friend from foe, so they won't be able to kill anyone: the result of their confusion will be universal peace.

Despite the script's cleverness, the presence of Tom Ewell, who is a first rate comedian and Oscar Homolka, who has long been a first rate actor, the entire film continually misses fire and fizzles out, like defective fireworks. And the chief reason, doubtless, is Marilyn Monroe's radiant presence. She is as out of place in a sophisticated comedy as she would be in a Tibetan lamasery, or, to be more exact, in a nunnery. She has been profoundly miscast in a Dumb Dora-Gracie Allen role and in relation to Tom Ewell as a Caspar Milquetoast-Walter Mitty character, both roles being foils for that classic situation of American farce: my wife's gone to the country, hurray.

Miss Monroe is neither a Dumb Dora nor a sophisticated come-dienne: neither intelligence nor stupidity have anything to do with her radiant, self-delighting image, which in this film is a distraction so immense that it becomes the chief interest, the kind of thing one would expect to happen had W. C. Fields played in *The Importance of Being Earnest* or a Restoration comedy. Nevertheless other film critics were wrong, I think, to question Miss Monroe's gifts as an actress when they described the failure of the film. To say that Miss Monroe is at fault is a colossal piece of irrelevance, one comparable to that of the little girl in Carl Sandburg's poem who, when she saw the midsummer moon arise, wanted to know what it was supposed to advertise.

Miss Monroe, like the true Hollywood beauties of old who preceded her as daughters of Venus, is a national phenomenon, like Buffalo Bill, the Mack Sennett bathing beauty, cross-word puzzles, Coca-Cola, Babe Ruth, and chewing gum. She can be understood only from one point of view, that of beauty, which is its own excuse for being, a truth which, as Emerson was but one among the first to recognize, must be pointed out to the American public time and again. Nothing that Miss Monroe says in any role can be quite as meaningful as the ways in which she sways: her poise and carriage have a true innocence: have a spontaneity, an un-selfconsciousness which are the extreme antithesis to the calculated sex of the strip tease and other forms of the propagation of prurience.

As an image and symbol, Miss Monroe represents an advance— or a regress, depending upon one's point of view—but in any case something new and different from her predecessors as screen sirens and queens. Most of them made sexual attractiveness quite as exciting as Miss Monroe does, but scarcely ever without making sexual beauty inseparable from evil, ruin, destruction, and all the stigmas imposed by Puritanism: the screen siren was a deadly vamp like Theda Bara, a honky-tonk Medusa like Marlene Dietrich, an unattainable Valkyrie who suggested Nirvana with a Swedish accent like Garbo, or a platinum blonde who suggested, like Jean Harlow, the blank and fatal beauty of an iceberg: but whatever her incarnation, she united love and death, beauty and evil, passion and demoralization as cause and effect.

Miss Monroe, however, is either beyond good and evil or prior to it. Sex is naughty, in a way, but very nice; it is naughty only as eating candy between meals might be, or getting a tan on the beach: it's not going to kill anyone, wreck a man's life, cause Anthony to lose the Roman Empire, inspire Nelson to win the Battle of Trafalgar; nor will it either precipitate or prevent another world war. Miss Monroe's attitude toward herself precludes such unnecessary overcomplications: she likes herself, she likes her body, she likes men, and she is having a wonderful time.

To speak thus of Miss Monroe as an image and a symbol and a

[459]

"sign of the times" is to risk seeming pompous, or jocose. The literal seriousness of the point can be made clear by citing two very different witnesses: women's clubs all over the nation protested when, two years ago, Miss Monroe appeared in *Niagara*, a film in which the Falls seemed less of a natural force than Miss Monroe; and in the preface to a recent pocketbook of photographs from the film production itself, George Axelrod, enchanted enough to disregard the disappearance of his comedy, says "Marilyn Monroe doesn't just play The Girl, She *is* The Girl." But clearly the whole truth belongs to the future and future social historians: the most one can say now is that Puritanism is no longer alive enough to inspire defiance; and the new attitude which Miss Monroe embodies with such natural and joyous ebullience first began to emerge in the lyric which Celeste Holm sang in *Oklahoma* in which she expressed much mock-distress at being just a girl who can't say no.

As the film of *The Seven Year Itch* shows, it would be wholly wrong to suppose that it does not matter what roles Miss Monroe plays, a comment which is prompted by Miss Monroe's interest in the heroines of Dostoevsky, an author who has suddenly become the object of mortal blows from all directions, including Jimmy Durante who announces in *Reader's Digest* that he can do without Dostoevsky but not without *Reader's Digest*. There are many other roles for which Miss Monroe is a natural: the one principle to be kept in mind is that, as long as the moonlight of Hollywood shines from coast to coast, it is just as important to be a star as to be an actress, provided that one is not a mixture or compromise but is, like Miss Monroe, a genuine star and nothing else. Among the plenitude of parts awaiting Miss Monroe are, for example, Venus in the drama of the judgment of Paris, Pocahontas, all the girls Ziegfeld wanted to glorify, and all the Miss Americas from 1920 to 1950 on the boardwalk or the beach at Atlantic City. Neurotic; unhappy-making roles, such as Grushenka, Hedda Gabler, Elizabeth Barrett Browning, and Iris March, ought to be left to actresses more divided in mind and heart, less wholesome, and less blessed with a pure physical confidence and a beautiful innocence of heart.

The subject is one I feel so strongly about (it is a great deal less important than a great many things that are wrongly supposed to be a great deal more important) that I have been inspired to conceive of two proper scenarios: in one Miss Monroe plays Lady Godiva: this is a slightly new version, for Lady Godiva's underlying motive is to impress her horse, who has shown himself insensitive to her charms; but better by far is a version of the drama of Original Sin free of all morbidity: Miss Monroe plays Eve, the serpent (Raymond Massey) comes along with the apple, which is turned down by Miss Monroe as Eve who declares that she is getting along fine with Adam, is happily married, and needs no fruit; and then either the serpent is sent away like an obstreperous salesman or Eve uses all of her female wiles to seduce the serpent into eating the apple himself, thus eliminating Satan, purging the universe of evil, and bringing about the most overwhelming, total, and conclusive of all the happy endings Hollywood has ever filmed. A part like this would reveal how Miss Monroe differs from all other actresses. However pure and virginal they are as ingenue heroines, they seem to have by contrast an irreducible, inescapable resemblance to Mata-Hari and her Philistine forebear, Delilah.

Underwater! AND *The Blackboard Jungle* (1955)

In *Underwater!*, Howard Hughes' cheesecake opera, a priest goes along with Jane Russell, the Cuban wife of Richard Egan, and with Gilbert Roland, his chum, to search for sunken treasure, the gold bullion worth millions which has been submerged in a Spanish galleon off the Cuban coast for three hundred years. The plot concentrates with a single-minded intensity which is ingenious and disingenuous on getting Miss Russell into the water as often as possible. It succeeds so well that she is totally immersed in the depths of the Caribbean for more than a third of the film. Miss Russell wears a Bikini, bears an oxygen tank upon her back, and her face is covered by the top part of her aqualung.

Yet her glamor and beauty are not diminished in the least, but rather heightened by the dignity of her silence as she cruises and glides about, larger than life on the Superscope screen, a singular performance which must be unique among the feats of the actresses

[461]

of all time. For neither Bernhardt nor Duse can ever have been silent and masked for so long a period in a starring role. This extraordinary tribute to the female torso is so vivid and sleek—it possesses in its stripped classic purity so much that suggests the birth of Venus or a Billy Rose Aquacade—that when Miss Russell returns to the surface, the magnificence of reality suffers. Since she is supposed to be Cuban, she begins sentences with a Spanish accent which she often abandons in mid-sentence, so that it is perhaps only courtly gallantry which makes Gilbert Roland begin sentences with an American accent and reverse the contrapuntal bilinguality. And there is a further originality in the fact that Miss Russell plays a wife with a warm and affectionate nature, but her crass husband rebuffs her advances because he cares only for the bullion at the bottom of the sea, which make for an indifference to Miss Russell's charms on the part of the male sex which is without parallel and beyond credulity until one grasps the underlying spiritual message of the film.

This message eluded me until I read another critic's comment: "The underwater photography is exciting and even exalting in a strange, other-worldly way." This immediately made everything clear and profound, including the benediction which the priest pronounces at the start of the expedition and the otherwise baffling conclusion. It is at the conclusion that Richard Egan throws all the gold ingots overboard, after toiling and risking his life for six reels to salvage them, declaring that principle is more important than gold. Since the production cost more than three million dollars, something must be more important than gold: cheesecake itself has never been that expensive.

Mr. Egan's squirming annoyance whenever Miss Russell wants to cuddle prepares the way for his final renunciation of all the precious lucre; his motive is not the mercenary obsession it seems but a spiritual vocation, like the quest of the Grail, and sets an edifying example for all who might forget that to look at a woman with adultery in one's heart is to commit that sin, and hardly condoned by sustained provocation in technicolor. So too, in an exalting other-worldly light, Miss Russell clearly becomes a symbol of the pieces which passes understanding except under water. And finally it is superficial and cynical to interpret the priest's presence as an effort to protect the film from the carnal meaning the coarse might impute to it. No reason whatever is given for his participation in the expedition, but this is a delicate parable of the degree to which faith is beyond reason.

One may very well know less about juvenile delinquency after seeing *The Blackboard Jungle* than ever before. The systematic confusion of the film as of the novel on which it is based is likely to increase the misunderstanding of a serious and complex problem, just as it forces one to observations which are outside the film.

The film itself concerns the experience of Glenn Ford as an innocent and high-minded prig who has begun to teach at a vocational school in a big city. He is immediately insulted and assaulted by his students and told by the other teachers that he had better concentrate upon policing the barbarians and forget his exalted conception of education.

Governed by an attitude of self-righteousness which he and all the other teachers never recognize as such, he misunderstands whatever occurs as he gropes about for some reason to explain the fact that adolescent schoolboys are terrifying gangsters. Thus after he has rescued a pretty young teacher from rape by a student, she attempts to seduce him, and he is merely baffled when she explains her eagerness as caused by the boredom of teaching. And the self-righteousness which helps him to resist temptation prevents him from seeing that her boredom has a significance which has nothing to do with his desire to be faithful to his pregnant wife. When one of his pupils asks him: "Did you ever try to fight thirty-five guys, Teach?", the question of personal courage obstructs the real problem of schools and classes so crowded that no teacher, no matter how gifted, could accomplish very much. He regards the passive resignation of older teachers as cynical cowardice. The fact that one teacher has gained the tolerance of his students by telling them of how he won the Purple Heart seems to him the evasion of a braggart, trading on his laurels. And finally his indignation about the low salaries which teachers are paid is equally distorted by self-righteous pride as wrong merely because plumbers, carpenters and "even household cooks" make more money.

[463]

In each of these and other like instances he stumbles upon and fails to recognize the chain reaction which causes juvenile delinquency and the outbreak of terror in the classroom. A bored teacher is boring. A discouraged teacher has too little self-esteem to win the esteem of students. A teacher who feels that his job marks him as a failure or a mediocrity in what is not only a competitive society but also a competitive educational system suffers from a self-contempt which makes him the object of contempt, particularly when he has to maintain order in an over-crowded class; and when he is forced to resort to external authority, he becomes an object of hatred, and the chain reaction is complete.

For although there is almost always a prior and primary breakdown of authority in the family itself, there is also an intense expectation very often that the school and the teacher, like the world itself, will be superior to the parent and the family. This expectation is bound to be severely disappointed whenever a teacher has to resort to some form of coercion or tyranny, whether because of personal reasons, classroom conditions or both, combined with an institutional decline in morale. Authority is bound to be hated unless it is loved, particularly in adolescence; and the natural inclination of the adolescent to identify prestige with power, strength, poise, confidence and self-mastery is such that the gangster becomes the most available image of the heroic and masculine ideal, and the cruelty which authority exercises to maintain itself in the family or school seems to be the only genuine kind of power worthy of admiration.

The Blackboard Jungle, like most films with a social purpose, problem plays, and novels with a thesis, requires a didactic comment and hardly merits any other kind. As an effort to deal with a social issue, it is a film with a problem in search of a thesis which it never discovers, and hence the temptation to provide one is irresistible. The one I have suggested is an unavoidable oversimplification, although based on long experience as a schoolboy in the New York public school system and even more upon the experience of a teacher of freshmen, fresh co-eds, and students fresh from the Pacific, during the war, in the Navy V-12 program. And the oversimplification is more than that; it is quite false, if it seems to single out the teacher as the primary root of what is wrong. But the teacher and the school can be strengthened far sooner than family life can be modified or the social order improved.

The sole cause of juvenile delinquency has been said to be democracy, liberalism, mass culture, universal education, industrialism, agnosticism, human nature, psychoanalysis and the New Deal. When none of these frees the adult of responsibility, the children are blamed. This is precisely the same as saying that marriage is the chief cause of divorce, just as the belief that comic books are the chief cause of teen-age crime resembles nothing so much as the assertion that Proust was the cause of the fall of France.

Films and TV (1955)

Among the motion pictures presented during recent weeks on television—presented, moreover, on TV and nowhere else—were *Open City, Stagecoach, The Private Life of Henry VIII, The Blue Angel, Beauty and the Beast,* and *Our Town.* All these films are not only excellent to some degree, but they are superior to any of the new films. And if the list were comprehensive, not special and small, an adequate summary of what TV provides now with casual largesse would show clearly that the owner of a TV set has the greatest of all cathedrals of the motion picture right in his own living room. Thus the immense collection of films made during the past forty years has scarcely been touched.

Most films are headed sooner or later for the TV plate. And it would be clear that a spectre is haunting Hollywood without any evidence drawn from films shown on TV: the continual widening of the screen is sufficient in itself to show how troubled and helpless Hollywood is. It is, in fact, in a state which can only be called *acutely* transitional. This is also true of TV as a whole and of the entire entertainment industry since the new medium may dominate or devour all the older forms. But less obvious, I think, and just as important, or more important, is the fact that the filmgoer himself is in a state of profound flux.

The beginning of the revolution can be marked with more ease in the making of films than in the filmgoer's experience. Thus, the tendency of actors to commute between Hollywood and the

TV studios increases for the perfectly good reason that TV pays well, as Ray Milland, one of the most successful commuters, freely avowed; and TV's enormous audience is bound to make it the final arbiter of a film's financial success, gradually or rapidly modifying the way in which films are made.

The experience of the filmgoer—the viewer of TV, to use the awkward and somehow unsavory name coined for him—is, as direct inspection for a short period will demonstrate, subject to a profound and continual change about which, so far as I know, almost nothing has been said. As the viewer moves back and forth between the TV plate and the motion picture screen, the screen continually becomes larger, whether or not its actual physical size has once more been increased.

The TV plate may become larger than the present span of seventeen, twenty-one or twenty-four inches. Its limit is probably the dimensions of the living room wall, but even if this unlikely growth should occur, the TV plate as a visual area will remain smaller than that of the screen and the stage also. Yet it will also remain the primary visual norm and hence exercise a profound influence and result in many unpredictable effects. But one fairly probable effect is that the visual area of the TV plate will be the frequent visual medium within which the director, the scenario writer and thus the actors tend to operate.

One possibility, to judge by the unreliable and ambiguous evidence of all forms of TV—the TV drama, variety show, and spectacular as well as the film made solely for TV presentation—is a fatal blow to the magnetism of the screen star. The evidence for this eventuality is too fragmentary and too dubious to be set down in detail: one can say that the Hollywood stars in TV shows do lose much of their radiance and the true TV star does not appear in TV films or dramas but only, like Liberace, in comparative isolation, or like Sid Caesar in complete domination of his own company which is natural enough in a variety show but may be unnaturally difficult otherwise. This may be due, however, not to the TV plate as a medium of acting, but to the fabulous cost of TV time and production combined with the popularity of the variety comedian. Whatever the fate of the screen star may be in future films which will at the very least appear on TV as well as on the screen, it is certainly hard to doubt that the close up and the aural powers of the actor will come to possess a new or renewed importance, and the chief reason is again the comparative smallness of the visual area of the TV plate.

This is merely one illustration of any number of possibilities, but most of them can hardly be described with any greater degree of concreteness, save perhaps by someone close rather than distant from the production of films. But what is perhaps the most important change in the attitudes and expectations of the filmgoer and viewer of films on TV is a complex, but unquestionable fact. It has been the object of very little serious attention, so far as I can make out, and yet it seems the most radical of all modifications and the most difficult to evaluate. The filmgoer who now views films as often or more often on TV loses what must be called, for lack of a better phrase, that portion of his "escape from freedom" which he found when he saw a motion picture on the screen. Once the filmgoer made his choice of a film, if, in fact, choice and not habit governed him, he was done with the anxiety of choice for the length of the picture show: and the double feature was but one attraction which made the motion picture theatre resemble a luxury liner, a rest cure and a pipe dream. But as a viewer the escape from the continual daily pressure of freedom and choice not only has been annulled, but the alternatives of choice have increased. The result is that one may look at the same film on the screen as on the TV plate and yet have two experiences which differ because the viewer is continuously aware that he possesses the choice of other brave new worlds and can reach them by extending his hand and turning the dial.

If you think only of TV, the change may not seem as radical as it is, particularly since there are so many attractions on TV other than motion pictures; one has only to think of such proven favorites as Congressional investigating committees and the major league pennant races. And besides, the experience of TV is at once so new and so various that, apart from the children, a set of primary expectations has not taken any abiding form and when it does it may be as free and fluid as that of the circus. But this is not true of watching a motion picture on TV—or for that matter a baseball game—and when one concentrates on the screen as the

[467]

only medium of motion pictures, one gets a fresh sense of the entire constellation of conditions which supported the escape from freedom of choice, and the hypnotic spell of the screen. The darkness and the omission of intermissions both may seem—as in fact they probably were at first, technical and accidental traits of the film upon the screen. The poor lighting and camera work of the early films may have been the initial cause of the degree of darkness: and the intermissions of the stage may have been forgone either for the sake of the financial benefits of continuous performances or, at the very start, because no stage company requires a breathing spell nor were there sets that took time for installation and removal. But whatever their origin, these and other characteristics of the experiences of films continued and flourished so much that any change was troubling enough to be protested. And for a very good reason; a lesser degree of darkness means that the dream quality of a film experience is diminished while intermissions are clearly for those opinionated people who are interested in talking all the time. The enchantment of the dream is broken by intermissions, light, self-appointed commentators on life, love and crime, as well as the TV alternatives of one to twelve other channels.

In a *New Yorker* cartoon last winter, a wife turns to her husband at the performance of a play and says, "If this were on TV, we would turn to another channel." In last week's *TV Guide*, there is a piece recommending the ownership of two TV sets by every family: "Surest way of avoiding arguments," and the article continues by discussing the menace of TV's choices to domestic tranquillity, omitting naturally only the logically foolproof alternative of returning to the primitive condition of no TV set. These two instances of the intuitive awareness of how powerful the fact of choice is in the experience of any kind of TV program and its inevitable reverberations on other forms of entertainment testify to two very different audiences: the sophisticated reader of *The New Yorker* will hardly modify the making of films, but the weekly *TV Guide*, directing itself to the largest audience of all time and existing to provide that enormous heterogeneous audience with a complete list and partial account of its wealth of choice should suggest the vast competitive arena in which Hollywood has hardly ventured. The TV viewer knows that he has a variety of choice; the maker of films knows that he must deal and cope with this variety and with an audience which may become more fickle. It is within these boundaries that Hollywood filmmaking has to move.

The Big Knife (1956)

Clifford Odets is not only a very gifted though erratic playwright, but an excellent scenario writer, and his complete condemnation of Hollywood in *The Big Knife* has an important meaning despite the false or limited nature of the attack.

The villain responsible for Hollywood's evil in *The Big Knife* is an omnipotent Hollywood magnate. He has two capable assistants in his infamy, and there is some implication that as a satanic monster he is a symbol of Hollywood's "system" (as one might say the capitalistic system), particularly of its commercialism. And the magnate certainly stops at nothing to protect the interests of the studio; his infamy includes eaves-dropping by tape-recorder, blackmail, and attempted murder. It is the interests of the studio which make him intervene in the private life of the male film star who is the hero of the Odets script. The film star has killed a child in a hit-and-run accident and his best friend has sacrificed himself and gone to jail for ten months as the culprit to save the star's reputation with the public. The hushed-up scandal serves as the magnate's blackmail weapon by means of which he compels the star to sign a new seven-year contract instead of departing from Hollywood's corruption. The best friend's wife also uses the same means to induce the film star to sleep with her. When the best friend finds this out he spits in the star's face, a repudiation which is final proof to the star of his own degradation and self-betrayal and the immediate cause of his suicide.

The allocation of guilt is typical of the confusion of the entire script: the star condemns himself and the film magnate; the best friend condemns the star and not his own wife, although the lady has a permanent and democratic inclination to adultery. The star's wife condemns the magnate and Hollywood as a commercialized system. She names some of the heroic directors and stars who have succeeded in surmounting Hollywood's organized degradation, yet her conviction that Hollywood itself corrupts her husband extends to the strange belief that departure will redeem their marriage, since her husband would be less tempted to infidelity elsewhere in America. The reason for her view is not at all clear, but possibly she believes that her husband's tendency to casual fornication is the result of the frustration of his exalted artistic aspirations.

I mention these, rather than other details of the story, to indicate how confused *The Big Knife* is as a condemnation of Hollywood. For no matter how monstrous and commercial the villainous magnate may be, the magnate's aims and despotic power are hardly the cause of the hit-and-run accident, the star's surrender to infatuated starlets, his betrayal of friendship and his self-betrayal. It is true that the magnate uses these failings for his own evil purposes, but this does not account for what is wrong with Hollywood films.

The real problem is not so much commercialism's domination as commercialism's impotence to master the causes of box office success and failure, which is essentially a failure to understand the public. It may be that this unrecognized impotence has much to do with making survival in Hollywood a matter of being willing and quick at cutting the throats of others (which someone once described as the higher form of unselfishness, since by cutting one's friend's throat one prevented him from becoming a cutthroat himself). But the primary problem remains, not the· presence of cutthroats, but of Hollywood's troubled relationship with the fickle and unpredictable public which awards box office success or denies it for reasons which elude the most intent commercialisms of the filmmakers.

When *The Big Knife* appeared on Broadway it was freely predicted that there would be no film version, so savage is the attack on Hollywood as a whole and so recognizable the Hollywood magnate. The filming of Odets' play does not suggest a new era of integrity, purity of heart or openness to criticism, but whether or not it was prompted by the success of *The Country Girl*, it suggests the possibility that Hollywood has reached a point of bewildered desperation which makes the magnate a welcome enough scapegoat. Apart from speculation, however, the important point

[470]

is that *The Big Knife* as a condemnation is melodrama and over-simplification and in direct contrast to the compassion and acute delicacy of recognition which Odets gave to the ordeal of the Broadway actor in *The Country Girl*, and which Hollywood's version rendered with perfect sympathy.

There are touches in *The Big Knife* which remind one of Odets' gifts as a writer, particularly the Hollywood magnate's appearance, his smoked glasses and hearing aid and his total self-dramatization. He wears the smoked glasses indoors and though he takes them off now and then, there is the suggestion that they are worn not to diminish the glaring sunlight and help him to see, but to indicate to others how they are to see him: as a being of mystery, wise, hidden and unique. The hearing aid has its customary function; but it breaks down when the magnate hears what he does not want to hear, and he is clearly only willing to listen to what he has indicated he wants other human beings to say to him. These and other details of his personality are mostly passed over or left undeveloped, but Rod Steiger's performance as the magnate is superior to the role itself (this is true also of Wendell Cory as his hatchet man and of Ilka Chase as a Hollywood columnist). What the smoked glasses and the hearing aid suggest as symbols is that the magnate exists in a state of ignorance of the public, of all other human beings, and above all himself. It is the kind of ignorance which is intensified by a sense of isolated superiority. It is this isolation from oneself and hence from all others that shows itself again and again on the telltale screen in one film after another.

The attempt in *The Big Knife* to make the magnate and commercialism the primary source of evil suggests a continuation and extension of the remarks I made about Hitchcock's career in Hollywood. The crucial error is not, I repeat, commercialism, but the mistaken assumption that one knows what the public wants. Thus Hitchcock, though he has more freedom of choice, in casting particularly, is probably regarded just as most directors and stars are: they can direct or act, but the front office has the knowledge of what the public wants and hence must tell these gifted beings *what* to direct or what roles to perform. The ignorance involved is like the logic of lunatics, proof against any correction by experience: success and failure are equally available as evidence that the public consists of children and fools, a half-truth which is true enough of the adult public to be more deceptive than simple falsehood.

For example, the belief that success provides the basis for a formula continues to be one of the worst of Hollywood's assumptions, along with the view that there must be *some* formula for success in pleasing the public. If there were, then it would have been long since discovered and sufficient effort would produce not only successful films but Broadway hits and best sellers with dependable regularity; and the information provided by the box office or by the public opinion agencies would suffice. But the public which is like everyone else, including the beings of Hollywood, does not know what it is going to want next month. This natural state of mind is not entirely fickle and arbitrary, however; the public likes cheesecake and filet mignon, but not so much that a repetition of both three times a day seven times a week, 12 months a year will not become unbearable. And although one important cause of the fickleness of the public is the constantly shifting anxiety which human beings feel in modern life, nevertheless the public is constant in its desire for news of the nature of experience which is genuine.

This is as close to a formula as one can come, and it is close enough. It is not always easy to distinguish between the genuine and the bogus, but it can be accomplished much of the time by introspection. If you don't think a joke is funny or a story is interesting, the chances of making anyone else laugh or be interested are very much reduced, and this criterion, thus formulated with unavoidable over-simplification, is a better guide by far than the box office, which will tell you what the public liked last week, but at the same time deceive you about what the public is going to like next month. There are other complications, including those special to Hollywood or any art directed to a vast mass of anonymous human beings, or involving co-operative effort and enormous financial risk. Only item by item of illustration would make the positive point—that the public wants everything to be genuine—entirely convincing.

The Big Knife as a version of what is wrong with Hollywood film making may be accurate enough in certain instances. But the truth is never accurate, Matisse remarked in a like connection, and neither villainy nor nobility, commercialism or a purity of aim account for more than two generations of Hollywood's successes or failures. It is when nothing human is alien to you that you have a chance to hold the attention of human beings in vast numbers. The magnate's smoked glasses and hearing aids are symbols not of despotism and avarice but of self-alienation and an alienation from other human beings; everything characteristic of Charlie Chaplin connected him and related him to the entire human race.

THE BADNESS OF MOST RECENT FILMS (1955)

The badness of most recent films is such that in attempting to review them, description sometimes turns to satire in the midst of a sentence. This is the original temptation of the film critic and clearly a waste of time, most of the time. Sixty million human beings go to the motion pictures every week in the United States: they may be wrong, but the conscious experience they so faithfully seek is not merely a subject of comedy. *The Long Gray Line, Captain Lightfoot, Untamed* and *Mambo* are all typical of Hollywood's groping, grabbing at anything, its uncertainty, and its disorganized energy. *Mambo* was made in Italy, but the same desperate principle of composition occurs: the greater the uncertainty about the film, the greater the tendency to cram every kind of effect into it. Nevertheless these four films and a great many other things related to recent films have the one virtue of suggesting questions about the making of films. The questions are hardly answerable except by means of speculation without conviction. But the questions are answers, in a way. Each one of them defines what is wrong either in a new film or in the mind of the beholder.

Thus *The Long Gray Line* was directed by John Ford. The question here is how the same man who directed *The Informer, Stagecoach, When Johnny Comes Marching Home,* and several other first-rate films managed to turn out something so poor. The picture is another one of the long gray line of biographical films which draw upon the passage of the years an inexhaustible source of sentimentality, to mention only that quality of the film which Ford's best pictures sometimes attack beautifully.

Captain Lightfoot presents a like problem. It is based upon W. R. Burnett's most recent novel, and this in itself of course would not be enough to make the perplexity so pointed. But the film is as dreary as the novel is delightful, although Burnett himself adapted the novel for the screen. Burnett's gifts as a novelist, which are underestimated or ignored are not relevant here except for the fact that since beginning his career his fiction has provided the substance of some of the best and most characteristic Hollywood films. *Little Caesar*, which appeared more than a generation ago, was one of the first of his novels to make an excellent picture, and to lend genuine and serious perceptions to the gangster film at a time when the genre was still developing. Since then there have been so many other films based on novels by Burnett—among them, *The Asphalt Jungle*—that it is difficult to think of another practicing writer of fiction who has provided so much good screen material and difficult to doubt that some natural affinity was responsible for the excellence of the films which were the result. To phrase the question with the utmost sharpness: how is it that the worst of all films based upon Burnett's fiction should be not only one of his most engaging novels but should also be the one which the novelist himself adapted for the screen? It is possible that the process of adaptation is itself an extremely special skill.

The script of *Mambo* was written by an excellent Italian writer too, and the cast includes Katherine Dunham and her company in addition to Silvana Mangano and Shelley Winters, yet the result is nothing but an immense waste of talent. After the opening episode, which has an extraordinary dramatic vitality, Katherine Dunham and her dancers seldom get a chance to bend a knee, but instead they sit and stand about expressing their understandable depression about the lack of enthusiasm for dancing upon the part of the heroine and other leading characters. The intention appears to be to make a truly American film, and of this instance, as of most others, one can say that the more American the intention of an Italian film the more the result is *Rigoletto* all over again, or some other pure ham, which remains *prosciuto* no matter how it is sliced. Here the real question is: why should the makers of Italian films want to imitate Hollywood?

[474]

The worst of these films is *Untamed,* and though there have been worse films, the energy of the new picture makes one forget the others. Among other traits which make it remarkably bad is the fact that Susan Hayward as the heroine causes the death of her husband and gives birth to an illegitimate child with an impunity which verges upon triumph. Instead of suffering the proverbial wages of sin, she enjoys the handsome compensation of Tyrone Power. Wholly apart from the conventional morality of motion pictures, the vicious and barbarous part played by Miss Hayward compels one to think of the placards which appeared on the screen in the halcyon days of the silent film: *"No pictures will be shown here which are not perfectly moral and clean."* This is precisely the kind of film which ought to be cited as truly immoral whenever the question of the morality of films arises.

These films have moments or passages which link them with many other films of the past year in one important way, the persistent and apparently irresistible magnetism of the Western as a genre. Thus James Cagney, so long the classic Hollywood gangster, is a sheriff in *Run for Cover.* Victor Mature, who has moved through every era of man, including the prehistoric, but seemed most himself in the Ice Age, becomes, as the title indicates, an Indian in *Chief Crazy Horse.* There are many other examples of a great variety: the Western is no longer restricted to the old West, nor it is limited to North America.

In *Untamed* the classic migration of the pioneer occurs, although the covered wagons are smaller, the prairie is replaced by the veldt, and the redskins by Zulus, when the settlers are surrounded, and the covered wagons form a circle to resist the Zulus' attack, the essential pioneer drama makes the difference between North America and South Africa meaningless. In a like way, *Captain Lightfoot* becomes exciting only at the end when, during a struggle between Irish rebels and English soldiers, the situation and the terrain combine to make the difference between redcoats and redskins disappear. A final instance which ought to be described in more detail is the way in which even historical films are transferred into Westerns by making the most of movement of nomads upon horses over wide open spaces.

The Western has always been popular, but the hold it now

[475]

exercises is so great that it hardly seems a genre any longer. And this phenomenon clearly is the same kind of thing and has the same roots as the present eminence of Davy Crockett in the role of the purely American hero. *Time's* comment on the latter fashion must be quoted:

> Why should Davy Crockett . . . whose story has been around for a long time suddenly click as a meaningful figure to Americans, young and old . . . Myths have meaning . . . Davy Crockett is the epitome of a man who can lick any problem with his wits and his own two hands.

This is the chief reason for the renewal of the Western too, but the explanation can be made far more concrete and exact; in *A Bullet is Waiting* which appeared last fall, the story is set in the present, and this is probably why the film was not labeled a Western, although it resorts to every typical Western element: the fugitive bandit, the sheriff in pursuit, the girl, the gun play, and the great outdoors. What is most illuminating is the motive of the heroine's father, an English author; it was the news of the atom bomb which made him depart from England and seek complete isolation for himself and his daughter in God's country. It is this sense of the present, in one or another form and intensity which makes the old West the image of the heroic age as never before. When human beings feel more and more that survival, happiness and the quality of life depend on uncontrollable and hidden powers, when they feel certain only that they are helpless in the face of history, what could be more attractive than an epoch in the past when a gun was enough to keep a man alive and a horse sufficed to ride to destiny? It makes one think of an immortal remark of the immortal William S. Hart: "I got along finely with most Eastern boys, but they did not understand me or my ways." The way that things have been panning out, it looks like us Eastern fellows can hardly understand anything else but old William S. Hart, home on the range, contending with nothing more complex than Comanches and cattle rustlers.

Bibliography of Publications by Delmore Schwartz

Essays and Reviews: First Appearances

"The Stars of Joseph Gordon Macleod." *Mosaic* 1 (Spring 1935): 8–17.

"Adroitly Naive" (review of *Poems* by Louis MacNeice). *Poetry* 48 (May 1936): 115–17.

"Defective Sincerity" (review of *Straight or Curly?* by Clifford Dyment). *Poetry* 50 (July 1937): 233–36.

"John Dos Passos and the Whole Truth" (review of *U.S.A.* by John Dos Passos). *Southern Review* 4, no. 2 (1938): 351–67.

Review of *The Man with the Blue Guitar, and Other Poems* by Wallace Stevens. *Partisan Review* 4 (February 1938): 49–52.

"Ezra Pound's Very Useful Labors." *Poetry* 51 (March 1938): 324–39.

Review of *Mr. Witt Among the Rebels* by Ramon J. Sender. *Common Sense* 7 (April 1938): 24.

"Primitivism and Decadence" (review of *Primitivism and Decadence* by Yvor Winters). *Southern Review* 3, no. 3 (1938): 597–614.

"The Critical Method of R. P. Blackmur." *Poetry* 53 (October 1938): 28–39.

"Ernest Hemingway's Literary Situation." *Southern Review* 3, no. 4 (1938): 769–82.

"The Politics of William Butler Yeats" (letter), *New Republic,* October 12, 1938, p. 272.

Review of *The Oxford Book of Light Verse,* ed. W. H. Auden. *Partisan Review* 6 (Winter 1939): 122–23.

"The Two Audens." *Kenyon Review* 1 (Winter 1939): 34–45.

Review of W. C. Williams' *Collected Poems: 1906–1938. Common Sense* 8 (February 1939): 24.

"The Poet as Poet" (on Yeats). *Partisan Review* 6 (Spring 1939): 52–59.

"A Great Poem, in English" (review of *Duino Elegies* by R. M. Rilke, translated by J. B. Leishman). *Partisan Review* 6 (Summer 1939): 119–21.

"The Criterion, 1922–1939." *Kenyon Review* 1 (Autumn 1939): 435–39.

"The Enigma of Robinson Jeffers." *Poetry* 55 (October 1939): 30–38.

"Rimbaud in Our Time." *Poetry* 55 (December 1939): 148–54.

"Mr. Eliot and Old Possum" (review of T. S. Eliot's *Old Possum's Book of Practical Cats*). *Nation*, December 30, 1939, pp. 737–38.

"Poetry and Belief in Thomas Hardy." *Southern Review* 6, no. 1 (1940): 64–77.

"The Poetry of Allen Tate" (review of *Selected Poems* by Allen Tate). *Southern Review* 5, no. 3 (1940): 419–38.

"The Fiction of William Faulkner." *Southern Review* 7, no. 1 (1941): 145–60.

"Neither Historian nor Critic" (review of *New England: Indian Summer* by Van Wyck Brooks). *Kenyon Review* 3 (Winter 1941): 119–23.

"The Isolation of Modern Poetry." *Kenyon Review* 3 (Spring 1941): 209–20.

"The Writing of Edmund Wilson." *Accent* 2 (Spring 1942): 177–86.

"An Unwritten Book" (on Yeats). *Southern Review* 7 no. 3 (1942): 471–91.

"Poet's Progress" (review of *Person, Place, and Thing* by Karl Shapiro). *Nation*, January 9, 1943, 63–64.

"Merry-Go-Round of Opinion" (review of *Brownstone Eclogues* by Conrad Aiken). *New Republic,* March 1, 1943, 292–93.

"Anywhere Out of the World" (review of T. S. Eliot's *Four Quartets*). *Nation*, July 24, 1943, pp. 102–3.

"The Shock of Recognition" (review of *The Shock of Recognition* by Edmund Wilson). *Partisan Review* 10 (September–October 1943): 439–42.

"The Poetry of Millay" (review of Edna St. Vincent Millay's *Collected Lyrics*). *Nation*, December 18, 1943, pp. 735–36.

"The Hero in Russia" (review of *The Hero in History* by Sidney Hook). *Kenyon Review* 6 (Winter 1944): 126–29.

"Under Forty" (part of a symposium). *Contemporary Jewish Record* 7 (February 1944): 12–14.

"New Writing in Wartime" (review of *Cross Section* by Edwin Seaver). *Nation*, August 12, 1944, pp. 190–91.

"A Man in His Time" (review of *Dangling Man* by Saul Bellow). *Partisan Review* 11 (Summer 1944): 348–50.

"Delights and Defects of Experience" (review of *New Directions, 1944*). *Nation*, October 21, 1944, pp. 476–77.

"He Too Has Lived in America" (review of *The World of Washington Irving* by Van Wyck Brooks). *Partisan Review* 12 (Winter 1945): 128–30.

"The Early Joyce" (review of Joyce's *Portrait of the Artist as a Young Man* and *Stephen Hero*). *Nation*, January 27, 1945, p. 106.

"T. S. Eliot as the International Hero." *Partisan Review* 12 (Spring 1945): 199–206.

"Gertrude Stein's Wars" (review of *Wars I Have Seen* by Gertrude Stein). *Nation*, March 24, 1945, pp. 339–40.

"A Poet and His Prose" (review of a selection of Whitman's prose and poetry). *Nation*, September 22, 1945, pp. 289–90.

"Virginia Woolf's Fiction" (review of Joan Bennett's *Virginia Woolf: Her Art as a Novelist*). *Nation*, October 13, 1945, p. 378.

"Aldous Huxley's Philosophy" (review of Huxley's *The Perennial Philosophy*). *Nation*, October 27, 1945, pp. 438–39.

"A Middle Western Anthology" (review of an anthology of the literature of the Middle West). *Nation*, November 3, 1945, pp. 468, 470.

"Karl Shapiro's Poetics" (review of Karl Shapiro's *Essay on Rime*). *Nation*, November 10, 1945, p. 498; also reply by Shapiro in issue of December 22, pp. 690–92, and reply to that by Schwartz in same issue.

"The Dream from Which No One Wakes" (review of *Little Friend, Little Friend* by Randell Jarrell). *Nation*, December 1, 1945, pp. 590–91.

"A Literary Provincial" (on Yvor Winters). *Partisan Review* 12 (Winter 1946): 138–42.

"The Sick City and the Family Romance" (review of *The Individual and His Society* and *The Psychological Frontiers of Society* by Abram Kardener). *Nation*, January 12, 1946, pp. 46–48.

"Wanted: A Literary Consciousness" (review of *Cross Section* by L. B. Fischer). *Nation*, January 19, 1946, pp. 77–78.

"The Meaningfulness of Absurdity" (review of Albert Camus' *Mythe de Sisyphe* and *Le Malentendu* and *Caligula*). *Partisan Review* 13 (Spring 1946): 246–50.

"Two Chapters from 'The Myth of Sisyphus' by Albert Camus" (translation). *Partisan Review* 13 (Spring 1946): 188–91.

"The Poetry of Hopkins" (review of G. M. Hopkins by the Kenyon Critics). *Nation*, March 23, 1946, pp. 347–48.

"Film Chronicle." *Partisan Review* 13 (Summer 1946): 351–52.

"Instructed of Much Mortality: A Note on the Poetry of John Crowe Ransom." *Sewanee Review* 54 (July 1946): 439–48.

"Unpleasant and Important Fact." *American Scholar* 15 (October 1946): 553–54.

"The First and Last Question" (review of *Education of Modern Man* by Sidney Hook). *Partisan Review* 13 (November–December 1946): 595–96.

"An Intolerable Confusion" (review of *A History of American Poetry* by Horace Gregory and Marya Zaturenska). *Nation*, December 7, 1946, pp. 660, 662, 664.

" 'I Feel Drunk All the Time' " (review of *Selected Poems of Kenneth Patchen*). *Nation*, February 22, 1947, pp. 220, 222.

"Auden and Stevens" (review of Auden's *The Age of Anxiety* and Stevens' *Transport to Summer*). *Partisan Review* 14 (Fall 1947): 528–32.

"The Noble View" (review of *The Noble Voice* by Mark Van Doren). *Sewanee Review* 55 (October–December 1947): 707–9.

"Does Existentialism Still Exist?" *Partisan Review* 15 (December 1948), 1361–63.

"Raw Genius, Self-Delusion, and Incantation" (book review). *Partisan Review* 15 (December 1948): 1135–36.

"The Literary Dictatorship of T. S. Eliot." *Partisan Review* 16 (February 1949): 119–37.

"Views of A Second Violinist." *Partisan Review* 16 (December 1949): 1250–55.

"The Genius of W. C. Fields" (review of *W. C. Fields: His Follies and Fortunes* by Robert Lewis Taylor. *Nation*, February 11, 1950, pp. 135–36.

"Smile and Grin, Relax and Collapse" (review of *55 Short Stories from The New Yorker*). *Partisan Review* 17 (March 1950): 292–96.

"The Life of a Hero" (review of *D. H. Lawrence* by Richard Aldington). *Nation*, July 15, 1950, 64.

Introduction to Turgenev, *Fathers and Sons*, translated by Constance Garnett. Harper's Modern Classics. New York: Harper's, 1951.

"The Grapes of Crisis." *Partisan Review* 18 (January 1951): 7–15.

"The Dark Night of F. Scott Fitzgerald" (review of *The Far Side of Paradise* by Arthur Mizener). *Nation*, February 24, 1951, pp. 180–82.

"The Vocation of the Poet in the Modern World." *Poetry* 78 (July 1951): 223–32.

"The Fabulous Example of Andre Gide" (review of *Two Legends:*

Oedipus and Theseus and *The Journals of Andre Gide*). *Partisan Review* 18 (July–August 1951): 459–66.

"The Miraculous Ayme and Others" (review of *Man and Boy* by Wright Morris, *The Twilight of the Elephant* by Elio Vitterini, *Conjugal Love* by Alberto Moravia, *All About H. Hatterr* by G. V. Desani, *At Swim-Two Birds* by Flann O'Brien, *The Watch* by Carlo Levi, *The Miraculous Barber* by Marcel Ayme). *Partisan Review* 18 (September–October 1951): 575–81.

"Fiction Chronicle: Dear Uncle James" (review of John O'Hara's *Chosen Country*, Graham Greene's *The End of the Affair*). *Partisan Review* 19 (March–April 1952): 234–38.

"Fiction Chronicle: The Wrongs of Innocence and Experience" (review of *The Groves of Academe* by Mary McCarthy, *Who Walk in Darkness* by Chandler Brossard, *Let It Come Down* by Paul Bowles, *The Works of Love* by Wright Morris, *Invisible Man* by Ralph Ellison). *Partisan Review* 19 (May–June 1952): 354–59.

"Masterpieces as Cartoons." *Partisan Review* 19 (July 1952): 461–71.

"Our Country and Our Culture" (part of a symposium). *Partisan Review* 19 (September–October 1952): 593–97.

"Long After Eden" (review of *East of Eden* by John Steinbeck, *The Old Man and the Sea* by Ernest Hemingway, *Men at Arms* by Evelyn Waugh, *Hemlock and After* by Angus Wilson, *Testimonies* by Patrick O'Brian). *Partisan Review* 19 (November–December 1952): 701–6.

"The Duchess' Red Shoes," *Partisan Review*, 20 (January, May 1953): 55–73, 365–66.

"A Universal Mind" (review of *Cezanne* by Meyer Schapiro). *Partisan Review* 20 (July–August 1953): 442–43.

"Light in the Poet's Wasteland" (review of *Poetry and the Age* by Randall Jarell). *New York Times Book Review*, August 16, 1953, p. 1.

"The Dragons of Guilt" (review of *Brother to Dragons* by R. P. Warren). *New Republic*, September 14, 1953, pp. 17–18.

"Truth as Brutality" (review of *The Present and the Past* by Ivy Compton-Burnett). *New Republic*, October 19, 1953, pp. 18–19.

"The Self Against the Sky" (review of *Collected Poems* by Conrad Aiken). *New Republic*, November 2, 1953, pp. 24–25.

"Adventure in America" (review of *The Adventures of Augie March* by Saul Bellow). *Partisan Review* 21 (January–February 1954), 112–15.

"Speaking of Books" (on the popularity of pocketbooks). *New York Times Book Review*, January 17, 1954, p. 2.

"Our Literary Critics: An Appreciation." *New Republic*, May 24, 1954, pp. 17–18.

"Speaking of Books" (on W. B. Yeats). *New York Times Book Review*, June 13, 1954, p. 2.

"In the Orchards of the Imagination" (review of *Collected Poems* by Wallace Stevens). *New Republic*, November 1, 1954, pp. 16–18.

"T. S. Eliot's Voice and His Voices." *Poetry* 85 (December 1954, January 1955): 170–76, 232–42.

"Faulkner's *A Fable*." *Perspectives USA*, no. 10 (Winter 1955), pp. 126–36.

"The Fiction of Ernest Hemingway." *Perspectives USA*, no. 13 (1955), pp. 70–88.

Film review: *Animal Farm, New Republic*, January 17, 1955, pp. 22–23.

Film review: *Bridges at Toko-Ri. New Republic*, January 14, 1955, pp. 28–29.

Film review: *The Country Girl. New Republic*, April 4, 1955, p. 21.

Film review: *Underwater!, Blackboard Jungle, New Republic*, April 11, 1955, pp. 29–30.

Film review: *East of Eden. New Republic*, April 25, 1955, p. 22.

"Mary Pickford: The Little Girl in Curls" (review of *Sunshine and Shadow* by Mary Pickford). *New Republic*, June 6, 1955, pp. 17–20.

Film review: *The Long Gray Line, Captain Lightfoot, Untamed, Mambo. New Republic*, June 27, 1955, pp. 21–22.

"Films—TV." *New Republic*, July 18, 1955, pp. 21–22.

Film review: *The Seven Year Itch* (on Marilyn Monroe). *New Republic*, August 8, 1955, pp. 22–23.

"Wallace Stevens: An Appreciation." *New Republic*, August 22, 1955, pp. 20–22.

"French Taste in American Writing." *New Republic*, September 5, 1955, pp. 21–23.

Film review: *To Catch a Thief, New Republic*, November 28, 1955, pp. 21–22.

Film review: *The Big Knife, New Republic*, January 9, 1956, pp. 19–20.

"Omnibus and the Egg-Heads" (letter). *New Republic*, January 23, 1956, p. 22.

Film review: *The Man with the Golden Arm, New Republic*, February 6, 1956, p. 22.

Film review: *The Court Jester, New Republic,* March 5, 1956, p. 21.

"Graves in Dock: The Case for Modern Poetry." *New Republic,* March 19, 1956, p. 20–21.

"Survey of Our National Phenomena." *New York Times Magazine,* April 15, 1956, pp. 28–29, 59–60.

"Guys, Dolls, and Vivian Leigh" (film review). *New Republic,* April 23, 1956, p. 20.

"The Man Who Read Kant in the Bathtub" (review of *Further Speculations* by T. E. Hulme, *New Republic,* May 21, 1956, pp. 21–22.

"Ring Lardner: Highbrow in Hiding." *The Reporter,* August 9, 1956, pp. 52–54.

"The Present State of Poetry" (lecture presented under the auspices of the Gertrude Clarke Whittall Poetry and Lecture Fund, Library of Congress, 1958). In *American Poetry at Mid-century, 1958.* Washington, D.C.: Library of Congress, 1958.

"The Nightmare of History" (review of *Ulysses in Nighttown*). *New Republic,* March 30, 1959, pp. 16–17.

"Novels and the News." *New Republic,* April 13, 1959, pp. 16–17.

"The Cunning and the Craft of the Unconscious and the Pre-conscious" (review of *Words for the Wind* by Theodore Roethke). *Poetry* 94 (June 1959): 203–5.

"The Art of Marianne Moore" (review of *O To Be A Dragon*). *New Republic,* January 4, 1960, p. 19.

"Ezra Pound and History" (review of *Thrones de los Cantares* by Ezra Pound). *New Republic,* February 8, 1960, pp. 17–19.

"The Traveler's Flight" (review of *The Age of Happy Problems* by Herbert Gold). *New York Times Book Review,* July 1, 1962.

" 'The Terror is Absolute' " (review of *An Age of Enormity* by Isaac Rosenfeld). *New York Times Book Review,* August 12, 1962.

Short Stories: First Appearances

"The Commencement Day Address." In *New Directions in Prose and Poetry.* New York: New Directions, 1937.

"In Dreams Begin Responsibilities." *Partisan Review* 4 (December 1937): 5–11.

"The Statues." *Partisan Review* 4 (May 1938): 11–18.

"An Argument in 1934." *Kenyon Review* 4 (Winter 1942): 62–74.

"New Year's Eve." *Partisan Review* 12 (Summer 1945): 327–44.

"A Bitter Farce." *Kenyon Review* 8 (Spring 1946): 245–61.

"The Child Is The Meaning of This Life." *Partisan Review* 14 (May–June 1947): 255–77.

"The World Is a Wedding." *Partisan Review* 15 (March 1948): 279–87.

"The Fabulous Twenty-Dollar Bill." *Kenyon Review* 19 (Summer 1952): 378–405.

"Tales From the Vienna Woods: An Inside Story." *Partisan Review* 20 (May 1953): 267–81.

"An American Fairy Tale." *Commentary* 26 (November 1958): 420–24.

"The Track Meet." *The New Yorker*, February 28, 1959, pp. 28–34.

"The Gift." *Partisan Review* 26 (Summer 1959): 453–60.

"Successful Love." In *Avon Book of Modern Writing*, no. 2 (New York: Avon, 1959).

POEMS: FIRST APPEARANCES

"E.A.P.—A Portrait," "The Saxophone," "Automobile," "Darkness." In *The Poet's Pack of George Washington High School*. New York: William Edwin Rudge, 1932.

"Two Poems." *Mosaic* 1 (November–December 1934): 9.

"Three Poems." In *New Directions in Prose and Poetry*. New York: New Directions, 1937.

"The Ballad of the Children of the Czar." *Partisan Review* 4 (January 1937): 29–31.

"Sonnets: You, My Photographer; Old Man in the Crystal Morning After Snow." *Poetry* 49 (February 1937): 252–53.

"Five Poems," In *New Directions in Prose and Poetry*. New York: New Directions, 1938.

"In the Naked Bed, in Plato's Cave"; "Heart, a Black Grape Gushing Hidden Streams." *Poetry* 51 (January 1938): 198–99.

"Poem." *Partisan Review* 4 (February 1938): 21.

"Sonnet: The Philosophers." *Common Sense* 7 (Spring 1938): 20.

"For One Who Would Not Take His Life in His Hands." *New Republic*, July 13, 1938, p. 273.

"Imitation of a Fugue." *Twentieth-Century Verse*, nos. 12–13 (September–October 1938), p. 97.

"Paris and Helen" (a play). In *New Directions in Prose and Poetry*. New York: New Directions, 1941.

"Shenandoah, or, The Naming of a Child" (a verse play). *Kenyon Review* 3 (Summer 1941): 271–92.

"The Starlight's Intuitions Pierced the Twelve." *Kenyon Review* 6 (Summer 1944): 383–85.

"Tired and Unhappy, You Think of Houses." *Scholastic* 47 (November 26, 1945): 22.

"The True, the Good, and the Beautiful"; "He Heard the Newsboys Shouting 'Europe! Europe!' "; "The Silence Answered Him Accusingly"; "Such Answers Are Cold Comfort to the Dead"; "The Silence in Emptiness Accused Him Thus, 'A Privileged Character'." *Partisan Review* 14 (March–April 1947): 146–49.

"My Mind to Me a Kingdom Is." *Accent* 10 (Winter 1950): 100.

"I Did Not Know the Spoils of Joy"; "Winter Twilight, Glowing Black and Gold"; "On a Sentence by Pascal"; "Dusk Shows Us What We Are and Hardly Mean." *Partisan Review* 17 (January 1950): 64–66.

"The Early Morning Light." *Kenyon Review* 12 (Spring 1950): 243–45.

Six poems: "Look, in the Labyrinth of Memory"; "Cartoons of Coming Shows Unseen Before"; "Don't Speak, Remember Once It Happened, So It May Again"; "One in a Thousand of Years in the Nights"; "Today is Armistice, a Holiday"; "Morning Light for One With Too Much Luck." *Commentary* 9 (March 1950): 227–28.

"Hope Like the Phoenix Breast Rises Again"; "My Love, My Love, My Love, Why Have You Left Me Alone?"; "Desperanto of Willy-Nully"; "Self-Unsatisfied Runs Everywhere"; "Chaplin Upon the Cliff, Dining Alone"; "Rumor and the Whir of Unborn Wings"; "Heart Flies Up, Erratic as a Kite"; "Why Do You Write an Endless History?"; "Self-Betrayal Which Is Nothing New"; "Twelfth Night, Next Year a Weekend in Eternity"; "True Recognition is Often Refused." *Poetry* 76 (April 1950): 1–9.

"Holderlin"; "Baudelaire." *Partisan Review* 21 (March 1954): 174–75.

"Fulfillment." *Art News Annual* 24 (1955): 90–91.

"The Children's Innocent and Infinite Window." *New Republic*, January 3, 1955, p. 19.

"The Innocence and Windows of Children and Childhood." *New Republic,* January 10, 1955, p. 19.

"Yorick"; "All of the Fruits Had Fallen." *New Republic*, January 31, 1955, pp. 20, 22.

"The First Morning of the Second World." *Kenyon Review* 17 (Fall 1955): 575–80.

"In Praise of Creation"; "Poem"; "A Little Morning Music." *Mutiny* 2 (Winter 1958): 17.

"Poem." *Partisan Review* 25 (Spring 1958): 225–26.

"The Kingdom of Poetry." *Poetry* 92 (May 1958): 63–66.

"Jacob"; "Poem"; "Sonnet." *Commentary* 25 (May 1958): 398–400.

"Candlelight and the Heart of Fall." *The New York Times*, May 22, 1958.

"O Child, When You Go Down To Sleep's Secession"; "Sequel"; "Once and For All"; "At a Solemn Musick"; "The Foggy, Foggy Playboy"; "Sonnet: The World Was Warm and White When I Was Born." *Kenyon Review* 20 (Summer 1958): 440–44.

"Poem: In the Green Morning, Before." *Partisan Review* 25 (Summer 1958): 373.

"Rumorous Dusk, Ominous Rain." *The New York Times*, July 2, 1958.

"Dark and Falling Summer." *The New Yorker*, September 6, 1958, p. 121.

"Kilroy's Carnival: A Poetic Prologue for TV." *New Republic*, December 1, 1958, pp. 15–16.

"Vivaldi." *The New Yorker*, December 6, 1958, p. 50.

"The Mind Is an Ancient and Famous Capital" (from *The Studies of Narcissus*). *New Republic*, December 15, 1958), p. 17.

"During December's Death." *The New Yorker*, December 20, 1958, p. 32.

"The Conclusion." *Partisan Review* 26 (Winter 1959): 56.

"The Dread and Fear of the Mind of the Others" (from *The Studies of Narcissus*). *New Republic*, February 2, 1959, p. 18.

"Abraham"; "Sarah." *Commentary* 27 (March 1959): 221–22.

"A Little Morning Music." *The New Yorker*, April 16, 1959, p. 44.

"Mounting Summer, Brilliant and Ominous"; "Swift"; "River Was the Emblem of All Beauty"; "All"; "Summer Knowledge." *Poetry* 94 (May 1959): 104–10.

"Gold Morning, Sweet Prince." *New Republic*, May 25, 1959, p. 15.

"Passages from *The Studies of Narcissus*." *Chicago Review* 13 (Summer 1959): 121–23.

"Philology Recapitulates Ontology, Poetry is Ontology"; "Poem"; "Song." *Prairie Schooner* 33 (Summer 1959): 154–56.

"Spiders," *New Republic*, July 27, 1959, p. 29.

"Cupid's Chant." *New Republic*, July 27, 1959, p. 29.

"The Choir and Music of Solitude and Silence." *New Republic*, September 28, 1959, p. 27.

"Poem: On That Day of Summer, Blue and Gold." *New Republic*, October 19, 1959, p. 24.

"All Night, All Night." *New Republic*, March 21, 1960, p. 18.

"Speaking at Twilight, Singing in the Morning." *Prairie Schooner*, 34 (Summer 1960): 123–27.

"This is a Poem I Wrote at Night Before the Dawn." *New Republic*, October 23, 1961, p. 24.

"Words for a Trumpet Chorale Celebrating the Autumn." *New Republic*, November 13, 1961, p. 12.

"Two Lyrics from Kilroy's Carnival, a Masque." *Sewanee Review*, 70 (Winter 1962): 12–13.

"To Helen (After Valery)." *New York Times*, February 6, 1962.

"Journey of a Poem Compared to All the Sad Variety of Travel." *Kenyon Review* 24 (Spring 1962): 304.

"Aria (from Kilroy's Carnival)." *New Republic*, April 23, 1962, p. 26.

"Poem"; "Remember Midsummer: The Fragrance of Box, of White Roses." *New Republic*, July 16, 1962, p. 21.

"Apollo Musagete, Poetry, and the Leader of the Muses." *Poetry* (October 1962): 108–11.

"Poem: In the Morning, When It Was Raining." *New York Times*, October 27, 1962.

"The First Night of Fall and Falling Rain." *New York Times*, November 6, 1962.

BOOKS

A Season in Hell (translation of Rimbaud). Norfolk, Conn.: New Directions, 1939. Rev. ed. 1940.

In Dreams Begin Responsibilities (chiefly poetry). Norfolk, Conn.: New Directions, 1939.

Shenandoah (play). Norfolk, Conn.: New Directions, 1941.

Genesis, Book One (poetry). New York: New Directions, 1943.

The World Is a Wedding (stories). Norfolk, Conn.: New Directions, 1948.

Vaudeville for a Princess, and Other Poems (prose, poetry). New York: New Directions, 1950.

Summer Knowledge: New and Selected Poems, 1938–1958 (poetry). Garden City, N.Y.: Doubleday, 1959. New ed. New York: New Directions, 1967.

Successful Love, and other Stories (stories). New York: Corinth, 1961.

Index